A SEMANTIC AND STRUCTURAL ANALYSIS OF REVELATION

SIL International®

SEMANTIC AND STRUCTURAL ANALYSIS SERIES

JOHN TUGGY, GENERAL EDITOR

A SEMANTIC AND STRUCTURAL ANALYSIS OF REVELATION

Andrew Persson

SIL International®

© 2016 by SIL International®

Library of Congress Control Number: 2016936493
ISBN: 978-1-55671-380-4

Printed in the United States of America

The Greek text used in this SSA is from The Greek New Testament, fourth revised edition, Edited by Barbara Aland and others, © 1993 Deutsche Bibelgesellschaft, Stuttgart.

All Rights Reserved
No part of this publication may be reproduced, stored in a retrieval system, or transmitted in any form or by any means without the express permission of SIL International. However, brief excerpts, generally understood to be within the limits of fair use, may be quoted without written permission.

Copies of this and other publications of SIL International® may be obtained through distributors such as Amazon, Barnes & Noble, other worldwide distributors and, for select volumes, www.sil.org/resources/publications:

SIL International Publications
7500 W. Camp Wisdom Road
Dallas, Texas 75236-5629 USA

General inquiry: publications_intl@sil.org
Pending order inquiry: sales_intl@sil.org
www.sil.org/resources/publications

CONTENTS

Acknowledgements 9

Abbreviations 10

GENERAL INTRODUCTION 11
Theoretical Basis 11
Communication Relations and Paragraph Patterns 12
Structural Forms of Paragraph Pattern in Various Discourse Types 13
Chart of Communication Relations 14
The Format of an SSA 15
The Display of the Unit 15
Example of the Display 16
Statement of the author's Intent 18
The Exegetical Notes 18
The Evidence for the Analysis of the Unit 18

INTRODUCTION TO THE SEMANTIC STRUCTURE
OF THE BOOK OF REVELATION 19
The Author and Addresses 19
The Historical Setting 19
The Genre – Apocalyptic 20
Symbols and Figures of Speech 20
Organization of the Major Constituents of the Book of Revelation 21
Theme Statements of the Major Units of the Book of Revelation 22

THE PRESENTATION AND DISCUSSION OF THE SEMANTIC UNITS
OF THE BOOK OF REVELATION 25
REVELATION 1:1–22:21 (Book) 25
  Book Constituent 1:1–3 (Paragraph: Superscription of the Book) 27
  Book Constituent 1:4–8 (Complex Paragraph: Opening of the Book) 30
  Book Constituent 1:9–22:11 (Part: Body of the Book) 35
    Part Constituent 1:9–3:22 (Act: Step$_1$ of Body) 37
      Act Constituent 1:9 (Paragraph: Setting of 1:9–3:22) 38
      Act Constituent 1:10–16 (Paragraph: Step of 1:9–3:22) 39
      Act Constituent 1:17–3:22 (Section: Goal of 1:9–3:22) 42
        2:1–3:22 Nucleus of 1:17–3:22 45
          2:1–7 (Letter$_1$ of 2:1–3:22) 47
          2:8–11 (Letter$_2$ of 2:1–3:22) 51
          2:12–17 (Letter$_3$ of 2:1–3:22) 54
          2:18–29 (Letter$_4$ of 2:1–3:22) 58
          3:1–6 (Letter$_5$ of 2:1–3:22) 63
          3:7–13 (Letter$_6$ of 2:1–3:22) 67
          3:14–22 (Letter$_7$ of 2:1–3:22) 72
    Part Constituent 4:1–16:21 (Act: Step$_2$ of Body) 76
      Act Constituent 4:1–11 (Scene: Setting for 4:1–16:21) 78
        Scene Constituent 4:1 (Episode: Occasion for 4:2–11) 78
        Scene Constituent 4:2–11 (Episode: Outcome of 4:1) 80
      Act Constituent 5:1–8:5 (Scene: Step$_1$ of 4:1–16:21) 85
        Scene Constituent 5:1–14 (Episode: initiating incident for 5:1–8:5) 87
        Scene Constituent 6:1–8 (Episode: Step$_1$ of 5:1–8:5) 94
        Scene Constituent 6:9–11 (Episode: Step$_2$ of 5:1–8:5) 97
        Scene Constituent 6:12–17 (Episode: Step$_3$ of 5:1–8:5) 99

  Scene Constituent 7:1–17 (Episode Cluster: Interlude of 5:1–8:5) 101
   Episode Cluster Constituent 7:1–8 (Interlude Episode: Nucleus$_1$ of 7:1–17)................102
   Episode Cluster Constituent 7:9–17 (Interlude Episode: Nucleus$_2$ of 7:1–17)...............105
  Scene Constituent 8:1–5 (Episode: Goal of 5:1–8:5) 109
 Act Constituent 8:6–11:19 (Scene: Step$_2$ of 4:1–16:21)..111
  Scene Constituent 8:6–12 (Episode: Step$_1$ of 8:6–11:19)...113
  Scene Constituent 8:13 (Propositional Cluster: Prominence orienter for 8:6–11:19)............115
  Scene Constituent 9:1–11 (Episode: Step$_2$ of 8:6–11:19)..116
  Scene Constituent 9:12 (Propositional Cluster: Prominence orienter for 8:6–11:19)............119
  Scene Constituent 9:13–21 (Episode: Step$_3$ of 8:6–11:19)...120
  Scene Constituent 10:1–11:13 (Episode cluster: Interlude of 8:6–11:19)..........................123
   Episode Cluster Constituent 10:1–11 (Episode cluster: Nucleus$_1$ of 10:1–11:13)............124
    Episode Cluster Constituent 10:1–7 (Episode: Nucleus$_1$ of 10:1–11)..................125
    Episode Cluster Constituent 10:8–11 (Episode: Nucleus$_2$ of 10:1–11)................128
   Episode Cluster Constituent 11:1–13 (Episode: Nucleus$_2$ of 10:1–11:13)....................130
  Scene Constituent 11:14 (Propositional Cluster: Prominence orienter for 8:6–11:19)..........135
  Scene Constituent 11:15–19 (Episode: Goal of 8:6–11:19)..136
 Act Constituent 12:1–14:20 (Scene: Step$_3$ of 4:1–16:21)..138
  Scene Constituent 12:1–13:18 (Episode Cluster: Problem of 12:1—14:20) 140
   Episode Cluster Constituent 12:1–18 (Episode Cluster: Occasion of 12:1–13:18)..........141
    Episode Cluster Constituent 12:1–6 (Episode: Occasion of 12:1–18).......................142
    Episode Cluster Constituent 12:7–12 (Episode: Outcome$_1$ of 12:1–18)...................145
    Episode Cluster Constituent 12:13–18 (Episode: Outcome$_2$ of 12:1–18).................148
   Episode Cluster Constituent 13:1–10 (Episode: Outcome$_1$ of 12:1–13:18)...................150
   Episode Cluster Constituent 13:11–18 (Episode: Outcome$_2$ of 12:1–13:18).................154
  Scene Constituent 14:1–20 (Episode Cluster: Resolution of 12:1–14:20)...........................157
   Episode Cluster Constituent 14:1–5 (Episode: Setting of 14:1–20)................................158
   Episode Cluster Constituent 14:6–13 (Episode: Step of 14:1–20).................................161
   Episode Cluster Constituent 14:14–20 (Episode: Goal of 14:1–20)...............................165
 Act Constituent 15:1–16:21 (Scene: Goal of 4:1–16:21) 168
  Scene Constituent 15:1 (Propositional cluster: setting of 15:1–16:21)................................169
  Scene Constituent 15:2–4 (Paragraph: Interlude of 15:1–16:21)......................................170
  Scene Constituent 15:5–8 (Paragraph: Step of 15:1–16:21)..172
  Scene Constituent 16:1–21 (Episode: Goal of 15:1–16:21)..174
   Episode Constituent 16:1 (Propositional cluster: setting of 16:1–21)...........................175
   Episode Constituent 16:2–9 (Paragraph Cluster: Step$_1$ of 16:1–21)................................176
   Episode Constituent 16:10–11 (Paragraph: Step$_2$ of 16:1–21)......................................178
   Episode Constituent 16:12–16 (Paragraph Cluster: Step$_3$ of 16:1–21).............................179
   Episode Constituent 16:17–21 (Paragraph Cluster: Goal of 16:1–21)............................182
Part Constituent 17:1–20:15 (Act: Step$_3$ of Body)..184
 Act Constituent 17:1–19:10 (Scene: Step of 17:1–20:15)..185
  Scene Constituent 17:1–2 (Paragraph: Setting of 17:1–19:10).......................................186
  Scene Constituent 17:3–18:24 (Episode cluster: Situation of 17:1–19:10) 187
   Episode Cluster Constituent 17:3–6 (Paragraph: Problem of 17:3–18:24)....................188
   Episode Cluster Constituent 17:7–18 (Episode: Resolving incident of 17:3–18:24)......190
   Episode Cluster Constituent 18:1–24 (Episode: Resolution of 17:3–18:24)..................194
    Episode Constituent 18:1–3 (Paragraph: Situation of 18:1–24)..............................195
    Episode Constituent 18:4–20 (Paragraph Cluster: Reaction of 18:1–24)..................197
     Paragraph Cluster Constituent 18:4b–8 (Paragraph: Situation of 18:4–20)............198
     Paragraph Cluster Constituent 18:9–19 (Paragraph: Neg. Reaction of 18:4–20) ...201
     Paragraph Cluster Constituent 18:20 (Paragraph: Positive Reaction of 18:4–20)..205
    Episode Constituent 18:21–24 (Paragraph: Situation of 18:1–24 amplified)............206
  Scene Constituent 19:1–8 (Paragraph: Reaction of 17:1–19:10).....................................209
  Scene Constituent 19:9–10 (Episode: Coda of 17:1–19:10)..212

Act Constituent 19:11–20:15 (Scene: Goal of 17:1–20:15)	214
Scene Constituent 19:11–16 (Descriptive Paragraph: setting of 19:11–20:15)	215
Scene Constituent 19:17–21 (Episode: Step$_1$ of 19:11–20:15)	218
Scene Constituent 20:1–3 (Episode: Step$_2$ of 19:11—20:15)	220
Scene Constituent 20:4–6 (Paragraph: Step$_3$ of 19:11–20:15)	222
Scene Constituent 20:7–10 (Episode: Step$_4$ of 19:11–20:15)	225
Scene Constituent 20:11–15 (Episode: Goal of 19:11–20:15)	227
Part Constituent 21:1–22:5 (Act: Goal of Body)	229
Act Constituent 21:1–8 (Scene: Nucleus$_1$ of 21:1–22:5)	230
Scene Constituent 21:1–4 (Paragraph: Description of 21:1–8)	231
Scene Constituent 21:5–8 (Paragraph: Declaration of 21:1–8)	233
Act Constituent 21:9–22:5 (Scene: Nucleus$_2$ of 21:1–22:5)	236
Scene Constituent 21:9 (Propositional Cluster: Setting of 21:9–22:5)	237
Scene Constituent 21:10–27 (Sub-scene: Step of 21:9–22:5)	238
Sub-Scene Constituent 21:10–14 (Propositional Cluster: Description$_1$ of 21:10-27)	239
Sub-Scene Constituent 21:15–17 (Paragraph: Description$_2$ of 21:10-27)	240
Sub-Scene Constituent 21:18–21 (Paragraph: Description$_3$ of 21:10-27)	242
Sub-Scene Constituent 21:22–27 (Paragraph: Declaration of 21:10-27)	244
Scene Constituent 22:1–5 (Paragraph: Goal of 21:9-22:5)	246
Part Constituent 22:6–11 (Section: Denouement of Body)	248
Section Constituent 22:6–7 (Paragraph: Nucleus$_1$ of 22:6–11)	249
Section Constituent 22:8–11 (Paragraph: Nucleus$_2$ of 22:6–11)	251
Book Constituent 22:12–20 (Section: Epilogue of the Book)	253
Section Constituent 22:12–17 (Paragraph Cluster: Nucleus$_1$ of Epilogue)	254
Section Constituent 22:18–20 (Paragraph Cluster: Nucleus$_2$ of Epilogue)	257
Book Constituent 22:21 (Paragraph: Closing of the Book)	258
Bibliography	259

ACKNOWLEDGEMENTS

Like most other volumes in the *Semantic and Structural Analyses* series this one on Revelation has had an extremely long gestation. In the 1990s Grace Sherman did much initial work on the analysis and notes. At that time no *Semantic and Structural Analysis* had been produced on a largely narrative book such as Revelation, so a great debt of gratitude is due to her for laying the foundations and providing the building materials of this volume.

In 2001, around the time that Grace died, her unfinished work on Revelation was passed over to me by the then editor of the series, John Banker. Since then I have re-examined and completed the analysis and done all the work necessary to produce the book in its current form. But unfortunately this task has had to be fitted in around other major commitments over many years, so I have been extremely grateful to John Banker for his editorial patience and continued constructive advice during this time. It is very sad that John passed away in 2013 before he could see this volume in print. Thanks are also due to Stephen Levinsohn for the profound insights and advice on the finer points of the Greek discourse grammar that he has produced whenever asked. Finally it should be made clear that the actual publication of this work would not have taken place without the persistent efforts and input of the current series editor, John Tuggy.

It is my sincere hope that this publication will benefit both Bible translators and other serious students of the Bible. As I hope the analysis demonstrates, the apostle John's purpose in writing Revelation was not to frighten or mystify Christians about the end of the world, but to encourage them to stand firm in their faith despite the evil around them and to be sure of their place in God's new creation. I trust that this volume will help others to understand this, as it has me.

Andrew Persson
Kidlington, Oxon. GB
July 2014

ABBREVIATIONS IN THE DISPLAYS

cf. = compare	MET = metaphor
ch. = chapter	MTY = metonymy
desc = descriptive	ONOM = onomatopoeia
DOU = doublet	p. = page
e.g. = such as	¶ PTRN = paragraph pattern
emot = emotive	pl = plural
exc = exclusive	pp. = pages
expo = exposition	proc = procedural
hort = hortatory	PRS = personification
HYP = hyperbole	RHQ = rhetorical question
i.e. = that is	sg = singular
ibid. = previous reference	SIM = simile
inc = inclusive	SYN = synecdoche
	v. = verse

ABBREVIATIONS IN THE TEXT

BDAG	Bauer, Danker, Arndt, Gingrich
BDF	Blass, Debrunner, and Funk
CEV	Contemporary English Version
JB	Jerusalem Bible
JBP	J. B. Phillips
KJV	King James Version
LB	Living Bible
LXX	The Septuagint
NASB	New American Standard Bible
NCV	New Century Version
NEB	New English Bible
NIV	New International Version
NLT	New Living Translation
NRSV	New Revised Standard Version
REB	Revised English Bible
RSV	Revised Standard Version
SSA	Semantic and Structural Analysis
TEV	Today's English Version (Good News Translation)
TDNT	Theological Dictionary of the New Testament
TH	Translator's Handbook
TNT	Translator's New Testament
UBS	United Bible Societies
UBSGNT	United Bible Societies' Greek New Testament (4th rev. ed.)

GENERAL INTRODUCTION TO SEMANTIC AND STRUCTURAL ANALYSES

The Semantic and Structural Analysis (SSA) commentaries are designed to assist Bible translators and Bible translation consultants. Due to the careful attention to meaning at all levels of the discourse, they should also be useful for Bible scholars, teachers, preachers, and anyone interested in a thorough understanding of the biblical text. The analysis is firmly based on discourse linguistics and assumes that each New Testament book is an integrated whole. The analytical process involves detailed study of the grammar, lexicon and discourse structure of the Greek, with the aim of clearly presenting the meaning of the text and the linguistic evidence on which the meaning is established.

THEORETICAL BASIS

The theoretical basis of these studies is Beekman, Callow and Kopesec's theory of discourse analysis, presented in *The Semantic Structure of Written Communication* (1981) and further developed by Kathleen Callow in *Man and Message* (1998). However, other theoretical approaches have not been ignored. A large body of biblical scholarship has been considered, and some of the weaknesses in their works have been supplemented.

This commentary is called *A Semantic and Structural Analysis* because its primary interest is the organized meaning of the text. The aim is to present, as far as possible, the organization and meaning that the biblical author intended his audience to understand. The text is approached with several underlying assumptions about language as a communicative medium:

1. The writer used written language signals in his attempt to communicate meaning, emotion, and social relations to his readers.
2. The writer assumed a vast body of shared information with his audience, such as language, culture, world-view, social relations, socio-political circumstance, specific circumstances, and time of the writing. Beekman, Callow and Kopesec call this the "communication situation."
3. The writer's own intended purpose and communication meaning were prior to and have priority over the written surface forms, but today our main access to the biblical writer's purpose and meaning is through the written text.
4. Communicated meaning consists of units of meaning logically related to other units of meaning.
5. Some meaning units are nuclear, or central, while others are satellitic or supportive to these nuclear units. These bundles of meaning are also bundled together with other, larger, units of meaning. In other words, meaning units are organized hierarchically in a discourse, giving rise to the "natural prominence" of the units (so Beekman, Callow and Kopesec).
6. The ways in which units are related to each other, that is, their "communication relations", are relatively few. These relationships are basic to human intelligence and makeup and are used in all languages whether or not there is a corresponding surface form expressing them. Moreover, even in the same language a specific relation is not always expressed by the same surface form, and conversely one surface form may be used to express *more* than one semantic relation.
7. When two meaning units are related to each other, each unit in this relationship carries out a "communication role."
8. Every language has certain grammatical and lexical devices which may be used by an author to mark specific meaning units as prominent. This is called "marked prominence."
9. There are limited ways in which communication relations can be arranged so that a whole arrangement is a purposive and complete unit. Such an arrangement forms a communication paragraph, or "paragraph pattern".
10. Each unit has a "theme", that is, a central topic and an argument about that topic, understandable from the prominence structure of the unit. (This is not to be confused with *motif*, which is a prosodic and coherence feature that runs through units of various sizes.)

In order to present the meaning and structure of any written communication, the editors of the SSA series have developed their own metalanguage and diagramming devices, which are explained in what follows.

COMMUNICATION RELATIONS AND PARAGRAPH PATTERNS

Semantic relationships between propositions, "communication relations", are the basic joining elements at all levels of a discourse. "Paragraph patterns" are made up of these relations with the additional elements of purposiveness and completeness. (An explanation of the total array of semantic relations between propositions is available in Beekman, Callow and Kopesec.)

Of the two charts that follow, the first shows the paragraph patterns used in this analysis, and the second shows the communication relations and unit roles. Most of the terms in the charts are self-explanatory, but for further explanations see Tuggy (1992) and Beekman, Callow and Kopesec (1981).

In the chart of communication roles, the relations are given in the usual order in which they are found in the Greek of the New Testament, e.g. reason–RESULT. Where there is no natural prominence on one part (i.e. where there is only *contextual* prominence), both relations are shown in lowercase letters, e.g. generic-specific.

		SOLUTIONALITY	CAUSALITY	VOLITIONALITY
I D E A S	EXPOSITORY −sequence	+problem(expo) +SOLUTION ±evidence^n ±(complication +SOLUTION)	+cause^n +EFFECT or +major +minor +INFERENCE or +evidence^n +INFERENCE^n or +application^n +PRINCIPLE	+justification^n +CLAIM
	NARRATIVE +sequence	+problem +RESOLUTION ±resolving incident^n ±(complication +RESOLUTION)	+occasion +OUTCOME	+step^n +GOAL
E M O T I O N S	EXPRESSIVE −sequence	+problem(emot) +SOLUTION ±seeking ±(complication +SOLUTION)	+situation^n +REACTION ±belief	+belief^n +CONTROL
	DESCRIPTIVE +sequence	+problem(desc) +SOLUTION ±experience^n ±(complication +SOLUTION)	+situation^n +REACTION	+description^n +DECLARATION
B E H A V I O U R	HORTATORY −sequence	+problem(hort) +APPEAL ±evidence^n ±(complication +SOLUTION)	+basis^n +APPEAL or +APPEAL +application^n	+motivation +ENABLEMENT^n or +motivation^n +ENABLEMENT
	PROCEDURAL +sequence	+problem(proc) +SOLUTION ±step^n ±(complication +SOLUTION)	+APPEAL +outcome^n	+STEP^n +accomplishment

STRUCTURAL FORMS OF PARAGRAPH PATTERN IN VARIOUS DISCOURSE TYPES

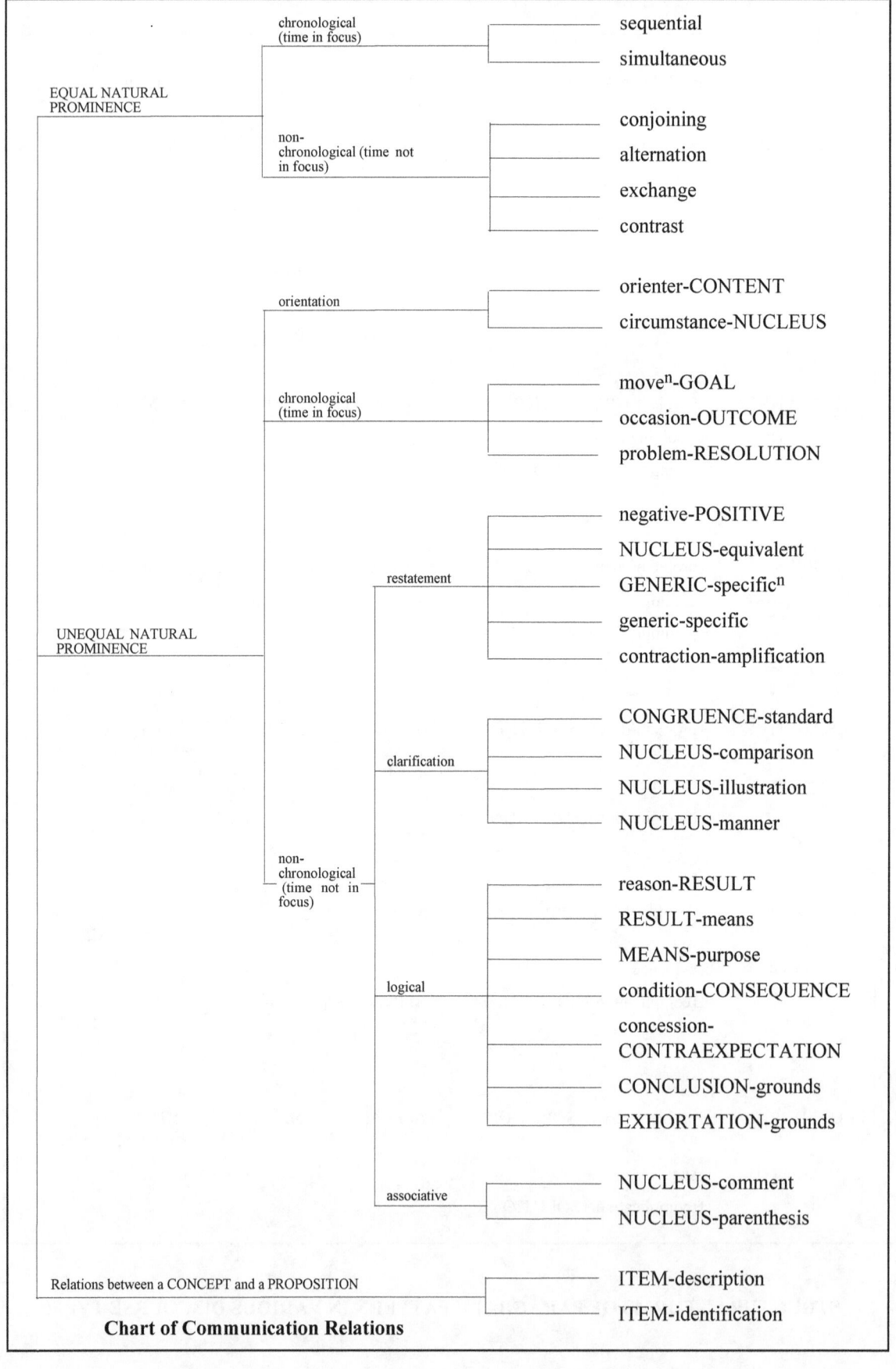

Chart of Communication Relations

THE FORMAT OF AN SSA

Following the General Introduction and a specific introduction to the book being studied, the main part of each Semantic and Structural Analysis (SSA) consists of displays and discussions of the semantic units which comprise the book. All units are considered, from the macrostructure or overall structure of the book, through the intermediate level structures such as parts and sections, down to the semantic paragraphs. Within each semantic paragraph smaller units are discussed, such as concepts, which relate to each other to form propositions (the basic unit of meaning) and the relationship of the propositions to one another.

Each semantic unit, whether semantic paragraph or something larger, is presented in the following order: (1) a display of the unit, (2) an explanation of the structure of the unit and a statement of how the original author intended to affect his audience by it, (3) exegetical notes about specific words and phrases as presented in the Display, and (4) arguments supporting the analysis of the unit under discussion as a whole.

THE DISPLAY OF THE UNIT

The Display is a schematic representation of the structure of the meaning of the unit. It contains a number of elements, as detailed in the following example (from the SSA of the Gospel of John):

PART CONSTITUENT 1:1-5 (Descriptive Paragraph: Generic Declaration1 of 1:1-5)

THEME: Jesus Christ expresses to us God's character being himself eternally God. He expresses by creating everything, giving humans life and knowledge, and by evil humans not overcoming him.

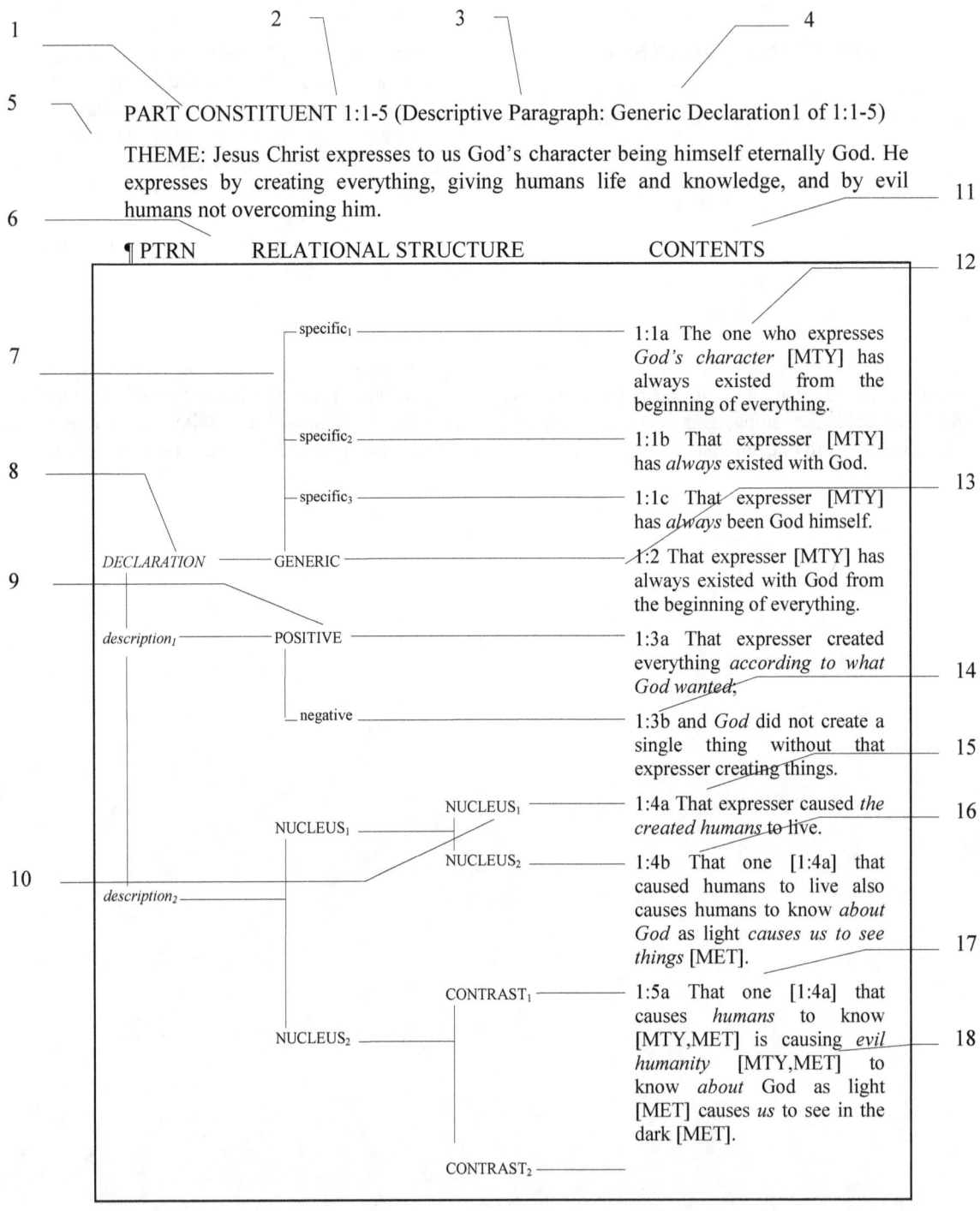

Key:

1. 'Part Constituent' shows that the unit goes together with some other similar unit(s) to form a 'Part', i.e. it gives the broader context of the unit.

2. '1:1-5' defines the specific text span of the unit.

3. 'Descriptive Paragraph' shows that the author was describing something with the intent of effecting the emotions of his audience (see the chart of Structural Forms of Paragraph Pattern, above) within the specific semantic level of this unit, which here is a semantic paragraph.

4. 'Generic Declaration of 1:1-5' states that the unit functions as a generic declaration within the larger context of the text span identified.

5. The second line is a statement of what the unit is all about. The Theme Statement presents the most prominent or nuclear parts of the unit, stating the topic and what is said about that topic.

6. The middle box contains column headers showing the type of information found below in the body of the Display.

The main body of the Display is in two main columns: on the left are the internal relations and structure of the unit, and on the right is the message content.

7. The text is assumed to be structured hierarchically and is therefore displayed with a form of tree diagram showing levels of dependency and branching.

8. The labels farthest to the left show the interdependent highest level units.

9. The next level from the left shows the units that support the highest level units.

10. Each succeeding column shows a lower supportive level and branching of units.

Units with labels in upper-case letters (capitals) are prominent or nuclear. In this particular example, the highest level of interdependent units are a declaration (prominent) with two descriptions supporting the declaration. The declaration is made up of four units, a generic statement with its specifics, as shown by the second level from the left.

It should also be noted that although the vertical lines indicate direct interdependency between units, a dotted vertical line is used to signify a proposition's relationship to those that follow as a group. (This is used mainly for the orienter–content relationship.)

11. The right-hand column of the display, under the title 'CONTENTS', has its own characteristics.

12. This column shows the results of a careful study of the grammatical structure of the Greek text and its semantic significance. The meaning is stated here in propositions with verbs in the active voice (as far as possible) and all participants explicit. The Greek text from which these propositions are derived may be a clause, a phrase, a verb, an abstract noun, or some other grammatical unit.

13. In the example the declaration unit is made up of four propositional statements. Each propositional statement is numbered as a part of a verse (1:1a, 1:1b, 1:1c, and 1:2). However, propositions are not numbered separately unless they require separate treatment. Here 1:3a is made up of two separate propositions in one propositional statement.

14. At the beginning of most propositional statements, a conjunction is used to signify its relationship to some other proposition. In 1:3b the negation is a restatement of the previous positive statement, and is therefore given the conjunction 'and'. In 1:5b the contrastive statement is introduced by 'but'.

15. The meaning is expressed unambiguously 'we are united to God'. In 1:4b the Greek term 'the life,' is expressed as 'the one that caused humans to live'.

16. The referents of pronouns and demonstratives are made explicit. In 1:4b the Greek has 'he' referring back in the text to 1:4a. This is signalled unambiguously in square brackets: 'that one [1:4a]'.

17. Italic words represent implicit information which is judged to have been part of the original message communicated by the writer. The exegetical notes give justifications for the inclusion of this information in the meaning of the message.

18. Abbreviations in square brackets indicate where a figure of speech (e.g. metonymy, metaphor) was used in the Greek.

In addition, words in bold face indicate focal words or phrases in the Greek that cannot be appropriately reflected in the grammar of written English.

THE STATEMENT OF THE AUTHOR'S INTENT

Following the Display is a section entitled 'Intent and Macrostructure' or 'Intent and paragraph pattern'. It deals with discourse type: how the biblical author intended the unit to affect his audience (in terms of chart of Structural Forms of Paragraph Pattern, above). Where there are alternative ways of interpreting the author's intent, the reasons for the preferred analysis are given. Also, the unit's structure is discussed in terms of the author's strategy for accomplishing the intended effect on the audience.

THE EXEGETICAL NOTES

The section entitled 'Notes' contains comments on words and phrases from the Display. Most of the notes consider the Greek text and its meaning, stating different opinions found in the commentaries and reasons for choices made in the analysis. In particular, discussion is focused on relationship with other units, prominence, purpose, meaning, plus historical and cultural matters required for understanding the text, and translational problems.

THE EVIDENCE FOR THE ANALYSIS OF THE UNIT

The Notes are followed by two sections that present the textual and semantic evidence for the analysis of the unit.

In the section entitled 'Boundaries and Coherence' argumentation is given for the analysis of the beginning and ending points of the unit. In view of the wide variation in ways that commentaries and translations divide the material of biblical books into smaller units (sections, paragraphs etc.) it is important to consider the linguistic evidence provided by discourse study of the Greek text. For each unit there need to be not only convincing indicators of its boundaries but also elements within it showing its coherence.

Under 'Prominence and Theme' the textual and semantic prominence features within the unit are set out. These include both the features of natural prominence, as in the relationships between propositions and sub-units, and the grammatical and lexical devices indicators of marked prominence, such as forefronting and emphatic words. In this section there is also an explanation of how these prominence features determine the unit's Theme Statement (as given in the Display).

INTRODUCTION TO THE SEMANTIC STRUCTURE OF THE BOOK OF REVELATION

This analysis is based on the principle that the proper understanding of any written document involves establishing the message which the original author intended to convey through the document to its original intended recipients. The first step in the analysis of Revelation is therefore to set out what is known about the writer, the recipients, the situation in which the book was written, and the assumptions that the writer and recipients would have shared about the way it was written, i.e. its genre.

For the full argumentation of these issues reference should be made to the most recent major commentaries. What follows is a summary of the positions which the current analysis adopts.

THE AUTHOR AND ADDRESSEES

Although the author of Revelation cannot be established with absolute certainty, he refers to himself four times as "John" (1:1, 4, 9; 22:8), calling himself a prophet, a witness, and brother of those to whom he writes. In the earliest external references to the book (Justin Martyr and Irenaeus, who wrote within two or three generations of the age of the apostles) this John was understood to be the apostle John. Such an identification is very significant evidence, since at that time there would still have been many clear memories of the apostle and the circumstances of his life.

There is also internal evidence within the book for its authorship by the apostle John. In the first place, the fact that this "John" offers no additional self-identification and yet he exercises unquestionable authority over all the churches of Asia argues strongly for his being the well-known apostle. Then it is striking that the main themes of Revelation, faithfulness to Christ and resistance to false teaching, are so close to the main themes of the Johannine epistles (see Sherman & Tuggy), and to prominent topics in John's Gospel. There are also specific terms that occur in the N.T. only in John's Gospel, the Letters of John and Revelation, notably the references to Christ as the λόγος 'word' in John 1:1, 1John 1:1 and Rev.19:13, and as the Lamb in John 1:29 and Rev. 5:6 etc.

One argument that is frequently used to deny that the apostle John could have written Revelation is that, unlike in John's Gospel and his Letters, the Greek of Revelation in several places ignores accepted grammatical rules. In fact, some commentators seem to find John's grammar as bizarre as the visions that he recounts. However, as the Notes in this analysis explain, many examples of what appears to be a cavalier disregard of grammatical rules can be explained on the basis of quotations, or echoes, of O.T. sources, e.g. 1:4c, 22:3c. Another possible explanation for the peculiarities of the Greek in Revelation may be that in the circumstances of its writing and original circulation the author did not have access to the sort of amanuensis or secretary who may have polished the style of other N.T. books. It may simply reflect the type of Greek that would have been written at that time by someone for whom it was their second or third language.

As this analysis shows, the book is encapsulated in the formal structure of a letter. That letter (and not just the subsidiary letters of chapters 2–3) is addressed to seven churches in the Roman province called Asia. However, 'seven' is used throughout Revelation to indicate a complete set (the spirits, seals, trumpets etc.), and there were obviously more than seven churches in the province, so it would appear that John was really addressing all the churches that were under his oversight.

THE HISTORICAL SETTING

The book contains numerous references to Christians being persecuted by the state authorities and to some of them being killed for their faith. This clearly places its writing in a period such as the rule of the emperor Domitian (81–96 AD) when public worship of the emperor began to be enforced throughout the Roman empire. This also agrees with the testimony of Irenaeus, c.180 AD, that "It *(the vision of Revelation)* was seen not very long ago, almost in our generation, at the close of the reign of Domitian" (*Against Heresies*, 5:30, 3).

It is important to note that this dating of Revelation places it right at the end of the apostolic age. To the Christians for whom it was written John would have been their last direct link with the life of Jesus and with Paul, who had brought the gospel to their area. In addition to persecution by the state, they would have been facing new challenges such as schisms and heretical teachings that were similar to the gospel but at variance with it. These are the sort of challenges that face any church as it grows beyond the lifetimes of its founding members.

THE GENRE – APOCALYPTIC

It is almost tautologous to say that Revelation is classified as apocalyptic in genre, since the literary genre of 'apocalypse' itself is named after this book and its first word, ἀποκάλυψις, meaning "revelation". It seems that the genre developed out of the Jewish tradition of prophecy in the inter-testamental period when the age of inspired prophecy had ceased. Its roots can be seen in the symbolic and visionary sections of Daniel (chs.7–12) and Zechariah (1:7–6:8). The Jewish non-Biblical apocalypses normally consist of a narrative in which an angelic figure discloses to some great historic personage the details of God's plans to intervene in human history bringing to an end all evil and unveiling the triumph of God's righteous people. These books mainly offer their message through symbols and mysterious events, some of which are interpreted by the angelic messengers.

Although this is the background against which the original readers would have read the book of Revelation, it nevertheless diverges from the non-Biblical apocalypses in several ways. Its visions are given not in a fictitious way to a notable character from the past, but to a real contemporary person. It also exhibits an overtly hortatory intent, with direct appeals to the readers for repentance in chs.2–3 and for steadfastness in the beatitudes scattered throughout the book. Moreover, although symbolism plays a huge part in the narrative of Revelation there is no angelic interpretation of the symbols as there is in other apocalypses. Finally, this apocalypse does not denigrate the present age in its focus on God's intervention in the future. It repeatedly affirms that God has already intervened for good through the sacrifice and resurrection of Christ, the Lamb, and in sustaining the church as it continues to proclaim his message, 'the testimony of Christ.'

These differences may derive from the fact that the author clearly sees himself as in the tradition of O.T. prophecy. John makes several references to his book being prophecy and he draws not only images but even phrases and quotations from the prophets, e.g. 18:2, 19:17.

SYMBOLS AND FIGURES OF SPEECH

Because Revelation is apocalyptic in genre it differs from other N.T. books as far as translation is concerned in that it requires the translator to distinguish between figurative language and symbolic language. Like figurative language, such as similes and metaphors, symbols also have an *image* (the symbol, or thing pictured) and a *topic* (the non-figurative meaning, the real thing referred to), as well as some point of comparison which links the *image* to the *topic*.

In translation the similes and metaphors of Revelation must be dealt with just as they are in other books. For instance, when Jesus says "I come like a thief" in 16:15, the *topic* is indisputably unexpectedness – not felonious intent! If necessary, this should be made clear in translation, possibly by additional wording (see the Display for that verse) or by a literal, rather than figurative, representation of the *topic*.

The difference between such figurative language and symbolism is that even if an *image*, such as the thief, recurs in a discourse it is never a participant in the narrative. It is always the *topic* of the figure that is relevant in the context. With symbols, however, such as the two beasts (ch.13) and the scroll (ch.5), it is the *image* that is important in the context, as either a participant in the narrative or an essential prop. The *topic* of such symbols is often hotly disputed. Since Revelation, unlike other apocalypses, does not give any interpretation of its symbolism, a translation cannot prejudge the debate and make any particular interpretation explicit. A translation can only relate what John said he saw in his vision, not the later events and characters that other people have interpreted it as referring to.

ORGANIZATION OF THE MAJOR CONSTITUENTS OF THE BOOK OF REVELATION

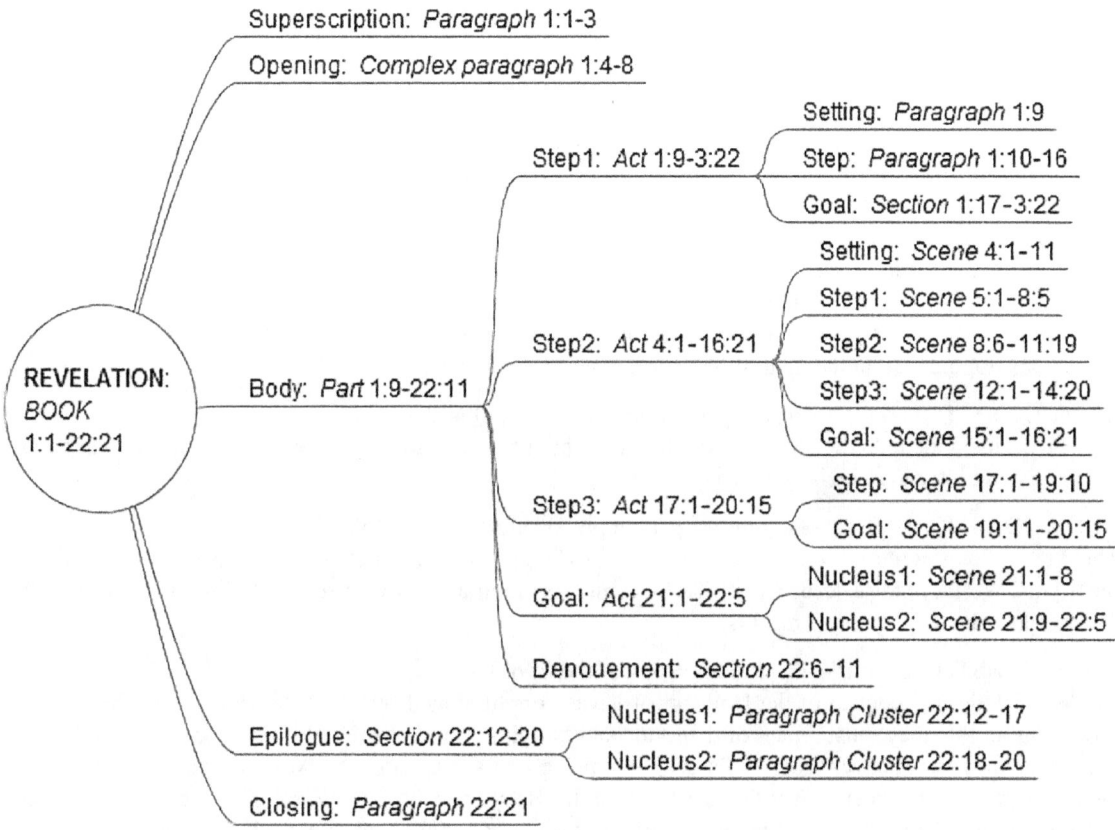

THEME STATEMENTS OF THE MAJOR UNITS OF THE BOOK OF REVELATION

REVELATION 1:1–22:21 (Book)
THEME: I, John, write to you who are in the seven churches of Asia to tell you that Jesus Christ is soon coming as king. Under the control of the Holy Spirit I was commissioned by Christ to send to the churches his proclamation that they must repent of their sins and be faithful and obedient to him. I saw God and Christ being worshipped in heaven, and God's people praising him as his judgment was enacted on the rebellious people of the earth. Then I saw the great prostitute, Babylon, who was drunk with the blood of God's people. She was being destroyed together with all those who rebelled against God. God judged all people by their deeds and all whose names were not in the book of life were thrown into the lake of fire. Finally I saw the Bride of the Lamb, the new city of Jerusalem, perfect in every way, where God will dwell permanently with his people. God declared that he had made everything new and everything was now accomplished. In the city God's servants have the abundant sources of eternal life, and they live forever as kings worshipping God in the light of his glory.

BOOK CONSTITUENT 1:1–3 (Paragraph: Superscription of the Book)
THEME: This book tells the message which Jesus Christ revealed to John. Therefore, Jesus' servants must read it, listen to it, and obey it.

BOOK CONSTITUENT 1:4–8 (Complex paragraph: Opening of the Book)
THEME: I, John, write to you who are servants of Christ in the seven churches in Asia. I pray God may bless you. We(inc) praise Jesus Christ. He is coming as king and all who rejected him will be distraught. The Lord God Almighty confirms this.

BOOK CONSTITUENT 1:9–22:11 (Part: Body of the Book)
THEME: Under the control of the Holy Spirit I was commissioned by Christ to send to the churches his proclamation that they must repent of their sins and be faithful and obedient to him. I saw God and Christ being worshipped in heaven, and God's people praising him as his judgment was enacted on the rebellious people of the earth. Then I saw the great prostitute, Babylon, who was drunk with the blood of God's people. She was being destroyed together with all those who rebelled against God. God judged all people by their deeds and all whose names were not in the book of life were thrown into the lake of fire. Finally I saw the Bride of the Lamb, the new city of Jerusalem, perfect in every way, where God will dwell permanently with his people. God declared that he had made everything new and everything was now accomplished. In the city God's servants have the abundant sources of eternal life, and they live forever as kings worshipping God in the light of his glory.

PART CONSTITUENT 1:9–3:22 (Act: Step$_1$ of Body)
THEME: When I was under the control of the Holy Spirit, the glorified Christ appeared to me and commissioned me to write down what would be revealed to me and to send it to the seven churches of Asia. He proclaimed that the churches must listen to his message exhorting them to repent of various sins and encouraging them to be faithful and obedient to him.

ACT CONSTITUENT 1:9 (Paragraph: Setting of 1:9–3:22)
THEME: I, John, who shares with you as we(inc) suffer persecution and serve our king Jesus, was on Patmos because I had proclaimed what God says and what Jesus witnessed about God.

ACT CONSTITUENT 1:10–16 (Paragraph: Step of 1:9–3:22)
THEME: Under the control of the Holy Spirit, I heard a voice ordering me to write down the vision and send it to the seven churches of Asia. I saw that the one speaking to me was the glorified Son of Man.

ACT CONSTITUENT 1:17–3:22 (Section: Goal of 1:9–3:22)
THEME: After the glorified Christ had told me not to be afraid and had commissioned me to write down what was to be revealed to me, he proclaimed that the churches must listen to his message exhorting them to repent of various sins and encouraging them to be faithful and obedient to him.

PART CONSTITUENT 4:1–16:21 (Act: Step$_2$ of Body)
THEME: I was told to come up to heaven and see the events that must happen. I saw God on his throne being worshiped, and Christ being worshiped as the Redeemer because he is worthy to open the sealed scroll. The opening of the seven seals and then the sounding of seven trumpets brought judgment on rebellious earth people, and God's servants were marked out, and there were cosmic manifestations of judgment. Satan and his agents caused all earth people to submit to them, but God's people were with Christ praising God as the final judgment was announced. Angels poured out the seven bowls of God's anger bringing terrible afflictions on the rebellious earth people in completion of God's punishment of them.

    ACT CONSTITUENT 4:1–11 (Scene: Setting for 4:1–16:21)
    THEME: I saw heaven open and was told to come and see the events that would happen next. I saw a throne at the centre of heaven and the elders and living creatures worshiping the glorious One sitting on it.

    ACT CONSTITUENT 5:1–8:5 (Scene: Step$_1$ of 4:1–16:21)
    THEME: : When the Lamb took the scroll from the One who sits on the throne, the whole created universe worshiped him as the worthy Redeemer. The opening of the first six seals brought judgment to rebellious earth people. Before the Lamb opened the seventh seal God's own servants were marked and those who had come safely through persecution praised God. When the Lamb opened the seventh seal, there was a silence and then cosmic manifestations of judgment occurred.

    ACT CONSTITUENT 8:6–11:19 (Scene: Step$_2$ of 4:1–16:21)
    THEME: At the sounding of each of six successive trumpet blasts, woeful judgment came upon the earth and its rebellious people. Before the seventh trumpet blast I was commissioned to prophesy and mark out the worshipers of Christ. Christ then sent two witnesses to prophesy to the nations. When the seventh angel sounded his trumpet, voices from heaven declared that the Lord God and his Messiah now rule over the world and the elders declared that the time had come for God's final judgment. Then the heavenly sanctuary became open to view and cosmic manifestations of judgment occurred on earth.

    ACT CONSTITUENT 12:1–14:20 (Scene: Step$_3$ of 4:1–16:21)
    THEME: Satan, as a powerful dragon, attacked God's Messiah but was defeated. Then his agents, two terrible beasts, attacked and defeated God's people. They caused all earth people to submit to them. But then I saw the Lamb on Mount Zion with all God's faithful people, and angels announced God's judgment on those who did not worship him. The Son of Man harvested the grain of the earth and the grapes of the earth were crushed in the winepress of God's anger against evil people.

    ACT CONSTITUENT 15:1–16:21 (Scene: Goal of 4:1–16:21)
    THEME: Those who had overcome the beast praised God and seven angels were given the seven bowls of God's anger. As these were poured out the people who had worshiped the beast suffered terrible afflictions and then the rulers of earth united for the final battle against God, but Jesus called on his people to be ready for him. When the last bowl was emptied God's punishment of people was complete, but they continued to curse him.

PART CONSTITUENT 17:1–20:15 (Act: Step$_3$ of Body)
THEME: I saw the great prostitute, Babylon, who was drunk with the blood of God's people. When she was destroyed I heard the inhabitants of heaven praising God and God's people rejoicing that the time had come for the marriage of the Lamb. Then I saw the King of kings going out to destroy the rebellious people of the nations. The beast and the false prophet led the people to fight against God's people but they were all destroyed, Satan was imprisoned, and God's people reigned as kings for a thousand years. After Satan led another rebellion against God, God had him thrown in the lake of fire. Then God judged all people by their deeds and all whose names were not in the book of life were thrown into the lake of fire.

ACT CONSTITUENT 17:1–19:10 (Scene: Step of 17:1–20:15)
THEME: I saw the great prostitute, Babylon, who was drunk with the blood of God's people. When she was destroyed the people of earth lamented and God's people rejoiced. Then I heard the inhabitants of heaven praising God for destroying her and I heard God's people rejoicing that the time had come for the marriage of the Lamb. I was told that those whom God invites to the Lamb's wedding are blessed.

ACT CONSTITUENT 19:11–20:15 (Scene: Goal of 17:1–20:15)
THEME: I saw the King of kings going out to destroy the rebellious people of the nations. The beast and the false prophet led the people to fight against God's people but they were all destroyed, Satan was imprisoned and God's people reigned as kings for a thousand years. After Satan led another rebellion against God, God had him thrown in the lake of fire. Then God judged all people by their deeds and all whose names were not in the book of life were thrown into the lake of fire.

PART CONSTITUENT 21:1–22:5 (Act: Goal of Body)
THEME: I saw the Bride of the Lamb, the new city of Jerusalem, perfect in every way, where God will dwell permanently with his people. God declared that he had made everything new and everything was now accomplished. In the city God's servants have the abundant sources of eternal life, and they live forever as kings worshipping God in the light of his glory.

ACT CONSTITUENT 21:1–8 (Scene: Nucleus$_1$ of 21:1–22:5)
THEME: I saw the new city of Jerusalem, where God will dwell permanently with his people and they will no longer experience suffering. Then God declared that he had made everything new and everything was now accomplished and he will provide abundant eternal life to all who trust him and punishment in the lake of fire for the wicked.

ACT CONSTITUENT 21:9–22:5 (Scene: Nucleus$_2$ of 21:1–22:5)
THEME: When I was told to come and see the Bride of the Lamb I saw the holy city, the new Jerusalem, perfect in every way. In the city God's servants have the abundant sources of eternal life, and they live forever as kings worshipping God in the light of his glory.

PART CONSTITUENT 22:6–11 (Section: Denouement of Body)
THEME: God has verified this revelation and Jesus reminds his people that he is coming soon, so they must obey the message of this book in order to enjoy God's blessings. I, John, am the one who heard and saw these things, and the angel who showed them to me told me not to keep this revelation secret.

BOOK CONSTITUENT 22:12–20 (Section: Epilogue of the Book)
THEME: Jesus warns that he is coming soon to recompense everyone according to their deeds. He proclaims that all who are free from sin will be blessed. He asserts that the message of this book has indeed come from him. The Holy Spirit and God's people respond by urging him to come. Whoever hears this is also urged to respond. Jesus then warns of the eternal consequences for anyone who tampers with the message of this book, and again declares that he is coming soon. I, John, respond by urging him to come.

SECTION CONSTITUENT 22:12–17 (Paragraph Cluster: Nucleus$_1$ of Epilogue)
THEME: Jesus warns everyone that he is coming soon to recompense them according to their deeds. He proclaims that all who are pure and free from sin will be blessed by God. He asserts that the message of this book has indeed come from him, the Messiah. The Holy Spirit and God's people respond by urging him to come. Whoever hears this is also urged to respond and accept the gift of eternal life.

SECTION CONSTITUENT 22:18–20 (Paragraph Cluster: Nucleus$_2$ of Epilogue)
THEME: Jesus warns of the eternal consequences for anyone who tampers with the message of this book, and he declares that he is certainly coming soon. I, John, respond by urging him to come.

BOOK CONSTITUENT 22:21 (Paragraph: Closing of the Book)
THEME: I pray that the Lord Jesus will bless you all.

THE PRESENTATION AND DISCUSSION OF THE SEMANTIC UNITS OF THE BOOK OF REVELATION

REVELATION 1:1–22:21 (Book)

THEME: I, John, write to you who are in the seven churches of Asia to tell you that Jesus Christ is soon coming as king. Under the control of the Holy Spirit I was commissioned by Christ to send to the churches his proclamation that they must repent of their sins and be faithful and obedient to him. I saw God and Christ being worshipped in heaven, and God's people praising him as his judgment was enacted on the rebellious people of the earth. Then I saw the great prostitute, Babylon, who was drunk with the blood of God's people. She was being destroyed together with all those who rebelled against God. God judged all people by their deeds and all whose names were not in the book of life were thrown into the lake of fire. Finally I saw the Bride of the Lamb, the new city of Jerusalem, perfect in every way, where God will dwell permanently with his people. God declared that he had made everything new and everything was now accomplished. In the city God's servants have the abundant sources of eternal life, and they live forever as kings worshipping God in the light of his glory.

MACROSTRUCTURE	CONTENTS
superscription	1:1-3 This book tells the message which Jesus Christ revealed to John. Therefore, Jesus' servants must read it, listen to it, and obey it.
opening	1:4–8 I, John, write to you who are servants of Christ in the seven churches in Asia. I pray God may bless you. We(inc) praise Jesus Christ. He is coming as king and all who rejected him will be distraught. The Lord God Almighty confirms this.
BODY	1:9–22:11 Under the control of the Holy Spirit I was commissioned by Christ to send to the churches his proclamation that they must repent of their sins and be faithful and obedient to him. I saw God and Christ being worshipped in heaven, and God's people praising him as his judgment was enacted on the rebellious people of the earth. Then I saw the great prostitute, Babylon, who was drunk with the blood of God's people. She was being destroyed together with all those who rebelled against God. God judged all people by their deeds and all whose names were not in the book of life were thrown into the lake of fire. Finally I saw the Bride of the Lamb, the new city of Jerusalem, perfect in every way, where God will dwell permanently with his people. God declared that he had made everything new and everything was now accomplished. In the city God's servants have the abundant sources of eternal life, and they live forever as kings worshipping God in the light of his glory.
epilogue	22:12–20 Jesus warns that he is coming soon to recompense everyone according to their deeds. He proclaims that all who are free from sin will be blessed. He asserts that the message of this book has indeed come from him. The Holy Spirit and God's people respond by urging him to come. Whoever hears this is also urged to respond. Jesus then warns of the eternal consequences for anyone who tampers with the message of this book, and again declares that he is coming soon. I, John, respond by urging him to come.
closing	22.21 I pray that the Lord Jesus will bless you all.

INTENT AND MACROSTRUCTURE

The overall structure of the book of Revelation is that of a letter. This is clear from the *opening* and *closing* units, which exhibit standard letter features of the time, as well as from the overt letters of 2:1–3:22. However, unlike other New Testament letters, much of the content of Revelation is narrative, relating the writer's visionary experiences.

This use of narrative in a letter framework explains the very many hortatory elements that are found, both within the narrative and in its setting. As a letter the book is addressed to the people of seven churches in the Roman province of Asia (1:4) and it contains unmitigated APPEALS to them in 2:1–3:22. Some of these APPEALS are to repent of sinful practices or lack of love for the Lord and others are to continue faithful to the end. But there are also mitigated exhortations at various points throughout the book. The seven beatitudes (1:3; 14:13; 16:15;

19:9; 20:6; 22:7, 14) are motivational and function as mitigated APPEALS. Their main hortatory theme is faithfulness. This suggests that the purpose of the narrative material itself is to encourage the saints to be faithful until the end.

Moreover, there are also expressive elements in the book that contribute to its hortatory purpose. They encourage the saints emotionally in the midst of their long and hard struggle by giving them hope. These passages concentrate on the greatness of God (e.g. 4:8–11) and on what God and Christ have done (e.g. 5:8–14, 7:9–12, 11:15–18, 19:1–8). The *epilogue* is also expressive, depicting the writer's eager reaction to the imminence of Jesus' return – which he wanted his audience to share.

Finally, even the narrative material encourages the readers to continue faithful to the end. It is clear from 1:9 and 2:1–3:22 that both the readers and the writer were enduring persecution for their faith, and much of the narrative deals with God's judgment on their persecutors, the people of earth who were in rebellion against him. This is followed by the final destruction of all evil and the establishment of the final order of all things, the "new Jerusalem" in which nothing exists except the saints and their God in a relationship of perfect peace, harmony and joy.

COHERENCE

One major indicator of the coherence of a discourse is whether its structure contains the typical constituents: introductory material, a main body of text, and closing material. These three elements are clearly seen in Revelation.

The *superscription* relates to the whole discourse and it is noticeable that the warnings to the recipients of the book in 22:18–19 echo the blessings in 1:3. For reasons why the *opening* and the *epilogue* are distinguished from the BODY see Boundaries and Coherence for those units, but they still deal with topics that are common to the whole book. The writer, John, speaks in the first person throughout, and his topic at all points is the imminent coming of Jesus Christ to bless God's people and to judge those who have rejected him. The *closing* completes the letter framework of the book in line with the *opening*.

PROMINENCE AND THEME

The BODY is obviously the most extensive and prominent part of the book, but some material from the introductory and ending units is also required in the theme. Because of the framing of the book as a letter, the identification of the author and addressees is required, together with the main topic of the communication – the imminent coming of Jesus Christ as king.

BOOK CONSTITUENT 1:1–3 (Paragraph: Superscription of the Book)

THEME: This book tells the message which Jesus Christ revealed to John. Therefore, Jesus' servants must read it, listen to it, and obey it.

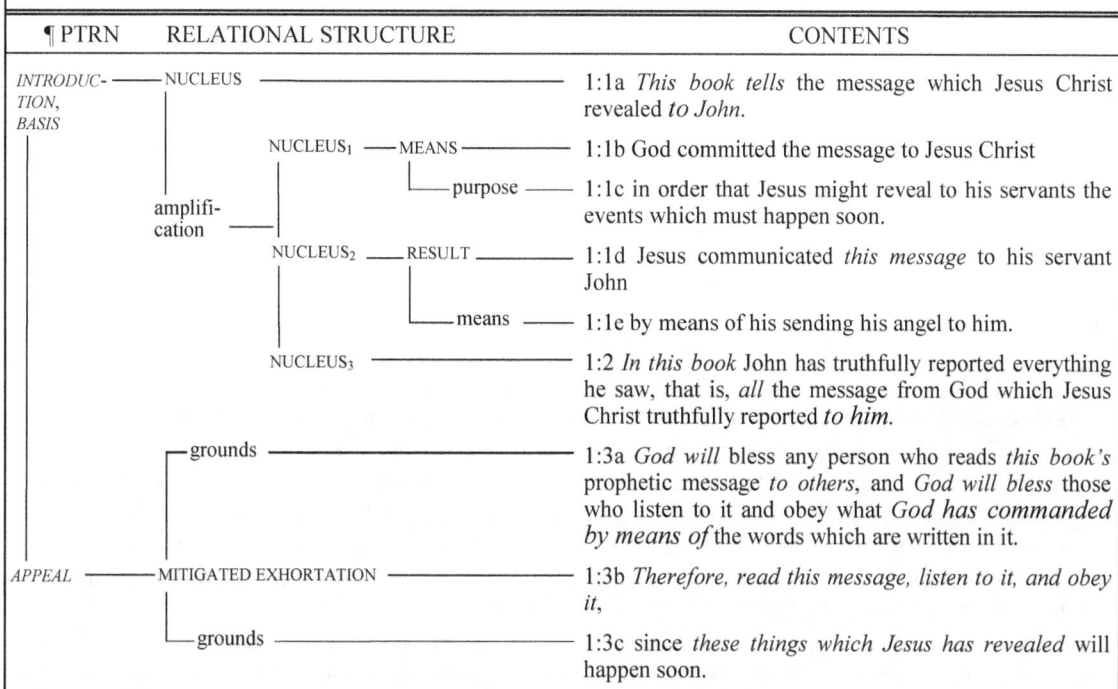

INTENT AND PARAGRAPH PATTERN

The unit is described as a *superscription* introducing the book as a whole. It designates the genre of literature, its source, purpose, and means of transmission. However, since the author's aim is that his book should be read, its intent is also hortatory, so the beatitude (1:3a) motivates to bring the appropriate response. The identity of the book, as originating in God and mediated through Christ and an angel, forms the *basis* for this mitigated APPEAL that it should be read and obeyed. But it is also prominent because of its position and structure, and its function as an introduction.

NOTES

1:1a *This book tells* These words supply the deictic information necessary in relating the topic, 'the revelation', to its concrete manifestation – 'this book'. But as far as ordering is concerned, note that in the Greek the phrase Ἀποκάλυψις Ἰησοῦ Χριστοῦ 'Revelation of Jesus Christ' stands at the very beginning of the discourse, showing the subject matter of the whole book.

the message which Jesus Christ revealed The construction 'revelation of Jesus Christ' is shown to be a subjective genitive by Jesus' activity in revealing the message (1:1c–d). Frequently such a genitive also carries some objective significance, and there are those who find this true here because the book continues to reveal the person of Christ. However, since the immediate context favours the subjective aspect, this analysis accepts it as more focal.

revealed A series of words from the same semantic field are used significantly. This starts with ἀποκάλυψις 'revelation', followed by δεῖξαι 'to show', and ἐσήμανεν (1:1d) 'make known'. It is the only place in the discourse that 'revelation' and 'make known' occur, though the noun 'sign' is used several times, and 'show' occurs frequently. The verbs 'show' and 'make known' seem to be chosen to reinforce the significance of the title of the book as a disclosure from God.

to John The implied indirect object is supplied in the display to satisfy the case frame. Although the revelation was ultimately for all God's people, in this proposition which defines the whole book John is the recipient of the revelation.

In this SUPERSCRIPTION the writer refers to himself in the 3rd person (1:1d) as ancient writers usually did. From 1:4 onwards, where the book takes on more of a letter format, he uses the 1st person.

1:1b-2 After the subject matter of the book has been introduced the rest of the Greek sentence restates it in greater detail.

1:1b committed The Greek word is ἔδωκεν 'he gave'. Thayer assigns here a meaning of 'to entrust'. The revelation was given to Jesus for a divine purpose, which he fulfilled by communicating it through John. In this verse the verb is immediately followed by the infinitive of purpose, δεῖξαι 'to reveal, show'.

1:1c his servants The servants belong to both God and Jesus Christ. Here we take the referent of the pronoun to be Jesus because of the sequence of pronouns in the verse: αὐτῷ 'to him', ἀγγέλου αὐτοῦ 'his angel', δούλῳ αὐτοῦ 'his servant'. The first of these clearly refers to Jesus. 19:5 shows that 'his servants' means all believers.

which must happen The word δεῖ 'must' is used several times in the book. Its use here is listed by BDAG under "of divine destiny or unavoidable fate." This means that these events will certainly happen, because God intends them to happen. A strong message of the book is God's control over people and events that touch their lives.

which must happen soon The phrase ἐν τάχει 'soon' is used in an eschatological sense and may be understood as 'suddenly', that is, 'without delay once the appointed time arrives' (see Morris), or in terms of the certainty of fulfilment. In prophecy the end time is always imminent (Mark 13:33) in a blending of the historical and the eschatological. There is also a strong eschatological significance in the use of ἐγγύς 'near' in 1:3c.

1:1d communicated The word in Greek is ἐσήμανεν 'communicated, made known'. The words ἔδωκεν 'he committed' and ἐσήμανεν 'he communicated' may appear to be parallel verbs in the Greek syntactic structure here, but the chain of revelation which is in focus requires that Jesus be the subject of ἐσήμανεν (see note on 1:1b above). Note that the Greek does not say that the angel was sent with the message, but that the message was sent "by means of" the angel. It is the communication to John that is in focus, not the sending of the angel.

1:2 truthfully reported The word ἐμαρτύρησεν 'he testified' has significance as a motif. It is used of what John is to write and of what Jesus disclosed to him. The verb is translated as *truthfully reported* because the English terms "testify" and "bear witness" imply a courtroom context, which is not present here. This is reinforced by the witness of Jesus in the epilogue (22:16). There is also the solemn warning of 22:18–19. The present perfect tense is used in the English here since it refers to the fact that John is in process of writing the book (Aune). The phrase *In this book* is also supplied to make this clear.

1:3a *God will* bless It is possible to translate μακάριος as a state, 'blessed, happy, fortunate', or with the transitive verb 'bless', showing how that state is occasioned, '*God will* bless'.

There are seven distinct pronouncements of blessing (beatitudes) in Revelation, each beginning with μακάριος 'blessed'. This is the first of these, and others are found in 14:13; 16:15; 19:9; 20:6; 22:7, 22:14. They tend to serve as mitigated commands.

reads...to others John envisages his book being read to an audience. At that time copies of books were very rare, and most people were illiterate.

those who listen to it and obey In οἱ ἀκούοντες...καὶ τηροῦντες 'those who listen to...and obey' there is only one article for both participles, so they must be taken together. The action of hearing is not complete without that of obeying.

what *God has commanded by means of* 'God has commanded by means of' is supplied in the display text since obedience is more universally understood as obedience to a personal being rather than to an abstract message.

1:3b–c *Therefore, read this message, listen to it, and obey it,* since *these things which Jesus has revealed* will happen soon The occurrence of γάρ 'for, since' with ὁ καιρὸς ἐγγύς 'the time (is) near' shows the basis for the addressees' carrying out the actions stated in the beatitude. Actually both the beatitude and the nearness of fulfilment act as motivation, clearly implying a command, thus this verse acts as a mitigated command.

BOUNDARIES AND COHERENCE

This is the beginning unit of the discourse. At 1:4 we find the normal initial component of a letter: the statement of the writer, and the recipients. This indicates a new section.

Coherence in the unit is shown by constant reference to the forefronted topic, that is, ἀποκάλυψις 'revelation'. It is referred to as τὸν λόγον τοῦ θεοῦ 'God's message' (1:2), τὴν μαρτυρίαν Ἰησοῦ Χριστοῦ 'what Jesus Christ truthfully reported' (1:2), ὅσα εἶδεν 'what he (John) saw' (1:2), and τοὺς λόγους τῆς προφητείας 'the prophetic message' (1:3a). It is not explicitly referenced in the verses following 1:3.

Another coherence feature is the fact that both parts of the superscription refer to the imminence of the events described (1:1c, 1:3c).

PROMINENCE AND THEME

The structure of the first sentence in the Greek, with no main verb, gives its opening words marked prominence. The theme statement consists of the main parts of the *INTRODUCTION/BASIS* (1:1–2) and the mitigated *APPEAL* (1:3).

BOOK CONSTITUENT 1:4–8 (Complex Paragraph: Opening of the Book)

THEME: I, John, write to you who are servants of Christ in the seven churches in Asia. I pray God may bless you. We(inc) praise Jesus Christ. He is coming as king and all who rejected him will be distraught. The Lord God Almighty confirms this.

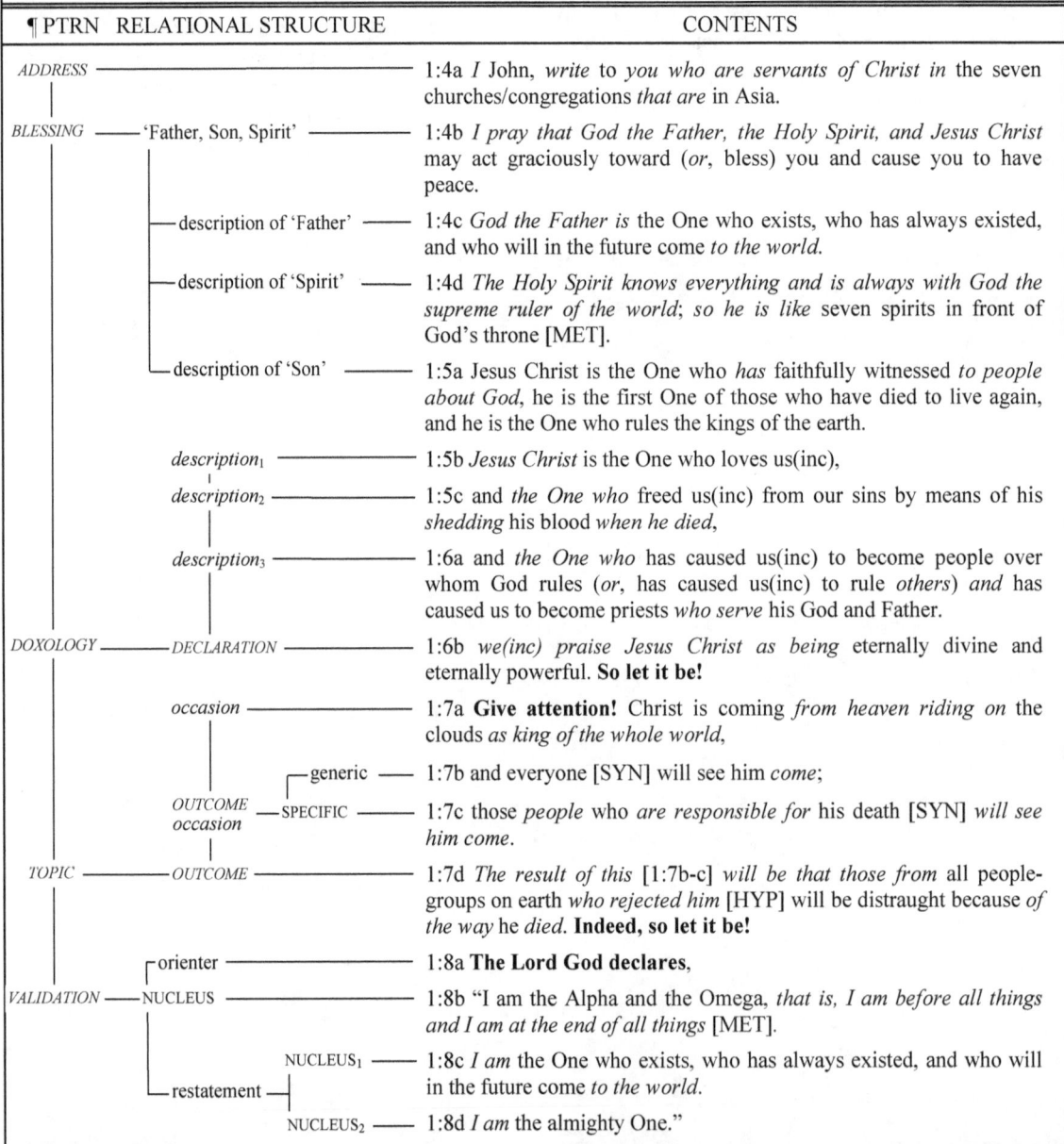

INTENT AND PARAGRAPH PATTERN

The unit begins with two features common to letters of the time, the ADDRESS and the BLESSING. The BLESSING is elaborated to include the three Persons of the Trinity with a special focus on Jesus Christ. This leads into three other features which can also be found (in different forms) in some of the NT epistles, namely the DOXOLOGY, the TOPIC of the letter, and the VALIDATION. Several epistles have a section of thanksgiving (e.g. 1Cor.1:4-9, 2Cor.1:1-3, Eph.1:3) following the Blessing section, and here it takes the form of a DOXOLOGY. This is followed by a dramatic presentation of the TOPIC of the book (1:7). This feature is not always so clearly shown in the opening of letters, but it is noticeable that in Rom.1:2-6 and Tit.1:1-3 Paul introduces the topic of his letter as part of the

Opening (before the Addressee). In each case the aim seems to be to validate the authority of the writer and his message. In Revelation the affirmation of God in 1:8 guarantees the fulfilment of the prophecies revealed in the book and this functions as a VALIDATION. Ladd calls it "the divine imprimatur."

Note that these labels are not paragraph pattern labels or normal communication relation labels. The relation between each of these units of the Opening is conjoining. This is indicated in the Greek by the juxtaposition of the units without any conjunctions.

NOTES

1:4a *write* to *you who are servants of Christ* There is no verb in the Greek, but 'write' is supplied since this is a letter. The reference to the recipients is in the third person ('to the seven churches') so 'you' is supplied from 1:4b. 'Who are servants of Christ' is needed to show the relationship the recipients have to the churches (i.e. congregations). This denotation of the recipients is appropriate to the discourse as 1:1c shows. As there, it does not refer to a special class of God's servants but to all believers.

the seven churches/congregations *that are* in Asia The definite article does not indicate that these seven churches constituted the whole church of Asia. There were other churches in Asia, but this was the group that John was commissioned (1:11) to write to. In the NT 'Asia' refers to the Roman province which occupied the western edge of Asia Minor.

1:4b *I pray that God the Father, the Holy Spirit, and Jesus Christ* These supplied elements are necessary in order to propositionalize the BLESSING, which is elliptical and complicated by the long descriptions of the agents of the blessing.

may act graciously toward you 'Grace' in this context represents an event, a benevolent action on God's part towards sinful mankind. It is used in a special Christian sense and since there is no specific English verb for such an event, 'act graciously' is used here. The closest alternative would be 'bless', which has somewhat of a wider range than 'grace'.

cause you to have peace J. Callow's comment on 'peace' (1983:28) in the similar context of Col.1:2 is helpful:

> It is generally agreed among the commentators that peace is the state enjoyed by the recipients of God's grace, and it is also generally considered that it is similar in meaning to the Hebrew word *shalom*, often translated by *eirēnē* ['peace'] in the Septuagint. The Hebrew word, however, means more than internal peacefulness or outward freedom from war, strife, etc. It corresponds more nearly to the English word "well-being", a state of blessedness or prosperity of body and soul. How far the ideas associated with the Hebrew word carried over into the Greek word *eirēnē* is very hard to say, especially when it is being used in a letter in the place where a conventional salutation would be used.

1:4c *God the Father is* the One who exists, who has always existed, and who will in the future come *to the world* The nominative case following the preposition ἀπό 'from' contravenes the rules of Greek grammar. It reflects the Greek of Exodus 3:14–15, where God disclosed his eternal existence to Moses saying that by the name ὁ ὤν 'the one who exists' he would be known perpetually. From its use in the Septuagint, the term became a name for God among Greek-speaking Jews.

The phrase ὁ ἦν 'the one who has always existed' is a use of the verb 'to be' in the past indicative tense to avoid the usual substitution of the past participle of γίνομαι 'to become'. The latter would not be in harmony with the doctrine of the immutability of God.

who will in the future come *to the world* The Greek text is ὁ ἐρχόμενος 'the one coming'. In the OT this term refers to the Messiah who will come into the world (Ps. 118:26; cf. Malachi 3:1). Here it completes the reference to God's past and present existence by showing that in the future he will come to bring this world to an end.

1:4d *The Holy Spirit knows everything and is always with God, the supreme ruler of the universe, so he is like* seven spirits in front of God's throne A large number of commentators accept the interpretation that 'the seven spirits' is a symbol of the Holy Spirit for the following reasons:

1. In the text at 1:4 the 'seven spirits' stand in a series of three sources, each introduced by ἀπό, from which the seven churches are to receive 'grace' and 'peace'. The first source is clearly understood as God, and the third is identified as Christ.
2. The seven spirits could not be angels for the following reasons:
   a. Angels could not be the source of 'grace' and 'peace'.
   b. Angels would not take linear precedence over the Son in this list (1:4c–5a).

c. 'Spirit' is not a term used for angels in Revelation.
3. In 3:1 Jesus says he has the 'seven spirits of God' so that they are possessed by both God and Jesus.

In Revelation the term 'Holy Spirit' does not occur, but 'the Spirit' is spoken of, as in 22:17. The number seven pervades the whole book, here no doubt pointing to the perfection and completeness of the divine nature and activity. In the Old Testament the number is symbolic of totality and completeness. Rev. 5:6 describes the Lamb as having seven eyes, which are interpreted as the 'seven spirits sent out into all the earth.' This imagery is drawn from Zechariah 4:2, 10b, and it symbolises the complete intelligence (as in 1 Cor. 2:10) and vigilance of the Holy Spirit.

The throne is a regular Biblical symbol for God as the supreme ruler of the world.

1:5a the One who *has* faithfully witnessed *to people about God* In the light of John 1:18 the witness of Jesus about God has the broadest possible meaning. He testified to the Old Testament message about God. Since he was God come in the flesh everything he did or said was a faithful witness about God.

1:5c freed us(inc) The Textus Receptus here reads λούσαντι 'washed' (i.e. 'washed us from our sins') instead of λύσαντι 'freed'. The oldest and best Greek manuscripts have the latter reading.

from our sins The concept of 'to free' normally implies being freed from some controlling power and so freedom not only from the guilt of sin but also from its power is implied here.

by means of his *shedding* his blood *when he died* The order of the words in the Greek shows that the focus of the sentence is on Christ's shedding his blood for us. GNB shows this focus in English: "by his sacrificial death he has freed us."

1:6a and *the One who* has caused us(inc) to become people over whom God rules (*or,* has caused us(inc) to rule *others*) and has caused us to become priests *who serve his* God and Father The Greek text is ἐποίησεν ἡμᾶς βασιλείαν, ἱερεῖς τῷ θεῷ καὶ πατρὶ αὐτοῦ 'he made us a kingdom, priests to the God and Father of him'. This idea is expressed in Exod. 19:6, also repeated in Rev. 5:9–10. In the New Testament βασιλεία most often has the meaning of a rule rather than a realm. The question here is whether the sense is 'believers ruled by God' or 'believers ruling over other people'. A substantial number of commentators understand it to mean reigning (with Christ) rather than being subjects in the kingdom. In 5:10 we read "You have made them to be a kingdom and priests to serve our God, and they will reign on the earth" (NIV, cf. 22:5). Caird says that John "believed that those whom Christ had released from their sins were called to be *a royal house*, not merely because he reigned over them as King, but because they were to share his regal authority over the nations (cf. ii. 26; iii. 21; v. 10; xx. 6)." However, there are certainly those who maintain that it means subjects of the kingdom, believers ruled by God, which would be its Old Testament meaning.

The relation of priests to God is made explicit by 'who serve' since a priest is one who is set apart, devoted to God in order to serve him. In 7:15 the redeemed are said to be before the throne to serve God day and night in his temple.

his God and Father While 'his' occurs only after 'Father' in the Greek, it probably qualifies both 'God' and 'Father' since a single definite article introduces both words.

1:6b we(inc) praise Jesus Christ as being eternally divine and eternally powerful The descriptions of Jesus Christ in 5b–6a function as part of the doxology, giving praise to him for his actions as well as for his glory and power.

In the New Testament when the term 'glory' is used of God it refers to his divinity as a unique quality which is his alone. Kittel and Friedrich understand it to express strictly the 'divine mode of being' (TDNT, vol. 2, p. 247) To give glory to God is to actively acknowledge or to extol his divine nature.

So let it be! This may be an appropriate translation for 'amen' here. However, it functions not as a proposition but as a prominence marker adding emphasis to the DECLARATION.

1:7a Give attention! The particle ἰδού occurs at the beginning of this verse. It is a prominence marker adding emphasis to this important announcement, which can be called the TOPIC of the book.

coming *from heaven riding on* the clouds Clouds in the Old Testament are associated with the divine presence (Exod.19:9) and with God's triumph over his enemies (Ps.18:9–14; 97:2–3). The picture here is drawn from Dan. 7:13–14 and is repeated several times in the gospels with reference to Christ's second coming (Matt. 24:30; 26:64). Different prepositions are used in the different references ('in/on/with the clouds') but the general idea is, as Bratcher and Hatton say, that the clouds are Christ's 'means of transportation.'

as king of the whole world This is supplied to make clear the implications of the passages in Daniel and Matthew cited above. Because of those passages, when John's audience heard that Jesus was coming 'with the clouds' they would have known that Jesus was coming with power and with God's authority to exercise his rule.

1:7b–d everyone will see him *come*; those *people* who *are responsible for* his death *will see him come*. *The result of this* [1:7b–c] *will be that those from* all people-groups on earth *who rejected him* will *be distraught* because *of the way* he *died* This is a definite, but indirect, quotation from Zechariah 12:10-14. It is also an echo of Matthew 24:30.

Taking 'every eye' to be completely universal, there is a generic-specific relation between 1:7b and 7c in which the specific aspect is more prominent than the generic because 7d has the most direct relationship with 7c.

In a sequence of finite verbs (ἔρχεται 'come,' ὄψεται 'see,' κόψονται 'be distraught') the final one is naturally highlighted. The people are distraught as an immediate result of recognizing him. This is the most prominent element because it points to the judgment, which is a main theme of the whole discourse.

everyone will see him *come* The Greek 'Every eye' is synecdoche for 'everyone'.

those *people* who *are responsible for* his death The Greek has ἐξεκέντησαν 'pierced,' but Jesus had already died when he was pierced. The piercing, perhaps because it proclaimed that Jesus actually died and also because John uses imagery here from Zech. 12:10, is used by synecdoche for the crucifixion as a whole.

Commentators in general agree with Mounce who says the classification of those who pierced him is not restricted to the Roman soldiers who stabbed Jesus on the cross nor to the Jews who wanted it done but "extends to all those of every age whose careless indifference to Jesus is typified in the act of piercing." This idea is made explicit in the display with the use of 'responsible for'.

those from all people-groups on earth *who rejected him* The Greek 'all people groups' is hyperbole, since those who have accepted Christ will clearly not be sad at his return.

will be distraught because *of the way* he *died* The English versions which translate κόψονται ἐπ' αὐτὸν as 'weep because of him' here are closer to the meaning of the Greek than those that use the term 'mourn.' The verb means 'to openly demonstrate deep sadness at the death of someone else,' literally 'to beat oneself.' The other person's death is regarded as a disaster for oneself. It does not necessarily indicate affection for the one who has died. In both this verse and Matthew 24:30 those who rejected Christ are seen as being originally indifferent to his death, but when they see his return in glory they will recognise it was really a disaster for them.

Indeed, so let it be! This may be an appropriate translation for 'yes, amen' here but note that both the words of the Greek text and 'so let it be' are primarily dialogue-oriented words. See the note on 1:6b. Here the ναί 'yes' adds an element of the writer's affirmation of the propositions it follows.

1:8a The Lord God declares In the Greek text this speech orienter comes after 'I am the Alpha and the Omega', and this change from the normal order highlights and emphasises the words of God. It reaffirms the eternal divine power and sovereignty needed to accomplish the events prophesied in the book.

Lenski understands κύριος 'Lord' as Christ, but the compelling reason for attributing the quotation of 1:8 to God the Father is that the description of the speaker is the same as that given of the Father in 1:4.

Many commentators understand the whole content of 1:8 as spoken by God the Father. But some consider only the statement 'I am Alpha and Omega' to be quoted, with the author John filling in the rest of the verse. We cannot be dogmatic about where the end of the quotation comes.

1:8b I am the Alpha and the Omega *that is, I am before all things and I am at the end of all things* The first and last letters of the Greek alphabet were used to represent a universal entirety, including all between the two extremes. This expression means the same as 'The first and the last' in 1:17, (see the note on 1:17f–18a) referring to the whole extent of whatever it designated. As in Isa. 41:4 and 44:6, it describes the comprehensiveness of God.

1:8d *I am* the almighty One In Greek κράτος 'power' denotes the presence and significance of force or strength rather than its exercise, and when used in a political sense it means legal and valid superior power. It has the sense of supremacy and victory. The related verb is often used to mean 'to conquer' or 'to rule'. The derived noun here, παντοκράτωρ 'ruler of all, almighty', occurs in the

Septuagint, where it often translates the Hebrew expression for 'Lord of Hosts'.

BOUNDARIES AND COHERENCE

As noted in Intent and Structure, 1:4–8 consists of brief units each with a different function. These could be handled as separate paragraphs, as some versions and texts do. They are handled here as a complex paragraph because they comprise the standard opening of a letter. This also delimits the boundaries of this unit, since 1:1-3 is non-epistolary and 1:9 begins the narrative BODY of the letter.

PROMINENCE AND THEME

The propositional clusters which comprise the unit are construed as equally important conjoined parts. However, as noted above, there are features of marked prominence in 1:6b, 7a, 7d and 8a, which highlight the DOXOLOGY, the TOPIC and the VALIDATION. The theme is constructed from the important features of each of the conjoined units.

BOOK CONSTITUENT 1:9–22:11 (PART: BODY OF THE BOOK)

THEME. Under the control of the Holy Spirit I was commissioned by Christ to send to the churches his proclamation that they must repent of their sins and be faithful and obedient to him. I saw God and Christ being worshipped in heaven, and God's people praising him as his judgment was enacted on the rebellious people of the earth. Then I saw the great prostitute, Babylon, who was drunk with the blood of God's people. She was being destroyed together with all those who rebelled against God. God judged all people by their deeds and all whose names were not in the book of life were thrown into the lake of fire. Finally I saw the Bride of the Lamb, the new city of Jerusalem, perfect in every way, where God will dwell permanently with his people. God declared that he had made everything new and everything was now accomplished. In the city God's servants have the abundant sources of eternal life, and they live forever as kings worshipping God in the light of his glory.

MACROSTRUCTURE	CONTENTS
STEP$_1$	1:9–3:22 When I was under the control of the Holy Spirit, the glorified Christ appeared to me and commissioned me to write down what would be revealed to me and to send it to the seven churches of Asia. He proclaimed that the churches must listen to his message exhorting them to repent of various sins and encouraging them to be faithful and obedient to him.
STEP$_2$	4:1–16:21 I was told to come up to heaven and see the events that must happen. I saw God on his throne being worshiped, and Christ being worshiped as the Redeemer because he is worthy to open the sealed scroll. The opening of the seven seals and then the sounding of seven trumpets brought judgment on rebellious earth people, and God's servants were marked out, and there were cosmic manifestations of judgment. Satan and his agents caused all earth people to submit to them, but God's people were with Christ praising God as the final judgment was announced. Angels poured out the seven bowls of God's anger bringing terrible afflictions on the rebellious earth people in completion of God's punishment of them.
STEP$_3$	17:1–20:15 I saw the great prostitute, Babylon, who was drunk with the blood of God's people. When she was destroyed I heard the inhabitants of heaven praising God and God's people rejoicing that the time had come for the marriage of the Lamb. Then I saw the King of kings going out to destroy the rebellious people of the nations. The beast and the false prophet led the people to fight against God's people but they were all destroyed, Satan was imprisoned, and God's people reigned as kings for a thousand years. After Satan led another rebellion against God, God had him thrown in the lake of fire. Then God judged all people by their deeds and all whose names were not in the book of life were thrown into the lake of fire.
GOAL	21:1–22:5 I saw the Bride of the Lamb, the new city of Jerusalem, perfect in every way, where God will dwell permanently with his people. God declared that he had made everything new and everything was now accomplished. In the city God's servants have the abundant sources of eternal life, and they live forever as kings worshipping God in the light of his glory.
denouement	22:6-11 God has verified this revelation and Jesus reminds his people that he is coming soon, so they must obey the message of this book in order to enjoy God's blessings. I, John, am the one who heard and saw these things, and the angel who showed them to me told me not to keep this revelation secret.

INTENT AND MACROSTRUCTURE

The surface macrostructure of the Body of the book can be seen to be narrative *step-GOAL*. The bulk of the narrative shows how God's final purposes for the world build up through three major *steps* towards the GOAL. This GOAL is the new creation which consists simply of God himself and his faithful people in the perfection of the new Jerusalem, where there is nothing of evil or suffering at all.

Following this GOAL there is a short final unit which acts as a verification of the vision that the narrative of the BODY relates. It is clearly part of the BODY but it does not extend the narrative of the vision. It is therefore designated as a *denouement* here.

See Boundaries and Coherence for 4:1–16:21 for discussion of an alternative division of the second and third *steps* (4:1–20:15).

While the overall framework of the Body is narrative in intent, since it relates what John saw in his vision, there is also an underlying hortative intent. This is overt in some parts, such as the letters to the churches (2:1–3:22) in STEP$_1$, where the hortatory intent is marked as highly prominent by devices such as τάδε λέγει 'these things says ...' (2:1 etc.), and in the warnings in the *denouement*. But a hortatory intent is also seen in the contents of the vision, as it shows that all the evil in the world and the people who reject God are under his purview and that he will definitely destroy them and vindicate those who are faithful to him. This would have the hortatory effect of encouraging John's audience to persevere in their faith whatever suffering it led them to face.

BOUNDARIES AND COHERENCE

This analysis takes the Body of the book to begin at 1:9 where the Opening's epistolary material ends and the narrative starts. Here John begins by identifying himself and relating his divine commission to write down the vision he was about to receive (1:9, 10–16). Similarly at the end of the Body, John again identifies himself and relates his angelic commission to publish what he has written (22:8–11). After that there is no further narrative and the Epilogue of the book consists of speech material that is expressive in intent.

Many analyses of Revelation take a different decision about the opening boundary of the BODY, putting it at 4:1, with the letters to the churches in a separate introduction to the book. It is true that the letters do have an introductory aspect and a different discourse style to the rest of the book, but separating them from the Body ignores their narrative framework (2:1a, 8a etc.). They are actually part of the speech which begins in 1:17 and which is in itself part of the narrative that starts in 1:9. The narrative continues at 4:1 with μετὰ ταῦτα εἶδον 'after this I saw'. Another factor that shows the coherence of 1:9–3:22 with the rest of the Body is the way in which the promises in the letters to those who overcome are shown as fulfilled in the GOAL:

1. The tree of life (2:7 cf. 22:2).
2. Deliverance from the second death (2:11 cf. 21:4, 8).
3. The name written in the Book of Life (3:5 cf. 21:27).
4. The new name (3:12 cf. 22:4).
5. Entrance into the Holy City (3:12 cf. 21:27).
6. Reigning with Christ (3:21 cf. 22:5).

However, if there are some disagreements about where the Body begins, there is very little agreement at all about its end. This has been placed variously at 22:5, 9 or 11. The description of the new Jerusalem ends at 22:5 and it is followed by heterogeneous material, the latter part of which is clearly an Epilogue. But the boundary between the Body and the Epilogue is not obvious. The current analysis takes the end of the Body to be at 22:11 because of the paragraph connectors in the Greek at 22:6 and 8, as explained under Boundaries and Coherence for 22:6–11.

The coherence of the Body is seen both in terms and themes that run throughout it and in specific topics that are introduced in earlier parts of the Body and then dealt with more fully in later ones.

One of the most striking terms that runs throughout the Body is the designation of Christ as the Lamb that had been killed but was alive. Noticeably this is used even where there is no direct reference to his sacrificial or redeeming role, such as 17:14 where he is the commander of God's army, and 19:7–9, 21:9 where the people of God are his bride.

A theme that links all the parts of the Body is the visionary nature of the narrative material. At or near the beginning of each of the parts of the Body, John states that he was ἐν πνεύματι 'in Spirit' (1:10, 4:2; 17:3; 21:10), meaning that he was specially under the control of the Holy Spirit in some way that enabled him to undergo supernatural experiences.

The literary device of introducing a topic well before it is treated in full has been mentioned above in connection with the promises in the letters (1:9–3:22) to those who overcome. It is also particularly noticeable in the case of the destruction of Babylon, which is mentioned very briefly at 14:8 and again at the end of STEP$_2$ (16:19), before being dealt with more fully in STEP$_3$, particularly in ch.18. This has the effect of giving coherence to these two Steps, as does the foreshadowing in 16:12–16 of the final battle against the forces of evil (19:19–21). Coherence between STEP$_2$ and the GOAL is indicated by the divine pronouncement Γέγονεν 'it has been accomplished', echoed by Γέγοναν '*(everything) has been accomplished*' at 21:6. Similarly STEP$_3$ is linked to the *denouement* by John's erroneous worship of the angel in 19:10 and his rebuke in terms of the proper spirit of prophecy, both elements of which are repeated in 22:6, 8–9.

PROMINENCE AND THEME

The GOAL, the vision of the new Jerusalem, is naturally prominent. However, the *steps* are not only necessary for the fulfilment of the GOAL, but are also prominent in themselves as major parts of the book. The theme of the body therefore comes from both the GOAL and the *steps*.

PART CONSTITUENT 1:9–3:22 (Act: Step₁ of Body)

THEME: When I was under the control of the Holy Spirit, the glorified Christ appeared to me and commissioned me to write down what would be revealed to me and to send it to the seven churches of Asia. He proclaimed that the churches must listen to his message exhorting them to repent of various sins and encouraging them to be faithful and obedient to him.

MACROSTRUCTURE	CONTENTS
SETTING	1:9 I, John, who shares with you as we(inc) suffer *persecution* and *serve* our king *Jesus*, was on Patmos because *I had proclaimed* what God says and what Jesus witnessed *about God*.
STEP	1:10–16 Under the control of the Holy Spirit, I heard a voice ordering me to write down the vision and send it to the seven churches of Asia. I saw that the one speaking to me was the glorified Son of Man.
GOAL (Hortatory)	1:17–3:22 After the glorified Christ had told me not to be afraid and had commissioned me to write down what was to be revealed to me, he proclaimed that the churches must listen to his message exhorting them to repent of various sins and encouraging them to be faithful and obedient to him.

INTENT AND MACROSTRUCTURE

Although this act has a narrative framework of SETTING – STEP – GOAL, it contains within its GOAL the most direct appeals in the whole book (2:1–3:22). Its primary intent is therefore hortatory.

Within this unit 1:9 functions as a SETTING since it introduces the narrator and his situation. 1:10–16 then functions as a STEP since it initiates the action, the appearance of Christ and his command to John to write to the churches. This is accomplished in the GOAL (1:17–3:22) where Christ issues his proclamation.

BOUNDARIES AND COHERENCE

The unit opens with a SETTING, in which John introduces himself and his relationship to his readers. The close of the act comes as Christ concludes his messages to the individual churches, that is, at the end of the message to the seventh church (3:22), and with announcement in 4:1–2 of an appropriate change of setting. Further means for determining the boundaries have been included in the discussion of the BODY.

Coherence is found throughout the unit in the references to the three main participants: John, Christ, and the churches, to whom the writing and revelation is addressed. Further evidence of coherence is seen in the statements identifying Christ at the beginning of each message, referring back to some part of the descriptions given in 1:12–16, 17–18 (2:1 cf. 1:13, 16; 2:8 cf. 1:17–18; 2:12 cf. 1:16; 2:18 cf. 1:14–15; 3:1 cf. 1:16; 3:7 cf. 1:18; 3:14 cf. 1:17).

PROMINENCE AND THEME

Natural prominence is recognized in 2:1–3:22 which is the nucleus of the GOAL. However, since the SETTING and the STEP are essential to the structure of the unit, the main points from these are also included in the theme.

ACT CONSTITUENT 1:9 (Paragraph: Setting of 1:9–3:22)

THEME: *I, John, who shares with you as we(inc) suffer persecution and serve our king Jesus, was on Patmos because I had proclaimed what God says and what Jesus witnessed about God.*

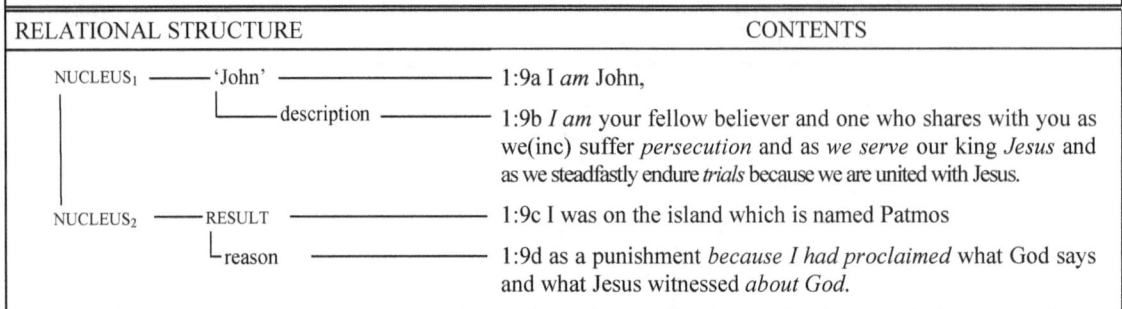

INTENT AND STRUCTURE

This descriptive paragraph actually gives the setting for the whole of the narrative BODY of the book. All the visions are presented as having been seen by John on Patmos. However, the setting does belong particularly to the first Act of the BODY since its main details, John's fellowship in suffering with his audience and his presence in a particular geographical region, are only of relevance to the first Act. After that, nothing of John's experience or location is relevant as he is addressed and moved around by an angel.

NOTES

1:9b your fellow believer The expression 'your brother' is understood to denote a fellow-member of the Christian community. It is rendered in the display according to its true referential meaning. However, in many languages the word 'brother' functions like 'brother' in Greek in this situation and, in fact, may communicate the total meaning of the Greek text better than a literal translation of 'your fellow believer' would.

shares with you as we(inc) suffer *persecution* and *as we serve* our king *Jesus* and as we steadfastly endure *trials* One definite article governs the three Greek nouns that are here represented as 'suffer,' 'serve our king' and 'endure.' Therefore they are regarded as a group, all qualified by the phrase ἐν Ἰησοῦ 'in Jesus.'

The word βασιλεία 'kingdom' here is taken to mean participation as subjects in the kingdom of Christ.

as we steadfastly endure *trials* Hauck (TDNT, vol. 4, pp. 581–88) shows the difference between an Old Testament "quietistic waiting on God" and the New Testament meaning of ὑπομονή 'steadfastness', where faith and hope are more central. Hauck says: "In most of the NT passages ὑπομένειν ['to be steadfast'] refers to the steadfast endurance of the Christian under the difficulties and tests of the present evil age."

The variety of words used in modern versions to translate ὑπομονή 'steadfastness' indicates the difficulty of finding an adequate equivalent. Perhaps the best equivalent in English is 'steadfastness', though the word is not frequent in current speech.

because we are united with Jesus The phrase ἐν Ἰησοῦ 'in Jesus' is very similar to the phrase Paul often uses 'in Christ,' which is widely understood to mean union with Christ.

1:9c-d I was on the island which is named Patmos as a punishment *because I had proclaimed* what God says and what Jesus witnessed *about God*. The use of phrases very similar to διὰ τὸν λόγον τοῦ θεοῦ καὶ τὴν μαρτυρίαν Ἰησοῦ 'because of the word of God and the witness of Jesus' in 6:9 and 20:4 makes it very likely that John's stay on Patmos was a punishment.

BOUNDARIES AND COHERENCE

This descriptive unit is delimited by the beginning of the BODY at 1.9a and the beginning of the narrative at 1.10. Its coherence comes from its comprising the elements necessary for the setting of a first-person narrative: the narrator's identity and his location.

PROMINENCE AND THEME

As has been mentioned above, the reason for John's presence on Patmos is marked as more prominent than the actual location. The theme contains the main elements of both parts of the unit.

ACT CONSTITUENT 1:10–16 (Paragraph: Step of 1:9–3:22)

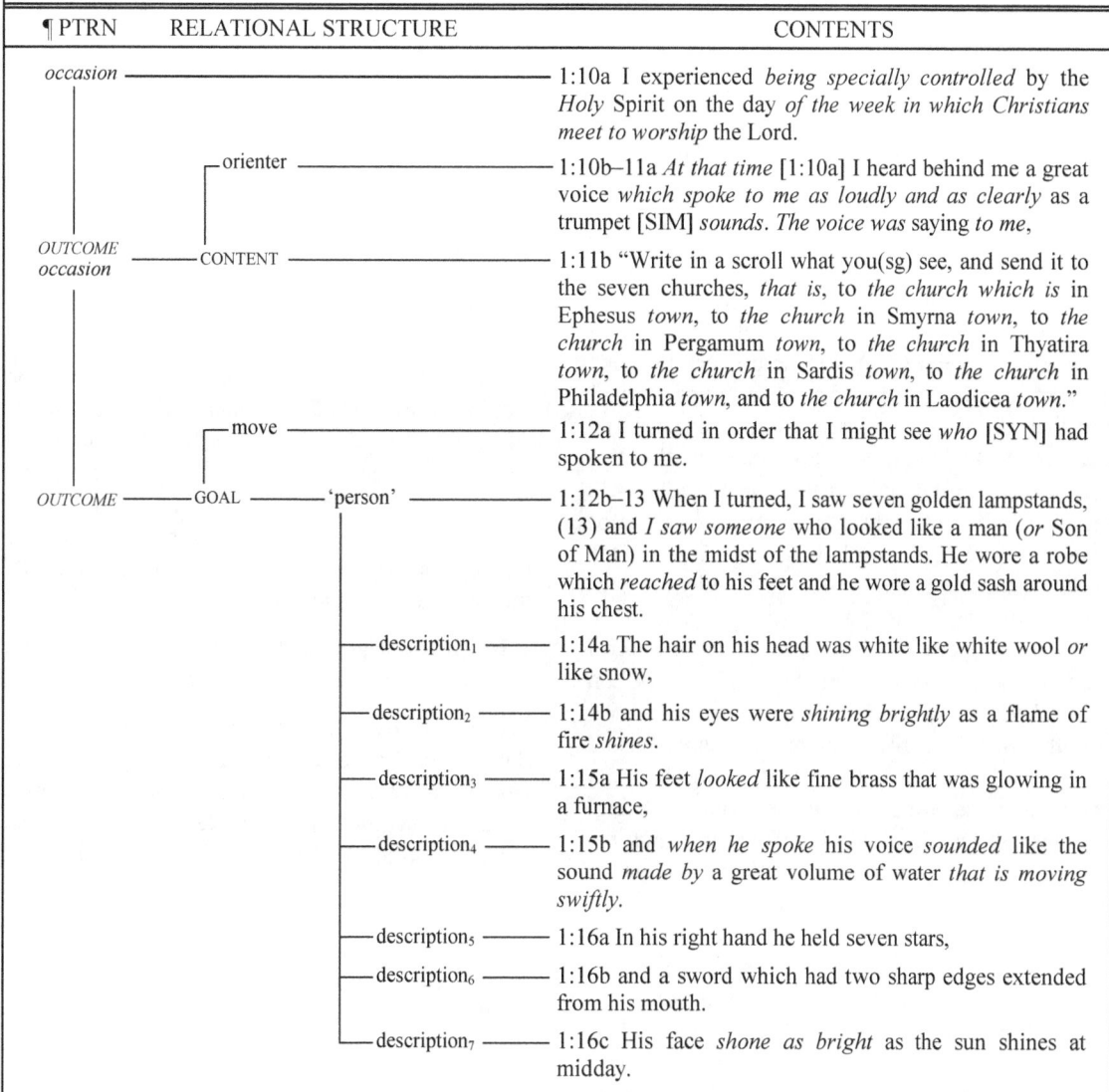

INTENT AND PARAGRAPH PATTERN

This narrative section relates three events in an occasion–outcome sequence: John's falling into a state of ecstasy, his hearing a voice ordering him to send an account of his visions to the churches, and his seeing the one who was speaking to him. This last constituent is expanded by a lengthy description.

NOTES

1:10a *specially controlled* by the *Holy* Spirit The Greek text has ἐν πνεύματι 'in spirit'. The expression is used four times in the book, once in each part of the BODY: this verse and 4:2, 17:3, 21:10. 'In spirit' is understood as a state of ecstasy in which John received a vision. It is not to be confused with Paul's term 'walking in the Spirit', which is his teaching of the normal life of the regenerated Christian, under the constant control of the Holy Spirit. Rather, it is a special state in which a person consciously experiences being guided supernaturally by God's Spirit.

1:11b in a scroll A book for John probably meant a scroll. The Greek has the object, 'What you see' first in the sentence as point of departure

(Levinsohn, pp. 7-8) indicating that the important part is 'write in a book'. A free translation in English might show this by saying, 'Take a scroll and write in it what you see'.

the seven churches This explains the reference in 1:4.

1:12b When I turned As a repetition of 1:12a this highlights the following proposition.

seven golden lampstands Since the lampstands are symbolic of the churches, seven, the number of completeness, would mean all of God's servants.

1:13 in the midst of the lampstands By repeating 'lampstands' John slows down his introduction of 'one like a son of man,' thus highlighting him.

a man (*or* Son of Man) The primary meaning of υἱὸς ἀνθρώπου 'son of man' is 'human being' and that is probably one sense intended here. The background for this use here is undoubtedly Dan. 7:13, "I saw in the night visions, and behold, with the clouds of heaven there came one like a son of man..." (RSV). Even though Dan. 7:13 is the background, this cannot bypass the use by Jesus of 'the son of man' in the gospels as a designation for 'Messiah', especially since Jesus used that term with the same background of Dan. 7:13. The person referred to here is the Son of Man, that is, Christ. And the use of 'one like a son of man' here is meant to allude to that fact. The Greek expression can handle both the designation of 'like a human being' and the allusion to the Messianic title, but the problem comes in translation into languages which cannot handle both. If one translates 'like a human being', the allusion is lost. However the reference to Christ will be clear from 1:17 and 18.

reached to his feet and he wore a gold sash around his chest The word ζώνη translated as 'sash' in the display is glossed by BDAG as 'belt' or 'girdle'. These words are not used in modern English for something that is worn around the chest, so 'sash' is used, indicating a cloth of gold worn around (not diagonally on) the chest.

1:15a like fine brass that was glowing in a furnace The Greek term is χαλκολίβανον or χαλκολίβανος, which has not been found in literature independent of Revelation and has never been clearly identified. However, it is a compound with the first part coming from χαλκός meaning 'copper, brass, bronze' and is usually translated as 'bronze' or 'brass'.

Another problem in this description is that πεπυρωμένης 'made red-hot' is a genitive participle that is not appropriately related syntactically to anything else in the clause. It would be expected to agree with the dative χαλκολιβάνῳ. However, semantically we must either assume a relationship to χαλκολιβάνῳ or that something is missing. Since the semantic relationship has at least the potentiality of coherence, it seems best to understand it as most versions do, for example, "His feet were like bronze glowing in the furnace." Weymouth translates: "like silver bronze when it is white-hot in a furnace." Phillips has: "like the finest bronze glows in the furnace."

1:15b his voice *sounded* like the sound *made by* a great volume of water *that is moving swiftly* The Greek text underlying the display rendering 'a great volume of water' is ὑδάτων πολλῶν 'many waters'. 'Many waters' is unnatural English and would be translated as 'much water', or 'many streams of water' if that were the intention, but it would seem that there would be a more distinct way of rendering the latter in Greek than ὑδάτων πολλῶν. Also, the implication is that the water is moving, otherwise there would be no sound. NIV translates as "rushing waters."

1:16a In his right hand he held The right hand symbolizes power, authority, and security.

1:16b a sword The word used here is ῥομφαία, 'large sword'. The New Testament uses two Greek words for 'sword'. John in Revelation uses μάχαιρα symbolically to represent war and bloodshed (6:4; 13:10, 14). He reserves the word used here for God's judgment, and it is his specific term used each time for the sword extending from Christ's mouth (1:16; 2:12, 16; 19:15, 21). This justifies the inference of Michaelis (TDNT, vol. 6, p. 998) that the only weapon used by Christ is his Word, and it accords with Isa. 11:4.

1:16c His face Most versions and commentators translate ὄψις here as 'face' (cf. John 11:44), but Lenski and Düsterdieck prefer 'appearance' (cf. John 7:24). This analysis uses 'face' simply because of the weight of opinion in favour of that translation. However, the argument for 'appearance' is not to be neglected. BDAG lists both meanings for this passage. Düsterdieck takes the shining to refer to the whole appearance of Christ because it comes last in the description, the head and eyes having been mentioned first, and because the overall impression in Daniel's vision speaks of the entire form (Dan. 10:6). Lenski also sees the description closed with a reference to the general appearance to sum up the picture. He refers to the transfiguration scene (Matt. 17:2), noting that in contrast πρόσωπον 'face' is used there.

A linguistic factor may have some bearing on the decision. The only place in the description where the conjunction δέ occurs is at the beginning of 1:14, where there is a switch from the topic of the person of Christ in general and what he was wearing to the subtopics of the different parts of his body. There are seven parts of the body described and this accords with John's symbolic use of the number seven for completeness. Thus that which is recorded in 1:13 appears to be introductory to the seven aspects which follow. This presentation of the seven parts of the body, which includes ὄψις in 1:16c, may suggest that ὄψις means 'face' rather than 'appearance'.

His face *shone as bright* as the sun shines at midday 'shone as bright as' provides the full point of comparison between the topic (Christ's face) and the image (the sun at midday). Literally midday is 'in the power of it'; the display rendering is a specific, concrete manifestation of this meaning.

BOUNDARIES AND COHERENCE

The unit begins with the switch to narrative in 1:10, after the descriptive Setting of 1:9. It ends with the resumption of the narrative, and the repetition of the verb εἶδον 'I saw' in 17a. The narrative structure gives the section coherence. It is a short chain of *occasion–OUTCOME* units linked by the conjunction καί 'and'.

PROMINENCE AND THEME

The main events of the narrative constitute the theme, together with a summary of the message John receives and a summary of the description of the one he sees, 'the glorified Son of Man.'

ACT CONSTITUENT 1:17–3:22 (Section: Goal of 1:9–3:22)

THEME: After the glorified Christ had told me not to be afraid and had commissioned me to write down what was to be revealed to me, he proclaimed that the churches must listen to his message exhorting them to repent of various sins and encouraging them to be faithful and obedient to him.

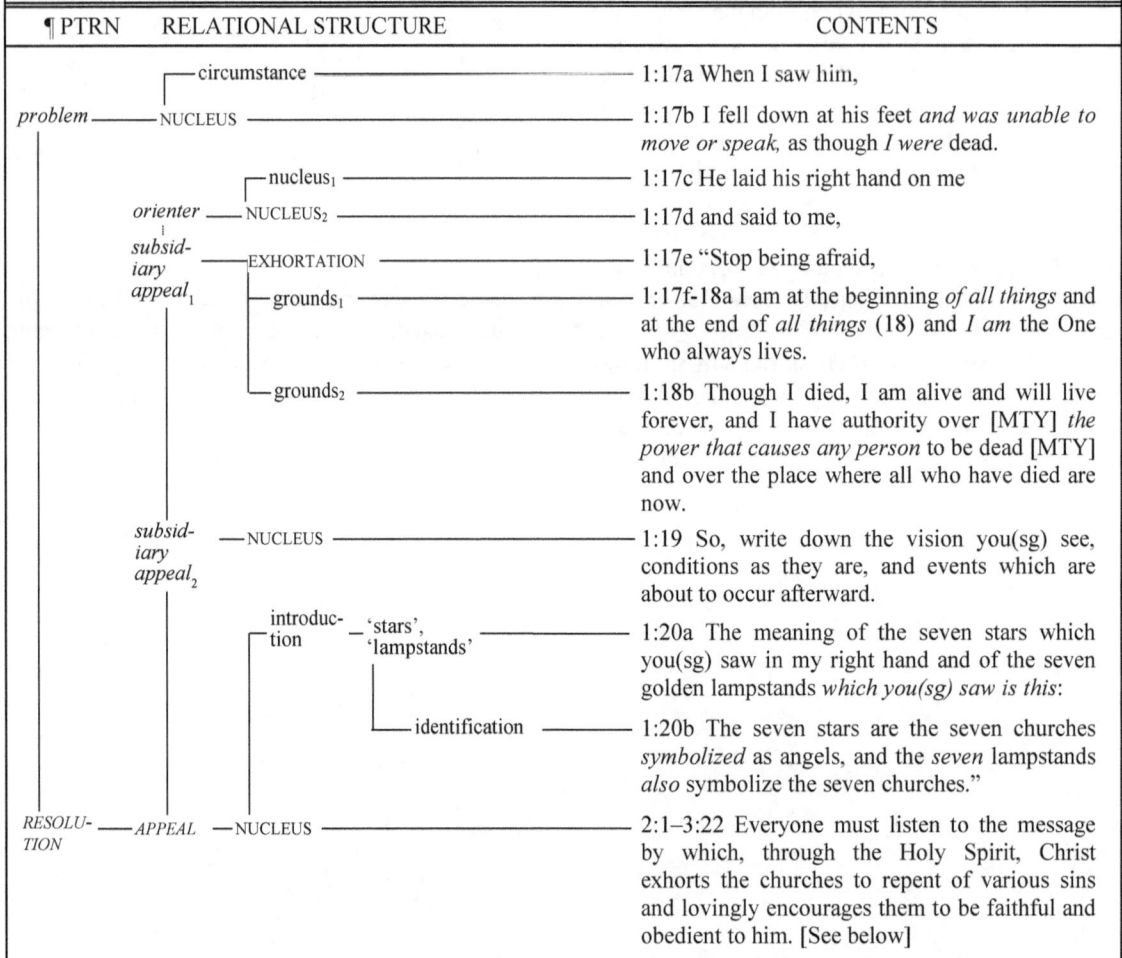

INTENT AND PARAGRAPH PATTERN

The main part of this unit, the speech of the glorified Christ (1:17c–3:22) is clearly hortatory, with two *subsidiary appeals* to John (1:17e–20) followed by the main APPEAL to the churches (2:1–3:22). However the unit itself is narrative, as John continues to narrate the course of his vision. Its internal structure is that of *problem–RESOLUTION*, since John's reaction to the sight of Christ interrupts proceedings. (As the APPEAL is so lengthy and consists of seven letters, it is dealt with in succeeding sections of this analysis, although it technically forms part of this unit.)

NOTES

1:17a When I saw him This repeating of 'I saw' from 1:12 indicates that the narrative is being resumed after the descriptive material of 1:13-16.

1:17b I fell down at his feet *and was unable to move or speak,* as though *I were* dead The constituent order of the Greek clause with 'as though dead' at the end indicates that the focus is on this phrase. This describes a physical reaction to the awesome vision, as at the transfiguration scene in Matt. 17:6. Some may ask whether John means to say he had fainted and thus received the vision in an unconscious state, or was simply motionless and speechless. Old Testament instances may also be cited, such as Dan. 10:4–11. Like John, Daniel was already experiencing a vision, but he reports falling into a deep sleep and being aroused by a hand placed on him and a voice telling him to stand to receive the divine message. Paul's experience on the way to Damascus (Acts 9:3–4; 22:7; 26:14) seems to have left him conscious though experiencing a supernatural revelation. Bratcher and Hatton suggest John had not fainted but was lying without moving or speaking. The italicized words in the display provide the point of comparison between the state of being dead and the presumed physical reaction John was experiencing.

1:17c-d He laid his right hand on me and said to me There are two simultaneous actions here. In both Old and New Testaments hands are laid on a person to ordain (1 Tim. 4:14), install in office (Acts 6:6), confer blessing (Mark 10:16), or impart healing (Luke 13:13).

1:17e Stop being afraid The negated present form forbids continuing what is already in progress. It is followed by the speaker's identification. As in Christ's reassurance to the disciples in John 6:20 the identification gives the grounds for the exhortation not to fear.

1:17f–18a I am at the beginning *of all things* **and at the end of** *all things* According to Kittel and Friedrich (TDNT, vol. 1, p. 1) 'the first and the last' means "the Creator and the Consummator," and comes from Isa. 44:6. Spelled out in a verbal form it shows God active in Christ initiating creation and faithful to consummate whatever he initiates. So an alternate rendering for the display would be 'I am the One who initiates all things and the One who will consummate everything I have initiated'. The Alpha and Omega of 1:8 is a comparable expression. In both passages divine activity is in focus. It is the eternal, almighty God in 1:8 and Christ his Son in 1:17f–18a.

I am **the One who always lives** Bratcher and Hatton say about 'the living one', "This means more than just 'I am alive'; it is the language of divine existence, of God, who by his nature has life in himself and cannot be thought of as not living."

1:18b though I died, I am alive The word ἰδού 'behold' occurs before ζῶν εἰμι εἰς τοὺς αἰῶνας τῶν αἰώνων 'I am alive for ever and ever'. Although Van Otterloo (p. 63) classifies this occurrence of ἰδού under "calling attention to a situation that requires action" (p. 59), the word order of the Greek clause shows that it is more appropriate under his category of calling special attention to something contrary to expectation. Thus 'though' is used in the display.

I have authority over Literally 'I have the keys of....'. 'Keys' can be understood as metonymy for their function: authority over something. It is questionable whether in translation 'keys' must be kept literally as a live figure, though it is advisable to do so if it can be done meaningfully and naturally.

over *the power that causes any person* **to be dead and over the place where all who die are now** In the expression 'the keys of death', 'death' is an abstract noun standing for the authority or power that causes people to die and keeps them dead. Christ's authority over Hades, the place of the dead, indicates that he has the power to cause the dead to live again, and this also seems to be the focus of 'the keys of death' here: Christ has the power to make the dead alive again.

1:19 So The conjunction οὖν introduces the repetition of the command of 1:11. Within the speech of Jesus it indicates the resumption of his main theme.

write down the vision you(sg) see 'The vision' in the display translates ἅ 'the things', which is a plural form referring to the singular ἀποκάλυψις 'revelation' (1:1), which Jesus showed to John. The aorist verb εἶδες 'you(sg) saw', does not need to mean something in past time (translated "see" in NCV, RSV). Aune shows that this is an 'epistolary aorist' indicating that when John comes to do the writing the 'seeing' will be in the past.

Undoubtedly the three parts of the command in 1:19 are meant to cover all the visions described in the book. If anything, the use of past, present, and future time is meant to be all-inclusive.

conditions as they are Some commentators believe that 'things which are' refers to conditions as found in the letters to the churches in 2:1–3:22 (Ladd, Walvoord). Others see this as contemporary events that may be seen scattered through all Revelation (Beasley-Murray, Düsterdieck, Lenski).

and events which are about to occur afterward Those who take 'things which are' as referring to chapters 2–3, understand this part to refer to chapters 4–22, while others see it as referring to Revelation as a whole.

1:20a The meaning of the seven stars which you(sg) saw in my right hand and of the seven golden lampstands *which you(sg) saw* At first sight 1:20 seems to be unconnected to the subject matter of 1:17e–19. However, Aune points out that it forms a link to 2:1–3.22. It introduces into the narrative of the vision the churches to whom Christ's message in 2:1–3:22 is addressed.

The meaning Swete says, "Here τὸ μυστήριον is the inner meaning of a symbolical vision." In the New Testament sense mystery finds its corollary in revelation. It must be understood that to say the stars and lampstands symbolize the angels and the churches does not fully explain them, because the full meaning is not yet revealed.

in my right hand The preposition used here is ἐπί, which has the primary meaning of 'on' (ἐν 'in' was used in the similar context in 1:16). The ἐπί has been variously interpreted as signifying a wreath or ring. But such minor details are hardly relevant in a vision unless they can be clearly shown to be contextually pertinent.

1:20b The seven stars are the seven churches *symbolized as* angels Stars have in common with angels that they are heavenly entities associated with light.

In the New Testament ἄγγελοι 'angels, messengers' nearly always refers to supernatural beings. In Revelation the word ἄγγελος 'angel' occurs 67 times, the only possible human application being the instances related to the churches. It seems unlikely that John would make an exceptional use of the term in this connection. It violates the symbolic system of the book. Understanding ἄγγελος as a human representative of the church is further rejected on the grounds that ἄγγελος as applied to humans means 'messenger', not 'representative'.

However, accepting the ἄγγελοι referred to in Rev. 1:20–3:22 as superhuman raises the problem that their circumstances are those of humans not celestial beings. For example:

   a. The problems they face (2:2).
   b. Sins of which they must repent (2:20).
   c. Their need to overcome evil in an earthly situation (2:10).
   d. Their prospect of reigning with Christ (3:21).

Mounce therefore says, "The most satisfactory answer . . . is that the angel of the church was a way of personifying the prevailing spirit of the church." Ladd says, "It is best to understand [angel] as a rather unusual symbol to represent the heavenly or supernatural character of the church." In other words, 'angel' is a symbol, rather than being a reference to an angelic being as such. So 'angel' in chapters 2 and 3 (and its introduction in 1:9–20) does not refer to any entity other than the individual church itself.

If there is a problem in interpreting the meaning of 'angel' here, there is an even greater problem in attempting to translate it into other languages. Possibilities for the symbolic interpretation are: 'The seven stars are the seven churches *symbolized as* angels'; and, for example, in 2:1: 'Write *this message* to the church in Ephesus, the church *symbolized as an* angel'; or 'Write this message to the church in Ephesus, *the church which, like an* angel, *belongs to heaven*'.

BOUNDARIES AND COHERENCE

As already mentioned, 1:17a as a repetition of 1:12b marks the resumption of the narrative at the beginning of this section. The end of the unit is marked by the end of the long speech by the glorified Christ and the end of the first Act. The cohesion of the unit comes from its being an interaction between John and the glorified Christ. Within the speech the *subsidiary appeals* are clearly addressed to him, and even within the main APPEAL each of the letters begins with an instruction to John: 'Write this message to the church in…'. As mentioned above (1:20a) 1:20 also provides a link between the *subsidiary appeals* and the APPEAL.

PROMINENCE AND THEME

Since the APPEAL comprises the vast bulk of this unit it is clearly the most prominent part. However, the *subsidiary appeals* are also basic to the theme since in them Christ resolves the writer's immediate problem (his fear) and commissions him to write the book.

2:1–3:22 Nucleus of 1:17–3:22

THEME: Everyone must listen to the message by which, through the Holy Spirit, Christ exhorts the churches to repent of various sins and lovingly encourages them to be faithful and obedient to him.

MACROSTRUCTURE	CONTENTS
LETTER$_1$	2:1–7 Christ exhorts the church at Ephesus to repent and to begin again to love him and each other. Everyone must listen to the message which the Holy Spirit speaks to the churches.
LETTER$_2$	2:8–11 Christ exhorts the church at Smyrna not to fear what they will suffer, but to trust in him even if they must die because they trust in him. Everyone must listen to the message which the Holy Spirit speaks to the churches.
LETTER$_3$	2:12–17 Christ exhorts the church at Pergamum to repent of permitting some of its members to follow teaching that encourages eating food offered to idols and sexual immorality. Everyone must listen to the message which the Holy Spirit speaks to the churches.
LETTER$_4$	2:18–29 Christ rebukes the church at Thyatira for tolerating a teacher who encourages sexual immorality and eating food offered to idols, and he announces that he will punish her and her followers. He exhorts the rest of the members to remain loyal to him. Everyone must listen to the message which the Holy Spirit speaks to the churches
LETTER$_5$	3:1–6 Christ exhorts the church at Sardis to become aware of its spiritual need and repent. But he promises that those who are worthy will live with him. Everyone must listen to the message which the Holy Spirit speaks to the churches.
LETTER$_6$	3:7–13 Christ promises the church at Philadelphia that they will be in his kingdom, that those who oppose them will acknowledge that he loves the church, and that he will keep the church from harm during the period of testing. He exhorts them to continue to obey his word and to be faithful. Everyone must listen to the message which the Holy Spirit speaks to the churches.
LETTER$_7$	3:14–22 Christ exhorts the church at Laodicea to accept his provision for their spiritual needs and to repent of their sins. He promises to fellowship with any who will respond to his call. Everyone must listen to the message which the Holy Spirit speaks to the churches.

INTENT AND MACROSTRUCTURE

Each of the letters contains *APPEALS*. While *APPEALS* do occur elsewhere in the book, those here are significant in that they are concentrated and that they are addressed to the recipients of the book rather than to John or participants in the vision itself. Thus 2:1–3:22 is the major hortatory part of the book. The question is whether the macrostructure within this unit is to be seen as that of a conjoined set of letters to distinct churches or a conjoined set of *APPEALS* to the church in general. Since the message to one church would not fit the situation of another, it seems better to label the relationship between the seven letters as that of conjoined *LETTERS*.

BOUNDARIES AND COHERENCE

The cluster of paragraphs containing the seven messages to the individual churches follows the commission to write to the churches. It closes at the end of the seventh message, thus coinciding with the end of the first act; this final boundary has been discussed earlier.

Coherence is shown by the fact that the letters all have very similar structural patterns and by the use of almost identical opening and closing parts:

1. Each message begins with Christ commanding John to write to the designated church.
2. This is followed by an orienter, addressed to the church and including an identification of the speaker, Christ, using terms mostly taken from the descriptions of him in 1:12-16, 17-18.

3. An appeal directed to all the churches to heed the Spirit's message is repeated verbatim at or near the close of each letter.
4. This is followed (in the first three letters) or preceded (in the last four) by a motivational basis in the form of a message to those who are victorious.

A study of the content of the messages shows the following chiastic structure, which may add to coherence of the unit:

A. To Ephesus there is the command to repent and the threat of rejection (2:5b, 5d–f).
  B. To Smyrna there is no rebuke, but wealth, the synagogue of Satan, suffering, and a crown are mentioned (2:9d, f, 10c, d).
    C. Christ commands Pergamum to repent lest he come quickly to judge (2:16a–d). A new name is promised (2:17c).
      D. To Thyatira the message comes from the Son of God, the one ready to judge and to reward with authority (2:18c, 26–28a).
    C'. Christ commands Sardis to repent lest he come quickly to judge (3:3c). He promises to recognize a name (3:5b).
  B'. Philadelphia is not rebuked, but strength, the synagogue of Satan, suffering, and a crown are mentioned (3:8c, 9a, 10b, 11c).
A'. Laodicea is threatened with rejection and called to repent (3:16b, 19b).

A further mark of cohesion is the fact that 2:2, at the start of the first letter, has σου 'your' in its default position, following the noun, in 'your works,' but when the same phrase occurs at the start of subsequent letters the σου is preposed to the noun, showing the switch of referent.

PROMINENCE AND THEME

Looking for the prominence of one message over the others is not very rewarding. There is some evidence for the prominence of the letter to Thyatira (2:18–29). It is the longest of the messages and is central, which also makes it central in the chiastic structure suggested above. However, the geographic location of the churches on a road circuit may have determined the order in which the letters occur. They are therefore viewed as equally prominent. The theme consists of the main parts which are identical or very similar in all the letters.

2:1–7 (Letter₁ of 2:1–3:22)

THEME: *Christ exhorts the church at Ephesus to repent and to begin again to love him and each other. Everyone must listen to the message which the Holy Spirit speaks to the churches.*

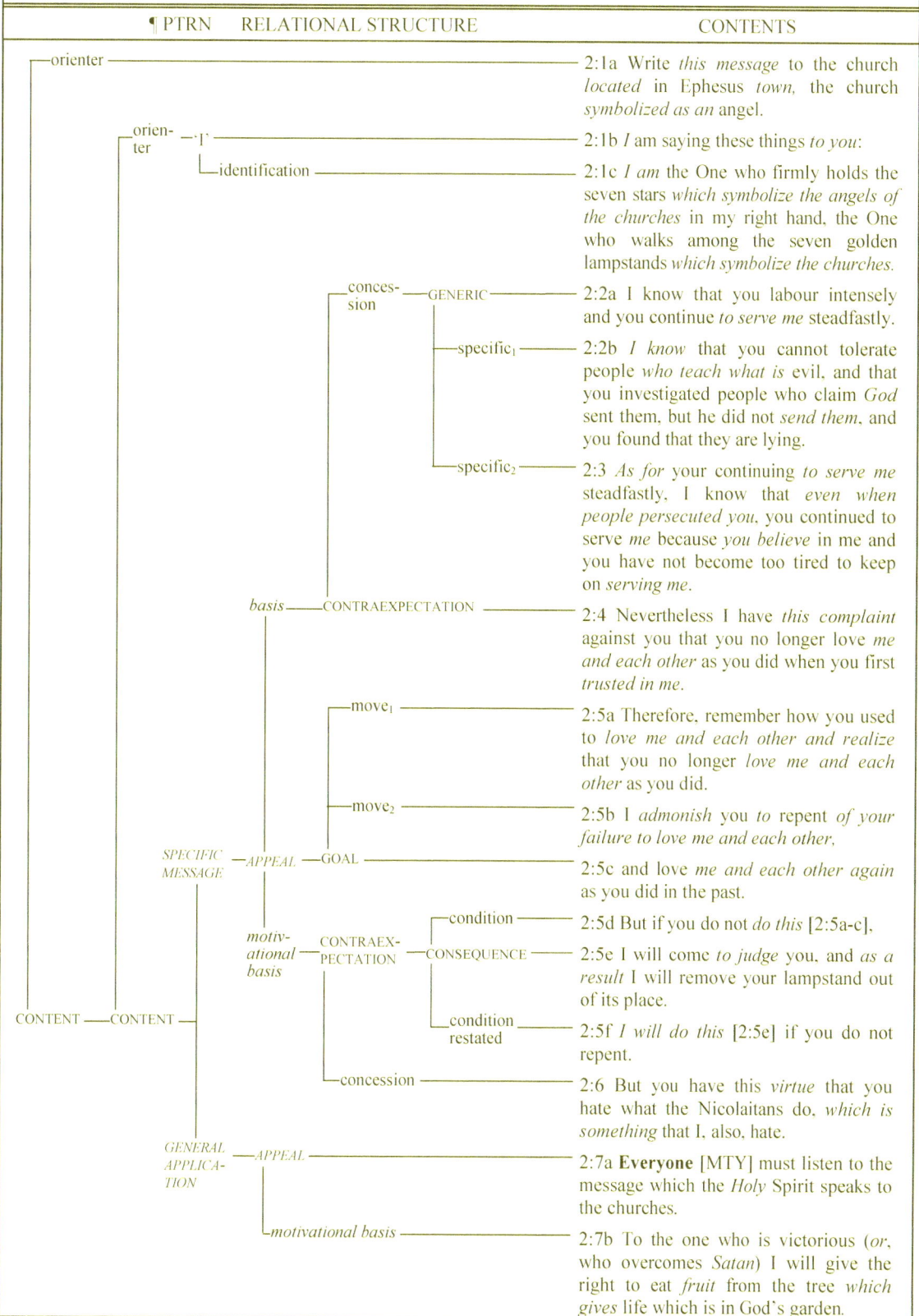

INTENT AND PARAGRAPH PATTERN

The content of each letter is essentially hortatory. This first letter is very clearly hortatory in its SPECIFIC MESSAGE to the Ephesian church. In each letter the GENERAL APPLICATION is also hortatory.

NOTES

2:1a the church *symbolized as an* **angel** For this interpretation see the note on 1:20b.

2:1b *I am saying these things to you* The usual formula for greeting in a letter does not occur at the beginning of each of these letters, but it has been given in 1:4 and the individual messages are meant for all the churches, so this is not surprising.

Though Christ uses second person singular almost exclusively in direct address to each of the angels, it is apparent from what he says that it is intended for the church. Charting second person singular and plural forms in the specific messages shows that the plural does not occur in the first letter nor in the last three. Probably there are definite reasons for the few occurrences of the plural form, as for instance:

1. In 2:10b the expression is partitive to indicate that not all the members of the Smyrna church will be imprisoned. The plural of 10c may be by attraction.
2. In 2:13e the plural is not in direct address and refers to the congregation as the group out of which one was singled for martyrdom.
3. The plural pronoun of 2:23 is appropriate following a reference to all the churches.
4. In 2:24–25 the pronouns are governed by τοῖς λοιποῖς 'the rest (of you)' as a group that, by their faithfulness, are distinguished from those being rebuked.

The conclusion is that the singular forms are used to represent 'the church' as an entity.

2:1c *I am* **the One who** The identification of the speaker here, as in each letter, is repeated from the general introductory material of the first chapter and, on that basis, is significant for all the churches. In most cases the identification is uniquely suited to the individual message. In this first letter the speaker's relationship to the seven churches is specified in the comprehensive terms of 1:20, though probably the mention of the lampstands also has a relationship to the statement in 2:5, 'I will remove your lampstand from its place'.

2:2a I know The Greek Οἶδα τὰ ἔργα σου 'I know your works', is a generic referring to the labour and patience which the church has shown, rather than as a separate specific action. This is similar to the meaning of 'your works' in 2:19, 3:1, 8, 15. The specifics of the labour and patience are spelled out in 2:2b and 2:3.

you labour intensely and you continue *to serve me* **steadfastly** As in English we speak of taking the trouble or pains to do something, so the word κόπος 'labour' (2:2b) includes these concepts.

2:2b *I know* **that you cannot tolerate people** *who teach what is* **evil** Here βαστάζω has the sense of 'tolerate'. The use of βαστάζω 'endure' in both a negative and a positive significance (2:2b and 3) seems intentional. The repetition highlights one of the main themes of Revelation—endurance—and one of the themes of the letters—resisting false teachers.

people *who teach what is* **evil** Here the accusative masculine plural form κακούς is used, so the denotation is people/beings who are evil in some sense. There is reason for understanding a difference in meaning between the two words κακός and πονηρός, though both may be translated 'evil'. Usage in the New Testament seems to point to a more sinister or diabolic connotation for the latter. For this reason caution may be used in translating κακός. Ladd says, "This does not refer to the evil conduct of their profane neighbours but to the false teachers in the church." 'People *who teach what is* evil' seems a more focal meaning in this context than 'people *who do* evil'.

people who claim *God* **sent them** The Greek word is ἀποστόλους 'apostles'. Its simple meaning is 'people who are sent'. Usually in the NT it refers to those who have special authority because they have been sent by God, and it often refers to the twelve appointed by Jesus. Here 'people who claim *God* sent them' rather than 'apostles' is used, since 'apostles' in English usually carries the narrower sense.

2:3 *As for* **your continuing** *to serve me* **steadfastly** The word order of ὑπομονὴν ἔχεις 'steadfastness you have' shows that the verse is focusing on the steadfastness mentioned in 2:2b.

even when people persecuted you, **you continued to serve** *me because you believe* **in me** BDAG glosses βαστάζω for this reference as "*bear* *patiently, put up with . . . evil"* (i.e. enduring evil things done to one). 'Even when people persecuted you' is therefore implied here.

because *you believe* in me The Greek text is διὰ τὸ ὄνομά μου 'because of the name of me'. Often in scripture the 'name' stands for the person and his character. The question is whether this phrase gives (1) the reason for the persecution, as "have suffered for my name" (JB) might signify, (2) the reason they endured, as "bearing up for my name's sake" (RSV) might signify, or (3) the means by which they were able to endure the persecution, 'you endured persecution through believing in me'. Of these, the second presupposes the first, so is used in the display.

2:4 Nevertheless I have *this complaint* against you The display follows NLT. Although 'complaint' is an abstract noun it seems to be the best way to render the sense in English. Another rendering would be: 'I criticize you because you no longer love . . . '. Living Bible has "Yet there is one thing wrong".

The conjunction ἀλλά 'but' marks the contraexpectation, but at the same time this proposition forms the basis for the main specific appeal of 2:5a–c.

you no longer love *me and each other* The object of their love is not made specific. Some restrict it to love for God (most specifically love for Christ in this context) and some make it apply only to people. Mounce says, "The expression includes both love of God and love of mankind at large, but seems to refer mainly to their love for one another", noting that "It seems probable that desire for sound teaching and the resulting forthright action taken to exclude all impostors had created a climate of suspicion in which brotherly love could no longer exist". Because love for Christ in the New Testament must include love for people, it is proper to include both Christ and people as objects of the love here.

2:5a remember This is the first in a series of three imperatives in the admonition. It is in the present tense and understood as the first step in repentance. Its action continues through the action of the next two imperatives, which are in the present tense. What they must remember first is how they used to love; remembering would help them respond in repentance.

***realize* that you no longer *love me and each other* as you did** 'Fallen' indicates that they are not only to remember what their love was like at an earlier time but to realize that they no longer love in the acceptable way they once did. 'Fallen' is a dead metaphor and the image need not be translated.

2:5b repent *of your failure to love me and each other* This is the second imperative of Christ's command. It is axiomatic that repentance is defined not only in one's attitude toward the wrong one has done (sorrow, regret) but most importantly in changing one's actions to doing what is right. This latter component is represented in the next imperative clause, 'do the works you did at first'.

2:5c love *me and each other again* as you did in the past This is the third imperative of the command. In the display the generic 'do' of the Greek is rendered specific to this situation as 'love'.

The phrase τὰ πρῶτα 'the first things' here means 'the former things', referring to 2:4.

2:5e I will remove your lampstand out of its place In 1:20 we are told that 'the seven lampstands are (i.e. symbolize) the seven churches'. This would indicate that this is a warning that the church would lose its existence in some way (cf. Charles, Swete, Ladd, Mounce). It gives the motivational basis for the appeal of 2:5a–c.

2:5f if you do not repent The severe consequence, highlighted by repetition, emphasizes the importance of repentance.

2:6 Nicolaitans Little is known for certain about the Nicolaitans. The best description of their practices is found in Revelation 2:14, assuming that 2:15 can be understood to say that the Nicolaitans advocated the same practices as what is called the teachings of Balaam in 2:14, eating food sacrificed to idols and immorality. The name almost certainly means 'people/followers of Nicolaos,' but it is not known who this Nicolaos was.

2:7a <u>Everyone</u> The Greek text has 'the one having an ear'. Since everyone is expected to have ears, all the addressees of the book are being asked to carry out the exhortation. This is an example of metonymy where the ear is put for its function of hearing. This expression is to emphasize the need to pay careful attention and no doubt to carry out the admonitions in one's own life.

In Matt. 11:15 and other passages Jesus appeals to "those who have ears" as he seeks a spiritual response to his message. This admonition seems to occur chiefly after parabolic or prophetic declarations when they are figuratively expressed, as in these letters to the churches.

the message which the *Holy* Spirit speaks to the churches The reference of 'message' is not simply to the following proposition, since that is not an appeal but a motivational promise. The reference is to all that which has preceded in this letter and to the messages to each of the other churches, as the plural 'churches' shows (Alford, Beasley-Murray, Swete).

2:7b the one who is victorious (*or*, who overcomes *Satan*) The ultimate victory is frequently expressed in Revelation by use of the verb νικάω 'to conquer/be victorious' without an object, though in some languages an object may be obligatory either grammatically or semantically and so an object is given in the alternate rendering in the display. See 1 John 2:13 where this object ('the evil one') is explicit. The picture is not of believers attacking Satan and defeating him (which is Christ's saving role), but of believers being attacked by Satan, through temptation, and overcoming.

I will give the right to eat *fruit* In each of the letters, the promise to the victor involves an action on the part of Christ. In five of them the word δώσω 'I will give' is used.

the tree *which gives* life The genitive construction 'tree of life' has the function of indicating the source of life, though, of course, in a figurative sense.

in God's garden The term 'paradise' occurs only three times in the New Testament. In the Greek it referred to the parks of Persian kings and nobility. It was also applied to the Jewish concept of the Garden of Eden, hidden and lost, but destined for restoration in the full redemption of Israel. The description of the New Jerusalem in Rev. 22:1–2 justifies the interpretation of 'the paradise of God' as 'God's garden'.

BOUNDARIES AND COHERENCE

The unit begins with Christ telling John which church to address the letter to. The beginning of the next letter in 2:8 shows that 2:7 ends the first letter. This is the boundary pattern of all the seven messages. Coherence in each unit is obvious as the address to a particular church is made and the appropriate commendation and warning are given. In each letter there is an address by Christ and a specific APPEAL to the particular church together with its *basis*. This is followed by a second APPEAL which is understood to be addressed to the churches in general, since the plural 'churches' is used and the same words are repeated each time. While the *basis* for this APPEAL is a motivating promise, there is also the idea that heeding the Spirit's message leads to victory. Even though in each letter it ties into the specific message for the particular church and every member is called to be victorious in his own situation, yet there is no promise given which would not be made to all. This combination of general and specific application helps to reinforce the idea that the seven messages are really one message and are for all 'God's servants' (1:1c).

Within the first letter, coherence within the specific message is evident in the *basis*-APPEAL-*basis* structure of 2:2–6.

PROMINENCE AND THEME

The APPEAL to the church at Ephesus is in natural prominence, supported by the *basis* for it. It is also given marked prominence by the motivational basis in 2:5d–f, which includes the repetition of the command to repent from 2:5b. Conjoined to the specific message is the general application. It is prominent as a command, and because this is repeated exactly in each message its prominence is also recognized on a higher level. The theme includes the SPECIFIC MESSAGE and the GENERAL APPLICATION.

2:8–11 (Letter₂ of 2:1–3:22)

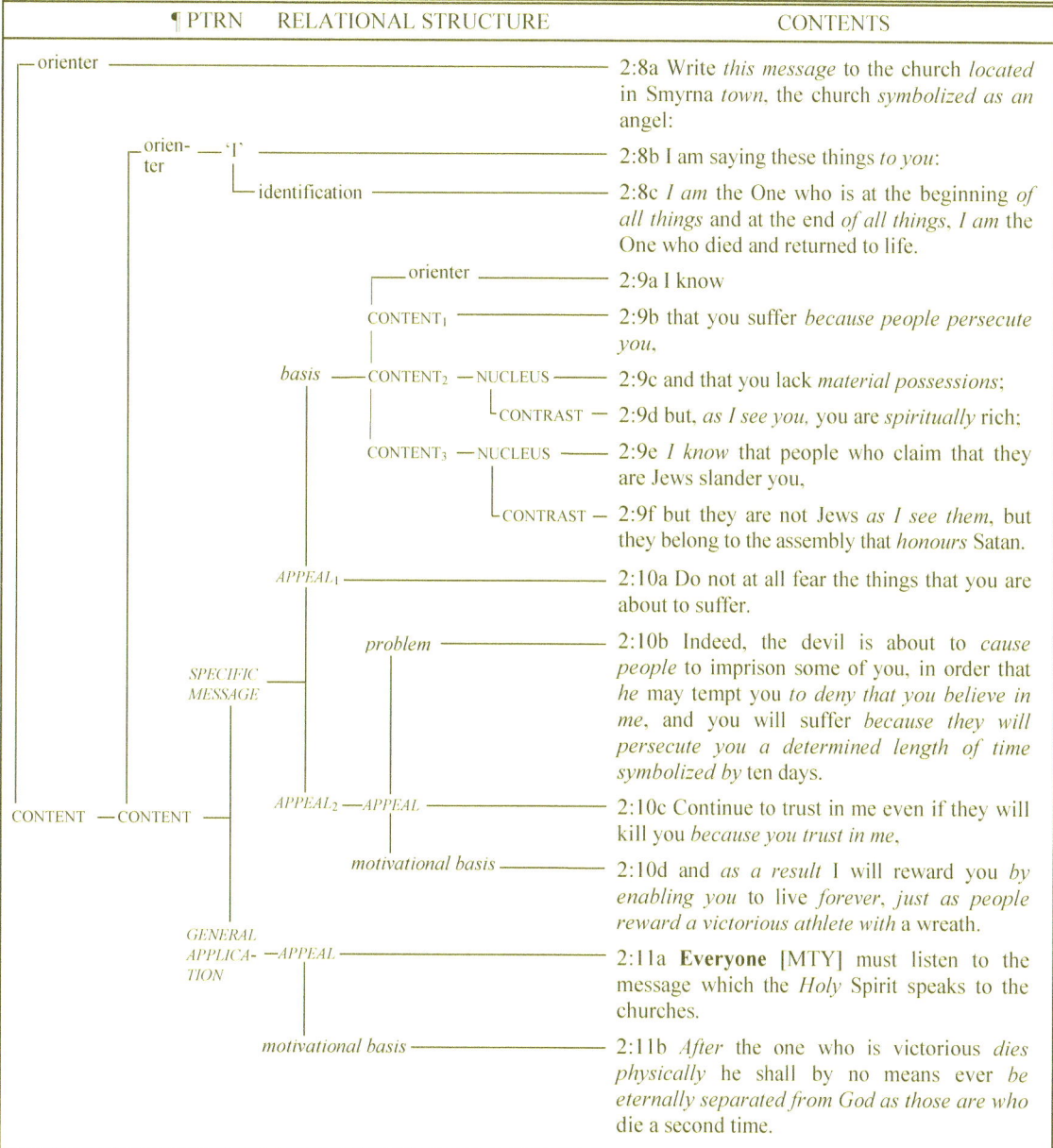

INTENT AND PARAGRAPH PATTERN

There are two imperative constructions in this second letter: μηδὲν φοβοῦ 'fear nothing' (2:10a) and γίνου πιστός 'be faithful' (2:10c). These two exhortations constitute the APPEALS of the SPECIFIC MESSAGE to the church in Smyrna. They are preceded (2:9) by Christ demonstrating that he knows the situation they are in, and in fact he knows it better than they do (see note 2:9c–f). This is the *basis* for the APPEALS. For the second exhortation, 'Be faithful unto death', ἰδού (2:10b) appears to mark the *problem* requiring obedience to the APPEAL; the result clause 2:10d acts as a *motivational basis* for the APPEAL.

NOTES

2:8c the One who died ... The relative pronoun ὅς 'who' gives a connection with the preceding clause similar to an amplification because of its demonstrative force (Dana-Mantey, p. 125). Christ's experience of death gives him authority to exhort the church not to fear death and to promise them eternal life (2:10).

returned to life The verb is ἔζησεν 'lived, came to life', an aorist referring to the event of resurrection. John 5:25 is an instance of this verb used with the meaning of a return to life.

2:9b you suffer *because people persecute you* Since θλῖψις so often denotes suffering caused by someone else and the context shows that persecution is being referred to in this paragraph, the display makes clear that persecution rather than sickness is in focus.

2:9c–f that you lack *material possessions*; **but,** *as I see you,* **you are** *spiritually* **rich;** *I know* **that people who claim that they are Jews slander you, but they are not Jews** *as I see them,* **but they belong to the assembly that** *honours* **Satan** In these contrasts, the descriptions of the circumstances serve as NUCLEI, since as actual circumstances they are thematic, being the situation to which the believers are not to react with fear. The function of the corrections or qualifications beginning with ἀλλά 'but' are part of the encouragement and therefore are to some extent acting as support for the exhortations not to fear but to be faithful. For these reasons both factors of the contrasts are construed as prominent.

2:9c–d that you lack *material possessions*; **but,** *as I see you,* **you are** *spiritually* **rich** The Greek is Οἶδά σου...τὴν πτωχείαν, ἀλλὰ πλούσιος εἶ 'I know ... your poverty, but rich you are'. Since people cannot be materially rich and poor at the same time, one of the words is figurative. The context shows that 'rich' is obviously the figurative word and that the reference is to the multitude of spiritual blessings. In both English and Greek 'rich' has a secondary meaning of 'abundance' and so, even though the contrast between 'rich' and 'poor' here is built on a live figurative relationship, the figure is handled in the display by modifying 'rich' with 'spiritually', rather than spelling out the grounds of comparison. If the grounds of comparison were spelled out, the propositionalization might be 'you have been blessed by God in many ways just as a rich person has many possessions'.

2:9f they belong to the assembly that *honours* **Satan** The display uses 'assembly' to show it is not a building which is referred to, but an organized group of people. The Jews are referred to as 'a synagogue of Satan' because they rejected and opposed the gospel of Christ. The function of 'synagogue of Satan' is made clear as 'assembly that *honours* Satan', with the implication that true Jews honour and obey God. In all probability they were actual Jews because at this time there was a strong Jewish population in Smyrna.

2:10 Although the two APPEALS of 2:10 are in negative-positive form, they are separated by the *problem*. Also, the relationship between the contents of the two is not one of purely negated antonyms. On this basis the exhortations are labelled as being in conjoined relationship rather than negative-*POSITIVE* and 'but' is not used to introduce the second exhortation.

2:10a Do not at all fear Some manuscripts have μή 'do not,' which is grammatically correct, as the negative adverb used with the imperative. But the UBS committee chose μηδέν 'nothing' on the basis that it would be more probable for a copyist to revert to correct grammar than to introduce the grammatical difficulty of μηδέν (singular) followed by the plural ἅ 'which' (Metzger:1971). BDAG lists μηδέν in this passage under "accusative of the inner object" with the gloss 'not at all, in no way'. The present analysis accepts the textual reasoning of the UBS committee recognizing that the strong negative fits the context significantly.

2:10b Indeed Van Otterloo (p. 63) classifies this occurrence of ἰδού under "calling attention to a situation that requires an action" (p. 59). In this classification ἰδού occurs at the beginning of the statement of the situation requiring action, the action to be taken usually is indicated in the next construction, here the APPEAL 'Be faithful unto death' in 10c. As far as the paragraph pattern is concerned, constituent 10b acts as a *problem* that demands action.

Some versions have translated ἰδού here as "Listen!" (TEV) or "I tell you" (NIV), which are very possible. Also, there is an element of ascensiveness here. 'Indeed' acts as an attention-getting word in English and it also marks ascensiveness so it is appropriately used here in the display.

cause people **to imprison some of you** The clause 'throw some of you into prison' is unquestionably literal here, not figurative, as the display makes clear by its use of an explicit agent.

in order that *he* may tempt you The word used for tempting is πειράζω. In the New Testament it is frequently used with reference to Satan's effort to tempt Christians to disobey God.

In itself 'tempt' is a type of causative and so two events are involved: 'tempt' and what one is tempted to do. This is made fully explicit in the display: '*he* may tempt you *to deny that you believe in me*'.

***a determined length of time symbolized by* ten days** This is interpreted by perhaps a majority of commentators as signifying a rather short period of time. Others see the severity of the suffering, potentially leading to death, as a reason for accepting ten as signifying completeness. In the Old Testament 'ten' is used as comprehensive, for instance, in the ten commandments completing the legal code and in the ten plagues which completed God's judgment on Egypt. However, that a definite number is used must mean at least that the length of the period is determined by God.

2:10c Continue to trust in me The Greek text is γίνου πιστός 'be faithful'. Because the present tense is used, the display has 'continue to trust'.

even if they will kill you *because you trust in me* The phrase ἄχρι θανάτου 'until death' is to be taken as referring to severity rather than to extent of time. '*Because you trust in me*' makes it clear that the reason for execution would be their faith in Christ.

2:10d and *as a result* I will reward you Καί 'and' is often used after an imperative as an indicator of result (BDAG). The crown of life is promised as a result of their faithfulness. It acts as a motivation for carrying out the command, though it also signifies God's gracious care for his people.

I will reward you *by enabling you* to live *forever, just as people reward a victorious athlete with* a wreath 'Of life' is understood as epexegetical, indicating in what the wreath/crown consists. The Greek word here is στέφανος, for which BDAG gives 'prize, reward' for this reference. In New Testament times it frequently had its primary meaning of 'wreath of honour awarded to an athlete', and BDAG says this imagery becomes less and less distinct, which might indicate its being a dead metaphor. However, in 1 Cor. 9:24–27 where Paul uses several figures relating to the race, the crown seems to be a live metaphor. In the present passage it is a symbolic reward after the race or battle of life. The crown is one of victory, as in James 1:12 and Rev. 6:2. In Revelation more than in any other book of the New Testament the battle rages, and God's people must win the victory. Because of these considerations and the significant use of symbols in this book, we take it here as a live metaphor.

2:11b he shall by no means ever *be eternally separated from God as those are who* die a second time 'The second death' is explained in 20:6, 14 and 21:8 as eternal separation from God.

Note that in the statement 'he will not be harmed by the second death', the negative applies to the whole clause, not just the verb. This means that not only will the overcomer not be hurt by the second death, but he will not experience it at all.

BOUNDARIES AND COHERENCE

For the boundaries see under 2:1–8. The coherence pattern has also been set in the first letter. Coherence in the unit is very marked. It is the shortest and most compact of the messages and is held together by many contrasts:

1. Contrast is made between death and life (2:8b, 2:10c–d, 2:11b).
2. The material destitution of the church is contrasted with its spiritual wealth (2:9c–d).
3. The false Jews' claim contrasts with Christ's estimate of them (2:9e–f).
4. The attitude of fear contrasts with the trust on which faithfulness is based (2:10a–d).

PROMINENCE AND THEME

The *APPEALS* have natural prominence in this hortatory paragraph. The theme includes each of the *APPEALS*.

2:12–17 (Letter₃ of 2:1–3:22)

THEME: *Christ exhorts the church at Pergamum to repent of permitting some of its members to follow teaching that encourages eating food offered to idols and sexual immorality. Everyone must listen to the message which the Holy Spirit speaks to the churches.*

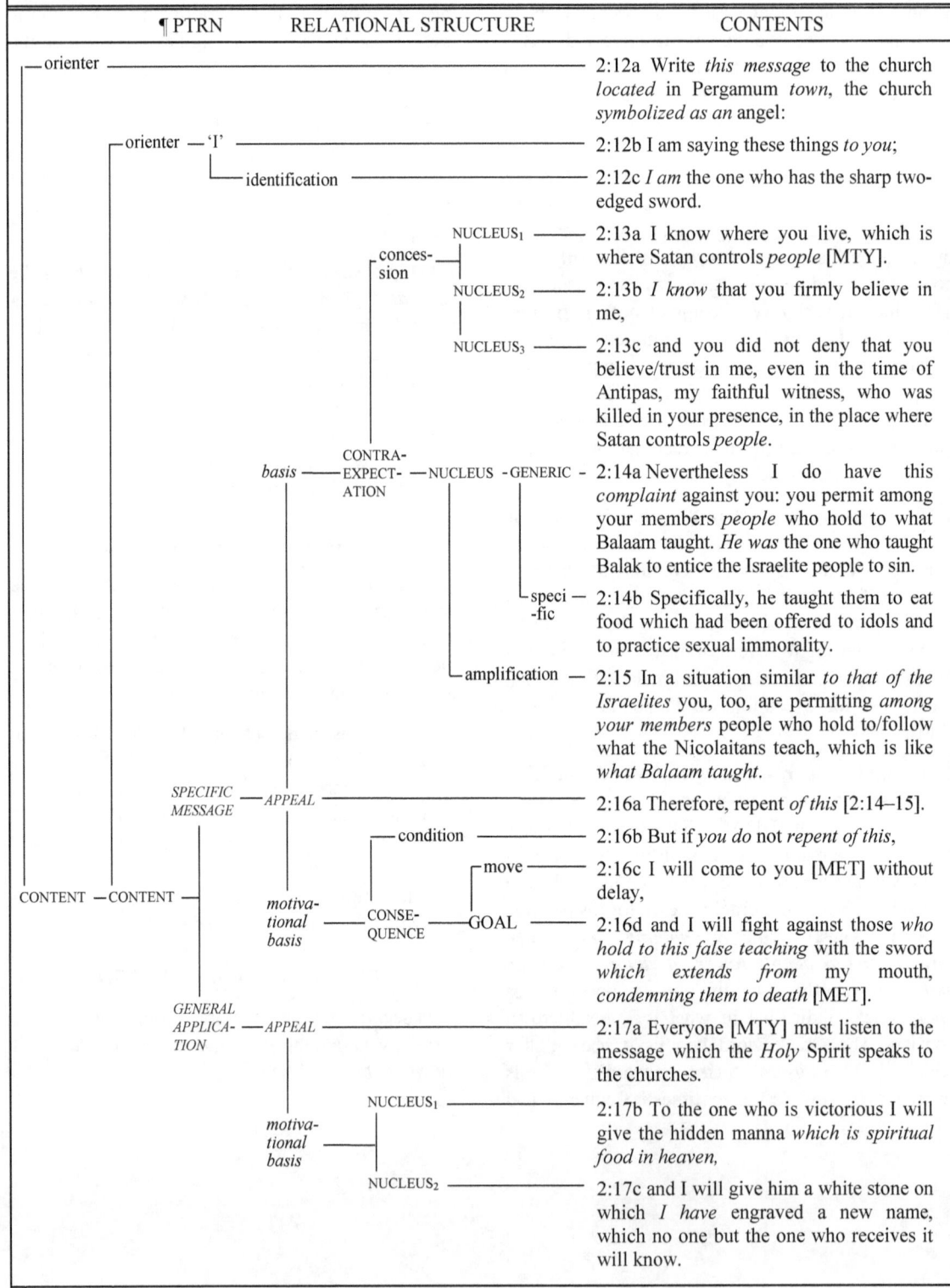

INTENT AND PARAGRAPH PATTERN

The SPECIFIC MESSAGE of this third letter has the imperative μετανόησον 'repent' at the beginning of 2:16, forming an APPEAL. As in the other letters the APPEAL is supported by *bases* both before and after it. 2:14 describes the situation which demands the APPEAL. 2:13 is concessionary to 2:14 and so does not form part of the situational *basis* as such but might be seen as building rapport and thus part of the *basis-APPEAL* dynamics. Following the APPEAL is the *motivational basis* in 2:16b–d, which is a warning.

NOTES

2:12c *I am* the one who has the sharp two-edged sword The decisiveness of war with the sword is in contrast to tolerance on the part of a church which allows false doctrine to spread among its members. The sword is clearly symbolic rather than figurative here because of the reference to it in 2:16d and the fact that it relates back to the vision of Christ in 1:16.

2:13a I know where you live, which is where Satan controls *people* The Greek is Οἶδα ποῦ κατοικεῖς, ὅπου ὁ θρόνος τοῦ Σατανᾶ 'I know where you live, where the throne of Satan *is*'. The double use of the locative 'where' indicates that the focus is on the second clause rather than on the first.

'Throne' here is metonymy for what is done by the one having authority to sit on the throne—'rule' or 'reign'—and so the display has 'where Satan controls *people*'. 'People' satisfies the case frame need for an object of 'control'.

2:13b you firmly believe in me The Greek is κρατεῖς τὸ ὄνομά μου 'you hold to my name'. The use of κρατέω 'to hold firmly' is applied to both faith in Christ and the tenacious following of false teaching. It is used here and in 2:14–15. It is significant that it is used to describe the loyalty of this church to Christ, 'his name' signifying himself, and again in connection with the heresy. BDAG lists both of these usages under the same heading: "*hold fast* (*to*) someone or something, and hence remain closely united" to the person or the teaching specified. The display has 'firmly believe in' for the relationship to the *person* of Christ and 'hold to' for the relationship to the heretical *teaching*.

2:13c you did not deny The aorist verb points to a time when they had been tested and remained faithful. Since this is connected with the reference to the faithful witness of Antipas and his martyrdom by the prepositional phrase ἐν ταῖς ἡμέραις Ἀντιπᾶς 'in the days of Antipas' indicating circumstance, it is taken as an historical event in which the believers at Pergamum maintained their belief in Jesus.

that you believe/trust in me There are two interpretations for 2:13c, though the difference between them is not great. They hinge on how τὴν πίστιν μου, literally 'the faith of me', is translated:

Some (Lenski, Walvoord) take τὴν πίστιν μου to mean the 'doctrine/teaching about me' or 'the doctrine I delivered', since ἡ πίστις in some contexts definitely does refer to that which is believed, in other words, teaching or doctrine.

However, other commentators (Beasley-Murray, Bratcher and Hatton, Düsterdieck, Morris, Swete) and English versions understand the clause to mean 'you did not deny that you believe/trust in me'. As in other instances in the New Testament the genitive τὴν πίστιν μου may be understood as 'believe in me' (Mark 11:22 and Eph. 3:12). This is an example of the objective genitive in which Christ is the object of the belief and a special relationship is indicated.

Both views can be justified by the context. Doctrine is certainly being talked about in this paragraph. However, it may be said for the second view that the central aspect of true Christian doctrine *is* faith in Christ (Acts 16:31).

even in the time of Antipas Some manuscripts omit καί 'even', failing to recognize its ascensive significance. However, this significance is clear from the fact that the temptation to deny the faith would be greater in a time of persecution severe enough to cause martyrdom. This analysis retains it, as does the UBS text. It is already clear from 2:13b that the church is faithful. The use of the ascensive conjunction gives added prominence to this proposition.

Antipas, my faithful witness Nothing is known of him with certainty, except the statement of his martyrdom. The name is a shortened form of Antipater.

The descriptive term 'faithful' may apply to those who proved the seriousness of their witness by suffering death. Christ is so designated in 1:5 with the same emphatic construction using the definite article with each word. The double use of the possessive in ὁ μάρτυς μου ὁ πιστός μου 'my witness my faithful (one)' also gives special emphasis.

where Satan controls *people* The Greek has 'where Satan lives'. The significance here seems to be of a settled control of people since, as a restatement of 2:13a where his throne is mentioned, it has a political overtone.

2:14a I do have this *complaint* **against you** It would seem that the use of ὀλίγα 'a few things' is not enumerative in the sense that it states the number of things Christ is going to mention since he only specifically states one complaint and ὅτι 'that, because' connects ὀλίγα with that complaint. Alford says that ὀλίγα "is used as a word of comparison with the far greater number of approved things which remained, and is plural, inasmuch as ὀλίγον would refer, not to the objective fewness, but to the subjective unimportance, of the grounds of complaint; which latter was not so." 'One thing' would also have downplayed the significance of the error.

who hold to what Balaam taught Other scripture passages refer to the Balaam incident as an evil example (Num. 25:1–9, cf 31:16; Neh. 13:1–3; Mic. 6:5; 1 Cor. 10:8; 2 Pet. 2:15–16) of which 2:14 gives the contemporary manifestation.

to entice the Israelite people to sin The meaning of σκάνδαλον in focus here is 'enticement to sin' (see BDAG).

2:15 you, too, are permitting *among your members* 'You have (people) holding to' means 'among your members/adherents there are those who hold to', and it also means 'you are permitting', especially since the imperative 'repent' is in second person, showing the responsibility of the church as a whole for what was going on.

like *what Balaam taught* Some consider Balaam's teaching and that of the Nicolaitans to be different heresies. This analysis accepts the two teachings as being similar and the reproof as one (Beasley-Murray, Ladd, Lenski, Mounce, Swete), since the words οὕτως 'so', καί 'also', and ὁμοίως 'likewise' indicate that 2:15 is an explanation or amplification of 2:14.

2:16a repent *of this* Since the second person singular is used in the imperative verb, the APPEAL is also directed to the church as a whole demanding that they no longer allow such false doctrine to be taught and practiced among the adherents of the church (Beasley-Murray, Düsterdieck, Lenski, Mounce, Swete).

2:16c I will come to you Instead of its primary meaning of 'physical motion toward', 'come' is sometimes used in scripture to denote other types of action taken on the part of the agent toward those involved and so is a type of metonymy. In some cases it is appropriate to substitute the specific action taken, e.g. 'I will punish you without delay', but here the punishment in 16d is against 'them' rather than 'against you'. Since 'I will come to you' places responsibility on the church as a whole, both entities need to be mentioned separately.

However, the use of the present tense in the Greek verb here indicates that the focus is on the following verb in the future tense.

without delay Here ταχύ means that as soon as it is determined they have not repented, Christ will immediately visit them in judgment.

2:16d I will fight against those *who hold to this false teaching* In the Greek text this is πολεμήσω μετ' αὐτῶν 'I will war with them'. Since this contrasts with the you(sg) of μετανόησον 'repent' which indicates the church as a whole, 'them' must refer to the other participants in the context: those who hold to the false teaching.

with the sword *which extends from* **my mouth,** *condemning them to death* That the sword is considered to be symbolic rather than metaphorical has been mentioned under 2:12c. Beckwith commenting on 2:12 says, "this epithet of Christ taken from 1:16 . . . and expressing the destroying power of his sentence of condemnation is chosen with special reference to the visitation threatened in v.16".

2:17b hidden manna *which is spiritual food in heaven* For the first readers of the letter, the figure of manna would call to mind the events of Exodus 16 and might even remind them of Jesus' teaching that he was the bread that came down from heaven (John 6:50, 51). In Jewish eschatology manna was the food of the blessed. The general understanding of the reward is that it is conferred after the earthly life is completed, so that the display specifies 'in heaven'. It is not physical food like the manna of the Old Testament. This hidden manna and the fruit from the tree of life (2:7) are both symbols of the same thing. Technically food is that which gives or sustains life, but the meaning of both symbols would seem to include (maybe focus on) the eternal life itself.

The manna is hidden in the sense that it has not yet been fully revealed and in that it will only be revealed to those who confess Christ.

2:17c I will give him a white stone Because of a frequent use of 'white' in Revelation to describe what is pure and pertains to heaven, it is often called the 'heavenly colour'. Since the Greek word also has the meaning of 'bright, glistening', some commentators read the term here as 'glistening stone'.

on which *I have* engraved a new name The implied 'I have' is made explicit to avoid a passive expression and need not mean a personal act of Jesus but something he causes to be done.

Whose name is engraved on the stone is not said. Many think it is the name of Christ, but his name would be known by all who received the stone—which does not seem the intention of 'no one knows except the one receiving it'. More probably the new name reflects the character of the victor (Morris, cf. Alford). That the new name is known only to the one who receives it indicates an individual relationship such as Jesus expressed in John 10:3 of the good shepherd, who calls his sheep by name, leading them out.

BOUNDARIES AND COHERENCE

For the boundaries see under 2:1–8. Coherence is also provided by the parallelism of the structure to that of the other letters (particularly the first two) and by internal contrasts:

1. The verb κρατέω 'hold' is used of the church's faith and the contrasted false belief of some (2:13b contrasted with 14a, 15).
2. Eating food offered to idols is contrasted with the heavenly manna (2:14b and 17b).
3. The martyr's death contrasts with divine judgment (2:13c and 16d).

PROMINENCE AND THEME

The *APPEAL* to repent has natural prominence. It is central in the *SPECIFIC MESSAGE* and supported by the *bases*. Conjoined to the *APPEAL* of the *SPECIFIC MESSAGE* is the *GENERAL APPLICATION*, the positive result of which should lead to the required repentance.

2:18–29 (Letter₄ of 2:1–3:22)

THEME: *Christ rebukes the church at Thyatira for tolerating a teacher who encourages sexual immorality and eating food offered to idols, and he announces that he will punish her and her followers. He exhorts the rest of the members to remain loyal to him. Everyone must listen to the message which the Holy Spirit speaks to the churches.*

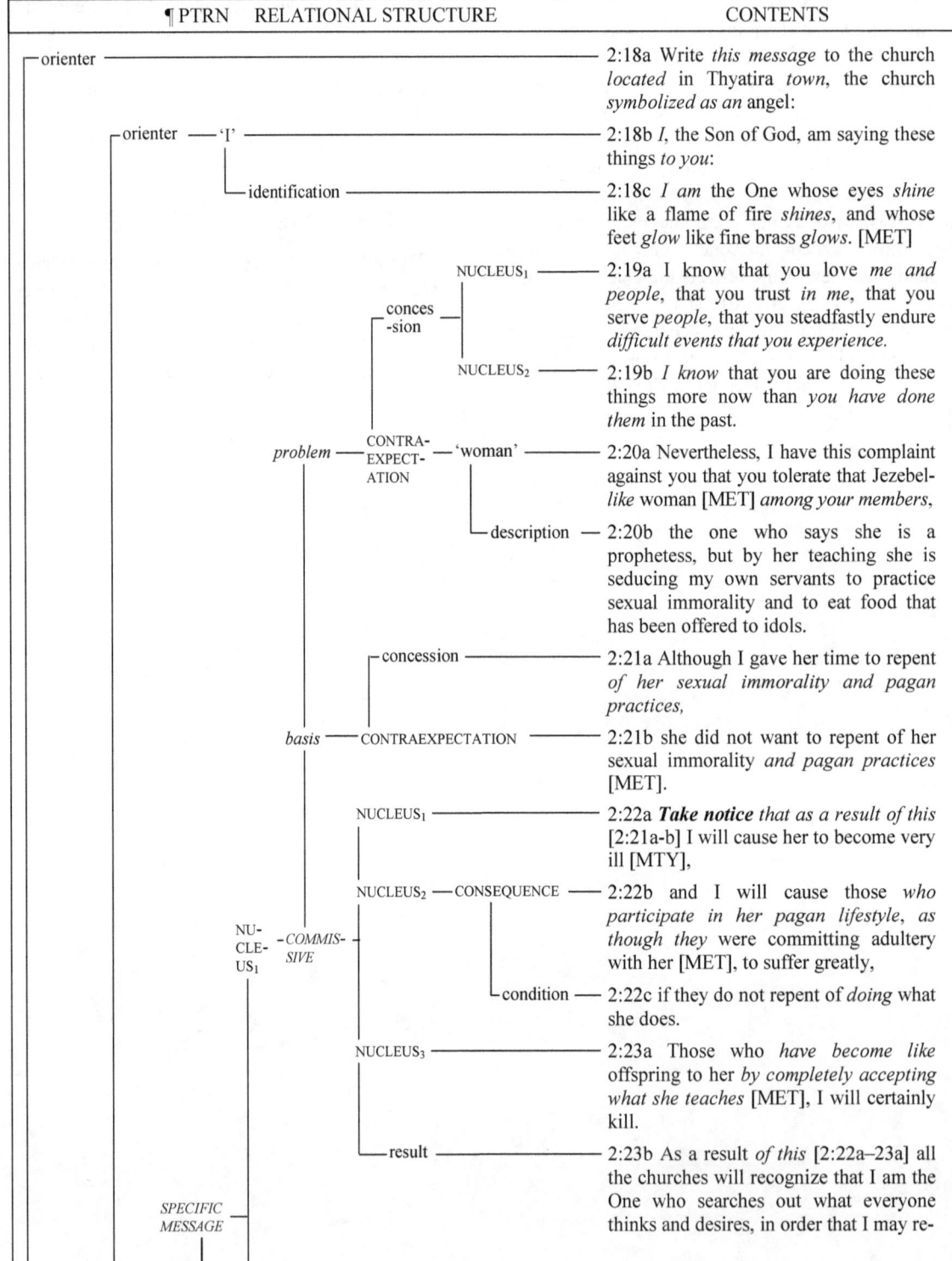

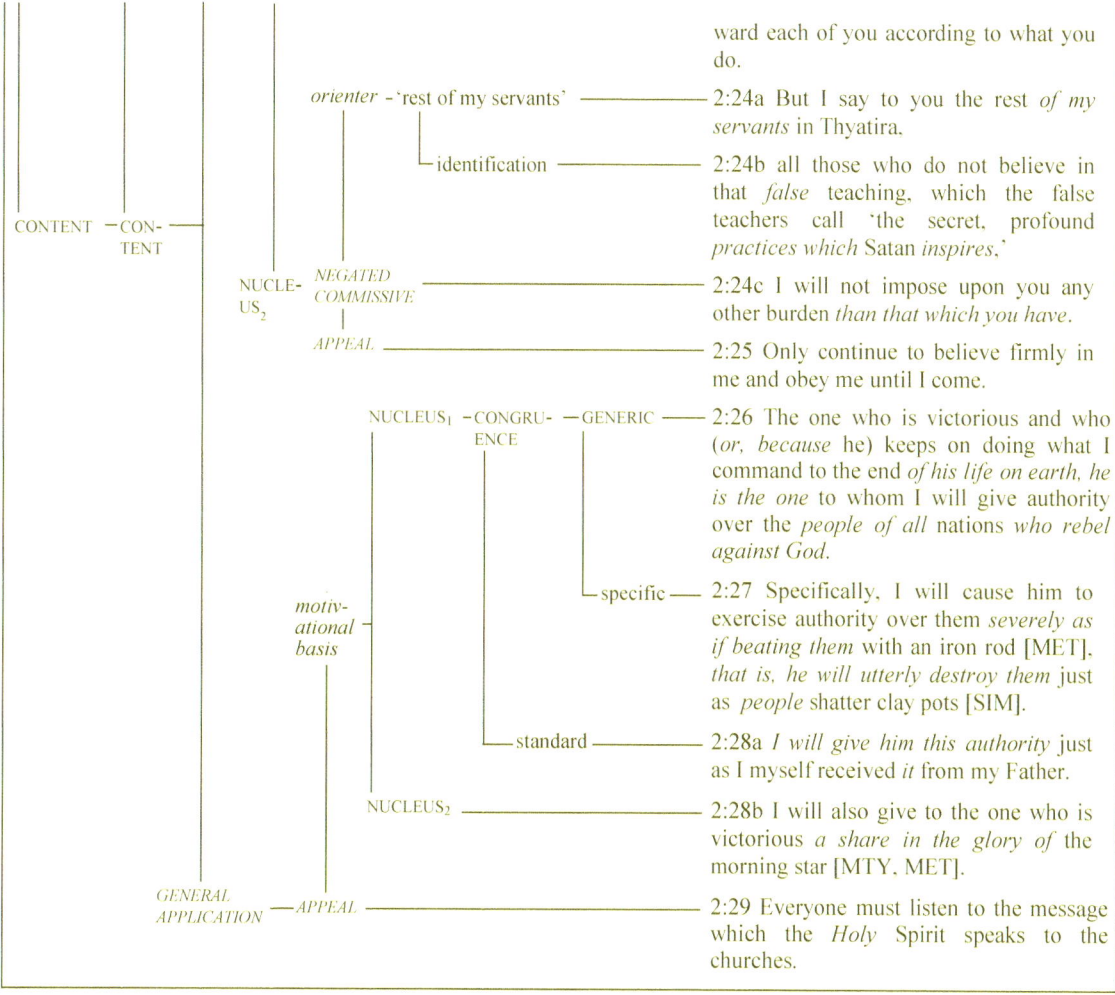

INTENT AND PARAGRAPH PATTERN

The SPECIFIC MESSAGE of Letter 4 may be seen as divided into two parts. The first part is 2:19–23 in which the focus is on the problem of immorality and pagan practices in the church at Thyatira. There is a hortatory solutionality paragraph pattern, but there is no explicit APPEAL directed to those who are doing wrong. Instead, there is a three-part COMMISSIVE, addressed to those who have remained faithful, in which Christ commits himself to solving the problem by bringing judgment on the offenders.

The second part of the SPECIFIC MESSAGE (2:24–25) is an APPEAL (2:25) addressed to those who do not follow the false teaching, preceded by what might be called a NEGATED COMMISSIVE, 'I will not impose upon you any other burden' (2:24c).

NOTES

2:18c whose eyes *shine* The shining eyes symbolize the penetrating gaze of the judge.

whose feet *glow* The points of comparison are missing in both the simile of the flame of fire ('shine') and of the fine brass ('glow') and so are made explicit in the display.

2:19a I know See the note on 2:2a.

you love *me and people*, that you trust *in me*, that you serve *people*, that you steadfastly endure *difficult events that you experience* The italicized words denote the satisfying of the case frames.

2:19b you are doing these things more now than *you have done them* in the past This concept would contrast with the decline in works based on love found in the Ephesian church (2:5). There seem to be several comments in the various letters that could be seen as being in contrast to something in another of the messages, making for coherence on a higher level.

2:20a that you tolerate The meaning of the Greek word ἀφεῖς in this passage is 'to allow, to permit, to tolerate'.

that Jezebel-*like* woman The name is recognized as symbolic. The symbolism of Jezebel wife of Ahab seems appropriate if some false teacher or cult is seen to be influencing the church as the historical wife influenced Ahab (1 Kings 21:25). Some commentators consider that the name refers to the false cult as a whole, not its leader in particular. Alford argues that it could reasonably apply to a prominent faction in the church, one that claimed prophetic powers.

2:20b by her teaching she is seducing my own servants to practice sexual immorality and to eat food that has been offered to idols The specific sins identify the cult with that of the Nicolaitans. Note that here fornication is mentioned first in the Greek text as in Num. 25:1–2, rather than in the order used in Rev. 2:14b. The immorality is literal here because idolatry which is sometimes expressed figuratively as adultery is specified separately and nonfiguratively. By posing as a prophetess her teaching is aimed at seduction to sin.

2:21a I gave her time to repent The aorist verb indicates a definite time in history. Alford sees this time for repentance as related to the verb 'tolerate' in 2:20a, so that the church was being censured for its persistence in the tolerance over an extended period.

of her sexual immorality and pagan practices While this clause does not explicitly state what she is to repent of, the next clause does—sexual immorality. But her practice and teaching of eating food offered to idols is mentioned in 20b. See the following note.

2:21b her sexual immorality *and pagan practices* While it is pointed out that πορνείας 'sexual immorality' must be translated literally because the idolatry for which it often stands is mentioned separately in 2:20, here the phrase must be inclusive of both immorality and idolatry. This basic figure, from the Old Testament, is metaphorical in that being sexually unfaithful is the image for Israel being spiritually unfaithful to God.

2:22a Take notice This is a translation for the attention-getting ἰδού. Van Otterloo classifies this occurrence of ἰδού under "used to call special attention because the statement is contrary to hearer/reader's expectation" (p. 54) and says the segment it introduces is "an unexpected pronouncement of judgment" (p. 57). It calls attention to the serious consequences Christ is going to carry out.

as a result This introduces the way in which Christ will deal with the sin. The church is not asked to physically discipline the wayward, though, of course, it should not tolerate their activity. Christ himself will physically discipline them.

His action is shown under three different statements because three distinct entities are in error (2:22–23a). Time for Jezebel's repentance has passed because she does not want to repent. Those participating with her are deceived and are threatened to be disciplined by great suffering unless they repent. But those completely adopting her pattern of living are her progeny and potentially as dangerous as she is. To show them as distinct from those who have been deceived τὰ τέκνα αὐτῆς 'the children of her' is in topicalized position (a point of departure).

I will cause her to become very ill There are other readings for κλίνην 'bed.' An important manuscript reads φυλακήν 'prison,' which seems to be taken from 2:10, where ὁ διάβολος 'the devil' is the agent. But 'bed' is classified as an 'A' reading in the UBS apparatus and occurs in the Majority Text; and the very diversity of less attested readings makes them suspect. The 'bed' is a metonymy for illness. Illness as punishment for sin was generally accepted in the period of this writing, and in 2:22a the verb βάλλω 'throw' confirms the idea of punishment. There are also passages in the Old Testament and Apocrypha which corroborate the figurative usage of 'bed' for illness (e.g. 1 Macc. 1:5).

2:22b those *who participate in her pagan lifestyle*, *as though they* were committing adultery with her This verse has μοιχεύω 'commit adultery,' so often used figuratively of being unfaithful to God (Alford, Düsterdieck, Swete).

2:22c what she does Though some manuscripts read the plural pronoun αὐτῶν 'their' (ἔργων αὐτῶν 'their works') here, the singular αὐτῆς 'her' is classified as an 'A' reading by UBS and appears in the Majority Text; it is accepted in this analysis as in harmony with the αὐτῆς 'her' of 2:22b. It is suspected that the two plural words preceding the pronoun may have led a copyist to inadvertently write the plural ending. Or it may be an intentional change, the scribe not understanding that 'her works' here does not stand for 'the things that she herself does' but for 'doing the same things that she does.' There is a continuing focus on 'Jezebel', though, of course, those participating with her are responsible for their own sins.

2:23a Those who *have become like* offspring to her *by completely accepting what she teaches* It seems unlikely that these are literal children since the context is cast in figurative style. Forefronting them as a point of departure shows them as distinct from those referred to in 2:22b, whose discipline has already been specified and whose call to repentance holds hope for their restoration. The 'children' are understood by commentators to be not only practicing the sins but fully accepting them as their own manner of life. The term probably has the idea of duration and fixed attitude, to describe a new generation of heretics ready to destroy the church.

I will certainly kill The severity and finality of their doom is emphasized by the expression with double reference to death, ἀποκτενῶ ἐν θανάτῳ 'I will kill with death.' This emphasis is expressed in the display text by 'certainly'.

2:24a But I say to you the rest *of my servants* The exhortation to the faithful comes only after the discipline or judgment is given. It is introduced with forefronted ὑμῖν δέ 'but to you(pl)' indicating the switch of topic to the faithful.

In 2:20b Christ uses the term 'my servants' to refer to Christians in Thyatira so it seems best to repeat that term here to provide a noun for the phrase which consists only of a nominalized adjective in the original text.

2:24b all those who do not believe in that *false* teaching which the false teachers call 'the secret, profound *practices which* Satan *inspires*' The relative pronoun οἵτινες 'whoever' is generally used to indicate that those mentioned belong to a certain class or group. 'The depths' or 'deep things' (τὰ βαθέα) is used figuratively to refer to a profound or secret ideology.

Basic to the interpretation is the identity of the third person plural agents in ὡς λέγουσιν 'as they say'. The question is whether the faithful of the church (those referred to in οἵτινες 'whoever', the subject of the main clause and nearest explicit antecedent) use the phrase ironically, or whether Jesus is actually quoting the heretics (also very possible because of the context). While the relatives ὅσοι 'as many as' and οἵτινες 'whoever' are third person, the reference is actually second person plural, so that it is very possible that the third person plural marker on the verb λέγουσιν refers to someone other than the addressees, that is, the false teachers.

The next question is whether the false teachers would have really called their teaching 'the deep things of Satan' or if they would have called it 'the deep things of God' and Jesus is saying that these deep things are actually the deep things of Satan. This is the view accepted by Alford. But many commentators maintain that 'the deep things of Satan' is actually what the false teachers called their own teaching (Lenski, Morris) and this would certainly be possible on a grammatical basis since 'as they say' follows the complete phrase 'the deep things of Satan'.

2:24c–25a I will not impose upon you any other burden *than that which you have*. Only continue to believe firmly in me and obey me until I come There are significant reasons for understanding βάρος 'burden' to refer to something difficult to bear. Its lexical meaning itself and its use in similar contexts support this (see Matt. 20:12, Acts 15:28, Gal. 6:2), as does the use of βάλλω 'cast' here.

It would seem that the most difficult burden would be faithful perseverance in the face of the terrible temptations to compromise both from the pagans and from fellow church members who had already been tempted. In the display, 'continue' expresses the 'persistence' component of meaning present in 'hold to' and the continuing activity expressed by this verb in combination with 'what you have'. Though expressed as a verb in the Greek text the function of 'hold to' in this context is to semantically modify an implicit action or event. The 'event' might be expressed generically as 'believe firmly in me and obey me'.

until I come The Greek text includes the particle ἄν which shows that the coming is dependent on some circumstance and so might be translated as 'until whenever I come'. Since other references make the coming certain and its time unknown, the larger context indicates it is the time of his coming which to them is uncertain.

2:26 The one who is victorious and who (or, *because* he) keeps on doing what I command Although these two participial phrases are joined by καί 'and' in the Greek surface structure, the second may be understood as a reason (or means) for the first: 'The one who is victorious because he keeps on doing what I command'. The genitive phrase τὰ ἔργα μου 'my works' may be understood as 'the works/actions which I command' (Ladd).

to the end *of his life on earth* It is best to understand 'end' as a reference to end of life on earth rather than end of the age since the situational context shows that contemporary people were dying for their faith and so death is more in view in this context than the end of the age, as 2:10 shows: 'Be faithful until death'.

I will give authority over the *people of all nations who rebel against God* In Revelation the term ἔθνη 'nations' is most often used for inhabitants of the earth who are in rebellion against God. That this is the case here is strongly suggested by the rule of force and punishment described in the next verse.

2:27 he will exercise authority over them *severely as if beating them* **with an iron rod** The combination of ποιμαίνω which has a nonfigurative meaning of 'to shepherd' and ῥάβδος which may be used to designate a shepherd's staff might at first sight suggest a live metaphor, and some commentators do make allusions to shepherd and staff here. However, it can be shown that the Hebrew equivalent of ποιμαίνω had taken on the additional sense of 'rule' even before the second Psalm was written and the equivalent for ῥάβδος may designate other types of rods, so that NIV translates both Psalm 2:9 and Rev. 2:27 as "rule them with an iron scepter". However, there is still a live metaphor in the 'iron rod,' which indicates the severity of the rule.

that is, he will utterly destroy them **just as** *people* **shatter clay pots**. The second part of the doublet is similar in meaning but is cast in passive form without an agent. As a result 'that is' is used to indicate the likeness in meaning and the general agent 'people' is supplied. The implied topic of the simile is made explicit: *'he will utterly destroy them'*.

2:28a *I will give him this authority* **just as I myself received** *it* **from my Father** The clause 'as I also have received *it* from my Father' relates back to 'I will give him authority' in 2:26.

2:28b *a share in the glory of* **the morning star** Christ himself is the morning star (22:16), and sharing his glory with him is alluded to in many other Scripture passages, such as Rom. 8:17. The display is based on the morning star being understood as metonymy, the star put for the glory of it. Lenski says, "The symbolism of the morning star is that of royal splendor".

Some take the statement as a metaphor with Christ as the nonfigurative meaning. Ladd says, "... many commentators feel that this is a promise that Christ himself will be given to the victor; but this is a difficult idea".

2:29 Everyone must listen to the message In this letter and the three that follow the APPEAL is given last.

BOUNDARIES AND COHERENCE

For the boundaries see under 2:1–8. As in the other messages, coherence is shown by the address to one church in particular and by the parallelism of structure. Another coherence factor is the focus throughout the SPECIFIC MESSAGE on 'Jezebel' and her followers.

PROMINENCE AND THEME

The theme statement consists of the most naturally prominent constituents of both parts of the SPECIFIC MESSAGE and of the GENERAL APPLICATION. As part of the paragraph pattern the *problem* and *basis* for the COMMISSIVES are briefly mentioned. However, the COMMISSIVE in the second part of the SPECIFIC MESSAGE is not included in the theme since it is a negated one.

3:1–6 (Letter₅ of 2:1–3:22)

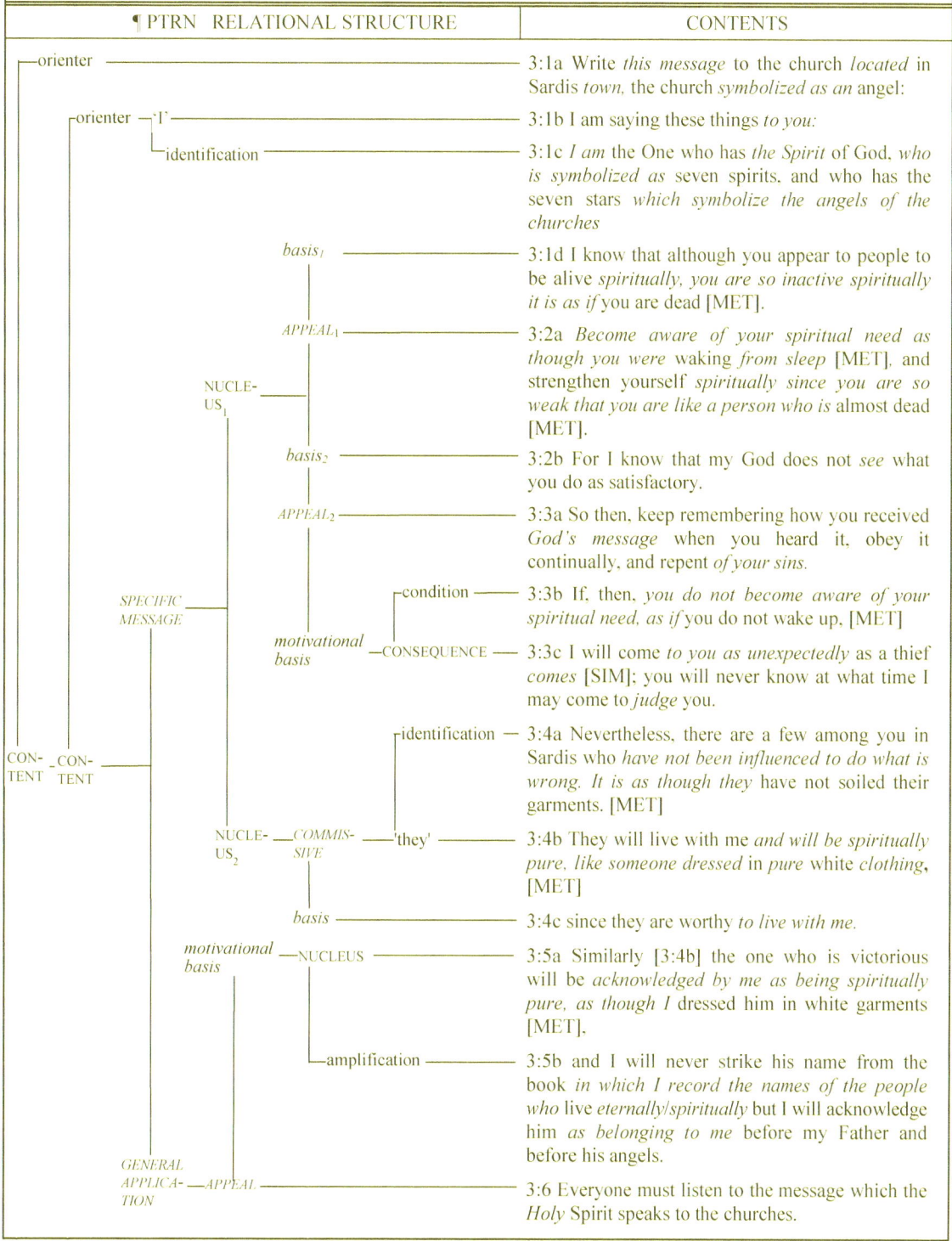

INTENT AND PARAGRAPH PATTERN

Again in this letter there are two groups addressed separately within the *SPECIFIC MESSAGE*. For those in Sardis who need to repent, a hortatory paragraph pattern is used (3:1d–3c). For those who have kept themselves morally pure there is a promise, 'they shall walk with me in white garments' (3:4). This can best be understood as a *COMMISSIVE*: 'I commit myself to enabling them to walk with me in white garments'. 'Since they are worthy' (3:4c) is considered as a *basis* for the *COMMISSIVE*. Note that while the *COMMISSIVE* is an encouragement to those who have been faithful, it is also motivational to some extent for the addressees to strive to be faithful.

NOTES

3:1c who has *the Spirit* of God, *who is symbolized as* seven spirits This expression is understood to refer to the Holy Spirit here and in various passages in which it appears in Revelation. See the note on 1:4d. In the display, '*who is symbolized as* seven spirits' is used in order to indicate that in Revelation the metaphor of 'the seven spirits' has become a fixed symbol for the omniscient Holy Spirit.

the seven stars *which symbolize the angels of the churches* This points back to the revelation of the meaning of the symbol of the seven stars in 1:20. Since it is immediately followed here by Christ's statement that the Sardis church gave a false impression of itself, it is probably significant that Christ describes himself as having not only the 'seven stars' symbolizing the churches, but also the 'seven spirits' symbolizing the omniscience of the Holy Spirit. In other words, he could not be deceived.

3:1d you appear to people to be alive The word order of ὄνομα ἔχεις 'you have a name', with the object preposed, indicates that the focus here is on the contrast between what they appear to be and what they are.

***you are so inactive spiritually that it is as if* you are dead** In these messages to the churches and in the New Testament generally it is expected of those who are living spiritually that they will do good works. But there are also those who are living physically yet are spiritually dead (Eph. 5:14; 1 Tim. 5:6). In BDAG the use of νεκρός here is listed as figurative in that the church "is inactive, remiss".

dead The figure is classified as a live figure of speech since it is continued in the commands to *wake up* and to *strengthen* the things which are left that are about to die.

3:2a–3a *Become aware of your spiritual need as though you were* waking *from sleep* and strengthen yourself *spiritually*. . . . keep remembering how you received *God's message* . . . , obey it continually, and repent *of your sins* Of the five imperatives of the rebuke, γίνου γρηγορῶν 'wake up', στήρισον 'strengthen', μνημόνευε 'remember', τήρει 'obey', μετανόησον 'repent', the second and fifth are in the aorist tense, showing that they are the prominent commands in this string. The present imperative 'wake up' is a preparatory step to 'strengthen yourself,' and the two present imperatives which follow appear to lead up to the decisive step of the last aorist imperative 'repent', the basic requirement for restoration.

3:2a *Become aware of your spiritual need as though you were* waking *from sleep* The command is full of meaning. It is contrasted with the inactive state attributed to the church. Since that condition is described figuratively, the command must be interpreted according to the figure. While some commentators and translators maintain that the sense intended is 'be watchful' here, the juxtaposition of νεκρός εἶ 'dead you are' with γίνου γρηγορῶν strongly suggests that the latter means figuratively 'rise up from sleep (death)' and referentially 'be aware of your spiritual need and do something about it'.

and strengthen yourself *spiritually since you are so weak that you are like a person who is almost dead* 'The remaining' (τὰ λοιπά) would appear to refer to the amount of effort that is being given to Christian works and character and not to specific characteristics that are still being practiced to the exclusion of those that are no longer being practiced. 'What remains which is about to die' indicates a very weak condition.

3:2b For I know that my God does not *see* what you do as satisfactory In propositionalizing 'your deeds complete before my God', the implicit event of 'seeing' needs to be made explicit.

Since this proposition comes between the two *APPEALS* and is linked to them by γάρ 'for' and οὖν 'therefore', it clearly functions as *basis* for both.

The article before ἔργα 'works' in some Greek texts is questioned. The reading with the article is listed as 'C' in the UBSGNT apparatus in its third revised edition, but in the fourth revised edition the article is included without any reference to a variant reading. It is true that in Rev. 2–3 the nine other occurrences of 'works' have the article. Without it the clause would mean that no work of the church is viewed by God as acceptable, which is more consistent with its being spiritually dead. However, since 3:4 indicates that there were a few faithful members, a comprehensive sense of 'no acceptable work' would be hyperbole used to show the awful condition of the church as a whole.

3:3a how you received *God's message when* you heard *it* In the Greek text the verbs 'received' and 'heard' do not have objects and the display has used 'God's message' to supply that lack in English. Some commentators translate πῶς as 'that'; others translate it as 'what', thus supplying an object. But the display follows Alford, who holds to the manner significance of 'how', which certainly makes good sense when God's message is taken as the object.

3:3b If then, *you do not become aware of your spiritual need, as if* you do not wake up Here again the nonfigurative meaning is made explicit in the display.

The οὖν 'then, therefore' in 3:3b is marking the result of refusing to react correctly to 3:2b, 'for I have not found your works complete before my God', refusing to carry out the commands in 3:2a and 3:3a. It cannot have an inferential relationship based directly on 3:3a, because that is a positive action. This οὖν marks the rejection of the APPEAL, 'you do not wake up', and the result of that rejection in the CONSEQUENCE, 'I will come like a thief....'

On the paragraph pattern level, 3:3b–c functions as the *motivational basis* for carrying out the commands in 3:2–3.

3:3c I will come *to you as unexpectedly* as a thief *comes* Many passages use the figure of the thief as demanding watchfulness (Matt. 24:43; 1 Thes. 5:4–6; Rev. 16:15).

you will never know at what time I may come to *judge* you Notice that 'you will not know at what time I will come upon you' is the point of comparison between the manner of a thief's coming and that of Christ's coming.

The function of the coming, judgment, is made explicit in the display. It is clearly an implicit action in this situation.

3:4a-b there are a few among you in Sardis who *have not been influenced to do what is wrong. It is as though they* have not soiled their garments.

They will live with me *and will be spiritually pure, like someone dressed* in *pure* white *clothing* The live figure of clothing is common in the New Testament. The word μολύνω 'to soil' stands not only for sexual impurity but also for religious and cultic defilement, especially for idolatry. It is used figuratively in both the Old and New Testaments. The nonfigurative meaning of these figures has been made explicit in the display.

live with me As often in the letters of Paul and John περιπατέω 'to walk' is a dead metaphor meaning 'to live'. Here 'walk/live with' has the sense of 'fellowshipping with'.

3:4c since they are worthy *to live with me* 'Worthy' is a word that takes a complement. Its conceptual meaning is not complete in itself. Here the complement is 'to live with me', taken from the immediate context.

3:5a Similarly the one who is victorious will be *acknowledged by me as being spiritually pure as though I* dressed him in white garments As in 3:4b, to which 'similarly' links this segment, the white garments are a metaphor of spiritual purity. However, the passive verb 'will be clothed in' extends the metaphor and implies an agent who acknowledges the victorious one as spiritually pure.

Similarly Instead of the adverb οὕτως 'in this manner' some manuscripts have οὗτος 'this (one)'. The Fourth Revised Edition UBSGNT gives the adverbial form a B ("almost certain") rating. This reading emphasizes the connection between 3:4 and 5a.

3:5b the book *in which I record the names of the people who* live *eternally/spiritually* Moses speaks of being blotted out of the book which God has written (Exod. 32:32, 33), and the record book is mentioned several times in Revelation. In 21:27 it is referred to as 'the book of life of the Lamb', which gives validity for seeing Christ as the agent of the writing, though the genitive might also represent the idea that only through the Lamb is there access to the book of life (13:8).

I will acknowledge him *as belonging to me* 'Acknowledge' is basically an orienter and so the proper content is needed to fill out the meaning. Since ἐξαλείφω 'erase, strike out' is a technical term in Greek for cancelling a person's citizenship, it is clear that what Christ 'acknowledges' is the believer's allegiance to him.

BOUNDARIES AND COHERENCE

For the boundaries see under 2:1–8. Coherence is shown by the similarity of the structure to that of the other letters. The use of similar terms in different parts of the structure gives added coherence to the letter, namely:
1. Life/death is mentioned in the SPECIFIC MESSAGE in 3:1d–2a and in the GENERAL APPLICATION in 3:5b.
2. The noun ὄνομα 'name' is used, though with different senses, in 3:1d, 3:4c, and twice in 3:5b.

PROMINENCE AND THEME

Christ addresses two contrasting groups of people in the church, and his words of exhortation to one group and of commitment to the other are in natural prominence as the focal point of the SPECIFIC MESSAGE. For the first group he uses five imperatives (3:2a, 3a) which also highlight his rebuke. One of these imperatives, γίνου γρηγορῶν 'become awake', is marked for prominence, being repeated (3:3b) in negative form as the condition relation in the *motivational basis* (warning). The theme comes from the prominent constituents of the SPECIFIC MESSAGE and the GENERAL APPLICATION.

3:7–13 (Letter₆ of 2:1–3:22)

THEME: *Christ promises the church at Philadelphia that they will be in his kingdom, that those who oppose them will acknowledge that he loves the church, and that he will keep the church from harm during the period of testing. He exhorts them to continue to obey his word and to be faithful. Everyone must listen to the message which the Holy Spirit speaks to the churches.*

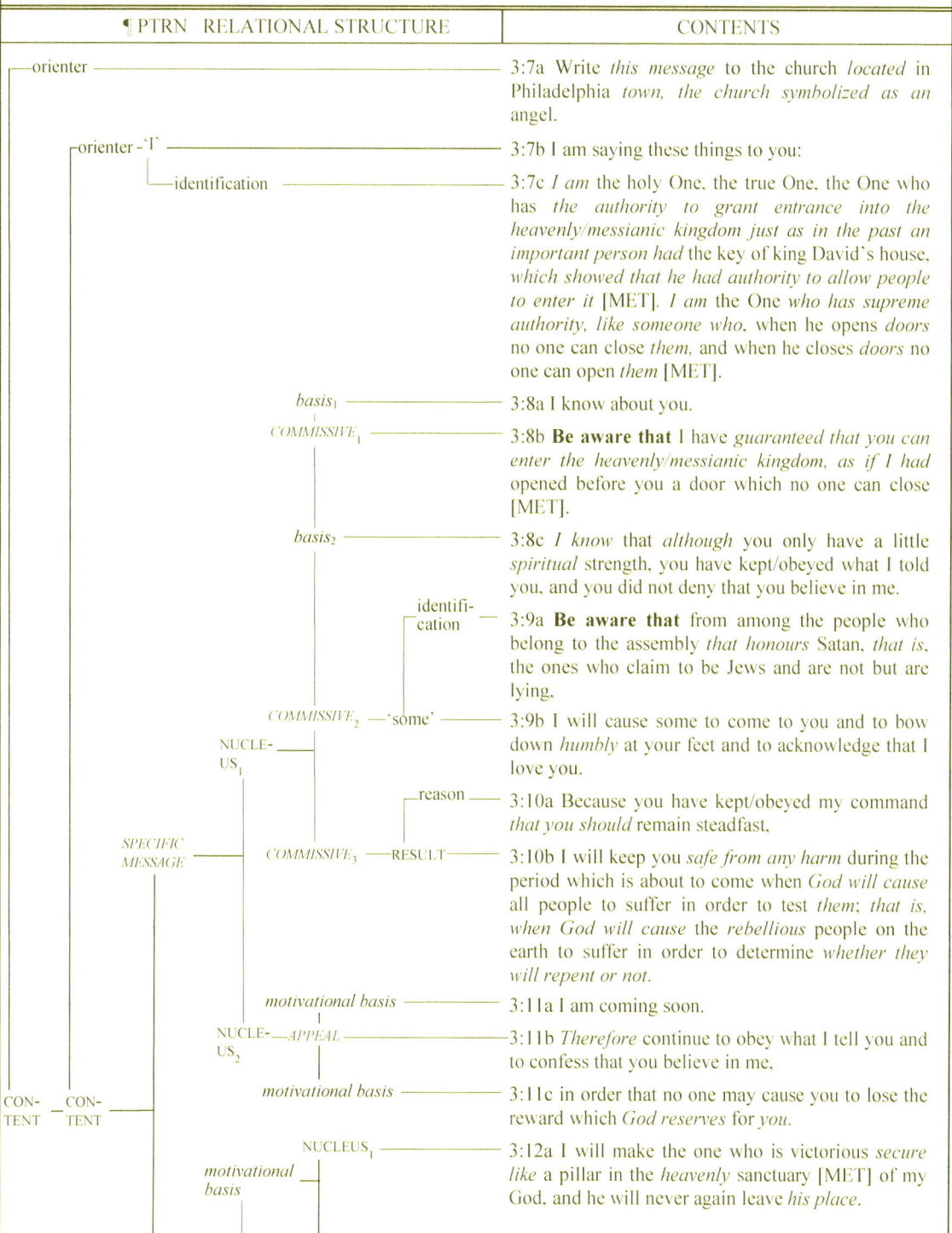

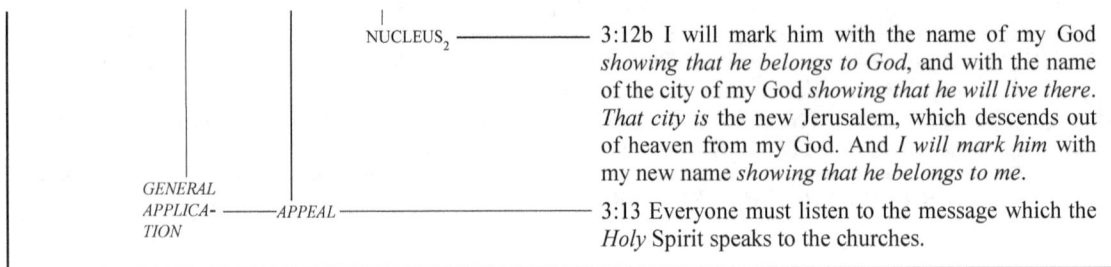

INTENT AND PARAGRAPH PATTERN

Since Christ saw no specific sin needing attention among the believers at Philadelphia, the *APPEAL* is a generic one to remain faithful. Most focal in the letter are Christ's three promises (*COMMISSIVES*) of what he will do for them. Since the believers are not strong and yet are faithful (3:8a, c as *basis*), he commits himself to strong action on their behalf.

NOTES

3:7c the holy One When 'holy' is used to modify God or Christ, it may indicate not only his moral perfection, as in Lev. 11:44–45; 1 Pet. 1:16, 'You shall be holy since I am holy', but also the uniqueness and perfection of all that God is, his divine essence and powers. The question in Rev. 3:7 is whether the comprehensive sense of 'holy' in relation to Christ is meant or whether it is his moral perfection that is in focus. Since his authority is in focus in the immediately following context of the key of David, the comprehensive sense seems more appropriate.

the true One Truth and holiness have much in common. Some understand ἀληθινός here in its sense of 'genuine' (BDAG) in contrast to the false messiah which unbelieving Jews estimated him to be. It is true that Christ makes no empty claims or pretence. But Charles wants a broader interpretation, more in line with Old Testament usage. In BDAG the occurrence here is listed as "*true, dependable*". It is associated with a righteousness which is faithful in word and purpose. Barclay translates: "The one whose nature is holiness and truth".

***I am . . . the One who has** the authority to grant entrance into the heavenly/messianic kingdom just as in the past an important person had* **the key of king David's house,** *which showed that he had authority to allow people to enter it* This relates back to the prophecy concerning Eliakim, who was vested with the key to the king's house, referred to as 'the house of David', in Isa. 22:20–25.

The key is a figure for complete authority. But there is also the figure of 'David', or possibly more fully, 'the house of David', as in Isa. 22:22. To fully unpack and propositionalize these figures would be quite complicated, e.g. 'As a key gives a person the authority/ability to open a door and let in whomever he may choose, so I have the authority to let in to the messianic kingdom, typified by the house of King David, whomsoever I choose'. Alternative ways of translating this would be:

1. Translate literally and let the function of a key, which is known in many cultures, carry the concept of authority to grant entrance. The significance of 'house of David' would have to be taught.
2. Instead of translating the figure of the key itself, use its nonfigurative meaning and also make explicit the nonfigurative meaning of 'house of David', at least to some extent, for example: 'I have the authority to grant entrance *into the messianic/heavenly kingdom typified by king* David's *earthly kingdom*'.
3. Try to retain both figures but with a manageable amount of implicit nonfigurative information made explicit, for example: 'I have the key of king David, *I have the authority to grant entrance into the heavenly/messianic kingdom typified by his earthly kingdom*'.

I am** the One **who has supreme authority, like someone who,** when he opens **doors** no one can close **them**, and when he closes **doors** no one can open **them This is a metaphorical way of referring to the complete authority of the one who has the keys to the royal household.

3:8–9 Relationships in these two verses depend much upon how the opened door is interpreted. The two views most widely accepted for the significance of the opened door are: (1) that it provides entrance into the messianic kingdom and glory (Beasley-Murray, Ladd, Morris, Mounce,); or (2) that it is a door of service for the church, offering opportunity for effective evangelism (Alford, Caird, Düsterdieck, Lenski, Swete).

The main problem with the door of service interpretation is that evangelism is not a theme in Revelation, whereas entrance into the messianic kingdom certainly is. Moreover, there appears to be a direct relationship between the key of David and the opening and shutting that Christ alone is able to do.

Many commentators see 3:8b as a parenthesis, interrupting 3:8a–c, but none explain why there should be a parenthesis here. More likely is the relationship given in the display (implicitly supported by Moule), which sees both 3:8a and 3:8c as equal *bases* for the COMMISSIVES of 3:8b, 9b and 3:10b.

3:8b *Be aware that* Here and in 3:9a the particle ἰδού gives the COMMISSIVE emphatic force.

3:8c *I know* that It is most likely that ὅτι here relates back to Οἶδά 'I know' introducing a further segment of the content of that orienter (Mounce, NIV, NRSV).

***although* you only have a little *spiritual* strength** The Greek text is μικρὰν ἔχεις δύναμιν 'you have little power', with 'little' forefronted before the verb, thus emphasizing it as 'only a little'. The church is in no way reprimanded for having little strength. The emphasis here does not rest on the lack of strength because the quality of the strength is specified in terms of the ability to honour Christ's word and confess his name. The 'little power' may be due to the fact that the church in Philadelphia only had a limited number of members, but this is not specifically mentioned here.

you have kept/obeyed what I told you In English it is difficult to give an equivalent with specific meaning and yet retain the author's intentional repetition of τηρέω 'guard, honour, obey' in 3:8c, 10a and 10b. In 8c and 10a τηρέω is rendered as 'keep/obey'. The repetition in 10b is understood as 'keeping safe from harm'.

3:9 The verbs διδῶ 'I will cause' and ποιήσω 'I will make' encode the one instance of the notion of 'cause', that is, causing the Jews to do homage before the believers. The reason for the double encoding is because a verbal repetition is required by the long reference to the object of the first verb, 'I will cause'.

3:9a *Be aware that* Note that the occurrence of ἰδού immediately before both διδῶ 'I will cause' and ποιήσω 'I will make' corroborates the fact that the verbs are expressing the same action.

the assembly *that honours* Satan See the note on 2:9f.

3:9b and to acknowledge that I love you The verb γινώσκω 'know (by experience)' is used, which with the homage amounts to acknowledgment. Use of the aorist ἠγάπησα 'loved' does not limit the love to the past. It is used because these Jews will become aware of specific past evidence of the fact that God loves the believers.

3:10a–b Because you have kept/obeyed my command ... I will keep you *safe from any harm* In 3:10a 'kept/obeyed' is used for ἐτήρησας (cf. 'obey' for the same form in 3:8c). The repetition of the same word (τηρήσω) in 3:10b is understood with a different sense, 'guard from harm'. The author emphasizes the parallelism by κἀγώ 'also I,' and preposing the object pronoun: 'you kept ... , I also will keep you.'

3:10a my command *that you should* remain steadfast The phrase τὸν λόγον τῆς ὑπομονῆς μου 'the word of the steadfastness of me' is interpreted by some as 'the message that I remained steadfast'. However, the fact that this ὅτι 'because' clause is preposed in the Greek sentence probably indicates that it is resumptive of the almost identical phrase in 3:8b ἐτήρησάς μου τὸν λόγον 'you obeyed my word.'

3:10b keep you *safe from any harm* during the period which is about to come when *God will cause* all people to suffer in order to test *them* The Greek text for the first part of this segment has σε τηρήσω ἐκ τῆς ὥρας τοῦ πειρασμοῦ 'you I will keep/guard from the hour of testing'. There are differences of opinion about the use of ἐκ 'from'. Some have based the idea of a pretribulation rapture on this verse, to the effect that God will remove his people 'from' the earth before the time of testing comes. But others cite the use of ἐκ in John 17:15, where Jesus specifically requests in his prayer that his disciples not be taken out of the world but 'kept from' (ἐκ) the evil one.

There are some important questions to be answered: (1) If the meaning of σε τηρήσω ἐκ τῆς ὥρας is 'I will keep you from adverse effects during the hour of πειρασμός', does πειρασμός mean 'temptation' or 'testing' or 'tribulation'? (2) If the πειρασμός refers to testing or temptation, does it only involve the rebellious people of the earth or are believers tempted or tested too? Certainly in the use of 'testing, trial' in this verse a significant component of meaning is the tribulation involved in the testing. But it is probably not the only component of meaning in focus here, since the primary meaning of the word is 'test' or 'tempt' and if affliction or tribulation only were meant there are other words that would have been used. Probably the best answer to these questions is that God will use affliction to test everyone on the whole earth and at the same time the devil will use it for his own purposes.

The conclusion based on translating τηρήσω ἐκ as 'remove out of' is that a promise of deliverance is made by which the church would be taken out of the world instead of being kept from spiritual harm while living through the time of trial. If the translator wishes to follow that conclusion, the proposition for that interpretation might read as follows: 'I will keep you from going through the time when *God will cause people* to suffer in order to test *them*'.

that is, when *God will cause* the *rebellious* **people on the earth to suffer in order to determine** *whether they will repent or not* In order to show the agent, which is God, and his purpose in causing the tribulation, this is made specific in the display.

the *rebellious* people The characteristic use of the designation 'the ones dwelling on the earth' in Revelation is for reference to mankind in rebellion against God (see 1:7). A majority of commentators agree that this is the meaning here.

3:11a I am coming soon Reference is to the second coming of Christ. This thought is a keynote of the book. The phrase is repeated three times in the epilogue (22:7, 12, 20) and greeted with eager response. For the churches of Ephesus (2:5e) and Pergamum (2:16c) it is used to motivate repentance, but for Philadelphia it is to motivate continued faithfulness.

Some English versions (KJV, NASB, NLT) translate ταχύ as 'quickly', while others (CEV, NCV, NIV, REB) translate it as 'soon'. However, the primary, or at least potential, meaning of 'I am coming quickly' in English, and probably in many other languages, is that the action of 'coming' is already in progress and the subject is moving rapidly. This is certainly not the intended meaning of the Greek text.

3:11b Therefore Since 11a functions as a *motivational basis* for the APPEAL in 11b, 'therefore' is used to signal the relationship in the display.

continue to obey what I tell you and to confess that you believe in me In 3:8c the church is commended for obeying Christ's command and for not denying faith in him. It is highly probable that ὃ ἔχεις 'what you have' is a generic representation of this commendation (cf. Mounce). Since 'have' in some languages would not collocate with actions or characteristics and in order to clarify the very generic 'what you have', a more specific representation is made here in the display. 'Not denied' is understood to mean 'confessed'.

3:11c in order that This purpose clause functions as a *motivational basis* for the APPEAL in 11b.

no one may cause you to lose the reward which *God reserves* **for you** The στέφανος is the victory wreath. TEV translates as 'victory prize'. It is the reward given to the faithful. See the note on 2:10d. It is clear that another would not be able to take the reward for himself, but the church might forfeit it (cf. Bratcher and Hatton) through yielding to the temptation to relax her hold on the essentials provided for her.

3:12a *secure like* **a pillar in the** *heavenly* **sanctuary** 'Pillar' stands for permanence, as the following statement 'he will never leave' shows. The pillar is secure in contrast to the 'peg' of Isa. 22:23, 25 which was in a sure place, but nevertheless removed. The figure is live because of the details given, such as the heavenly sanctuary and the security promised through it.

'*Heavenly* sanctuary' is not inconsistent with the statement in 21:22 that there is no temple in the holy city because the whole may be understood as a temple. Both 'pillar' and 'sanctuary' are metaphorical. Also, the writer is not careful to reconcile the details of his visions.

he will never again leave *his place* In the Greek text, this statement is strengthened by repeated signals for the same function or semantic component: ἐξ- on the verb ἐξέλθῃ plus ἔξω to signal 'out'; the double negative οὐ μή plus ἔτι '(no) more' to signal the negative sense. The strong assurance of permanence may be taken prophetically, that is, not only that no power will be able to move him from God's presence, but also, he will not of his own choice leave it.

3:12b I will mark him with the name of my God *showing that he belongs to God*, **and with the name of the city of my God** *showing that he will*

live there. That city is* the new Jerusalem, which descends out of heaven from my God. And *I will mark him* with my new name *showing that he belongs to me The threefold inscription speaks of a profound relationship with God and Christ, describing the victory for the one who is faithful.

I will mark him Grammatically this could be either on the person or the pillar, since both of these words are masculine in Greek. Some commentators have referred to ancient customs of inscribing names on pillars, but a thought more consistent with the context finds reference in 14:1 and 22:4, where the saints are marked on the forehead.

BOUNDARIES AND COHERENCE

For the boundaries see under 2:1–8. As in the other letters coherence is shown by the parallelism of structure. Repetition of the same or similar terms in different parts of the structure provides added coherence:

1. Opening and shutting doors in the orienter (3:7a) and the first COMMISSIVE (3:8b).
2. The verb τηρέω 'keep/guard' three times in the COMMISSIVES (3:8c, 10a, b) and probably referred to by κράτει 'hold on to' in the APPEAL (3:11b).
3. The noun ὄνομα 'name' in the *basis* for the COMMISSIVES (3:8c) and in the *motivational basis* of the GENERAL APPLICATION (3:12b).

PROMINENCE AND THEME

Both the APPEALS and the COMMISSIVES are naturally prominent and comprise the theme.

3:14–22 (Letter₇ of 2:1–3:22)

THEME: Christ exhorts the church at Laodicea to accept his provision for their spiritual needs and to repent of their sins. He promises to fellowship with any who will respond to his call. Everyone must listen to the message which the Holy Spirit speaks to the churches.

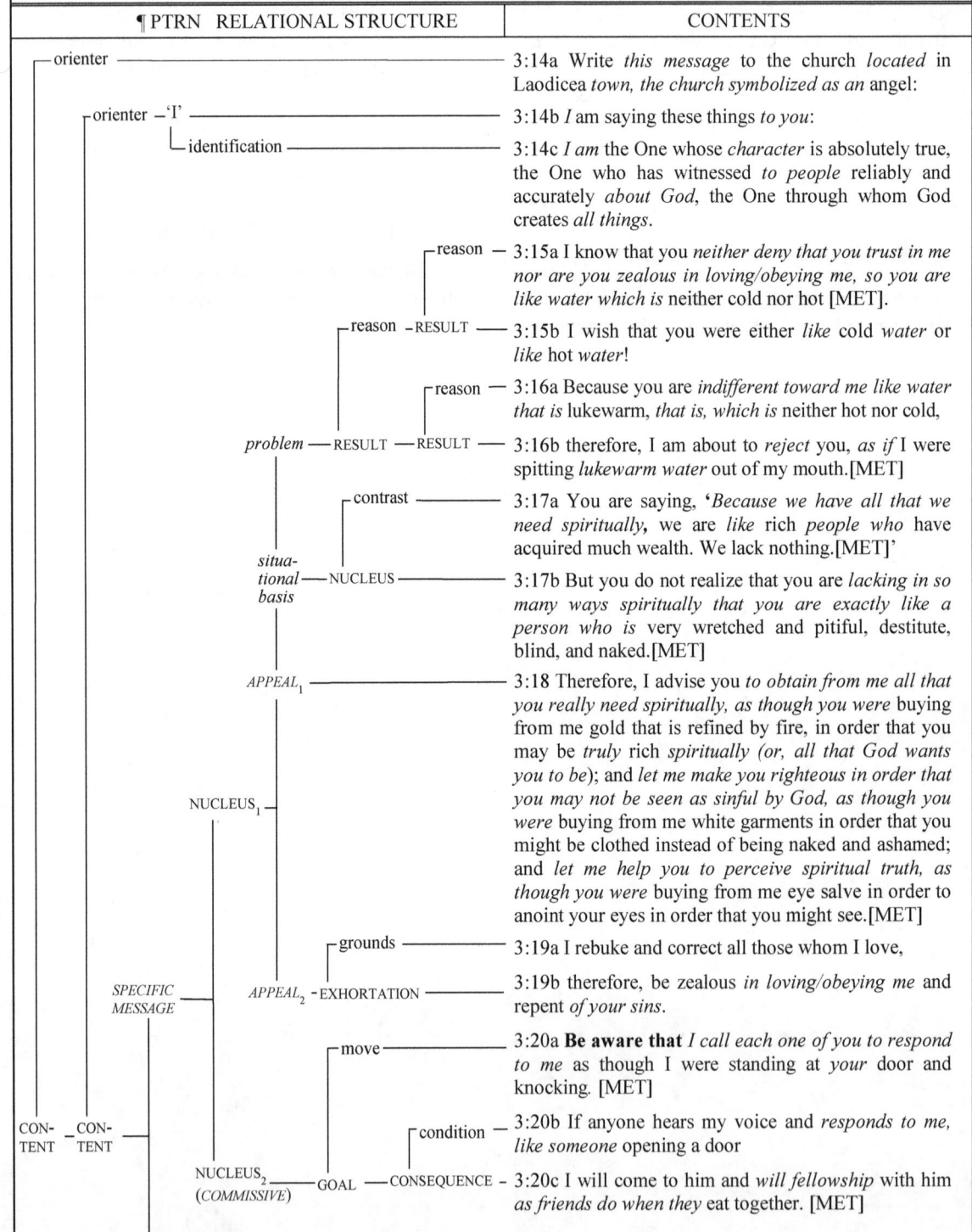

| | | 3:21 I will grant to the one who is victorious to sit with me on my throne *ruling over all the universe*, just as I was victorious and sit with my Father on his throne. |
| | | 3:22 Everyone must listen to the message which the *Holy* Spirit speaks to the churches. |

INTENT AND PARAGRAPH PATTERN

This hortatory subscene is analysed as one of the solutionality type since 3:15–16, which describes the believers' indifference, is taken as presenting the *problem*. Unlike the other APPEALS in these seven letters, that of 3:18 appears as a mitigated command, introduced by συμβουλεύω 'I advise...'. An alternate analysis would understand 3:15–16 as a *motivational basis* for the APPEALS. 3:17 is labelled as a *situational basis* for the APPEALS since it is introduced by ὅτι 'because' and describes the wretched state of the Laodicea church which is the reason for its need to repent and appeal to the Lord for help.

In the surface structure 3:20 appears to be a COMMISSIVE and has been presented as such in the display diagram. But it also might be seen as a mitigated command, the form of which is most clearly shown in the condition 'if anyone hears my voice and opens the door'. The APPEAL would then be 'Heed my voice and open the door'. (See Longacre, p. 7; Sherman and Tuggy, pp. 2, 6, 7, 27.) However, one of the reasons for analysing this constituent as a COMMISSIVE is that Christ's promise to come and fellowship is marked as significant by the reciprocal phrases 'I ... with him, and he with me'. So this should probably be seen as the most prominent part of the verse. Thus it may well be that the command is mitigated as a supporting, conditional clause for reasons of prominence rather than for reasons of rapport, the latter being the common reason for mitigation.

Being last in the series of seven messages, this unit has some aspects of transition. Christ's identification is given in details that are not mentioned in John's vision of him (1:9–20) but that emphasize his place in the Godhead. The promise to the victor has more reference to Christ's final reign (3:21) than that found in the other messages. These emphases make a fitting transition to the vision of the throne of God in heaven (4:2–11).

NOTES

3:14c whose *character* is absolutely true The Greek text for this is ὁ ἀμήν 'the Amen'. The root of the Hebrew word means that which is sure, firm, valid, and binding. God's righteousness and faithfulness are basic to the meaning. In the Hebrew of Isa. 65:16, God is 'the Amen', translated 'the God of truth' or 'the faithful God'. That Jesus is 'the Amen' refers to his essential being of truth and righteousness (John 14:6; 1 John 5:20).

who has witnessed *to people* reliably and accurately *about God* The Greek text is ὁ μάρτυς ὁ πιστὸς καὶ ἀληθινός 'the witness faithful and true'. Both the concepts of trustworthiness and absolute truth are carried over from the Old Testament concept of 'amen'. The phrase corresponds to Christ's being 'the amen' and expands the meaning. Barclay translates: "the witness on the truth of whose words you can rely". See also the note on 1:5.

through whom God creates Even though lexically ἡ ἀρχὴ τῆς κτίσεως τοῦ θεοῦ could mean 'the first one created by God', such an interpretation is obviated by those passages which show Christ to be the agent of creation, as John 1:1–3; Heb. 1:2.

all things The product (direct object) of creating is added to fill out the case frame.

3:15a I know that See the note on 2:2a.

you *neither deny that you trust in me nor are you zealous in loving/obeying me, so you are like water which is* neither cold nor hot The figure here is considered live since there is a series of related metaphors (3:15b–16). There is general agreement on the interpretation of the figures as representing the extremes of denial of Christ (or even hostility toward him) and of fervent love for him. Alford rejects the suggestion that 'cold' is symbolic of a love that had deteriorated, on the grounds that that would be too similar to the indifference described as the lukewarm state.

zealous in loving/obeying me Whereas 'hot' is generally understood as describing zeal, being zealous describes the manner of an action rather than indicating what that action is and so a representation of the action itself must be made explicit to indicate the meaning fully. In this context where fellowship with Christ is a goal (3:20c) and Christ makes reference to his love (3:19a), loving, or its corollary obeying, may well be in focus.

3:15b I wish that you were either *like* cold *water* or *like* hot *water*! This is kept figurative in the display to help maintain the vividness of the Greek text. An alternative would be to render it nonfiguratively: 'I wish you would either deny that you trust me or be zealous for me!' There is probably some use of irony here, since 3:19b makes it clear that Christ's real desire for the church is that they would be zealous for him. It is as if he is saying 'I wish you would be zealous for me. But even if you would reject me that would be better than this indifference!'

3:17 The ὅτι 'because, that' at the beginning of 3:17 is best taken as indicating a grounds (*situational basis*) for the following APPEAL in 3:18. 'Therefore' in the display text for 3:18 expresses this *basis-APPEAL* relationship.

3:17a You are saying, '*Because we have all that we need spiritually*, we are *like* rich *people who* have acquired much wealth. We lack nothing.' The church may have had material wealth but in this context the speaker's concern is more with spiritual attitudes and his offers have to do with spiritual values. Real material poverty in the church at Smyrna was contrasted with spiritual wealth, but the boast of the Laodiceans is understood as having reference to spiritual values. The point of similarity of the metaphor is 'having all that one needs'. In the Greek text there are three statements that are similar in meaning. These three appear in the display text, but the third of these, which is nonfigurative, is also repeated as the reason why they are like rich people to make clear the meaning of the metaphor.

***who* have acquired much wealth** Use of the perfect tense after the declaration of the earlier part of 3:17a ('I am rich') points to the perfect of existing state in which attention is called to the result of past action. This 'having become rich' points to self-effort (Charles, Swete).

3:17b you are *lacking in so many ways spiritually that you are exactly like a person who is* very wretched and pitiful, destitute, blind, and naked The wretchedness and pitiableness are general terms and overlap in meaning, to a certain extent. 'Pitiable' as a literal translation of ἐλεεινός transfers well into English, but it involves a verbal idea ('to pity') even though it is an adjective. For many languages it will be more appropriate to use a word like 'pitiable' or 'miserable' that describes the state of the person.

The specific terms which follow are tied in with the remedies advised in 3:18. The use in the Greek of the nominalized form 'the one who …' gives the idea that the condition is extreme: that wretched and pitiful one *par excellence*. The one article holds the descriptive clause together. That the specific terms are used figuratively with a spiritual significance is indicated by the correction required for them (3:18). The spiritual significance (the nonfigurative part of the metaphor and the point of similarity) is signalled in the display with the words 'lacking in so many ways spiritually that you are exactly like a person…'.

3:18 Note that for each of the three figures in this verse an attempt is made to provide the nonfigurative meaning of the metaphor.

***obtain from me all that you really need spiritually, as though you were* buying from me gold that is refined by fire, in order that you may be *truly* rich *spiritually* (*or, all that God wants you to be*)** The contrast between the false spirituality of the Laodiceans and the genuine spirituality that Christ will give must be kept in focus. Gold refined by fire certainly represents genuineness. It may also include the idea of faith or spirituality that has been proven by testing. Genuineness is represented in the display nonfiguratively by 'really' and 'truly'.

and *let me make you righteous in order that you may not be seen as sinful by God, as though you were* buying from me white garments in order that you might be clothed instead of being naked and ashamed Spiritually the garments represent character or life. The splendour of the white raiment they may obtain from Christ is in its whiteness, symbolic of purity, righteousness, and heaven. The truly righteous character of Christ is needed instead of their self-righteousness.

and *let me help you to perceive spiritual truth, as though you were* buying from me eye salve in order to anoint your eyes in order that you might see The use of the figure for spiritual blindness is appropriate to their inability to observe their true condition and to distinguish between true and false values. For languages which do not have a word for 'spiritual', one suggestion would be 'help you to understand what you are truly like and that you need to repent'.

3:19a I rebuke and correct These are the words used to promote repentance and there is considerable overlap of meaning. The verb ἐλέγχω 'rebuke' carries the concept of reproof in the exposing and convincing of educative discipline. This may mean punishment, but emphasis tends to be more on the words of teaching and admonition calling for repentance. The rabbis took it as showing brotherly love. The verb παιδεύω 'educate, correct' is used of the educative dealing of God with the people of Israel. It is associated with the discipline of punishment and suffering. Heb. 12:7–11 presents a lofty goal as the purpose of such discipline.

those whom I love The verb 'love' here is φιλέω, but there is considerable debate about whether this indicates any difference of meaning from ἀγαπάω, the more common verb for 'love' in the NT. Those who hold to a difference of meaning between φιλέω and ἀγαπάω claim that the former is the more emotional love and the latter is governed by will. In that case the translation here might be 'those whom I affectionately love.'

3:19b be zealous *in obeying me* and repent *of your sins* The first imperative here, ζήλευε 'be zealous' is in the present tense, and the second, μετανόησον 'repent' is aorist. As in 3:2a–3a this probably shows that the first is a preparatory step to the second. This verb ζήλευε 'be zealous' probably echoes ζεστός 'hot' in 3:15–16 both in sound and in meaning. As in 3:15a it requires an indication of the activity referred to (see note on 3:15a).

repent *of your sins* The object of 'repent' is made explicit as 'of your sins' to fill out the case frame.

3:20a *Be aware that* Van Otterloo classifies this occurrence of ἰδού under "calling attention to a situation that requires action" (p. 59). The situation is 'I stand at the door and knock' and the action called for is an implicit one: 'Open it' (p. 63). See Intent and Paragraph Pattern for more discussion of an implied call for action here.

I call each one of you to respond to me as though I were standing at your door and knocking Here again the non-figurative meaning of the metaphor is made explicit in the display. The figurative 'standing ... and knocking' indicates an appeal to the persons concerned to respond to the one who is knocking and asking to be let in.

3:20b If anyone hears my voice and *responds to me* See Intent and paragraph pattern for discussion of 3:20b as a mitigated command.

3:20c I will come to him and *will fellowship* with him *as friends do when they* eat together The common meal was shared as the most intimate proof of friendship in the Middle East. In this verse eating together is a figure which represents the close fellowship of friends.

3:21 grant the one who is victorious to sit with me on my throne *ruling over all the universe* Throughout the NT 'throne' represents ruling. See the Note on 1:4d.

BOUNDARIES AND COHERENCE

For the initial boundary see under 2:1-8. The end of this unit coincides with the end of Step₁ of the Body (1:9–3:22). As in the other letters coherence is shown by the parallelism of structure. Coherence is also provided by themes which link different parts of the letter:

1. There is a contrast between Christ, who in the orienter (3:14c) is described as an accurate witness, and the church, which in the *situational basis* of the APPEALS (3:17) gives a false picture of itself.
2. There may be a link between Christ as the one through whom God created all things (3:14c) and his instruction to the church that all their needs could be met through him (3:18).
3. In the COMMISSIVE (3:20c) Christ promises that the one who responds to him will share a meal μετ' ἐμοῦ 'with me' and in the GENERAL APPLICATION (3:21) he states that the one who is victorious will share the heavenly throne μετ' ἐμοῦ 'with me'.

PROMINENCE AND THEME

The APPEALS of 3:18–19 are naturally prominent. In 3:20 the COMMISSIVE, the condition for which may be seen as a mitigated command, strongly brings out the whole purpose of the SPECIFIC MESSAGE. It is appropriate to consider the APPEALS and the COMMISSIVE as the most naturally prominent parts of the SPECIFIC MESSAGE.

PART CONSTITUENT 4:1–16:21 (Act: Step₂ of Body)

THEME: I was told to come up to heaven and see the events that must happen. I saw God on his throne being worshiped, and Christ being worshiped as the Redeemer because he is worthy to open the sealed scroll. The opening of the seven seals and then the sounding of seven trumpets brought judgment on rebellious earth people, and God's servants were marked out, and there were cosmic manifestations of judgment. Satan and his agents caused all earth people to submit to them, but God's people were with Christ praising God as the final judgment was announced. Angels poured out the seven bowls of God's anger bringing terrible afflictions on the rebellious earth people in completion of God's punishment of them.

MACROSTRUCTURE	CONTENTS
setting	4:1–11 I saw heaven open and was told to come and see the events that would happen next. I saw a throne at the centre of heaven and the elders and living creatures worshiping the glorious One sitting on it.
step₁	5:1–8:5 When the Lamb took the scroll from the One who sits on the throne, the whole created universe worshiped him as the worthy Redeemer. The opening of the first six seals brought judgment to rebellious earth people. Before the Lamb opened the seventh seal God's own servants were marked and those who had come safely through persecution praised God. When the Lamb opened the seventh seal, there was a silence and then cosmic manifestations of judgment occurred.
step₂	8:6–11:19 At the sounding of each of six successive trumpet blasts, woeful judgment came upon the earth and its rebellious people. Before the seventh trumpet blast I was commissioned to prophesy and mark out the worshipers of Christ. Christ then sent two witnesses to prophesy to the nations. When the seventh angel sounded his trumpet, voices from heaven declared that the Lord God and his Messiah now rule over the world and the elders declared that the time had come for God's final judgment. Then the heavenly sanctuary became open to view and cosmic manifestations of judgment occurred on earth.
step₃	12:1–14:20 Satan, as a powerful dragon, attacked God's Messiah but was defeated. Then his agents, two terrible beasts, attacked and defeated God's people. They caused all earth people to submit to them. But then I saw the Lamb on Mount Zion with all God's faithful people, and angels announced God's judgment on those who did not worship him. The Son of Man harvested the grain of the earth and the grapes of the earth were crushed in the winepress of God's anger against evil people.
GOAL	15:1–16:21 Those who had overcome the beast praised God and seven angels were given the seven bowls of God's anger. As these were poured out the people who had worshipped the beast suffered terrible afflictions and then the rulers of earth united for the final battle against God, but Jesus called on his people to be ready for him. When the last bowl was emptied God's punishment of people was complete, but they continued to curse him.

INTENT AND MACROSTRUCTURE

This second act of the Body of the book consists of narrative, unlike the first act. The greater part of it relates the destruction of the ungodly people of earth, and this is clearly something that God has already chosen to do and carries out by his sovereign will. Thus it is a volitionality discourse with a *step-GOAL* structure. The carrying out of God's predestined will is most clearly represented in the three series of seven punishments of rebellious mankind, in which the progression toward a final goal is marked and inevitable (see below, Prominence and Theme).

BOUNDARIES AND COHERENCE

The second act begins with the transfer of John by the Spirit from earth to heaven (4:2) as he responds to the voice calling him to come up (4:1) and see the events ἃ δεῖ γενέσθαι 'that must happen'. It closes with the voice from heaven that declares γέγονεν 'it has happened/come to pass' (16:17). There are also cosmic manifestations, a pronouncement against Babylon, and blasphemy by the people of earth (16:18–21). These four features indicate a finality. In 17:1 John is again summoned by an angelic voice and transferred by the Spirit to another location, indicating that another act has begun.

A feature which gives coherence to the unit is the parallelism of structure in the narration of the three series of judgments: the seven seals (6:1–8:5); the seven trumpets (8:6–11:19); and the seven bowls (15:1–16:21). The opening of the seals follows a general pattern shown in each of the three series: the first four of the judgments seem to be related in some way, the fifth and sixth have elements in common, and the seventh forms a transition to the next series. Even in the third series the last judgment, the seventh bowl, is transitional with its reference to the destruction of Babylon pointing forward to the next act.

Another feature linking the three series is the manifestation, at the close of each, of thunder, lightning, and earthquake (8:5; 11:19; 16:18–21).

In addition to the theme of judgment running through the unit there are also repeated references to the fate of God's people. The saints are separated from those who refuse to worship God (7:1–17, 11:1–3), persecuted by Satan and his agents (7:14, 11:2, 12:17–13:18) and triumphant with Christ (7:15–17, 11:12, 14:1–4, 15:2–4). It is noticeable that all these references occur in units which are analysed as *interludes* in the series of judgments, or in the scene 12:1–14:20, which forms a sort of interlude between the first two series of judgments and the third.

An alternative analysis of this unit would be to understand it as ending with 11:19. 12:1 would then begin a new act in which the conflict of Satan and his agents against God and his saints would be the major theme, ending in the final destruction of Satan and all who follow him at 20:15. This is a possible analysis since it is not until chapter 12 that Satan is clearly introduced and much of the discourse has to do with him and his henchmen in chapters 12–20. However, since the three series of seven judgments have such clear cohesion, it is best to see the introduction of Satan and his agents as part of a separate participant structure overlaid on the formal discourse structure.

PROMINENCE AND THEME

The final scene is the focal point toward which the action of the unit is directed, making it the GOAL, the naturally prominent passage in the act. This progression towards a goal can be seen in the three series of seven judgments. In the first series, the opening of the seals, there is an emphasis on what is allowed (notice ἐδόθη 'was allowed' in 6:2, 4, 8) and on the partial nature of the judgment (the olives and the vines are spared in 6:6, only a quarter of the people are killed in 6:8, and in 6:14 the mountains and islands are displaced, not abolished as in 16:20). Then in the second series, the trumpets, the destruction is extended to all the vital resources of life on earth, but its scope is still restricted to one third (8:7, 9, 11, 12, 9:15). Finally, the pouring out of the bowls brings unlimited destruction (16:3, 18–21), and all the rebellious people of earth are terribly afflicted (16:2, 6, 9, 11, 21).

Another feature which emphasizes the prominence of the GOAL is its focus on finality. This is seen in its opening statement (15:1) and in the dramatic pronouncement from heaven γέγονεν 'it has happened/come to pass' in 16:17.

The *setting* of this unit (4:1–11) also has marked prominence since it gives the narrator's location and the heavenly setting of the rest of the body of the book.

The theme is therefore a summary of the *setting*, the *steps* and the GOAL.

ACT CONSTITUENT 4:1–11 (Scene: Setting for 4:1–16:21)

THEME: *I saw heaven open and was told to come and see the events that would happen next. I saw a throne at the centre of heaven and the elders and living creatures worshiping the glorious One sitting on it.*		
MACROSTRUCTURE		CONTENTS
occasion		4:1 I saw heaven open and was told to come and be shown the events which must occur next.
OUTCOME		4:2-11 I saw a throne in heaven with One sitting on it. He was the center of every creature and object in heaven. The elders and the living creatures worshiped him as the holy and mighty Creator.

INTENT AND MACROSTRUCTURE

The opening boundary of the second act indicates a major break in the discourse and to some extent 4:1–11 supplies the setting for the whole of the rest of the Body of the book, since it opens with an invitation to enter heaven to see "the events which must follow" (4:1). However, this unit is more specifically the narrative setting for the events of the second act (4:1–16:21) since it shows how John came to see these events and sets the scene in heaven against which they are played out. It has an *occasion*–OUTCOME structure, with the heavenly call forming the *occasion* and John's vision of the scene in heaven being the OUTCOME.

BOUNDARIES AND COHERENCE

The beginning boundary of the 4:1–11 scene coincides with that of the second act and is marked by the end of the letters to the seven churches and the beginning of the narrative of the heavenly visions. The closing boundary is marked by a switch from setting-type material to a stimulus-response chain of events starting at 5:1. The unit has coherence in that both parts of it are made up of setting-type material. The location of heaven is central to both.

PROMINENCE AND THEME

Since this unit to some extent gives the setting for all the rest of the Body, both its parts are prominent. They are crucial in both setting the scene and in showing how the author came to see it.

SCENE CONSTITUENT 4:1 (Episode: Occasion for 4:2–11)

THEME: *I saw heaven open and was told to come and be shown the events which must occur next.*			
RELATIONAL STRUCTURE			CONTENTS
NUCLEUS₁	orienter		4:1a After these things [1:9–3:22] I, *John*, experienced *another scene*
	CONTENT		4:1b *in which I saw that* there was a doorway open into heaven
NUCLEUS₂	orienter		4:1c and *I heard* the voice like a trumpet which I had heard before [1:10b]. It was saying to me,
	CONTENT	EXHORTATION	4:1d "Come up here,
		GROUNDS	4:1e since I will show you events that must happen after these things [1:9–3:22]."

INTENT AND PARAGRAPH PATTERN

This is a narrative unit which details John's initial vision that formed the *occasion* for his larger vision of the events in heaven. This initial vision consists of something seen and something heard.

NOTES

4:1a After these things [1:9–3:22] I, *John*, experienced *another scene* The command to John in 1:19 is to write 'what you see, that is, conditions as they are and events which are about to occur afterward'. (See note on 1:19.) There is no overt suggestion that Revelation comprises many visions. The implication is that it is one vision going from scene to scene. So in this verse we can speak of John's seeing another 'scene' when he says εἶδον 'I saw'. However, it may be better to translate this verb as 'I experienced' since the content that follows includes a voice, which he heard without seeing the speaker.

4:1b there was a doorway open into heaven The phrase θύρα ἠνεῳγμένη 'a door opened' refers to the state of a doorway being open, not to the action of a door being opened. It is the equivalent of 'the heavens opened' in Matt. 3:16 and Acts 7:56.

This clause is preceded in the Greek by καὶ ἰδού 'and behold, and lo'. Since ἰδού immediately precedes θύρα ἠνεῳγμένη 'a door opened', it is marking the open doorway as thematic (Van Otterloo p. 46). The open doorway is what gives John the means to enter heaven and observe what happens there.

4:1d "Come up here" The response to this invitation is not specified as a bodily change of location for the seer and does not necessarily indicate that his body will no longer be on earth. Many of the subsequent scenes may be interpreted as viewed from heaven, but his position is not given specifically. In the vision he is seeing events happen on earth as well as those which take place in heaven. For instance, 5:3 and 13 seem to include both spheres.

4:1e since I will show you events This constitutes the grounds for the exhortation of 4:1d, but since it refers to the main purpose of the narrative it clearly has marked prominence. This is common for grounds-exhortation constructions like "Come/Go and …".

that must happen This is the same phrase as in 1:1. See the note on that verse.

BOUNDARIES AND COHERENCE

The opening words of chapter 4, μετὰ ταῦτα 'after these things', mark a new unit since they close out the preceding unit (1:9–3:22) and begin a new one. In 4:2 another time word, εὐθέως 'immediately', marks the transition to John's main vision of heaven. Within the unit coherence is provided by the focus on heaven, and by the two-part structure detailing what John saw and what he heard.

PROMINENCE AND THEME

In this short unit the theme consists of the main points of the CONTENT of John's vision, including the grounds 4:1e, which have marked prominence.

SCENE CONSTITUENT 4:2–11 (Episode: Outcome of 4:1)

THEME: I saw a throne in heaven with One sitting on it. He was the center of every creature and object in heaven. The elders and the living creatures worshiped him as the holy and mighty Creator.

¶PTRN	RELATIONAL STRUCTURE	CONTENTS
	orienter	4:2a Immediately I experienced *being specially controlled* by the *Holy* Spirit, *and I saw*
DESCRIP-TION	NUCLEUS₁ — NUCLEUS₁	4:2b *that* there in heaven was a throne,
	NUCLEUS₂ — 'One'	4:2c and on the throne One was sitting (*or, sitting as a ruler*).
	└─ description	4:3a The appearance of the One who was sitting on the throne shone like a *brilliant* diamond and like a *brilliant red* carnelian jewel. [SIM]
	nucleus₂	4:3b There was a rainbow which *shone* like a *brilliant* emerald jewel around the throne.
	nucleus₃ — NUCLEUS₁	4:4a Around the throne there were twenty-four thrones.
	NUCLEUS₂ — 'elders'	4:4b On these thrones were seated twenty-four elders.
	└─ description	4:4c *The elders* were wearing *pure* white garments and *were wearing* golden victor's wreaths on their heads.
	nucleus₄	4:5a From the throne there came lightning and rumblings and thundering.
	nucleus₅	4:5b Seven torches of fire were burning in front of the throne. These symbolize God's *Holy Spirit who knows all things and so he is like* seven spirits. [MET]
	nucleus₆	4:6a In front of the throne *there was what looked* like a sea *made of* glass which was as clear as crystal. [SIM]
	nucleus₇ — 'living creatures'	4:6b Nearest to the throne and around the throne there were four living *creatures*, which had many [HYP] eyes in front and behind.
	└─ description	4:7 The first living *creature* was like a lion. The second living *creature* was like an ox. The third living *creature* had a face like a human face. The fourth living creature was like an eagle *that is* flying.
	┌─ description	4:8a These four living *creatures,* each of them had six wings, and they had many [HYP] eyes all around *their bodies* and under *their wings,*
	orienter — 'they'	4:8b and day and night they never cease to say/sing:
situation	CONTENT	4:8c "Holy, holy, holy is the Lord God, the almighty One, the One who has always existed, who exists, and who will in the future come to the world."
	circumstance	4:9 Whenever the living *creatures* glorify, honour, and thank the One who sits on the throne, *that is,* the One who lives forever and ever,
DECLAR-ATION	SIMULT-ANEOUS NUCLEUS₁ — SIMULTANEOUS NUCLEUS₁	4:10a the twenty-four elders prostrate themselves before the One who sits on the throne,
	SIMULTANEOUS NUCLEUS₂	4:10b and worship the One who lives forever and ever,

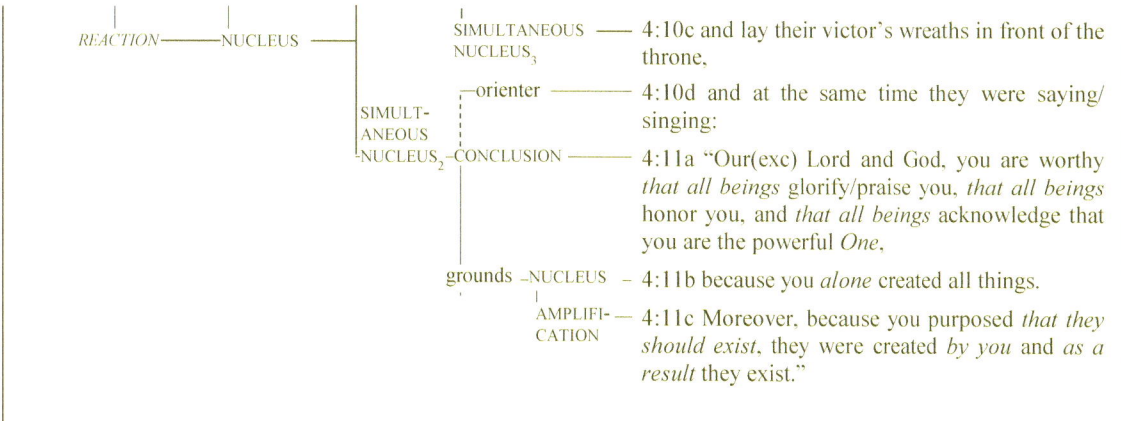

INTENT AND PARAGRAPH PATTERN

The 4:2–11 paragraph is obviously descriptive. As we would expect, it has a sequential ordering, beginning with a description of the central and most prominent point, the throne and the One sitting upon it, and then a description of the beings or items around the throne. In one sense 8–11 might be seen as further description, but it seems better to understand it as the DECLARATION, a reaction to the greatness and holiness of the enthroned Creator, since what the beings around the throne say is more prominent and thematic than a description of their actions alone. This prominence is shown by the amount of redundancy in the build-up to the speeches: in 4:8 'had many eyes' partly repeats 4:6b, and 'day and night' is duplicated by 'they have no rest'; in 4:9 the preceding speech is recapitulated; and 4:10 consists of a triple repetition in which the descriptions of God are repeated from 4:9.

In this particular *description-DECLARATION* paragraph pattern the description of the One on the throne is marked as highly prominent, so the *description* is capitalized.

NOTES

4:2a I experienced *being specially controlled* by the *Holy* Spirit See the note on 1:10a.

4:2b–7 This DESCRIPTION of what John first saw and heard in heaven is presented as seven items. The throne is mentioned first and God is merely presented as 'the One sitting on the throne,' probably to avoid saying that John actually 'saw God.' Similarly, the thrones of the elders are mentioned before the elders themselves, perhaps to avoid making them more prominent than God. All the items are described in terms of their position in relation to the throne of God, more or less starting with those nearest the throne and then moving outwards. However, it is noticeable that the 'living creatures,' who are referred to as being nearest the throne, are mentioned last. This may be to provide a link with the DECLARATION that follows (in which the living creatures are the first actors) or because the elders are given more prominence since the focus of the book is on God's plans for his people, who the elders represent.

4:2b–c there At the beginning of 4:2b there is another καὶ ἰδού 'and behold, and lo' immediately preceding θρόνος 'throne' and so marking 'throne' as thematic. Such translations as NIV's "There before me" and 'There in heaven' may capture some of the intended sense of emphasis.

4:2b–c in heaven was a throne The verb ἔκειτο 'was set' is descriptive of place rather than action and does not indicate that John saw the throne being put there.

a throne, and on the throne One was sitting (*or*, sitting *as a ruler*) The word 'throne' is used to represent the sovereign power of kings (2 Sam. 3:10, 14:9) and of God (Ps. 89:14, Heb. 1:8, 4:16). Throughout Revelation 'throne' is highly significant, especially in its reference to God, since it symbolizes his absolute sovereignty. Thus not only is God often described or identified as 'the One sitting upon the throne' but very often 'the throne' may be seen as being used by metonymy for God himself, as in this unit (4:4-6, 10), .

Some languages may not have a word that specifically means a throne, but the important thing is to communicate the idea of sovereignty and ruling. With this in mind an alternate propositionalization for 4:2c is 'and on the great seat One was sitting *as a ruler*'.

4:3a The appearance of the One who was sitting *on the throne* Since 'appearance' is an abstract noun, a verb with agent may have to be used in some languages, for example, 'the One sitting on the throne looked like a diamond shining very brightly'.

shone like a *brilliant* diamond and like a *brilliant red* carnelian jewel What John saw was the brilliance and colour akin to that of precious stones. The names used for gems in the Biblical texts are not all comparable to modern designations. Here *diamond* translates ἴασπις 'jasper', but jasper found in the orient at the present time is usually an opaque stone used for pavement. This seems not to fit with the other stones mentioned here, and many commentators find the description of ἴασπις 'jasper' in 21:11 more in harmony with the present context. There it is said to be as clear as crystal and probably means a diamond (Lenski, Walvoord). Because of the many manifestations of God in terms of light, the brilliance of the diamond seems preferable to the opaque quality of modern jasper. It should be noted that when these precious stones are referred to in Revelation it is their appearance that is focal, not the identity of the jewel itself. 'Brilliant' is used in the display to reinforce the idea of the glorious splendour of the appearance of God.

The carnelian is a very precious red stone.

4:3b a rainbow ... around the throne There is some difference of opinion on the description of the rainbow. Some picture it as a complete circle, while others understand it to be a half circle. But the verb κυκλόθεν 'around' seems to make the circle specific. The Greek term ἶρις means primarily 'rainbow' but secondarily any circle of radiance or bright light. Some prefer 'rainbow' here because of its covenant significance (Gen. 9:13), but this does not fit well with its being described as 'like an emerald.'

like a *brilliant* emerald jewel The most common understanding of the colour of the emerald is green.

4:4b elders There is much conjecture about the identity of the elders. There is no evidence that they are human elders, and in the Greek text they are not called angels but are classified with them as a separate group in 7:11. As celestial beings they may in some way represent God's human servants of the old and the new covenants.

4:4c *pure* white garments It is most likely that the white garments symbolize purity and holiness (cf. 3:18). In the display, 'pure' is used to modify 'garments' as a word that may communicate both material and moral purity.

4:5a lightning and rumblings and thundering These manifestations have to do with the presence of God (Exod. 19:16–19; Ps. 77:18), "symbolizing the divine power and glory" (Ladd).

rumblings Some have translated φωναί as 'voices', but many consider that it refers to the sounds of the storm as in the Exodus passage. In Rev. 11:19 lightning, φωναί, and thunder are also mentioned, but there they are listed with an earthquake and hail, which tends to indicate that here also in 4:5a it refers to the rumblings of thunder rather than the voice of God.

4:5b Seven torches The fiery torches are a reminder of the smoking fire of the Sinai experience and of God's presence (Exod. 19:18).

These symbolize God's *Holy Spirit who knows all things and so he is like* seven spirits See the notes on 1:4d.

4:6a there was what looked like a sea *made of* glass which was *as clear* as crystal The Greek text translated literally is 'as a glassy sea like/similar to crystal'. NIV and TEV translate "clear as crystal", which indicates the point of similarity since ancient glass tended to be semi-opaque (Swete).

4:6b Nearest to the throne The Greek is ἐν μέσῳ τοῦ θρόνου 'in middle of the throne'. The exact position is not clear. It cannot mean the centre of the throne because that is clearly the position of the One who sits upon it. Probably ἐν μέσῳ 'in (the) middle' describes the living creatures as inside the circle of elders. This would harmonize with 7:9–11 which seems to picture concentric circles, with the believers surrounding the angels, who encircle the elders, and the four creatures in the centre nearest to the throne.

were four living *creatures* The words τέσσαρα ζῷα 'four living (ones)' form a substantive phrase (the form is neuter plural) in which the Greek does not explicitly indicate the type of being. Because of their activity in this unit we know them to be creatures. The emphasis is on their living. Hughes says that they "represent the whole order of animate creation", an interpretation that is taken by various commentators.

had many eyes Figuratively the eye is used to indicate watchfulness, intelligence, and discernment. The eyes are highlighted by repetition in 4:8a.

The verb γέμοντα 'being full of' is commonly used by hyperbole for 'having a lot of' something. Obviously the creatures were not completely covered with eyes or it would not have been possible for John to distinguish them from one another, as he does in 4:7.

4:7 The first living *creature* was like a lion. The second living *creature* was like an ox. The third living *creature* had a face like a human face. The fourth living *creature* was like an eagle *that is* flying. The symbolism for the living creatures at least seems to indicate high points in God's creation. They suggest power, strength, intelligence, and swiftness as he carries out his plan through creation. It is hard to picture an eagle flying yet positioned with the other living creatures around the throne. But we realize that in visions the meaning intended to be conveyed by the symbols is more important than conformity to real life structure.

4:8a and they had many eyes all around *their bodies* and underneath *their wings* The Greek is κυκλόθεν καὶ ἔσωθεν γέμουσιν ὀφθαλμῶν 'around and within are full of eyes'. The question may be asked as to where on the living creatures the eyes mentioned here are located. There are some (Alford, Düsterdieck, NLT) who think the eyes mentioned here are on the wings, a possibility since the wings are the most immediate prior reference to a part of the body. In any case, the statement about the eyes in 4:6b indicates a more general position of the eyes on the body, so that 'within' here could easily make reference to a position underneath the wings whether there is a direct reference back to wings or not. But the main point of the positions mentioned both in 4:6b and 4:8a is not to help an artist transfer it to a drawing board, but to symbolize universal watchfulness.

4:8b day and night they never cease to say/sing Although the primary meaning of λέγω, the orienter for the praise, is 'say', some versions translate it as 'sing' (JB, NEB, RSV, TEV). While λέγοντες 'saying' is also used to introduce the elders' declaration of praise in 4:10, the declaration of praise to the Lamb in 5:9 is introduced with καὶ ᾄδουσιν ᾠδὴν καινὴν λέγοντες 'and they sang a new song, saying'. The fact that the participle λέγοντες has the function of introducing that quote, with a minimal reference to the form of the speaking (cf. 5:9), may indicate that it is not necessary to understand a specific reference to normal speech here. So there seems to be no substantial reason for not using 'sing'.

4:8c Holy, holy, holy is the Lord God Here the word for 'holy' is ἅγιος. The Holy God is separate from everything creaturely, let alone unclean and sinful. The repetition uses the heavenly number three. He is called 'the Holy One' (Isa. 40:25), expressing his very nature by his name.

the almighty One See the note on 1:8d.

the One who has always existed, who exists, and who will in the future come *to the world* See the notes on 1:4c.

4:10a-b prostrate themselves . . . and worship The Greek for 'prostrate' is πεσοῦνται 'will fall'. This is a dead metaphor; the movement is not unintentional as in the primary meaning of 'fall'. The meaning is that they prostrate themselves to the ground in order to properly worship God. In 4:10b προσκυνήσουσιν also carries the idea of prostrating oneself, but may be translated 'worship'.

4:10c They lay their victor's wreaths in front of the throne The Greek verb is βάλλω 'throw', a forceful word in its primary meaning. But that is not what is intended here. To avoid the idea of violent action, the display uses 'lay' in English, listed by BDAG as a secondary meaning.

4:10d and at the same time they were saying/singing The present tense Greek participle λέγοντες 'saying', indicates that the following words (4:11) were uttered simultaneously with the actions of worship that the elders were performing (4:10a-c).

4:11a Our(exc) Lord and God, you are worthy *that all beings* glorify/praise you, *that all beings* honour you, and *that all beings* acknowledge that you are the powerful *One* The Greek is ἄξιος εἶ, ὁ κύριος καὶ ὁ θεὸς ἡμῶν, λαβεῖν τὴν δόξαν καὶ τὴν τιμὴν καὶ τὴν δύναμιν 'worthy are you, our Lord and God, to receive glory, and honour, and power'. It is obvious that 'to receive honour' may be propositionalized as 'honour you'. But there is no way in which God will receive any kind of 'power' from anyone or anything. The elders are ascribing to God great power and acknowledging that power (Barnes, Beasley-Murray, Swete). It is more difficult to know the exact meaning of 'to receive glory' in this context. It may be fairly synonymous with 'to receive honour', and in that sense could be translated 'praise'. On the other hand, it could be seen to function as 'power' does here (a description of God's nature) and be propositionalized as 'acknowledge that you are glorious'. Either way 'to give glory to God' means to recognize the full import of his deity revealed in all scripture.

4:11b because you *alone* created all The word σύ is the free form of the pronoun 'you', and whenever it is put before the verb, emphasis of some type is being shown. Here it emphasizes the uniqueness of God as creator and so is rendered as 'you alone' in the display.

4:11c because you purposed This translates διὰ τὸ θέλημά σου 'by your will,' which is put in the emphatic position at the beginning of the sentence, showing that here the reason is more in focus than the result.

they were created *by you* and *as a result* they exist The Greek order is 'they were/existed and they were created'. Several English versions have reversed the order within 4:11d since chronologically creation comes before existence. NIV has "by your will they were created and have their being." Logically there is a cause-effect relation between 'they were created' and 'they exist'. Düsterdieck says: "After the divine work of creation is mentioned (ἔκτισας), the idea recurs to the same point with vivid clearness: as all things *were*, which before were not. The καὶ ἐκτίσθησαν is, then, not synonymous with the ἦσαν, but presents expressly the precise fact upon which the ἦσαν depends: 'they were created.'"

While ἦσαν is imperfect, it is more natural in English to translate as 'they exist' rather than to imply only a past time orientation with 'they were existing' or 'they existed'.

BOUNDARIES AND COHERENCE

The unit begins with a time word εὐθέως 'immediately', introducing the orienter for the vision which comprises the bulk of the unit. It is the throne which dominates the scene. A doxology closes the unit as the elders lay down their crowns before the throne and worship the One sitting upon it. Another indication of the final boundary is that after the occurrence of Καὶ εἶδον 'And I saw' (a common marker of a new unit in Revelation) in 5:1 a stimulus-response chain begins.

Numerous coherence factors may be pointed out in the unit, such as:
1. The throne is referred to in almost every constituent of the unit, and every person or thing is described in relation to the throne.
2. The activity of worship is described as directed to the central figure on the throne.
3. The action in the DECLARATION is carried out by the two animate groups mentioned in the DESCRIPTION, the elders and the 'living creatures.'
4. No change of time or location is given.

PROMINENCE AND THEME

In a *description-declaration* paragraph both components are necessary for the theme, even more so in this paragraph where the *description*, especially of the One on the throne, is highly prominent.

ACT CONSTITUENT 5:1–8:5 (Scene: Step₁ of 4:1–16:21)

THEME: When the Lamb took the scroll from the One who sits on the throne, the whole created universe worshiped him as the worthy Redeemer. The opening of the first six seals brought judgment to rebellious earth people. Before the Lamb opened the seventh seal God's own servants were marked and those who had come safely through persecution praised God. When the Lamb opened the seventh seal, there was a silence and then cosmic manifestations of judgment occurred.

MACROSTRUCTURE	CONTENTS
initiating incident	5:1–14 When the victorious Lamb took the scroll from the right hand of the One who sits on the throne, the whole created universe worshiped him as the worthy Redeemer.
step₁	6:1–8 When the Lamb opened each of the first four seals of the scroll, each of the four living creatures called forth a horseman who brought judgment to earth people.
step₂	6:9–11 When the Lamb opened the fifth seal, the souls of God's servants who had been killed because of their faith appealed to him to judge the earth people. They were honoured by God and told by him to rest until they were joined by all the others who would be killed for their faith.
step₃	6:12–17 When the Lamb opened the sixth seal of the scroll, the natural world began to fall apart causing the rebellious earth people to hide because the time had come for God to judge them.
interlude	7:1–17 An angel commanded four other angels to continue restraining the destructive winds. Then some angels marked one hundred and forty-four thousand people to show that they were God's servants. A triumphant crowd of those who had come safely through persecution acknowledged that their deliverance had come from God and the Lamb, and so the angels, the elders, and the living creatures worshiped God in praise.
GOAL	8:1–5 When the Lamb opened the seventh seal there was silence in heaven. Seven angels each received a trumpet, and another angel offered up to God the prayers of all the saints. Then this angel threw fire onto the earth and cosmic manifestations of judgment occurred.

INTENT AND MACROSTRUCTURE

In the previous unit (4:1–11) God has been presented as the Creator and Ruler of the universe and appropriately praised. As the present unit opens he holds in his hand a scroll which is sealed. The context indicates that the contents of the scroll represent the fulfilment of his purpose for the created universe. To reveal the contents of the scroll the seals must be broken, and the Lamb is found worthy for this. As each seal is broken there is a cry for the purpose to move forward. Even the sixth seal contributes toward that end because the rebels acknowledge God will punish them. The *interlude* (7:1–17) shows how God protects and encourages his servants in times of suffering and judgment. Schooling says, "...interludes are usually located in the heavenly realm and project a sense of certain hope for God's people" (p. 112).

Since the events in the episodes clearly manifest step by step progress toward a goal, the relationship within the scene is *step-GOAL*. But it is important to note that the opening of the seals brings about not a knowledge of the contents of the scroll but rather the actual events of judgment. Also, whereas in real life we would expect that all seven seals of the scroll would have to be opened before there was any action or revelation of its contents, here the action begins with the opening of the first seal. In fact the opening of the scroll is never mentioned anywhere in the narrative of the book, even when the last seal is broken open. Nor is there any definite explanation of its contents.

This may be why it is difficult to determine what the GOAL really is and how much the seventh seal encompasses. Some commentators understand it as only encompassing 8:1, the half-hour silence in heaven. Others understand it as encompassing 8:1–5. It may be best to understand the action of the angel in 8:5 of casting fire from the altar upon the earth as the judgment set into motion by the seventh seal. It is also possible to see this action as representing the judgment to be accomplished by the blowing of the seven trumpets. This might explain why the seven trumpets are first introduced in 8:2. If the silence of 8:1 is connected with the hearing of the prayers of the saints (Charles, Beasley-Murray), then the introduction of the trumpets in 8:2 is a preview of the judgment that follows with the actual blowing of the trumpets, and is meant to show that God does answer the prayers of the saints, as 8:3–5 goes on to show more explicitly.

Some commentators see the seventh seal as in some sense encompassing all of the judgments brought about by the trumpets, a sort of telescoping effect in which the trumpets fit into the seventh seal. It seems better, however, for reasons of prominence and hierarchical structure, to keep only 8:1–5 as the GOAL of the *steps* of the scene.

However, if the content of the scroll is understood as God's final acts of judgment, then the breaking of the seals is preparatory, just as the judgments it reveals seem to be. Two other series of seven judgments follow, and they represent God's wrath to the full, closing with γέγονεν 'finished' (16:17). In the first two of these three series the seventh judgment seems to introduce the next series (8:2; 10:7, cf. 15:1).

BOUNDARIES AND COHERENCE

The scene begins with the introduction of the scroll in God's hand and of the Lamb who accepts it in order to open its seals. It closes when he has broken the last of the seals. It is true that the seven trumpets are first introduced in 8:2, but, as mentioned in Intent and Macrostructure for this unit, it seems best to take this as a preview rather than as the actual beginning of the scene in which the seven trumpets are the basic distinguishing factor.

The end of the unit is signalled by a cosmic manifestation like that at certain other places in the vision, as 11:19, 16:18–21, where it also marks the end of a scene.

There are numerous evidences of coherence, for instance:

1. The continuity of the opening of seven seals.
2. The Lamb is active in this scene and referred to by pronoun at the opening of each seal. After this he is not called 'the Lamb' until his wedding is announced in 19:7.
3. The judgments in this scene are not administered by angels until the very last action in which an angel throws the fire from the altar onto the earth (8:5). With the opening of the next scene they immediately sound their trumpets to announce judgment.
4. Throughout the scene there is an anticipation of judgment. On the opening of each seal except the sixth some voice is raised calling for judgment (the living creatures in 6:1, 3, 5, 7 and the martyrs in 6:10), and it is assumed that the prayers of the saints in 8:3–4 are also calling for God's judgment, because of the action of the angel with the censer.

PROMINENCE AND THEME

The most naturally prominent episode of the scene is 8:1–5, the scene in which the last seal is broken, but in a step-goal construction the steps themselves are prominent enough to be represented in the theme. Here they are represented generically with the statement "The first six seals brought judgment to rebellious earth people". It is also true that the prominence of the GOAL depends on the fulfilling of the purpose called for in the *initiating incident*, where it seemed thwarted since John wept for fear no one would be able to open the seals (5:4). Marked prominence is shown in the *initiating incident* (5:1–14) by the fact that it introduces the main participant of the scene, the Lamb, using a *problem-RESOLUTION* structure. The theme, therefore, also includes the *initiating incident*.

SCENE CONSTITUENT 5:1–14 (Episode: initiating incident for 5:1–8:5)

THEME: When the victorious Lamb took the scroll from the right hand of the One who sits on the throne, the whole created universe worshiped him as the worthy Redeemer.

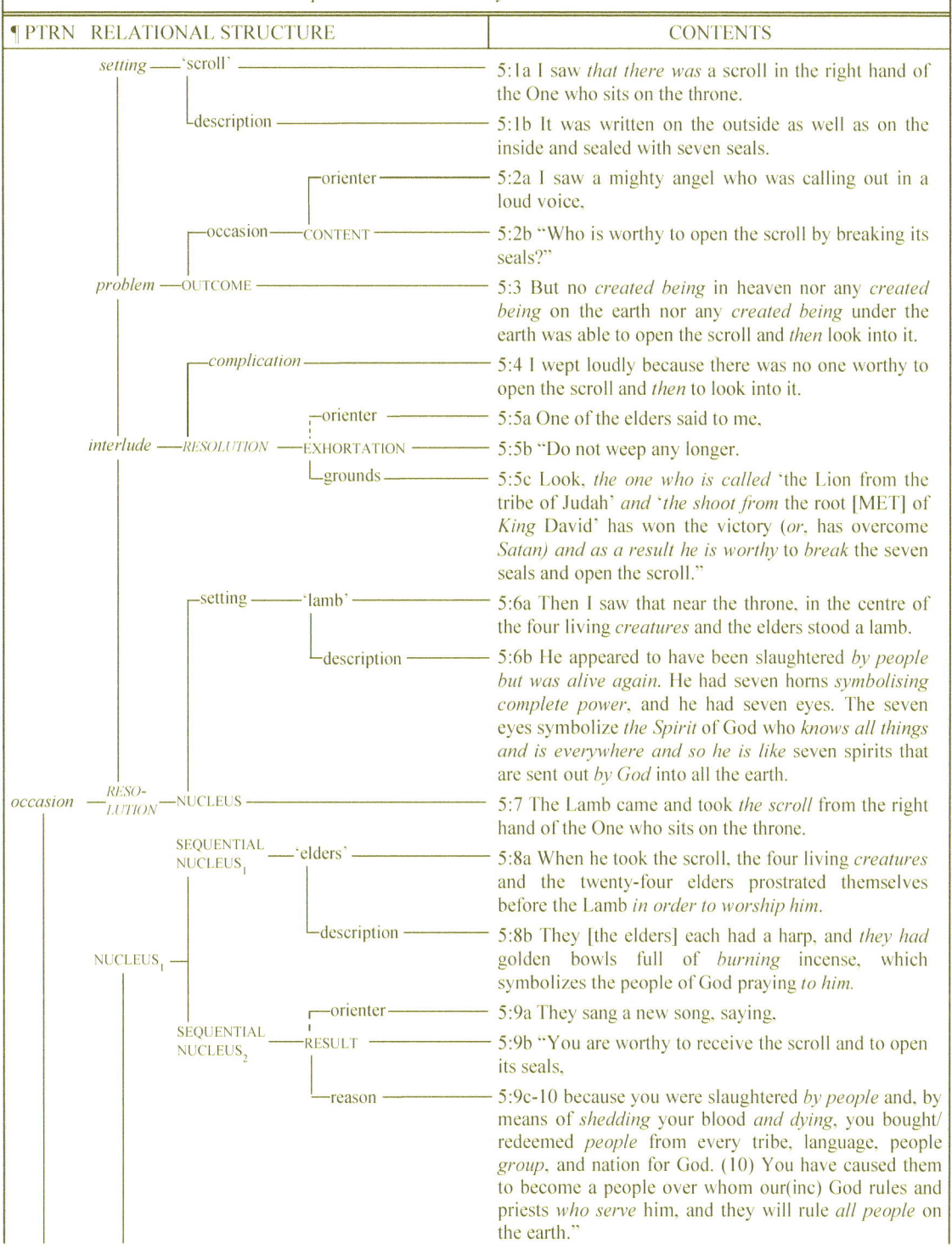

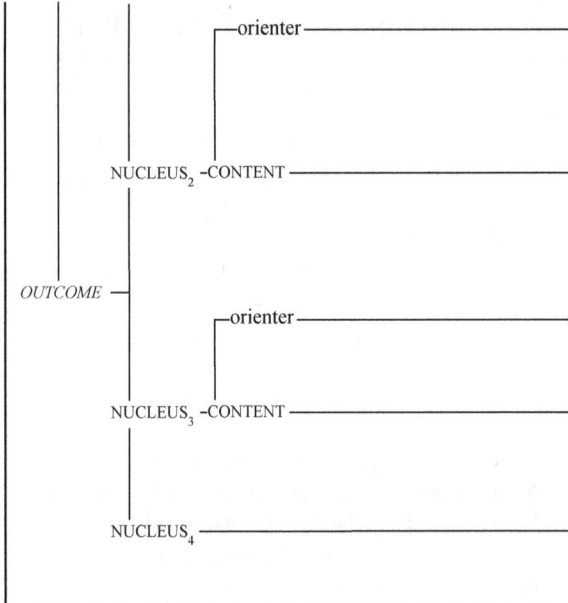

INTENT AND PARAGRAPH PATTERN

Chapter 5 contains a dramatic *problem-RESOLUTION* sub-unit reaching a peak in the Lamb being the only one found worthy to open the seals of the scroll. However, the fact that the main verb of the *RESOLUTION*, 'took' in 5:7, is backgrounded (see note on 5:7) indicates that it is not the climax of the unit but a focal point which highlights the praise and worship of the Lamb as the worthy and mighty Redeemer by the whole created universe (5:8–14). It also leads to the opening of the first seal in 6:1 and the whole judgment plot of the discourse. The repetition, or 'tail-head' linkage, in 5:7–8, "took.... When he took ...", confirms that this constitutes the major boundary within the unit.

While this paragraph is narrative, its paragraph pattern on the highest level can also be seen as expressive. The songs of the inhabitants of heaven and of the whole created universe are certainly highly expressive in form. At the same time the truths presented in the songs are so foundational to the message of Revelation that the intent could be seen as expository or even hortatory. It therefore seems best to diagram the unit with narrative paragraph patterns but to keep in mind this joining of the three intents.

NOTES

5:1a in the right hand of the One who sits on the throne While the proper sense of the preposition ἐπί with the accusative is 'on, upon' it is difficult to see how ἐπί plus accusative in 20:1 can mean 'a great chain on his hand' rather than 'a great chain in his hand'. All English versions translate with 'in' in both places.

5:1b It was written on the outside as well as on the inside and sealed with seven seals The UBSGNT text has ἔσωθεν καὶ ὄπισθεν 'inside and backside'. In the display 'outside' is used instead of 'backside' since it is somewhat more fitting in English to describe the opposite of the inside of a scroll as its outside rather than the back of a scroll. Thus the display is not based on the variant reading ἔξωθεν 'outside'. A scroll would be expected to have writing inside, but if the inside could not contain all the discourse, writing would continue on the other side. That would be the backside as the scroll was held for reading.

Because the writing on the outside of the scroll is the more unusual factor, 'as well as' is used in the display along with the appropriate switching of order of 'inside' and 'outside' that this construction necessitates.

sealed with seven seals There are different opinions about how the seals were affixed. One is that the scroll had seven sections and that each section had a seal, so that the sections could be opened successively as they are in 6:1–8:5. The other option is to interpret according to the usual custom of the era to seal the outside of the document only. John's use of seven seals instead of one fits the intended structure of the following discourse and is appropriate to the meaning of completeness that the number seven signifies. Because of the thoroughly figurative style of the book it is not necessary to reason out how the scroll could still have several seals on it, for instance, and yet most of its contents have already transpired.

5:2a a mighty angel Rather than the common gloss of 'strong' for ἰσχυρός the meaning here is more likely to be 'powerful,' 'mighty', 'having great authority', not a reference to the angel's physical strength (Walvoord, Aune).

5:2b "Who is worthy to open the scroll by breaking its seals?" The worthiness of the Lamb is strongly emphasized by repetition, by being the qualification for the task to be performed (5:2b), and by being in the direct quotations of the doxologies (5:9b; 12b). The Lamb's fitness for the task in this passage is not based just on his essential being, by which he has ἐξουσία 'authority,' the quality he has because he is the Son of God (Matt. 28:18). Rather, it is particularly based on his acts, that is, on what he has done (5:9c–10), both in his victory (5:5c) and in the sacrifice which made it possible (5:6b). The focus here is on his worthiness and δύναμις 'capability', which have been proved.

The content of the scroll is the prophecy of what must happen soon, the divine will, which is closely sealed. The seals must be broken to initiate the action (6:1–8:5). They constitute the *problem* which must be overcome in order to reveal the judgment of God and his ultimate triumph.

5:3 was able That ἐδύνατο 'was able' is used in the sense of worthiness is clear from the emphasis on ἄξιος 'worthy' in 5:2–4, 9b, 12b. Beside the significance of having strength, the word means to have suitability or to qualify for doing something. Followed by the aorist infinitive ἀνοῖξαι 'to open,' it is used with little stress on the idea of power and strength.

no *created being* in heaven nor any *created being* on the earth nor any *created being* under the earth This triple expansion of the simple οὐδείς 'no one' is a rhetorical device for slowing down the narrative and emphasising its climax in 5:6–7.

5:4 I wept loudly This interlude further slows down the narrative and gives emphasis to 5:6–7 by introducing an offline interaction consisting of another problem (i.e. *complication*), namely the writer's emotional breakdown, which requires its own RESOLUTION in 5:5.

loudly The primary meaning of πολύ is 'much', but BDAG glosses this occurrence as 'loudly'. CEV and NCV translate as "I cried hard" and NIV as "I wept and wept".

there was no one The use of εὑρέθη 'was found' in 'found worthy' here is like that in 2:2, 3:2, and in Phil. 2:7. The verb serves almost as an auxiliary. It is not so much the problem of finding a person as of the fitness of whoever might respond.

worthy to open the scroll and *then* to look into it Since much of the wording here is a repetition from 5:2–3 it is clearly another rhetorical device for emphasising the climax.

5:5a said to me In the Greek this is a historical present tense, a further device for pointing forward and highlighting 5:6.

5:5b "Do not weep any longer . . ." The Greek is μὴ κλαῖε, a negative plus the verb for 'weep'. But since the verb is in the present tense and John is already weeping the phrase signals a prohibition to continue what is in progress.

5:5c Look The particle ἰδού 'behold, lo' occurs immediately before ἐνίκησεν ὁ λέων 'the lion has conquered', emphasizing the victory of the Lion of the tribe of Judah. It indicates the grounds for the resolution of John's problem. Many English versions, and also the display, translate ἰδού here as "look", where 'look' has both the meaning 'to look' and functions as communicating emphasis. Other languages may have other ways to communicate the emphasis in this context.

the one who is called **'The Lion from the tribe of Judah'** Since there is no further reference to a lion it is clear that "the lion from the tribe of Judah" is a title applied to Christ (Bratcher and Hatton). Gen. 49:9 is the background for the title.

'the shoot from **the root of** *King* **David'** The Greek is ἡ ῥίζα Δαυίδ 'the root of David.' Bratcher and Hatton point out that this is another Messianic title being applied to Christ. The background of the title is in Isa. 11. In Isa.11:1 "the shoot from Jesse's stump" is descriptive of the Messiah, "There shall come forth a shoot from the stump [ῥίζης in the Septuagint] of Jesse, and a branch shall grow out of his roots [ῥίζης (singular) in the Septuagint]" (RSV). In this context 'shoot', 'branch' and 'roots' are all live metaphors and the picture is of Jesse, David's father, as the root from which the shoot (the Messiah) springs. But in Isa.11:10, "the root of Jesse will stand as signal to the peoples", ῥίζα 'root' stands for the shoot itself (the Messiah who is the hope of the Gentiles). In Rev. 5:5c the same figure of speech is used, but with the name of David replacing that of his father. This emphasizes the Messiah's relationship to David as Israel's most glorious king. In this verse BDAG glosses ῥίζα as

"*shoot ... growing from the root*". In Rev.22:16 'the root of David' is again used as a title of Christ, but now with an added description 'his descendant.'

has won the victory (*or*, has overcome Satan) See the note on 2:7b.

5:6a near the throne, in the centre of the four living *creatures* The Greek for the first part of this is, ἐν μέσῳ τοῦ θρόνου, literally, 'in the middle of the throne'. In 4:6 this phrase locates the four living creatures as nearer to the throne than the twenty-four elders. Here it locates the Lamb as nearer to the throne than the four living creatures.

stood a lamb The writer throws even greater highlighting on the Lamb by putting a long and complex locative phrase between the verb 'I saw' and what he saw.

5:6b slaughtered *by people but was alive again* 'People' is supplied to satisfy the case frame. Also, since 'slaughtered' in its normal meaning indicates a state that is irreversible, 'but was alive again' is added in the display to show that it is not so in this case.

He had seven horns *symbolizing complete power* 'Horn' indicates power, and 'seven horns' indicates 'complete power'.

The seven eyes symbolize *the Spirit* of God who *knows all things and is everywhere and so he is like* seven spirits that are sent out *by God* into all the earth The Lamb has the seven(fold) Spirit of God (1:4, 3:1). See the note on 1:4d. His having the Holy Spirit is referred to in such passages as Luke 4:18 and John 3:34. In the present passage the comprehensive ministry of Christ through the Spirit is shown by the number seven and by the sending out 'into all the earth'.

seven spirits The word ἑπτά 'seven' before πνεύματα 'spirits' is bracketed in the UBS text because evidence both for and against its authenticity is about equal. The meaning of the text would not be altered by including it or by omitting it.

5:7 The Lamb came and took *the scroll* The verb describing the action of the Lamb with regard to the scroll here and in 5:8a is λαμβάνω 'take' or 'receive'. The great majority of English versions use "take" (CEV, KJV, NASB, NCV, NIV, NLT), though REB uses "receive". There are other languages beside Greek which would have an overlapping of meaning for the verb. In this unit 'receive' might bring into focus the initiative of God in offering the scroll and the worthiness of the Lamb to receive the scroll. To translate 'took' could bring to mind the free acceptance of Christ in taking the responsibility involved in his incarnation. Both concepts are emphasized in scripture.

In the Greek the verb 'took' is in the historical present perfect tense, which is used when the writer wants to background one event in order to highlight the next one. In this case John is highlighting the event for which he is building up expectation throughout this chapter, namely the opening of the seals in 6:1ff. It is probably also highlighting the praise and worship of 5:8-14, although that scene may also be regarded as another interlude that builds up to the climax of 6:1. It is part of the plot that deals with the righteous rather than the condemned, and here specifically with their praise of the Lamb and the One sitting on the throne.

5:8a prostrated themselves...*in order to worship him* This supplies the function of the bodily action of prostrating themselves. See the note on 4:10a–b.

5:8b They [the elders] each had a harp The text does not specifically say that the living creatures did *not* have harps and golden bowls. A point in favour of understanding that they did have them is the inclusiveness of the worship described in the immediate context. Moreover, the grammatical point that ἔχοντες 'having' agrees more properly with πρεσβύτεροι 'elders' than with the neuter ζῶα 'living ones' carries little weight, since the author could certainly use masculine if he meant to include both groups. However, against including the living creatures is the view which is chosen by a majority of commentators (Alford, Beale, Düsterdieck, Lenski, Mounce, Swete). Mounce says, "Since the function of the living creatures is not priestly, it may be best to take the harps and bowls as applying only to the elders". It would seem more appropriate for the elders to present the prayers of the saints because of their relationship to God's servants. (See note on 4:4b.) But we recognize that the text is ambiguous on the point and could be interpreted either way.

harps It is difficult to know the exact form of the κιθάρα 'harp, lyre' envisioned here. Certainly it was smaller and had fewer strings than the modern harp, perhaps 10 or 12 strings. It was held on the arm or in the lap and played either with the fingers or a plectrum (pick).

and *they had* golden bowls full of *burning* incense, which symbolizes the people of God praying *to him* The noun θυμιάματα can refer either to 'incense' or to 'the burning of incense.'

Here, since it is symbolic of prayers ascending to God, it is appropriate to specify 'burning'.

The verbal noun προσευχαί 'prayers' represents the event of praying and is rendered as a verb in the display.

The noun ἅγιοι 'saints, holy ones' is translated as 'the people of God' since it is clearly used in Revelation as a designation of the faithful believers, not as a description of their holiness.

5:9a They sang a new song, saying The singers are specified only by the third person plural suffixes on the main verb and participle but they are probably the elders, since there is no indication of a change of subject from 5:8b.

The new song is in celebration of a new situation which will continue through eternity. The significance of καινός, the word chosen here for 'new', is new in kind and quality. It occurs frequently in Revelation as descriptive of the new name or character of the redeemed (2:17), the new Jerusalem (3:12), and the new heaven and earth (21:1).

In this clause the tense is present, which could be interpreted to mean the historical present or the continuative. The latter may be quite appropriate because the doxologies of 4:8 and 11 are stipulated as continuous, and the doxology in 5:13 could be understood as continuing forever and ever. On the other hand, the paragraph has a chronological timeline in which a strict continuative would be inappropriate. The use of the historical present would be to show that the words of the song are going to be fulfilled in the next main event (6:1).

5:9c–10 This unit beginning with ὅτι 'because' could be interpreted as the grounds, reason, or situation for 5:9b. Since the truths here are an established fact, not something to be proven, conclusion-grounds is ruled out. Thus it would be a result-reason relationship, but in the context of a song it potentially is also expressive and might be labelled as REACTION-*situation*. However, the words of 9b are more expository in import than expressive, so it is best to label it as result-reason. The truth expressed in 9b–c is extremely fundamental to the kingdom of God and the theme of the whole book.

5:9c by means of *shedding* your blood *and dying* Means relationships are presented in full propositional form in the display text and therefore two verbs expressing the implicit actions are supplied here. (Note that 'shedding your blood' by itself does not necessarily indicate death.)

you bought/redeemed There is no doubt that ἠγόρασας 'bought' in this context can mean 'redeemed, ransomed' (Beasley-Murray, Ladd, Lenski, Morris, Swete).

people The pronoun ἡμᾶς 'us' is found in some manuscripts and considered by most commentators to have been added in order to give the verb ἠγόρασας 'bought' a direct object, even though there is an implied object in the phrase 'from every tribe . . .'. A major problem with ἡμᾶς 'us' is that it would be the only reference in Revelation that classifies the elders as human. "People" seems a better object.

from every tribe, language, people *group*, and nation The final position of this phrase in the Greek sentence, and the lack of definite articles before the nouns, show that it is the most focal element of the proposition.

The purpose of the piling up of synonyms is to indicate the universality of the redeemed people. Therefore a translator does not necessarily need to seek the same distinctions for each word as in Greek.

5:10 a people over whom our(inc) God rules and priests *who serve* him The Greek has βασιλείαν καὶ ἱερεῖς 'a kingdom and priests' here. Like 1:6 this declaration has a background in Exod. 19:6. Israel was to be a people ruled by God and wholly consecrated to his service. See note on 1:6a.

our(inc) God Scripture speaks of God as the God and Father of Christ (Eph. 1:3). Though there is a difference in the way in which he is the God of Christ and of created beings, there is a common basic relationship. Since there is a common basic relationship to the same God and since Christ rather than God the Father is being addressed, an inclusive pronoun would normally be appropriate. However, in some languages there may be other features of the language which will necessitate the use of a form other than the inclusive in this situation.

they will rule *all people* on the earth The tense of the verb is in question because some manuscripts have the present and some have the future. Both UBSGNT and Hodges and Farstad have the future tense here. The immediate context, which seems to refer to their destiny, makes the future form more acceptable.

The object of the verb is given as 'all people' to supply the case frame, but throughout Revelation there is no focus at all on those who God's people will rule over. So an alternative translation would be 'they will be kings on the earth'.

5:11 As I *continued to* look This verse begins with καὶ εἶδον 'and I saw', a common device in Revelation, that moves the timeline along or introduces a new unit. Here what is in focus is the hearing rather than the seeing, since no explicit object is given for the seeing. Some versions translate καὶ εἶδον as "Then I looked" or "I looked again". CEV translates as "As I looked, I heard . . ." which indicates better the reality of what John was doing.

the voice of many angels It could possibly be understood that this voice included those of the living creatures and the elders. But, since their song has already been recorded in 5:9–10 and the angels are said to be around them as though distinct from them, the angels alone are considered responsible for the following doxology.

There were millions and millions of them The Greek is literally 'The number of them was tens of thousands of tens of thousands, and thousands of thousands.' This is obviously not a precise numbering but indicates an uncountable crowd.

5:12b "The Lamb . . . is worthy *that all created beings* acknowledge that he is *infinitely* powerful, *infinitely* rich, *infinitely* wise, and *infinitely* strong; and he is worthy *that all created beings* honour him, glorify him, and praise him." This ascription of the worthiness of the Lamb consists of a series of seven abstract nouns. Some of these nouns are attributes of Christ (power, riches, wisdom, strength) and transform as adjectives, while others indicate the action of honouring and praising Christ and transform as verbs. 'Glory' could be taken either way.

infinitely Even though there are no explicit lexical or grammatical signals as to the intensity of each of the attributes mentioned, without question the context implies that they are to the extent of infinity. The one article with the seven nouns in the light of the concept of seven as a number of completeness may be focusing on the completeness or totality of the attributes and worthiness of praise and honour; that is, that Christ has *all* the completeness of Deity.

One of the results of expressing the abstract nouns of the text in straightforward and unskewed propositions is that the significant numerical listing of the attributes may not be quite so obvious as in the Greek. Since the use of symbolic numbers in Revelation seems intentional, it would be an advantage to retain the form in translation wherever possible. However it would not outweigh the importance of clear presentation of the meaning.

5:13a I heard all the creatures The question arises as to what is included in πᾶν κτίσμα 'every created thing, every creature'. Some commentators specifically mention that 'every creature' includes the animals (Alford, Bratcher and Hatton, Düsterdieck). Some commentators may think that non-animate creation is also intended, but it is difficult to clearly tell that this is what they mean (e.g. Swete).

5:13b "*Let us(inc)* forever praise and honour and glorify the One who sits on the throne and the Lamb, and *acknowledge that they* reign all powerfully forever and ever." A doxology is not necessarily addressed to God in the second person, but may be expressed of him in the third person.

There is a question as to whether 'for ever and ever' modifies the action of praising or modifies the attributes, especially the power of God and the Lamb, to which it most closely connects. It is probably best to understand it as modifying each of the nouns of the doxology.

5:14 The four living *creatures* said, "So let it be" The "amen" of 5:14a expresses agreement with all that the doxologies have celebrated.

BOUNDARIES AND COHERENCE

The unit continues in the same situational setting as 4:1–11 because no change is indicated. However, we construe it to be a new unit, the first episode of the scene (5:1–8:5), because of new elements being introduced. Also it has *problem-RESOLUTION* and *occasion-outcome* paragraph patterns rather than a descriptive one as 4:1–11 has. Now narration begins to move with a sequence of events. This helps to define the initial boundary of the episode. Chapter 5 functions as the *initiating incident* for the 5:1–8:5 scene, starting the action (i.e. beginning the event-line) of the scene. The unit focuses on the Lamb as worthy to take the scroll. His taking it occasions his worship by all creation. The episode closes as the living creatures and the elders express their agreement with the universal worship.

The episode of 5:1–14 is in some ways coordinate with that of 4:1–11. First comes adoration of the One on the throne, then that of the Lamb, both of whom are praised in the closing doxology (5:13b). But the strongly cohesive factor of the scroll and its seals dominates the scene from 5:1–8:5. Also, 4:1–11, which presents the perfect and complete worship of the One on the throne, has an important introductory aspect which governs the rest of the body of the discourse. For this reason 4:1–11 is recognized as a separate unit with significance on a higher level. The new elements presented in 5:1–14 indicate a separate scene. The higher level structure is discussed elsewhere.

Coherence within the unit is shown by the repeated references to the scroll (five times in 5:1–5) and to the Lamb (ten times in 5:5–14). The 'tail-head' linkage at the major boundary (5:7–8) also gives coherence to the unit.

PROMINENCE AND THEME

The worship of the Lamb by all creation is naturally prominent as the OUTCOME of his action in taking the scroll from the One on the throne. His worthiness to do this is highlighted in the doxologies which his act occasioned. The theme is based on this OUTCOME, that is, worship of the Lamb. It expresses the occasion of the worship (the RESOLUTION of the *problem*), emphasizing the worthiness of the Lamb.

SCENE CONSTITUENT 6:1–8 (Episode: Step₁ of 5:1–8:5)

THEME: *When the Lamb opened each of the first four seals of the scroll, each of the four living creatures called forth a horseman who brought judgment to earth people.*

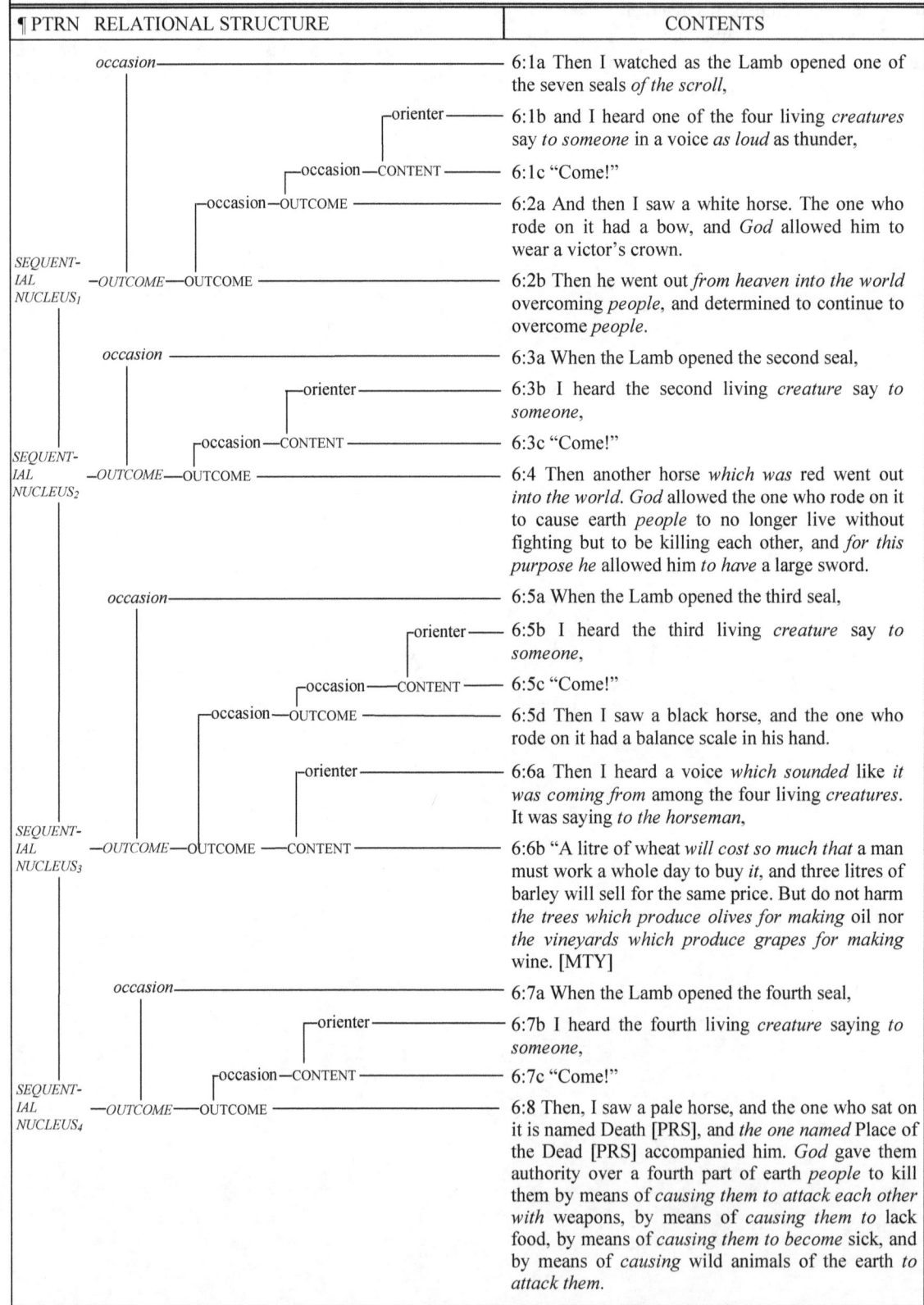

INTENT AND PARAGRAPH PATTERN

At this point in Revelation there begins the narrative part of John's vision of the end-time, following the hortatory material in chs.1–3 and the settings for the vision in chs.4 and 5. It is therefore natural that this unit, 6:1–8, should consist of a tightly-knit sequence of narrative sub-units. Each of these sub-units is built on an *occasion-OUTCOME* structure.

NOTES

6:1a I watched as The term εἶδον is usually translated as 'I saw,' but here it is followed by a 'when/as' clause rather than by an object. Since 'saw' requires an object in English, 'watched' is used here.

6:1b say *to someone* 'To someone' is supplied to satisfy the case frame. In many languages it may not be necessary to translate it. Because the voice comes before an introduction of the one addressed, 'someone' is used instead of a specific identification of the addressee.

in a voice *as loud* as thunder 'Loud' seems to be the most appropriate point of similarity between thunder and the sound of a voice in this simile.

6:1c "Come!" The best attested manuscripts have the one word ἔρχου 'come', but many, assuming that John is the one addressed, add καὶ ἴδε or καὶ βλέπε 'and see' after the command to come. UBSGNT has ἔρχου alone and gives it a B rating. For several reasons, this analysis follows those manuscripts which omit the second command (καὶ ἴδε or καὶ βλέπε 'and see'). It seems more logical for the simple command to be made to the horseman, who immediately appears. In this unit ἔρχου might also be translated 'go' if we think of the direction of the mission of the horsemen, which is toward the earth.

6:2a And then I saw Here there is a combination of καὶ εἶδον 'I saw' and καὶ ἰδού 'and behold'. The phrase is repeated in 6:5 and in 6:8. In each of these places καὶ ἰδού may function as introducing each new participant in the action. Van Otterloo (p. 34) says that one of the two major functions of ἰδού is "to focus special attention on a major thematic participant as he/she/it is introduced onto the event line of an episode."

The one who rode on it There are various opinions about the identity of this horseman, and some consider that he is Christ, identifying him with the horseman in 19:11. But the only thing these two riders have in common is the colour of the horses, which is not determinative because white horses were regularly chosen for Roman leaders in victory processions (see Charles). Also, this rider has a bow, which sets the context for conflict, but Christ's weapon is always the sword of his mouth (1:16; 19:15). The crown this rider was given is a στέφανος which stands for winning a contest, whereas 19:12 shows Christ crowned with many διαδήματα '(royal) crowns'. Rather than being identical these two horsemen may be considered antithetical, as John weaves a strain of antithesis throughout the book. That the first rider's mission is similar to that of the other three in this unit is the opinion of Beasley-Murray, Charles, and Mounce among others.

***God* allowed him to wear a victor's crown** The Greek text has ἐδόθη αὐτῷ στέφανος 'he was given a victor's crown'. For languages in which it would not be obligatory to supply the agent of 'give' it would be better not to add the agent here nor in the other occurrences in this chapter of ἐδόθη 'was given.' In fact, the symbolism of the vision would be skewed by having God physically 'give' a crown to the horseman. So it is clear that the meaning here is that God *allowed* him to wear the victor's crown. This fits with 6:4 where God *allows* the second horseman to take peace from the earth, using the same verbal form ἐδόθη. Caird says, "John uses this word three times of a gracious gift of God which is in keeping with his purpose of redemption (vi. 11; xii. 14; xix. 8); but more frequently he uses it of the divine permission granted to evil powers to carry out their nefarious work—the denizens of the abyss (ix. 1, 3, 5), the monster (xiii. 5, 7), and the false prophet (xiii. 14, 15)".

6:2b Then he went out *from heaven into the world* overcoming *people*, and determined to continue to overcome *people*. The verb ἐξῆλθεν 'went out' presumably implies 'from heaven,' since the rider is going into the world to carry out his task of conquering people.

6:4 Then another horse *which was* red went out *into the world* As in 6:2b the verb ἐξῆλθεν 'went out' presumably implies 'from heaven,' since the rider is going into the world to 'take peace from the world' (see next note).

to cause earth *people* to no longer live without fighting A literal translation of the Greek text is 'to take peace out of the earth'. 'Peace' is an abstract noun and there seems to be no problem in understanding 'to take peace out of the earth' as an idiomatic way of representing the same idea as the following ἵνα clause, 'so that people would kill one another'. Thus in the display these two clauses are taken as two ways of saying the same thing.

6:6a I heard a voice *which sounded* **like** *it was coming from* **among the four living** *creatures.* When John uses ὡς 'like' here, he is not in doubt about the nature of the sound, which he interprets as speech. The question is concerning its source. It seems to him to be ἐν μέσῳ τῶν τεσσάρων ζῴων 'in the midst of the four living ones.'

But since John does not identify the speaker, some take it to be the Lamb. In 5:6 the Lamb is said to be 'in the middle of . . . the four living creatures'. Others identify the voice as that of the One sitting on the throne, since he too is in the midst of the four living creatures. On the other hand, the fact that the identification is not precise may indicate that the four living creatures are the ones from whom the voice comes (Alford, Lenski).

6:6b A litre The term χοῖνιξ was a dry measure almost equivalent to a litre. When used for wheat, one χοῖνιξ 'litre' was a day's ration for one man. Three litres of barley would be a day's ration for a horse, although barley was also used as food by poor people.

will cost so much that **a man must work a whole day to buy** *it,* **and three litres of barley will sell for the same price** The Greek says that one litre of wheat will cost a 'denarius' which was a Roman silver coin. It was the standard day's pay for a soldier or for a labourer. Because translating using the name of a coin here would not communicate clearly, the equivalent to the value of the denarius is used in the display, 'a man must work a whole day to buy it'. To make it clear that lack of food is the significant factor in this judgment, 'will cost so much' is added. In New Testament times a denarius would normally buy about eight litres of wheat.

do not harm **the trees which produce olives for** *making* **oil nor** *the vines which produce grapes for making* **wine** The transitive use of ἀδικέω 'injure' with the accusative of an object means to damage or spoil it. There is a figure of speech of metonymy here as the effect taken for the cause, that is, the product for its source (Düsterdieck, Mounce, Swete). Wine and the oil that was made from olives were very important parts of the food and drink of people in John's days. Both grapevines and olive trees take several years before they start bearing useful fruit, so destroying them would be a very serious matter. The famine prophesied with the coming of the rider of the black horse is severe enough to cause distress, but it is limited like the other judgments of this series.

6:8 a pale horse The term χλωρός means 'pale green' when applied to vegetation, but when applied to people it refers to the skin colour of a sick person or a corpse. This association is probably in focus here.

the one who sat on it is named Death, and *the one named* **Place of the Dead accompanied him** The first three horsemen are not named but each has an object appropriate to the judgment being symbolized. However, it is the *names* of the fourth rider and of his companion that are appropriate. Death and Hades are linked as in other references in Revelation (1:18; 20:13–14). Here they may be seen as administrators of divine justice. Hades is taken for the place or abode of the dead. The word θάνατος is used for pestilence further on in this verse (see Louw and Nida, 23.158), but here, combined with Hades and the commission to kill, the translation is 'Death'.

a fourth part of earth *people* The fourth part of the earth is to be understood not geographically but as a proportion of the population of the earth. This is another indication of the limitation of the control granted to the agents of God's justice.

BOUNDARIES AND COHERENCE

The opening of the unit begins with the Lamb's opening the first seal at which point the first horse and rider are introduced. The close comes with the commissioning of the last of the riders and his companion. After this the living creatures no longer direct the action, and there are no more horsemen.

Several coherence factors bind the unit, as follows:

1. Each of the horsemen is called out by one of the living creatures.
2. Each time, the word ἤκουσα 'I heard' is repeated and refers to the voice of one of the living creatures.
3. The logical sequence of conquest, bloodshed, famine, and pestilence with death comes as the horsemen ride out.
4. Each of the horsemen is shown to be controlled by a higher power, either in respect of his authority (6:2a, 4), or by a limitation being placed on the scope of his action (6:6, 8).

In fact, the narratives of the openings of the first four seals have so many features in common with one another, and distinct from the other seals, that they are clearly a group of sequential actions which together constitute the first *step* towards the GOAL of the seventh seal (8:1–5).

PROMINENCE AND THEME

The theme is stated as a generalization of the four sequential events, which are described according to a single pattern.

SCENE CONSTITUENT 6:9–11 (Episode: Step₂ of 5:1–8:5)

THEME: *When the Lamb opened the fifth seal, the souls of God's servants who had been killed because of their faith appealed to him to judge the earth people. They were honoured by God and told by him to rest until they were joined by all the others who would be killed for their faith.*

¶ PTRN RELATIONAL STRUCTURE	CONTENTS
occasion	6:9a When the Lamb opened the fifth seal,
⎸ setting—'God's servants'	6:9b I saw under (*or*, at the base of) the altar *in heaven* the souls of God's servants
⎸ identification	6:9c who had been slaughtered *by people* because *they believed* what God said and because they proclaimed the message *which Jesus witnessed to people about God.*
⎸ orienter	6:10a They appealed loudly *to God* saying,
occasion—CONTENT	6:10b "Sovereign Lord, you are holy and true; how long *will it be* before you judge the people who live on the earth and punish them because *they killed us(exc) and shed* our(exc) blood?"
OUTCOME—OUTCOME	6:11 Each of them was given *by God* a long white robe, and they were told *by God* to rest a little longer until all their fellow believers who served *the Lord* with them who *were destined* to be killed were killed, just as they *had been killed.*

INTENT AND PARAGRAPH PATTERN

Episode 6:9–11 has a narrative *occasion-OUTCOME* paragraph pattern where the *occasion* is the Lamb's opening of the fifth seal and the OUTCOME is John's view of the souls under the heavenly altar with their plea for justice and God's response.

NOTES

6:9b under (*or*, at the base of) the altar *in heaven* The question has been asked about the identity of the altar. The term is mentioned seven times in the book (6:9; 8:3, 5; 9:13; 11:1; 14:18; 16:7). In these passages it is not identified with either the altar of burnt offering or the incense altar in the earthly Temple.

'In heaven' is supplied in the display to give a more specific indication of what altar is meant. Although it is true that the primary meaning of ὑποκάτω is 'underneath', it is difficult to know exactly what position is meant. Swete says, "Their souls (ψυχάς) are seen 'under the altar,' because in the Levitical rite the blood, which is the ψυχή (Lev. 17:11 ἡ γὰρ ψυχὴ πάσης σαρκὸς αἷμα αὐτοῦ ἐστίν 'for the soul/life of all flesh is its blood'), was poured out at the foot of the altar (Lev. 4:7)". Therefore the most significant relationship to be communicated is probably that between the blood of the sacrifice poured out at the base of the altar and the souls of the martyrs.

the souls This refers to the souls or spirits of these believers who have been martyred. Various cultures divide the manifestations of life differently and the translation here may not always be easily determined. Note that in English 'ghosts' would not be a proper translation.

6:9c *they believed* what God said A valid alternate translation would be '*they proclaimed* what God said'.

they proclaimed the message *which Jesus witnessed to people about God* The Greek is τὴν μαρτυρίαν ἣν εἶχον 'the testimony which they were holding'. The phrase has been interpreted to mean the testimony which the martyrs gave to people. But the other instances in Revelation in which a similar phrase occurs in connection with 'the word of God' seem to refer to the witness that Jesus made ('Jesus' is explicit in 1:2, 9; 20:4; note Caird, Lenski, Mounce). In any case they had been slaughtered because they would not deny the truth to which

Jesus witnessed and on account of which he was slaughtered. Therefore in this analysis the testimony is taken to be that of Jesus.

'The message *which Jesus* witnessed *to people about God*' is a propositionalization of the abstract noun 'testimony' as understood in this context.

6:10a They appealed loudly *to God* The prayer may have been addressed to either Christ or God. A reason for understanding it as addressed to God the Father is that judgment is described as the pouring out of God's wrath (16:1). It appears to be the majority opinion of commentators that God is the one addressed. It is Christ who is opening the seals, but acting as the agent of the One who sits on the throne (5:7), though Christ is recognized in equality with God throughout the book.

6:10b Sovereign Lord, you are holy and true The word δεσπότης 'master, lord' is used ten times in the New Testament. As in this verse, it is used of God in prayer in Luke 2:29 and Acts 4:24, but it refers to Christ in 2 Pet. 2:1 and Jude 4. In the Old Testament as well as here it puts emphasis on the omnipotence of God (Isa. 1:24; 10:33). Many versions translate "Sovereign Lord" (NIV, NEB, NLT, NRSV, RSV).

Since the adjectives 'holy' and 'true' modifying δεσπότης 'Master' follow the noun in the Greek, they are translated by a stative clause in the display. This may be regarded as the basis for the martyrs' appeal to God to judge the people of the earth.

how long *will it be* **before you judge the people who live on the earth and punish them because** *they killed us(exc) and shed* **our(exc) blood?** In the Greek the vocative 'sovereign lord holy and true' comes between the question words ἕως πότε 'until when' and the rest of the sentence. This gives added prominence to the question.

The question has elements both of a real question and a rhetorical one. The martyrs not only want to know how much longer it will be before God executes justice on those who have murdered them, but they are also appealing to him to act swiftly.

6:11 Each of them was given *by God* **a long white robe, and they were told** *by God* **to rest a little longer until all their fellow believers who served** *the Lord* **with them who** *were destined* **to be killed were killed, just as they** *had been killed* The factors involved in the complex outcome may be listed as follows:

1. The martyrs were given long white robes. This indicates that they have kept themselves pure by refusing to deny their faith. (See also 3:4–5).
2. They are to rest in confidence. They can no longer doubt the outcome of their suffering because the One who kept them from denying their faith will also keep all their fellow servants in the same way.
3. The time of waiting for complete victory will be short.

given *by God* God may be seen as the provider of the robes and as charging the saints to rest, at least as the principal source of the action, since he is the chief actor throughout the book.

to rest a little longer The verb ἀναπαύσονται 'they will rest' is in the middle voice. It could mean they should not continue to make their cry for God's justice, that they simply remain quiet, or that they should enjoy the peaceful rest with which they have been blessed. The context and the parallel passage (14:13) would emphasise the latter.

all their fellow believers ... who *were destined* **to be killed** For the fulfilment of prophecy πληρόω 'fulfil' is usually in the passive with ἵνα 'in order to.' Here, the form in the UBSGNT is the aorist subjunctive passive πληρωθῶσιν. With the passive form, there is the meaning of a measure or number to be completed by all the saints who are to be killed.

all their fellow believers who served *the Lord* **with them** The Greek has 'their fellow-servants and their brothers.' However, the commentators are agreed that this does not refer to two groups but to one, 'their fellow-servants, that is, their brothers.'

BOUNDARIES AND COHERENCE

The beginning of the 6:9–11 paragraph is at the opening of the fifth seal. It reveals the souls of the martyred saints under the altar in heaven. Thus there is a change of location and of persons. The horsemen were to carry out their judgment on the unrighteous people living on the earth. The present incident involves God's people who are no longer on earth but have been killed and are under the heavenly altar. They are in contrast to the unrighteous people mentioned when the next seal is opened. The close of the paragraph comes when the appeal of the martyrs is answered and the next paragraph begins in 6:12 with the common paragraph introducer καὶ εἶδον 'and I saw' and the opening of the sixth seal.

PROMINENCE AND THEME

In an *occasion-OUTCOME* paragraph pattern both components are essential to the theme. Here there are two layers of *occasion-OUTCOME* relationships and both *occasions* are essential. The *OUTCOME* of the episode is naturally prominent and perhaps forms the most significant part of the theme. However, the direct speech of the souls under the altar has marked prominence and its appeal for justice has significance beyond this one episode.

SCENE CONSTITUENT 6:12–17 (Episode: Step₃ of 5:1–8:5)

THEME: When the Lamb opened the sixth seal of the scroll, the natural world began to fall apart causing the rebellious earth people to hide because the time had come for God to judge them.

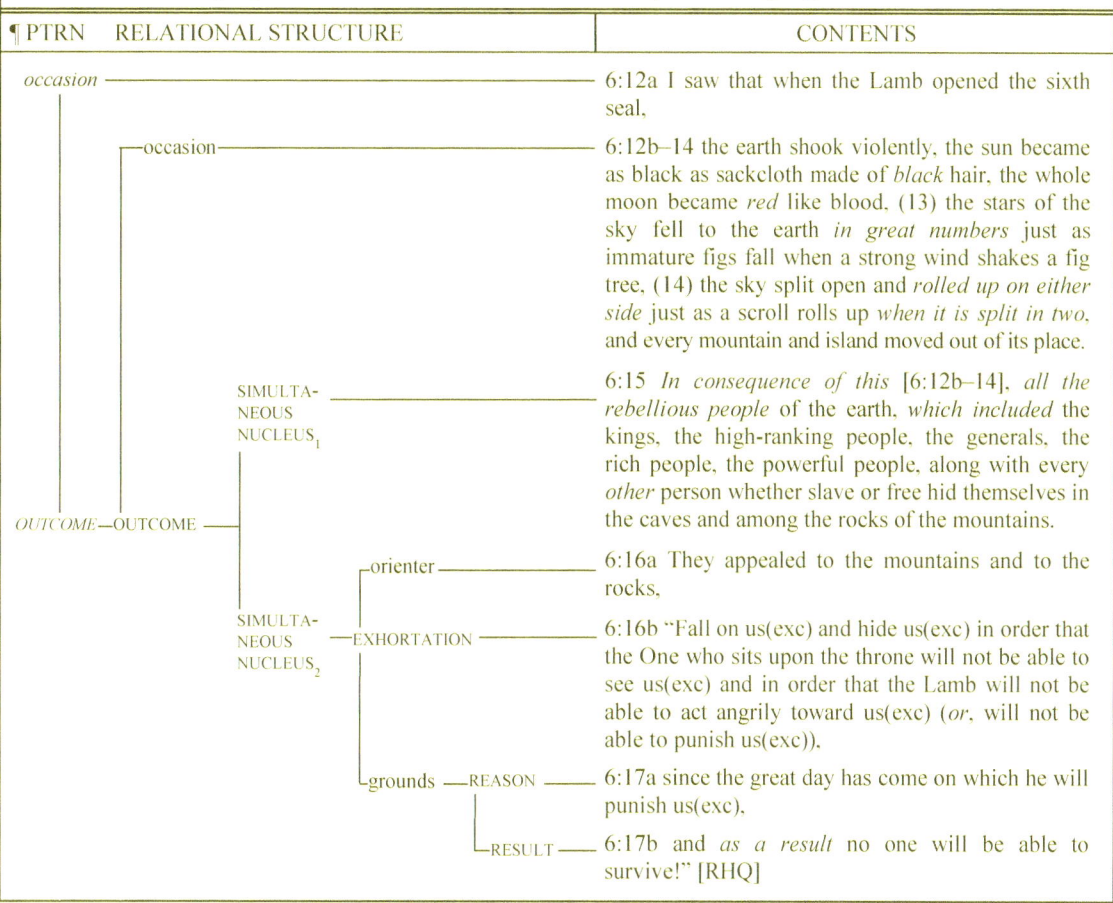

INTENT AND PARAGRAPH PATTERN

As with the opening of the fifth seal in the previous episode, the 6:12–17 episode has an *occasion-OUTCOME* paragraph pattern. Within the happenings occasioned by the opening of the seal, the calamities in nature occasion an outcome of fear in the hearts of the rebellious people of the earth. The impassioned plea to the rocks and mountains to fall on them and hide them from the face of God and the wrath of the Lamb may be seen as a warning to all in this present age who would rebel against God.

NOTES

6:12b–14 The position within the Greek sentence of the subjects 'sun,' 'moon,' 'stars', etc. here indicates that this is not a chronological sequence of events, but a description of many things that John saw at the same time. He was witnessing the whole natural world—the earth, the sky and all the fixed points in them—beginning to fall apart.

6:12b the earth shook violently In the prophecy of Jesus there are earthquakes in various places (Matt. 24:7), but 6:14b would indicate a general shaking of the whole world.

black as sackcloth made of *black* hair Swete says that σάκκος τρίχινος 'sackcloth made of hair/wool' was made of the hair of the black goat. In the display 'black hair' is a specific representation of the generic 'hair', which in English is not naturally associated with darkness.

the whole moon Literally this is 'the whole moon', but it can be translated as 'the full moon' (RSV). Or, 'whole' could be translated adverbially as TEV, "the moon turned completely red like blood".

6:13 the stars of the sky fell to the earth *in great numbers* just as immature figs fall when a strong wind shakes a fig tree The point of similarity is the ease and great number with which the figs and stars fell.

immature figs It would seem that here ὄλυνθος means figs that for some reason do not mature but fall easily in a windstorm.

6:14 the sky split open and *rolled up on either side* just as a scroll rolls up *when it is split in two* BDAG glosses the passive of ἀποχωρίζω as 'be separated' and this reference as 'the sky was split'. The description suggests an opened scroll that is torn across the middle. The two halves would roll back on themselves when the tension that held the scroll extended was released by the split (Mounce, Swete). What had been visible of the open scroll would have vanished. In language situations where scrolls are not known, the comparison with the scroll may need to be dropped.

6:15 *the rebellious people* of the earth The kings are designated as being 'of the earth', a phrase which is applied throughout the book to rebellious people. The phrase 'of the earth' is grammatically attached only to 'the kings', but it is understood as generic and intended to qualify semantically all the other groups of people mentioned. For this reason it is moved in the display to a position before the enumeration.

powerful people The word ἰσχυροί 'strong/powerful' refers primarily to physical strength and is often used in contrast to ἀσθενής 'weak/sick.' Coming as it does after 'rich' it may include strength of influence.

along with every *other* person whether slave or free Basically the message is that judgment is universal and without partiality. The surface structure of the Greek text begins with the most powerful and continues with those who might be expected to have little defence, that is, 'every slave and free person'. The seven-fold list indicates that all rebellious people are included, so that 'every' may be simply an emphasis on the completeness of the list, by repetition or by summary. Contrast with the other categories on the list is not in focus because 'slaves and free persons' would not be entirely exclusive of those already specified.

6:16a–b They appealed to the mountains and to the rocks: "Fall on us(exc) and hide us(exc) in order that the One who sits upon the throne will not be able to see us(exc) . . ." The content of the prayer of the earth people shows that they have rebelled against God.

The use of the historic present λέγουσιν 'they say/appeal' here at the end of the episode points forward to the enactment of the next set of judgments starting in ch.8.

and *in order that* the Lamb will not be able to act angrily toward us(exc) (*or*, will not be able to punish us(exc)) In its eschatological use ὀργή 'anger' refers both to an emotion and to divine reaction to evil in terms of judgment with punishment as its outcome. The wrath of God is his response to rejection of his manifestation of love in the provision of salvation through Jesus Christ (Rom. 2:5–9) and to man's disobedience in rejecting his just law.

6:17a since the great day has come As BDAG shows, μέγας may be understood in a superlative sense, especially with the article. To call it 'great' seems inadequate, and Bratcher and Hatton suggest 'terrible'. The term ἡ ἡμέρα ἡ μεγάλη 'the great day' is used in a special sense in that 'day' is not a literal twenty-four hour day but the set time for an event. As in 16:14 there is also the aspect of finality, since throughout Scripture 'the day', with or without modifiers (e.g. 'of the Lord'), is a technical term for the end time.

he will punish us(exc) Some manuscripts read τῆς ὀργῆς αὐτῶν 'their wrath' and others read τῆς ὀργῆς αὐτοῦ 'his wrath'. Since there is adequate textual evidence for the singular and many references associate Christ's wrath and judgment with God's (Acts 17:31; Rev. 19:15), this analysis uses αὐτοῦ 'his' referring to the great day of Christ's wrath, instead of αὐτῶν 'their' as in the UBSGNT, which would specify God's wrath as well as Christ's. As far as meaning is concerned, the difference is largely a question of focus.

6:17b and *as a result* no one will be able to survive The threat to survival echoes the Old Testament expression of the prophets in Joel 2:11; Nah. 1:6; Mal. 3:2. The rebels, by showing fear when punishment is involved, acknowledge guilt but are not repentant.

survive The literal translation is 'stand'. The word has various connotations in Greek and English, many of which might not be natural in other languages.

BOUNDARIES AND COHERENCE

The 6:12–17 paragraph opens with the Lamb breaking the sixth seal, and it closes with the cry of the rebellious people of earth when they recognize that the time for judgment has actually come. The next unit begins in 7:1 with μετὰ τοῦτο εἶδον, a marker of a new unit (cf. 4:1) and a new situation and new characters are introduced: angels and the 144,000 sealed servants of God.

God is dealing with rebellious people in 6:12–17 and their response is in focus. They do not respond in repentance, but tremendous fear grips them.

PROMINENCE AND THEME

In this third episode of the seal-breaking series the outcome of the cosmic upheaval is naturally prominent. It also has marked prominence by use of direct speech, emphasis on the inclusiveness of the list of people affected, and a strong emotional tone. The direct *occasion* (6:12b–14) for this OUTCOME is also given in considerable detail and for this reason is highlighted. Both the elaborate *occasion* with its marked prominence and the OUTCOME are represented in the theme statement.

SCENE CONSTITUENT 7:1–17 (Episode Cluster: Interlude of 5:1–8:5)

THEME: An angel commanded four other angels to continue restraining the destructive winds. Then some angels marked one hundred and forty-four thousand people to show that they were God's servants. A triumphant crowd of those who had come safely through persecution acknowledged that their deliverance had come from God and the Lamb, and so the angels, the elders, and the living creatures worshiped God in praise.

MACROSTRUCTURE	CONTENTS
NUCLEUS₁	7:1–8 An angel appeared and commanded the four angels who had authority to harm the earth and the sea that they should continue restraining the destructive winds. Then angels marked one hundred and forty-four thousand people to show that they were God's servants.
NUCLEUS₂	7:9–17 I saw a triumphant crowd of those who, I was told, had come safely through persecution and who now serve God and are sheltered by him. When they acknowledged that their deliverance had come from God and the Lamb, the angels, the elders, and the living creatures worshiped God in praise.

INTENT AND STRUCTURE

As noted in the Intent and Structure for 5:1–8:5, interludes focus on God's people and they provide encouragement for the saints. In 7:1–8, God's protection of his people is shown in the marking of the 144,000 with his seal of protection. In 7:9–17, the innumerable crowd of God's people before the throne praise him for their deliverance from the great tribulation with its severe persecution.

BOUNDARIES AND COHERENCE

An initial μετὰ τοῦτο εἶδον 'after this I saw' at the beginning of 7:1 signals the opening of the 7:1–17 episode cluster. (This is the only time in the book that the singular 'this' is used in such a phrase. It may point back to the speech of 6:16–17, rather than to the whole episode.) Another marker of the opening of the unit is the introduction of new participants. The unit closes at the end of the elder's declaration about the main participants of 7:9–17. The next unit, beginning at 8:1, returns to the main structural line of the scene, the opening of the seals.

Coherence is seen in the fact that the human participants are wholly God's people and that judgment upon the wicked is not being carried out, as it is in the context before and after this interlude.

PROMINENCE AND THEME

The two elements of the unit are equally prominent, and so the theme consists of a summary of them.

EPISODE CLUSTER CONSTITUENT 7:1–8 (Interlude Episode: Nucleus₁ of 7:1–17)

THEME: An angel appeared and commanded the four angels who had authority to harm the earth and the sea that they should continue restraining the destructive winds. Then angels marked one hundred and forty-four thousand people to show that they were God's servants.

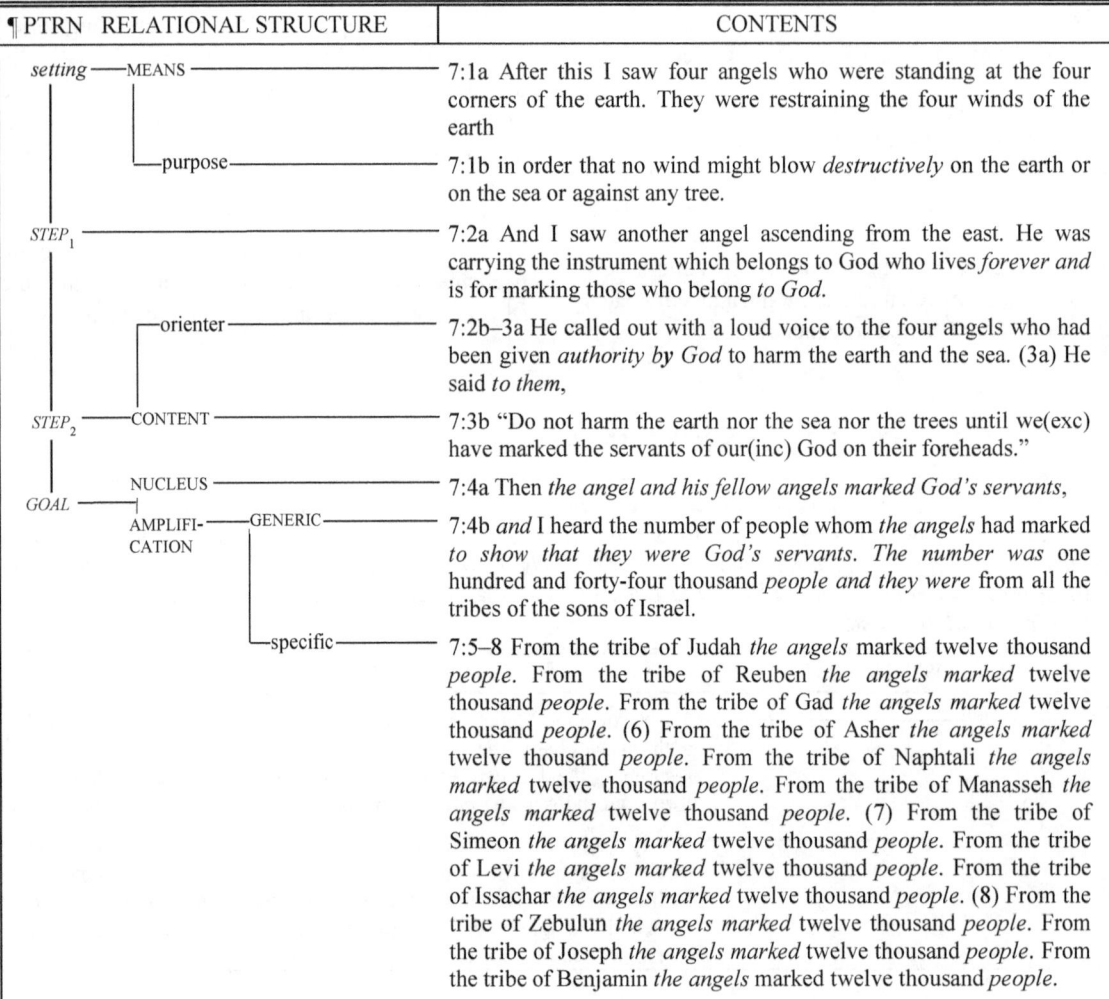

INTENT AND PARAGRAPH PATTERN

The 7:1–8 episode has a narrative *step-GOAL* paragraph pattern in that the action of the unit is basically that of one agent, the angel in charge of the sealing of the 144,000. This action takes place against the background of other angels who are seen holding back the destructive judgment of the four winds, as introduced in the *setting*.

The GOAL of the angel, the sealing of the servants of God, does not occur on the event line as an explicit act of the angel (and his fellow-angels). But the act of being sealed is referred to with the perfect passive participle ἐσφραγισμένοι 'having been sealed' four times in 7:4, 5, 8. This marks prominence on the patients (those sealed) rather than the agent(s). What is in focus is God's protection of his servants during the time of destructive judgment on the earth. The episode fits into the larger context of preparation necessary before the beginning of the time when God's wrath is completely poured out.

NOTES

7:1a standing at the four corners of the earth
The expression 'corners of the earth' is retained in the display because it is the way John records what he saw in his vision. In languages where it will not be possible, or very unnatural, to use 'corners of the earth', an appropriate substitute will need to be found.

7:1a–b restraining the four winds of the earth in order that no wind might blow *destructively* on the earth or on the sea or against any tree 'To restrain' or 'to control' is a secondary meaning of the verb κρατέω 'to take into one's possession'. The meaning of restraint is clear from the purpose clause which follows. It is inferred in 7:2b that these are destructive winds and this important factor is made explicit here in the display text.

In some languages winds may not normally be counted, but this might be handled as 'wind from (these) four different places/directions'.

7:2a the instrument which belongs to God who lives *forever and* is for marking those who belong *to* God In the display text the noun 'seal' is not used but the generic 'instrument' is used with the function of the seal, since σφραγίς 'seal' is not being used here with the same sense as in chapters 5 and 6.

In ancient times a seal, when used to mark an object or person, indicated ownership. The fact that those to be marked in this instance are said to be God's servants (7:3b) is in harmony with the objective.

God who lives *forever* In the phrase 'the living God', which occurs throughout scripture, 'living' means more than just being alive. Bratcher and Hatton say on the use of 'living' in 1:18 that "it is the language of divine existence, of God, who by his nature has life in himself".

7:2b who had been given *authority by* God The verbal form ἐδόθη 'given' is highly thematic throughout the book and here again indicates authority delegated from God.

7:3b until It is important to note the urgency with which the angel interrupts the process of imminent judgment. The setting, with its reference to the destructive winds, prepares the reader for judgment, but the deliberate pause makes room for the protection of the saints. One of the important objectives of the book is to give assurance and comfort to the readers in a time of great trouble that called for widespread martyrdom. It will be observed that the following unit (7:9–17) gives even stronger encouragement and hope.

on their foreheads The word for forehead occurs in the New Testament only in Revelation. It refers to the sealing by God in 7:3 and 9:4 and to the name of God on the forehead of the saints in 14:1 and 22:4. The mark of the beast is the reference in 13:16; 14:9; 20:4. In 17:5 the blasphemous name is on the forehead of the great whore. It will be noted that the mark of the beast is on the right hand or on the forehead (13:16) and that it is called a χάραγμα 'mark' or 'stamp', like something engraved or cut and thus not identical with the divine seal.

until we(exc) have marked The plural subject in σφραγίσωμεν 'we have marked' probably implies that other angels are also involved in the task.

7:4a Then *the angel and his fellow angels marked God's servants* The purpose for making this implied action explicit in the display is to represent the complete action of the underlying timeline, preserving the total *step-GOAL* relationship. However, the omission of explicit reference to this in the Greek text indicates that the focus is on the patients (those marked) rather than on the agents of the marking.

7:4b I heard the number of people whom *the angels* had marked *to show that they were God's servants. The number was* one hundred and forty-four thousand *people* Consistent with so many other numbers in Revelation, this number is clearly symbolic. Twelve is a number used of those governing under God, as the number of the tribes of Israel. This number is squared, multiplied by a thousand and understood as a limitless number. Thus it aptly shows the completeness of the number of God's servants. In the next unit (7:9–12), the redeemed are simply said to be beyond numbering.

all the tribes of the sons of Israel There are commentators (e.g. Düsterdieck, Thomas, Walvoord) who maintain that the 144,000 refers only to the literal sons of Israel. The basis for this is that actual names of tribes of Israel are used. But others (Alford, Barnes, Ladd, Lenski, Morris, Mounce) accept the names as symbolic, used in order to show that God's servants include both Jew and Gentile.

BOUNDARIES AND COHERENCE

See Boundaries and Coherence for 7:1–17 for discussion of the opening boundary. At 7:9 there is a time phrase μετὰ ταῦτα εἶδον 'after these things I saw' similar to the one in 7:1; it marks the beginning of the next episode. The end of the specific list of tribes of those sealed (the GOAL) marks the close of this episode.

Coherence is evident in that one action is begun and finished in the unit. The repeated use of σφραγίς 'seal' (6:2) and σφραγίζω 'to seal' (7:3, 4, 5, 8) also provides coherence.

PROMINENCE AND THEME

In a *step-GOAL* paragraph pattern, the *steps* and the GOAL are thematic. That the sealing of the 144,000 was accomplished is the prominent feature of the unit. The act of being sealed is referred to with the perfect passive participle ἐσφραγισμένοι 'having been sealed' four times in 7:4, 5, 8. The significance of the sealing is also highlighted by symbolic numbers which show it is comprehensive and by the specific naming of tribes.

EPISODE CLUSTER CONSTITUENT 7:9–17 (Interlude Episode: Nucleus₂ of 7:1–17)

THEME: I saw a triumphant crowd of those who, I was told, had come safely through persecution and who now serve God and are sheltered by him. When they acknowledged that their deliverance had come from God and the Lamb, the angels, the elders, and the living creatures worshiped God in praise.

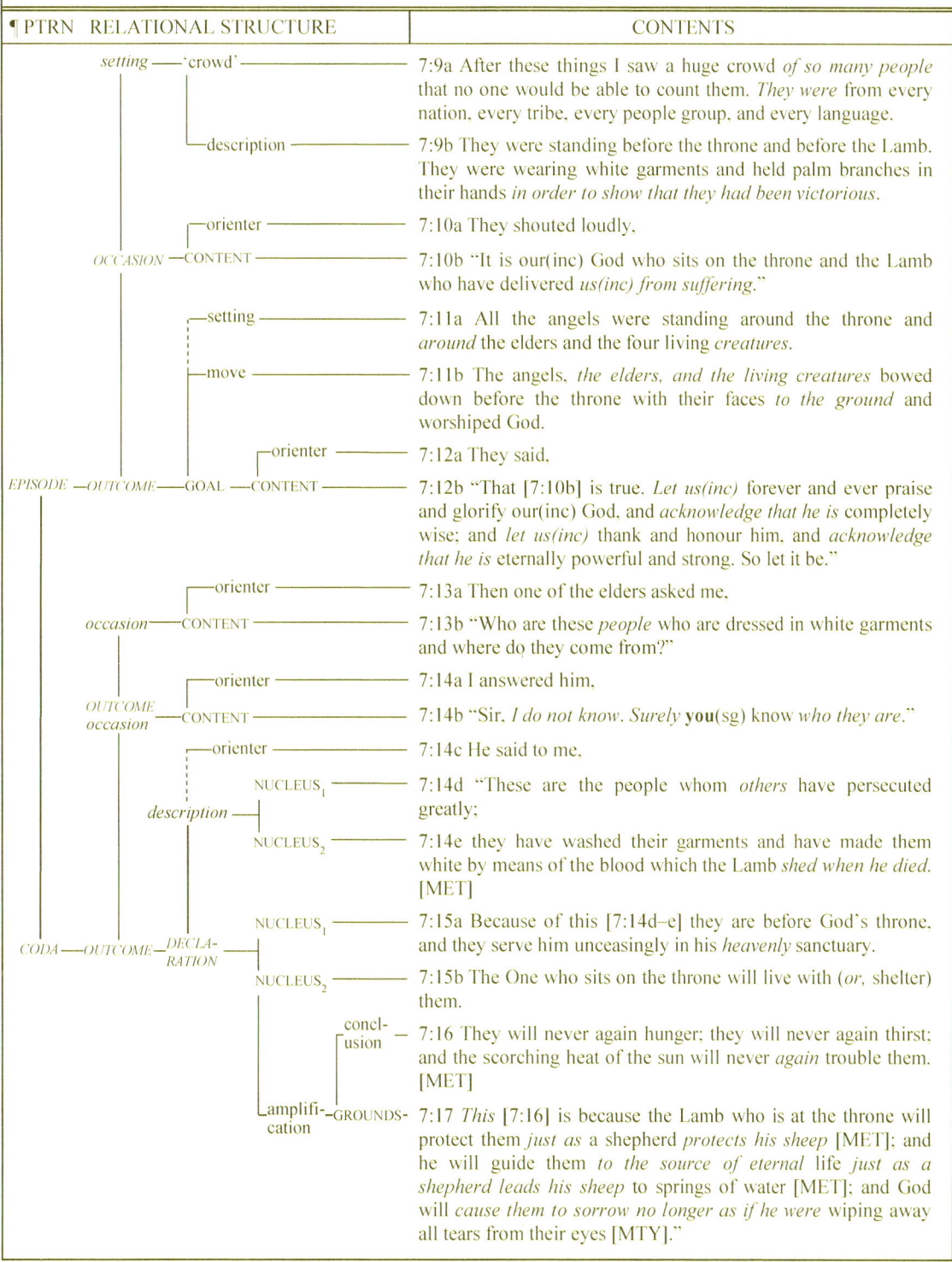

INTENT AND STRUCTURE

This unit, while primarily narrative, contains a CODA which has a descriptive function in giving more details about the main participants, the saints who had come through persecution. Yet this CODA also has a hortatory function in the overall framework of the book, encouraging the readers to persevere through suffering.

NOTES

7:9a After these things I saw Van Otterloo classifies the occurrence of καὶ ἰδού 'and behold' (occurring after μετὰ ταῦτα εἶδον 'after these things I saw') as marking the introduction of major thematic participants in a vision (p. 45). Thus καὶ ἰδού is marking the innumerable crowd as the major participants of this episode. Since English does not have a closely corresponding marker, some modern versions (CEV, NLT) do not translate it at all while others use the presentational form "there was": ". . .I looked, and there was a great number of people . . ." (NCV), ". . . I looked and there before me was a great multitude . . ." (NIV).

***They were* from every nation, every tribe, every people group, and every language** In 7:14, the people in this great crowd are identified as those who have come out of τῆς θλίψεως τῆς μεγάλης 'the great tribulation'. The fourfold list along with the adjective παντός 'all' indicate worldwide inclusiveness. The list is also used in 5:9, 7:9, 11:9, 13:7, 14:6, with a different order each time. Similar lists are in 10:11 and 17:15. The number four is frequently used symbolically of that which pertains to earth.

7:9b They were wearing white garments The στολή 'robe' is a long flowing garment, which would be laid aside for work and put on again after the work had been completed. White robes are symbolic of victory and of purity elsewhere also (3:5, 18; 4:4; 6:11; 19:14).

held palm branches in their hands *in order to show that they had been victorious* The palm branch was a common symbol of victory among Jews, Greeks, and Romans.

7:10a They shouted loudly Not only is the description of the saints one of people prepared for celebration, their praise is vigorous. This adds to the completeness of the deliverance for which they praise God.

7:10b "It is our(inc) God who sits on the throne and the Lamb who have delivered *us(inc) from suffering.*" The expression of praise, 'Salvation to our God who sits on the throne and to the Lamb', is somewhat elliptical. God and the Lamb are being praised by the attributing to them of the deliverance which the saints have experienced. The display expresses this as an acknowledgment by the saints that they owe their deliverance to those enthroned.

Some specifics of the deliverance are mentioned in 7:14–17. These verses show that what the saints have been delivered from is persecution (7:14d) and suffering (7:16) and sorrow (7:17).

As in 5:13 and 7:12 this doxology is not explicitly addressed to God in the second person. He is referred to in the third person in the surface structure. Even so, it is difficult to know who is being addressed (i.e. spoken to, not necessarily spoken about). If the redeemed are addressing each other and/or the angels and other beings in heaven, then 'our(inc)' would be the correct form for languages which make a distinction between first person plural inclusive and exclusive forms. If God and the Lamb are being addressed (spoken to), then the 'our' would be exclusive (see Bratcher and Hatton, p. 127).

7:11b The angels, *the elders, and the living creatures* bowed down before the throne It is true that in the syntax of the Greek text the elders and the living creatures are not clearly marked as bowing down and worshiping. And most commentators refer to those worshiping as angels without reference to the elders and living creatures. However, it would seem possible that in ἔπεσαν 'they fell down' the third person plural marker is intended to include all those just mentioned. And the fact that the elders and living creatures are mentioned, even though unambiguously only in reference to the angels' position, suggests that they are meant to be included in the worship. This is especially borne out by the fact that their exclusion from the worship, especially when they are already mentioned in the context, would seem strange when every other loyal creature in the universe is included. Aune, Lenski, Thomas, and Walvoord understand the elders and living creatures as taking part in the doxology.

**7:12b "That [7:10b] is true. *Let us(inc) forever and ever praise and glorify our(inc) God, and acknowledge that he is* completely wise; and *let us(inc)* thank and honour him, and *acknowledge that he is* eternally powerful and strong. So let it be." The first 'amen' is an expression of agreement with the declaration of the saints on the part of the heavenly beings and the second, a confirmation of their own praise.

Each attribute in the praise of the heavenly creatures has the definite article. This may be interpreted to mean that each attribute or expression of praise belongs to God to an infinite degree. The sevenfold ascription of praise indicates completeness—most likely with focus on the completeness of the worship and the complete worthiness of the One being worshiped. But compare with notes on 5:12b. In translation into languages where use of synonymous terms is difficult and does not produce the rhetorical effect of awe and grandeur, language-specific ways of producing these effects should be used.

forever and ever ... eternally In the Greek εἰς τοὺς αἰῶνας τῶν αἰώνων 'to the ages of the ages' appears to relate to the whole of the doxology. However, in English "forever and ever" collocates well only with the four ascriptions of praise. So "eternally" is used with "powerful and strong".

7:13a Then one of the elders asked me It is appropriate for an elder to explain the scene just as one of them cleared up the problem of who would be able to break the seals in 5:5.

The basic meaning of ἀπεκρίθη is 'answered,' but in the New Testament it is often used, as here, to introduce a speech which does not answer a previous one, but which responds to a previous event and represents a new initiative.

7:13b "Who are these *people* who are dressed in white garments and where do they come from?" The form of the question in Greek calls attention to the information given by putting it first in the sentence, 'These who are dressed in white garments, who are they and where do they come from?'

7:14b "Sir, *I do not know*. Surely *you*(sg) know *who they are.*" '*I do not know*' is supplied to fill out the direct answer to the elder's question, an obligatory step in some languages. The pronoun σύ 'you(sg)' is emphatic. It infers that John does not know and that the elder surely would know. This gives the elder the opportunity to explain the vision to John. Swete says, "Σὺ οἶδας is at once a confession of ignorance, and an appeal for information." On this basis an alternate propositionalization would be '*Surely* **you** know *who they are; please tell me*'.

7:14d These are the people whom *others* have persecuted greatly BDAG lists the participle ἐρχόμενοι 'coming' under the nonliteral use of the verb with the preposition ἐκ 'out of', glossing ἐρχόμενοι ἐκ τῆς θλίψεως as 'have suffered persecution'. It identifies and describes the saints as those who have been persecuted. His statement answers the question about who they are as well as where they have come from.

7:14e they have washed their garments and have made them white by means of the blood which the Lamb *shed when he died* The statement is obviously figurative; it expresses the fact that the death of Jesus is the basis on which sin is forgiven and purity is imparted to the believer. The figure of the cleansed white garment, signifying freedom from the guilt of sin, is significant in this context and is clearly connected to the blood of Christ, the only thing that can effect such cleansing.

The figure of washing garments and making them white in the blood of the Lamb is a type of metaphor in which the figure itself is so significant and symbolic that the metaphor cannot be restated as a simple simile. A complex restatement of it would be something like 'As people wash garments in water to make them pure white, in the same way these people have trusted in the Lamb's dying and shedding his blood on their behalf, and so they have become pure, with all their sins forgiven and removed'.

7:15a unceasingly The Greek is ἡμέρας καὶ νυκτός 'by day and night', but this is purely figurative language, since there is no implication that there is any night in heaven.

7:15b will live with (*or*, shelter) them BDAG suggests for this verse the meaning 'shelter' for σκηνώσει 'will live/dwell', since the verb occurs with the phrase ἐπ' αὐτούς 'over' or 'above them', rather than μετ' αὐτῶν 'with them' as in 21:3 or ἐν αὐτοῖς 'among them' (cf. John 1:14). 'Shelter' seems appropriate if, as in the display, the mention of dangers to which humans are exposed (7:16) is a restatement of this promise.

7:16 the scorching heat of the sun will never *again* trouble them The Greek has οὐδὲ μὴ πέσῃ ἐπ' αὐτοὺς ὁ ἥλιος οὐδὲ πᾶν καῦμα 'neither the sun nor any scorching heat will fall on them', which is probably a hendiadys (NLT, TNT) since 16:9 shows John using καῦμα 'scorching heat' with reference to the sun. There is also a metaphor in 'fall on' meaning 'affect, trouble.'

7:17 *This* is because The conjunction ὅτι 'because, for' marks this verse as the grounds for the previous one. However, in this case the grounds are marked as more prominent than the conclusion both by the fact that they are positive in contrast to the negatives of 17:16, and by the expanded noun subject 'the Lamb who is in the midst of the throne' being placed before the verb rather than after it.

the Lamb who is at the throne As in 5:6, ἀνὰ μέσον τοῦ θρόνου 'in the midst of the throne' is used to symbolize the Lamb's divine position of power and authority, positioned nearest to the throne of God himself. Some translations (JBP, NIV, TEV) render it as 'in/at the center of the throne'. This may be all right as long as it is not understood to exclude God the Father from his position which is at the centre of the throne.

will protect them *just as* a shepherd *protects his sheep*; and he will guide them *to the source of eternal* life *just as a shepherd leads his sheep* to springs of water The figurative expression continues as of a pastoral scene. BDAG gives 'protect' as one of the figurative (extended) meanings of ποιμαίνω 'to shepherd, herd'.

'He will guide them to the source of eternal life' might be alternatively rendered as 'he will enable them to live forever'.

God will *cause them to sorrow no longer as if he were* wiping away all tears from their eyes The figure now is metonymy in that the tears stand for the sorrows which have caused them to flow.

BOUNDARIES AND COHERENCE

The unit begins with μετὰ ταῦτα εἶδον, καὶ ἰδού 'after these things I saw, and behold'. This clause and similar phrases frequently introduce new units in the book. For the final boundary see Boundaries and Coherence for 7:1–17.

Coherence in the unit is based on the single location of the action and on the main participants, the victorious saints, who are introduced at the beginning of the unit and are described in detail at the end. There is also a focus throughout on God and the Lamb (7:9, 10, 11, 12, 14, 15, 17).

PROMINENCE AND THEME

Normally OUTCOME is more naturally prominent than *occasion*. However, here the participants in 7:9a are marked as thematically important (see note) and the focus of their doxology on the highly discourse-prominent feature of final deliverance/salvation marks the OCCASION (7:10) as prominent. The CODA is given marked prominence by the question and answer of 7:13a–14b, which add no new information but delay the *description–*DECLARATION, thus highlighting it. So the theme includes the declaration of God's deliverance and the heavenly worship, as well as the elder's DECLARATION from the CODA.

SCENE CONSTITUENT 8:1–5 (Episode: Goal of 5:1–8:5)

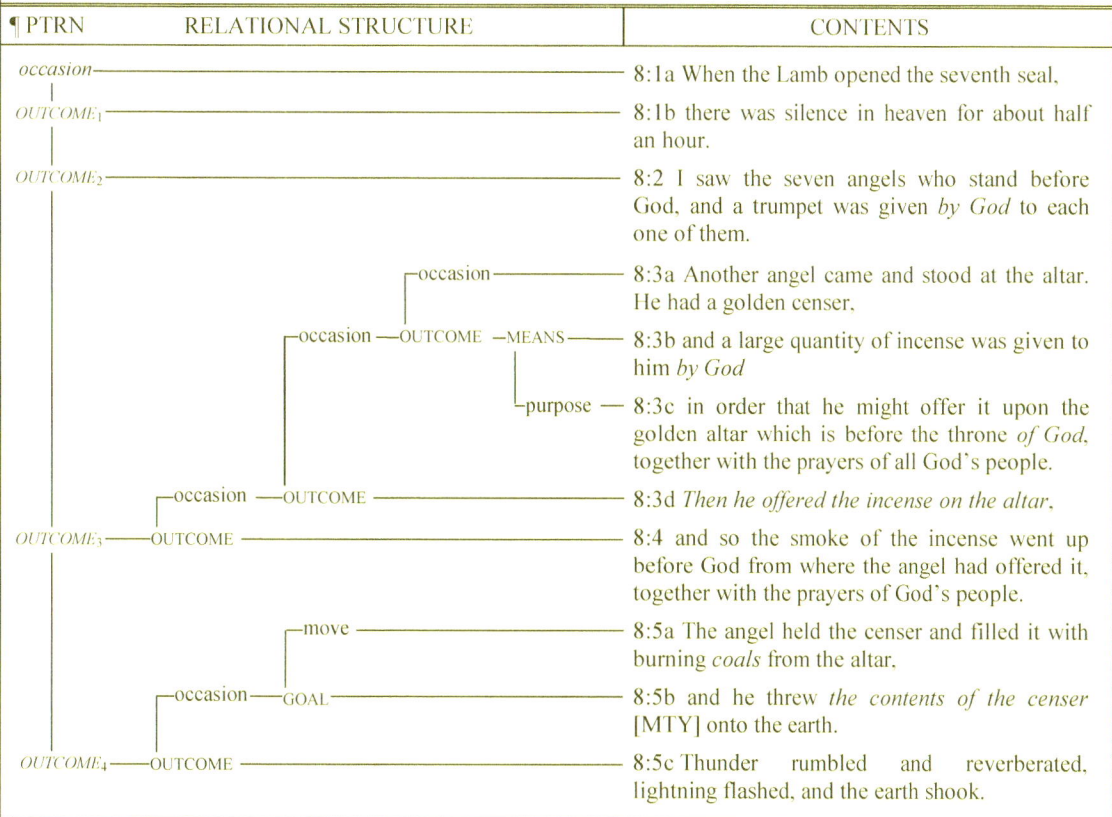

THEME: When the Lamb opened the seventh seal there was silence in heaven. Seven angels each received a trumpet, and another angel offered up to God the prayers of all the saints. Then this angel threw fire onto the earth and cosmic manifestations of judgment occurred.

INTENT AND PARAGRAPH PATTERN

In this unit again there is the *occasion-OUTCOME* paragraph pattern that is typical of the opening of the seals, this time the seventh seal. There appears to be a sequence of four outcomes to the opening of the seventh seal, each one more dramatic than the previous: firstly silence in heaven for half an hour, then the giving of the trumpets to the seven angels, then the offering up of the prayers of God's people, and finally the throwing of fire on the earth in judgment. Many commentators see the last two of these as being in a cause-effect relationship (the prayers of the saints bringing about judgment). However, in the Greek there is no explicit indication of this, and the use of a noun subject in 8:5a as well as the backgrounding of the first verb (see note on 8:5a) point to it being a separate *OUTCOME*.

NOTES

8:1a When This picks up the sequence of the repetitive action of seal-breaking from chapter six.

8:1b there was silence The silence, which sets the stage for the action of the unit, is usually interpreted as a dramatic hush which calls attention to the awesome events which are to follow. The noun form σιγή is used, having the primary meaning of absence of all noise or sound. There are many Old Testament references to silence in the presence of God (e.g. Hab. 2:20). This is the meaning accepted in this analysis.

There is also the question about whether or not there was absence of action as well. There is nothing in the text of 8:1–5 to demand cessation of activity, and commentators have concluded that the introduction of the trumpet angels and the offering of the saints' prayers took place during the silence.

The duration of the silence, specified as ὡς ἡμιώριον 'about half an hour,' is taken to be a brief time.

8:2 the seven angels who stand before God The article used with the angels of the trumpets (τοὺς ἑπτὰ ἀγγέλους 'the seven angels') could designate them as being well known in Jewish and Christian circles, as those who stand before God. However, their individual identity is not pertinent here for understanding the text. But it is important to know that the trumpet angels are those who stand in God's presence and, therefore, are directly commanded by him.

a trumpet was given *by God* to each one of them The trumpet is used in the Old Testament for eschatological announcements (Zeph. 1:16) and in the New Testament is referred to in connection with the return of Christ (1 Cor. 15:52).

Though ἐδόθησαν 'were given' implies that God is the ultimate agent of the giving, the question is whether an intermediate agent should be represented here in the display. Because of the immediacy of the angels' position before God, it would seem appropriate to use 'God' here as agent.

8:3a stood at the altar The altar of this unit is described in terms of the incense altar in the Temple in Jerusalem. It is golden and it is set before the throne (8:3c) just as the incense altar in the Temple was in front of the Holy of Holies.

He had a golden censer This was to be used for carrying the incense in. In this instance the incense was not burned in the censer but on the altar (8:3c).

8:3b and a large quantity of incense was given to him *by God* The passive ἐδόθη 'was given' is used here. Ultimately it represents what God is doing, but the complex activity of heaven, in which all is done according to his will, may use various agents. The passive serves to keep the angel with the censer as the thematic participant.

8:3c offer it…with the prayers of all God's people In the Old Testament sacrificial system there was to be incense offered with the grain offerings (Lev. 2:1–2). There is no direction in the description of the offerings for the incense to be 'mingled' with a sacrifice and the word 'mingled' is not used here in the Greek text. It is more accurate to say that the angel offered up the incense together with the offering. The dative form ταῖς προσευχαῖς gives the associative sense that the incense is offered with the prayers in order to permeate them with its smell.

prayers 'Prayers' is kept as an abstract noun in the display since in this context the prayers must be seen in some sense as an entity if they are to be offered up to God by the angel together with the incense. Since prayer is an event, the associated events here are praying and offering incense, and so the nonfigurative representation of the first would be the saints praying to God, an action which could be visually associated with the angel offering incense to God. Of course, the offering of incense is also figurative, and could even be understood as standing for the prayers of the saints (Bruce), though this appears to be a minority opinion.

8:3d *Then he offered the incense on the altar* The action of offering and burning the incense is implied by the mention of smoke in the next verse. This segment is supplied in order to fill out the event line of the episode.

8:4 the smoke of the incense According to Mounce the cloud of fragrant smoke was symbolic of God's acceptance of the prayers.

In the next unit the prayers begin to be answered, but the complete answer does not come until the fourth act of the drama.

from where the angel had offered it The Greek says literally 'from the hand of the angel' but 'hand' is being used figuratively here, meaning 'as a result of the angel's action'.

8:5a held the censer The use of the perfect tense in εἴληφεν 'took' shows that this action is not in focus. In fact, 'held' is a better translation, since the angel already had the censer in his hand (see 8:3a).

8:5b and he threw *the contents of the censer* onto the earth Although the censer is grammatically the object of ἔβαλεν 'he threw', it is obvious that the angel did not throw the censer to the earth, but the fire which it contained. The figure is metonymy.

8:5c Thunder rumbled and reverberated, lightning flashed, and the earth shook The plurals used in the Greek for the thunder and lightning may be to indicate the intensity of the manifestation. Judgment is clearly in focus here, so that through the angel and in the cosmic disturbance, God is acting in response to the prayers of all the saints.

BOUNDARIES AND COHERENCE

The opening of the unit announces the breaking of the seventh seal, and the close coincides with that of the close of the scene. (See the notes on

5:1–8:5.) The end of the unit is signalled by a cosmic manifestation like the ones at the end of the scene of the seven trumpets (11:19) and at the end of the scene of the seven bowls (16:18-21).

Some have thought the mention of trumpets in 8:2 violates the coherence of the unit because their use is not introduced until 8:6. However, this episode is transitional in nature, since besides being the GOAL of 5:1–8:5 it also introduces the main characters of the next episode.

Unity of location provides the coherence of the unit. The action takes place in the presence of God (8:2a) and before the throne (8:3c).

PROMINENCE AND THEME

The unit has four points of natural prominence, the four OUTCOMES of the opening of the seventh seal (see Intent and paragraph pattern). The last OUTCOME consists of the cosmic manifestations which signal the time for the trumpets to announce the new series of judgments. This episode is the goal of the steps (6:1–17) which prepare the way for the outpouring of God's wrath. The theme gives the action detailed under the occasion and each OUTCOME.

ACT CONSTITUENT 8:6–11:19 (Scene: Step₂ of 4:1–16:21)

THEME: At the sounding of each of six successive trumpet blasts, woeful judgment came upon the earth and its rebellious people. Before the seventh trumpet blast I was commissioned to prophesy and mark out the worshipers of Christ. Christ then sent two witnesses to prophesy to the nations. When the seventh angel sounded his trumpet, voices from heaven declared that the Lord God and his Messiah now rule over the world and the elders declared that the time had come for God's final judgment. Then the heavenly sanctuary became open to view and cosmic manifestations of judgment occurred on earth.

MACROSTRUCTURE	CONTENTS
step₁	8:6–12 As each of the first four angels sounded their trumpets a third of the natural resources of the land, sea, fresh water, and a third of the celestial lights were destroyed.
prominence orienter	8:13 An eagle flying high in the sky announced that rebellious earth people would suffer terribly when the three remaining angels blew their trumpets.
step₂	9:1–11 When the fifth angel sounded his trumpet, terrible locusts with stings like scorpions came out from the underworld and attacked the rebellious people of the earth. When the locusts tortured them, the people longed to die, but they could not.
prominence orienter	9:12 The first tragic event has occurred, but alas two more are coming.
step₃	9:13–21 When the sixth angel blew his trumpet, a huge army of horsemen killed a third of the rebellious earth people with the fire that came out of their horses' mouths. But the rest of the people did not repent of their false worship nor of their evil practices.
interlude	10:1–11:13 A mighty angel holding a small open scroll shouted and the thunders responded. Then he swore that God would no longer delay in completing his secret purpose. When I took and ate the scroll as I was instructed, I was commanded to prophesy again about all people. Christ told me to mark out his worshipers from the nations and he appointed two witnesses to prophesy to the nations. Afterwards the beast from the underworld killed them and the nations rejoiced over their dead bodies, but God resurrected them and took them to heaven. At the same time a great earthquake occurred, causing those who survived it to become afraid and acknowledge God as awesome.
prominence orienter	11:14 The second tragic event has occurred, and the third is coming soon.
GOAL	11:15–19 When the seventh angel sounded his trumpet, voices in heaven declared that the Lord God and his Messiah now rule over the world, and the elders declared that the time had come for God's final judgment. Then the heavenly sanctuary became open to view and cosmic manifestations of judgment occurred on earth.

INTENT AND MACROSTRUCTURE

As in the series of the seals, the series of the trumpets is a *step-GOAL* pattern leading to the declaration of God's supreme power to govern the world and the beginning of final judgment. Also, just as the first four seals comprised one unit, here the first four trumpet blasts comprise *step₁*.

Preceding the second and third *steps* and the GOAL are three announcements of doom for the rebellious people of earth (8:13; 9:12; 11:14). These are treated as *prominence orienters* since they mark the units that follow them and show that they are judgments to be considered very serious indeed.

Also as with the series of the seals, there is an *interlude* (10:1–11:13) before the GOAL. This builds up dramatic tension by switching the focus and delaying the GOAL. It deals with John's prophesying, an announcement that there will be no more delay in completing God's purpose, and an account of two witnesses prophesying to the nations. It thus deals with the activity of God's people and God's protection of them.

BOUNDARIES AND COHERENCE

The judgments of the seven trumpet blasts give coherence to the unit. The unit begins at 8:6 when the trumpet angels prepare to sound their instruments. It closes at 11:19 when the cosmic manifestations respond, as in 8:5.

The three pronouncements of woe (at 8:13, 9:12 and 11:14) also give coherence to the unit.

PROMINENCE AND THEME

In a *step-GOAL* pattern both the *steps* and the GOAL are considered thematic and the GOAL to which the *steps* lead is most prominent. As in the series of the seals, the *interlude* is also prominent, with its switch of scene and participants. The three pronouncements of woe are significant because of the emphasis they provide for the units they orient, but they are not thematic in themselves.

SCENE CONSTITUENT 8:6–12 (Episode: Step₁ of 8:6–11:19)

THEME: *As each of the first four angels sounded their trumpets a third of the natural resources of the land, sea, fresh water, and a third of the celestial lights were destroyed.*	
¶PTRN RELATIONAL STRUCTURE	CONTENTS
setting	8:6 The seven angels who had the seven trumpets prepared to sound them.
⎡occasion	8:7a The first angel sounded his trumpet,
⎢ ⎡occasion	8:7b and hail and fire mixed with blood were hurled (*or*, poured down) *by God* onto the earth.
SEQUENTIAL NUCLEUS₁ —OUTCOME —OUTCOME	8:7c *As an outcome of this* [8:7b], *the fire* burned up a third of *everything on* the *dry* land, *specifically*, it burned up a third of the trees and *a third of* every kind of green plant.
⎡occasion	8:8a The second angel sounded his trumpet,
⎢ ⎡occasion	8:8b and something like a huge mountain burning with fire was hurled *by God* (*or*, fell crashing) into the sea.
SEQUENTIAL NUCLEUS₂ —OUTCOME —OUTCOME	8:8c–9 *As an outcome of this* [8:8b], a third part of the sea became blood, (9) a third of the creatures in the sea died, and a third of the ships *on the sea* were destroyed.
⎡occasion	8:10a The third angel sounded his trumpet,
⎢ ⎡occasion—'star'	8:10b and a huge star, which was burning like a torch, fell from the sky into a third of the rivers and into *a third of* the water springs.
⎢ ⎣description	8:11a The name of the star is Wormwood/Bitterness.
SEQUENTIAL NUCLEUS₃ —OUTCOME —OUTCOME	8:11b *As an outcome of the star falling*, the water in a third *of the rivers and springs* became bitter, and many people died from *drinking* the water because it had become bitter.
⎡occasion	8:12a The fourth angel sounded his trumpet,
⎢ ⎡occasion	8:12b and disaster came on a third part of the sun, a third part of the moon, and a third of the stars,
SEQUENTIAL NUCLEUS₄ —OUTCOME —OUTCOME	8:12c so that a third part of the sun, moon, and stars became dark, and during a third of the day and *a third* of the night they gave no light.

INTENT AND PARAGRAPH PATTERN

The structure of this unit is very similar to that of 6:1–8, the opening of the first four seals. Here the events consequent on the blowing of the first four trumpets have many common features, and they are distinct from the last three trumpets. They can therefore be seen as a series of sequential actions constituting the first step towards the goal of the seventh trumpet (11:15–19).

NOTES

8:7b were hurled (*or*, poured down) *by God* onto the earth The verb βάλλω 'throw' is not a usual term to express hail falling. It suggests a powerful movement, to be interpreted as supernatural, particularly in the present context. It is often translated 'hurl'. An alternate propositionalization is suggested by TEV's "came pouring down." The 'pouring' (in English at least) maintains some of the force of βάλλω and there is no need to state the agent causing the action.

8:7c a third of *everything on* the *dry* land The interpretation of γῆ 'earth' as 'the dry land' is in harmony with the fact that in 8:7–12 the land, sea, water, and sky are each mentioned separately as being affected.

***specifically*, it burned up a third of the trees, and it burned up every kind of green plant** From the standpoint of the focus on part of man's resources being destroyed, that which is burned up in 8:7c may be interpreted as the earth's vegetation in general, and specifically the fruit trees and the fodder plants.

burned up The horror of the burning is clearly in focus here, as the Greek repeats the verb κατεκάη 'was burned up' three times in the verse.

***a third of* every kind of green plant** The Greek is πᾶς χόρτος χλωρός 'all green grass,' referring to plants that provide food for domestic animals. However, 9:4 says that the locusts were forbidden to harm the grass, which implies that not all the grass on earth is meant in this verse. Morris calls attention to this, but most English versions of the text still seem to understand 'all the grass' in contrast to 'a third of the trees'. Beckwith solves the problem by saying that 'all green grass' "refers, not to that of the whole earth, but to that of the third part here spoken of". 'A third of' does occur twelve times in this unit (8:7c, 8c, 9, 10b, 11b, 12b, 12c), and is usually interpreted as a partial destruction before the final judgment. For this reason, although it does not occur in connection with the grass, it is regarded as implicit here.

BDAG lists the occurrence of πᾶς in this verse under "*every kind of*", that is, "everything belonging, in kind, to the class designated by the noun".

8:8b burning with fire Some texts do not have πυρί 'fire'. The UBS text does have it. This analysis also includes the word because it is found in many texts and may have been omitted on account of καιόμενον 'burning' which follows it, so that some copyists considered it redundant. There is also a difference in versification found in some versions. This analysis follows the UBS division, beginning verse 9 after αἷμα 'blood'.

8:9 a third of the creatures in the sea died, and a third of the ships *on the sea* were destroyed It is probably to be understood that these catastrophes happened to all sea life (both the fishes and the large sea animals such as whales) and shipping in a third of the sea. If an agent is necessary for διεφθάρησαν 'destroyed' the mountain-like object might be used.

8:11a–b The name of the star is Wormwood/Bitterness. *As ... the water ... became bitter* The plant wormwood *(Artemisia absinthium)* is used in flavourings and medicines. It is not poisonous in itself, but one extract of it is highly toxic. In most forms it has a very bitter taste, and for that reason it is used in the Old Testament as a metaphor for sorrow and anguish (Prov. 5:3–4, Lam. 3:15). In this verse the star is named after its effect on the waters, so it is not necessary to give an exact equivalent of the plant name in translation. The display therefore uses 'Wormwood/Bitterness', and then 'bitter' where the Greek has 'became wormwood'.

8:12b and disaster came on The Greek has the passive ἐπλήγη 'was struck', but translating it as an active the agent 'God struck ...' might imply a physical striking by God. However, this verb πλήσσω 'to strike' is closely connected with the noun πληγή which has the meaning 'terrible disaster', although it is traditionally translated 'plague'. It is therefore appropriate to give the verb a similar translation in this verse.

8:12c they gave no light The blow on the celestial lights is said to affect a third of them so that the smitten parts could not shine. As a result of this mankind is left in total darkness for a third of each day and a third of each night. Darkness is a common theme of judgment throughout the Bible (Exod. 10:21–23, Joel 3:15, Mark 13:24).

BOUNDARIES AND COHERENCE

Concerning the boundaries there is room for difference of opinion, because the unit begins and ends with verses that are clearly transitional. Some have taken 8:6 to be a part of 8:1–5 since the trumpets were supplied in 8:2 and that unit leads up to their sounding. However, since that unit functions as the GOAL of 5:1–8:5 the beginning of a new scene is called for at 8:6. Evidence of this is seen in 8:6 in the use of an aorist active verb (ἡτοίμασαν) with an explicit object to state that the seven angels prepared to sound their trumpets. It begins the action of the trumpet series.

At the close of the unit, some have included 8:13, but the words καὶ εἶδον, καὶ ἤκουσα 'and I saw, and I heard', occurring as they frequently do in an initial position, point to a break. Also, the flying eagle announces new woes for earth dwellers in connection with the action of the three angels who have yet to blow their trumpets. This signals a new start before the last three trumpet blasts.

Again, a look at the larger context shows strong argument for the boundaries of the unit as presented in the display. That is, in many ways 8:6–12 is like 6:1–8, which gives the detail of the opening of the first four seals, and 16:1–8 with the detail of the first four bowls. In each of the three judgment series, the first four incidents are closely related and are given in rapid succession. There is both correspondence and contrast found in comparing the three similar units.

Several coherence factors bind the unit 8:6–12:

1. The identical structure of the four *occasion–OUTCOME* sequences.
2. The use of the same formula to introduce each of the four trumpets.
3. The fact that the judgments revealed cover the totality of man's resources on land (8:7), on the sea and in the sea (8:9), in the fresh water (8:11) and in the skies (8:12).
4. The fact that each of the judgments is only partial, being the destruction of one third of the resources.

PROMINENCE AND THEME

The theme statement is based on understanding the common factor of the four units as the loss of natural resources in the human environment.

SCENE CONSTITUENT 8:13 (Propositional Cluster: Prominence orienter for 8:6–11:19)

THEME: *An eagle flying high in the sky announced that rebellious earth people would suffer terribly when the three remaining angels blew their trumpets.*	
RELATIONAL STRUCTURE	CONTENTS
orienter	8:13a I saw an eagle flying high in the sky and I heard it saying in a loud voice:
CONTENT	8:13b "Very terrible *indeed* (*or*, Terrible, terrible, terrible *indeed*) will be the suffering of the *rebellious* people who live on the earth when *each of* the three remaining angels blow their trumpets. They are about to blow them."

INTENT

The 8:13 propositional cluster functions as a prominence orienter signaling the horrible consequences of the events that are about to be recounted. There is no doubt about the expressive nature of this propositional cluster, but its basic intent must be seen in connection with the drama itself to which it lends its support, especially since the propositional cluster does not have a full paragraph pattern.

NOTES

8:13a an eagle The cardinal number ἑνός 'one' may be interpreted as the indefinite article in English. There is some textual support for the word 'angel' instead of 'eagle', but this is too slight for it even to be mentioned in the UBS apparatus.

high in the sky The Greek phrase used here for showing the position of the eagle is ἐν μεσουρανήματι 'in midheaven', that is, where the sun is at its zenith. By this means it could be seen and heard by all. The message is for all the rebellious inhabitants of the earth.

8:13b "Very terrible *indeed*..." The threefold repetition of the announcement may indicate three separate sufferings to follow, but more likely it signifies the severity and certainty of the suffering.

BDAG classifies οὐαί 'woe' generally as an interjection and this occurrence as an exclamation with accusative of the person (1c). In English 'woe' is basically an abstract noun. For this reason the display renders οὐαί according to its meaning in context rather than more literally.

will be the suffering of the *rebellious* people who live on earth The judgment is directed against the inhabitants of the earth, seen as those in rebellion against God (3:10; 6:10; 11:10; 13:8; 17:2).

They are about to blow them The reference to the fact that the three angels are about to blow their trumpets shows the introductory aspect of the announcement and its urgency.

BOUNDARIES AND COHERENCE

The unit stands alone because it has significance on a higher level than that of the episode. It does not refer to the four trumpets that have been heard but announces the three which are to follow. Coherence is seen by the single announcement of the eagle.

PROMINENCE AND THEME

Prominence is found in the words spoken by the eagle (8:13b). The theme has the orienter and what the eagle says.

SCENE CONSTITUENT 9:1–11 (Episode: Step₂ of 8:6–11:19)

THEME: When the fifth angel sounded his trumpet, terrible locusts with stings like scorpions came out from the underworld and attacked the rebellious people of the earth. When the locusts tortured them, the people longed to die, but they could not.

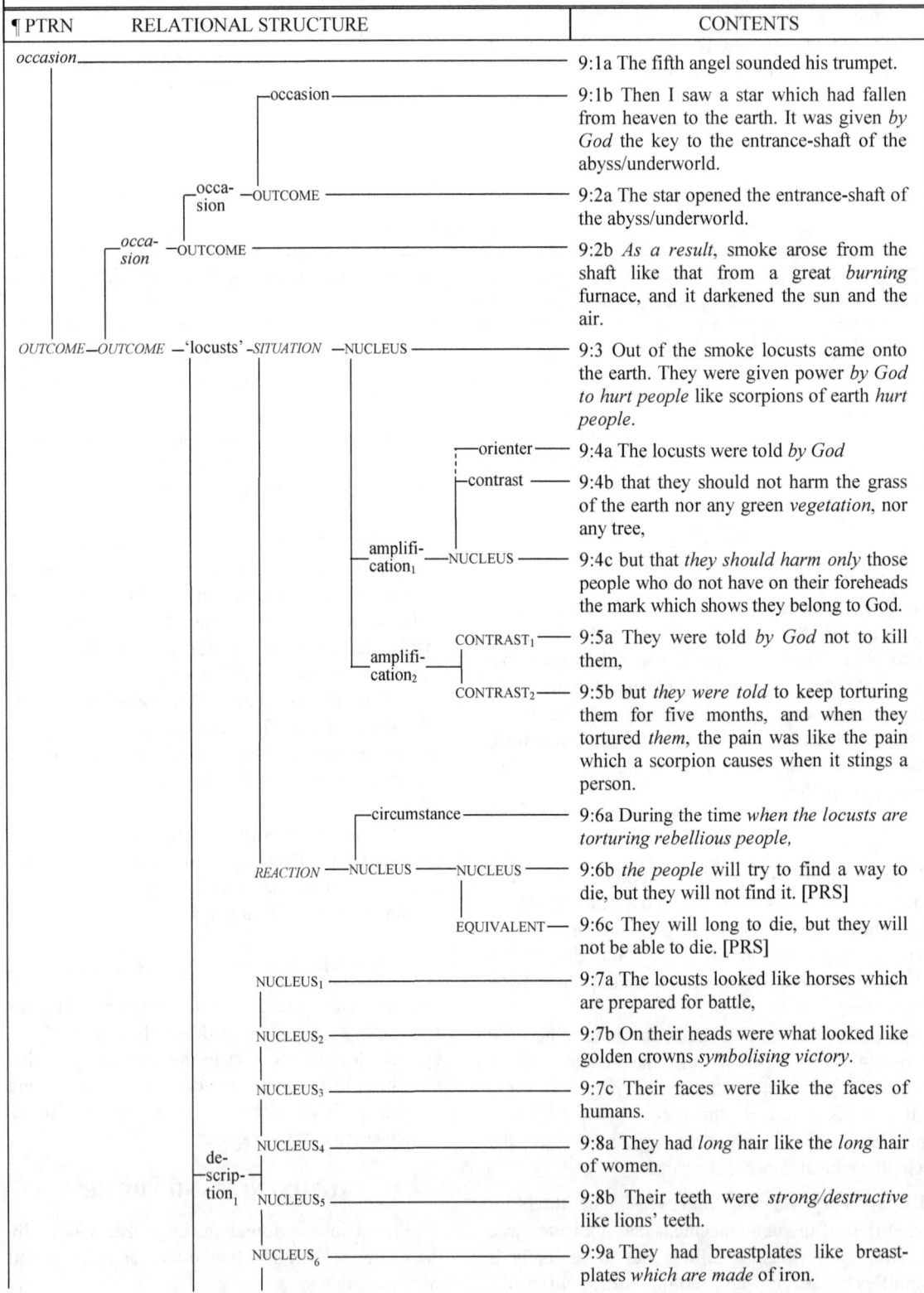

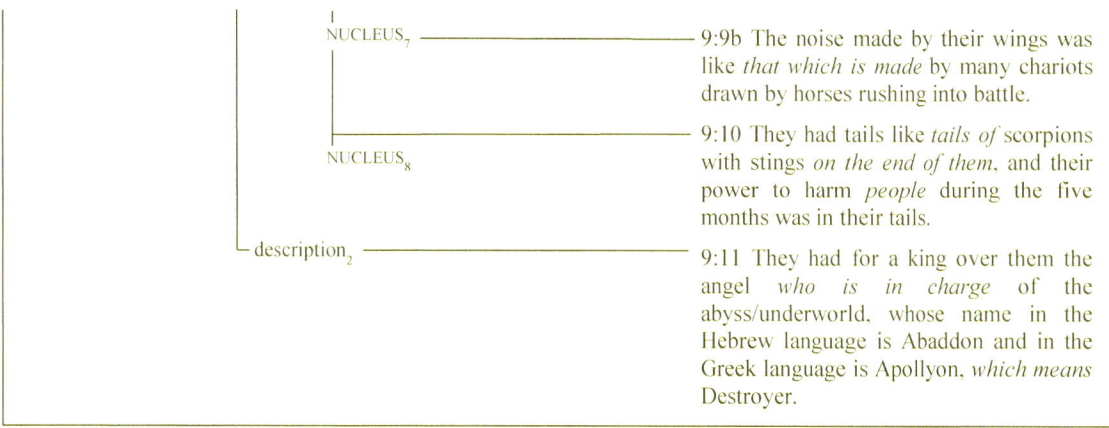

INTENT AND PARAGRAPH PATTERN

The 9:1–11 episode has an *occasion-OUTCOME* paragraph pattern indicating the consequences of the sounding of the fifth trumpet. Though the first part of the OUTCOME (9:1–3) has an *occasion–OUTCOME* structure, much of the episode is actually an amplification of the harm the locusts were allowed to do to rebellious earth people (9:4–6) and a description of their terrifying appearance (9:7–10). This suggests that at a deeper semantic level description is being used as a warning of the awful consequences of being among the rebellious earth people.

NOTES

9:1b a star From its actions it is clear that this star represents either an angel or possibly Satan himself. Isaiah 14:12 is traditionally understood as referring to Satan falling as a star from heaven. In Revelation stars have already been used to represent angels in 1:20.

There may be a problem in some languages trying to personify a star. One solution would be to say something like 'an angel who looked like a star'.

which had fallen from heaven In the Greek 'from the sky/heaven' comes before the verb 'fallen', probably indicating that this is the focal part of the description of the star. This would support the interpretation that the star represents Satan or an evil being (Alford, Moffatt).

entrance-shaft The word φρέαρ is often used for 'well' or 'pit' and in a general sense could be seen as synonymous with 'the abyss', and so TEV translates τὸ φρέαρ τῆς ἀβύσσου 'the pit/shaft of the abyss' as 'the abyss' only. However, the picture here is of a shaft leading downwards into the underworld.

abyss/underworld In Revelation the term ἄβυσσος 'abyss, depth, bottomless pit, underworld' is used seven times. In the present passage it has a ruling angel with whom destructive spirits are associated (9:11). In 11:7 it is the place from which the beast comes to fight and overcome the two witnesses. It is also the place of the beast's origin in 17:8. In 20:1–3 an angel who has the key to this place comes with a chain to bind Satan for a thousand years and imprison him there, so that during that time he may not deceive the nations.

9:3 Out of the smoke locusts came onto the earth The locusts are said to come out of the smoke as if the smoke were their vehicle, or as if the cloud of smoke turned into a huge swarm of locusts.

They were given power *by God* Mounce says, "The use of the passive voice in speaking of the release (v. 1, 'was given'), the empowering (v. 3, 'were given power'), and the limiting (v. 5, 'they were not given power to kill') of the locusts suggests that this plague, even though demonic, is under the sovereign control of God".

In certain languages 'power' is not used as an abstract noun and the concept of power in cases such as this is sometimes rendered by using the verbal form 'be able' or 'enabled'. '*God* enabled them *to hurt people* like scorpions of earth *hurt people*' would be an alternate propositionalization. However, it should be noted, both here and in the next verse, where the Greek passive ἐρρέθη αὐταῖς 'it was told to them' occurs, that focus is still on the locusts, not on God.

9:5a–b They were told *by God* not to kill them, but *they were told* to keep torturing them The use of the conjunction ἀλλά 'but' and the fact that the two segments it connects are not a simple negative-positive statement show that the first command, not to kill people, is just as important as the second. This is significant in view of 9:6.

9:5b for five months The limitation of five months gives the idea of continuous attack during that period. It could be interpreted as a limited period like the limited extent of other judgments announced by the trumpet angels. Added importance is given to this limitation by its repetition in 9:10.

9:6 The significance of the future tense in this verse is debated. It may be indicating that this is a new statement following the amplification of 9:3 in 9:5. This would be confirmed by the use of the time phrase 'in those days' at the beginning of the verse. It is certainly noticeable that the locusts' attacking people is not actually related as an event in this unit. It is simply assumed in 9:5b and in this verse. Thus in 9:6 John describes not what he sees in the vision but what will happen as the locusts carry out the commissioning they received in 9:4–5.

9:6c they will not be able to die The frustration of not being able to find escape in death is highlighted by being repeated and written in poetic form. The Greek text has two parallel figurative forms:

1. People seek death, but can never find it.
2. They long to die, but death flees from them.

In the first sentence, 'death' might be seen as personification or, at least, as an object which cannot be found. In the second, 'death' is personified in that it flees from one. Both of these are rendered completely nonfiguratively in the display, since in this type of figure there is nothing in the content of the figures themselves that is lost by rendering them nonfiguratively. What is lost is the effect produced by the rhetorical form and this should be rebuilt in the translation into any language, if possible.

9:8a *long* hair like the *long* hair of women The long flowing hair of a woman suggests the horse's mane. The point of comparison seems to be the length and free flow in the wind.

9:8b their teeth were *strong/destructive* like lions' teeth For most languages it may not be necessary to supply a word like 'strong' or 'destructive' here to make clear the point of similarity, except where lions are not well known.

9:9a They had breastplates like breastplates *which are made* of iron The Greek word θώραξ, may mean either 'breastplate' or 'chest'. In the context of 'horses prepared for battle' it would be likely for John to interpret what he saw (i.e. the first occurrence of θώραξ) as breastplates. Some English versions translate this first use of the word in this verse as 'chests' or 'scales', translating specific to the locust's scales. However, it is known that war horses were often protected by iron breastplates.

9:10 They had tails like *tails of* scorpions, with stings *on the end of them* In the description, 9:7 does not use finite verbs in the Greek. In 9:8 and 9 three verbs in the past tense are used. But the description becomes more vivid in 9:10a with the use of the present active ἔχουσιν 'they have.' This highlights the most important part of the description of the locusts, namely that their power to hurt people is in the sting on the end of their tails, like scorpions.

9:11 They had for a king over them Again the use of the historic present tense (cf. 9:10) highlights the identity of the locusts' ruler as the angel of the underworld. The relationship confirms the demonic origin of the locusts. The name given for the ruler in Greek is the present participle of the verb ἀπόλλυμι 'to destroy.' In English this would be translated "one who destroys". The name is expressed in both Hebrew and Greek for emphasis. The identification is clearly spelled out and anticipates the destruction in the next episode.

BOUNDARIES AND COHERENCE

The opening of the 9:1–11 episode is indicated by the sounding of the trumpet of the fifth angel. The episode closes in 9:11 with the identification of the king of the locusts, after which comes the second woe (9:12), announcing the last two trumpets, and the blowing of the sixth trumpet (9:13). The locusts and their attack on rebellious people are what gives coherence to the unit.

PROMINENCE AND THEME

The OUTCOME of the attack of the locusts is in natural prominence. The elaborate description of them and the harm they did has marked prominence because of its length and startling imagery, and so is also mentioned in the theme. The theme also includes the paragraph-level *occasion* of the sounding of the trumpet and mention of the source of the locusts, which is significant.

SCENE CONSTITUENT 9:12 (Propositional Cluster: Prominence orienter for 8:6–11:19)

THEME: *The first tragic event has occurred, but alas two more are coming.*	
RELATIONAL STRUCTURE	CONTENTS
┌─grounds ────────	9:12a The first tragic event is past.
└─CONCLUSION ────	9:12b Be aware that two tragic events are still coming after this.

INTENT

As with the 8:13 propositional cluster, this one in 9:12 functions as a prominence orienter signalling the horrible consequences of the events that are about to be recounted. See the Intent note for 8:13.

NOTES

9:12a There is no speech orienter for the statement in 9:12. This statement could be taken as also spoken by the eagle as in the similar announcement in 8:13. However, since there is no orienter here, it is best to bypass the question of who the speaker might be. The focus is on the statement itself.

9:12b Be aware We would expect that the announcement of the last two tragic events would have some connotational or rhetorical force. This is to some extent communicated in the word οὐαί 'woe' itself but also is being communicated with the use of ἰδού, which in this context might be translated as 'be aware that' or 'but alas'.

BOUNDARIES AND COHERENCE

The coherence of this unit is evident from the single topic of tragic events in sequence. It has significance on a higher level than that of the episode and so does not belong in the same paragraph as the episode before it or after it.

PROMINENCE AND THEME

The CONCLUSION of this unit is marked for prominence both by the emphasis marker ἰδού and by the historic present tense of the verb 'is coming'. The grounds is also included in the theme since it marks the place of this unit in the section 8:6–11:19.

SCENE CONSTITUENT 9:13–21 (Episode: Step₃ of 8:6–11:19)

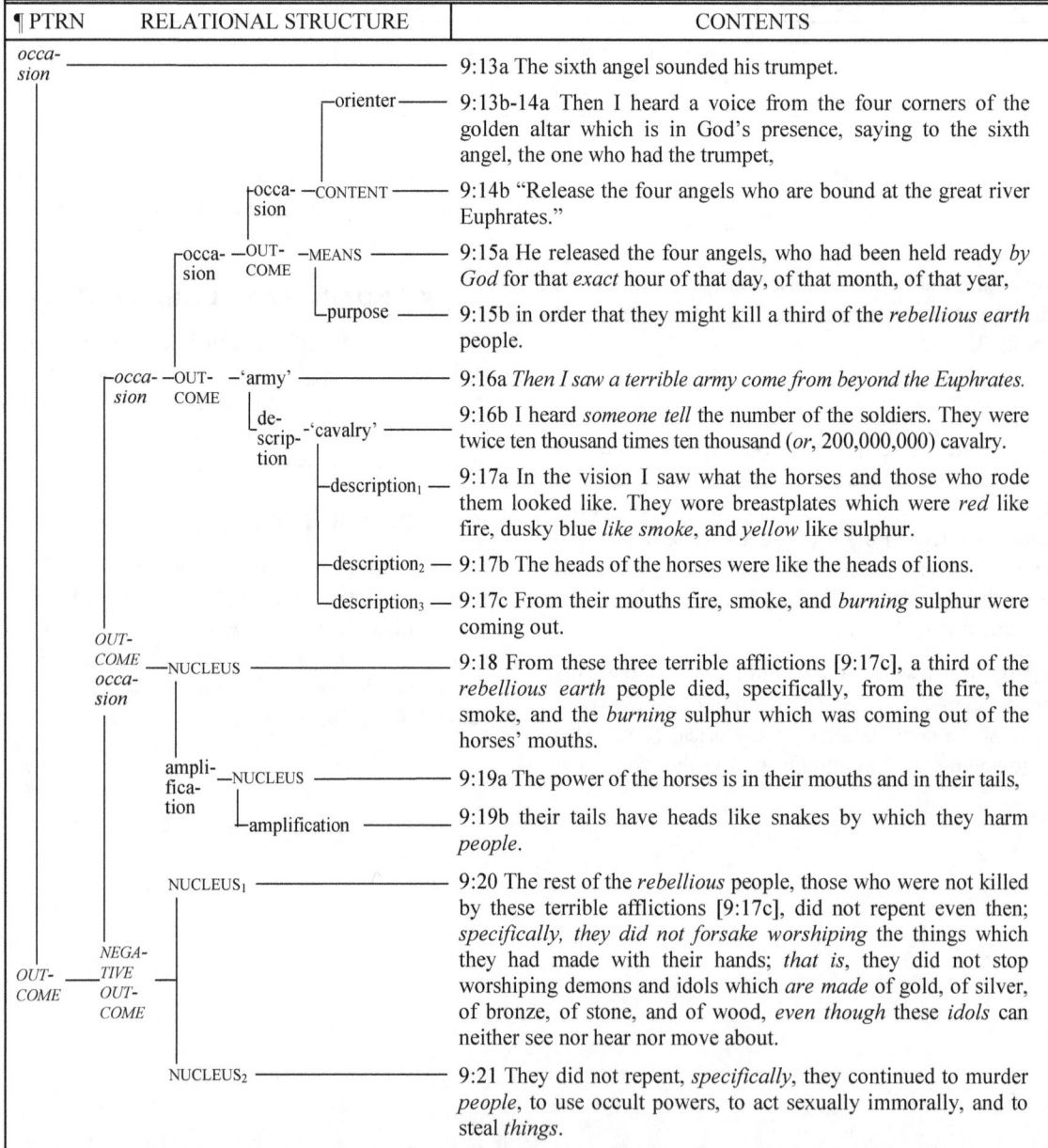

INTENT AND PARAGRAPH PATTERN

As in other episodes where a trumpet is blown or a seal is opened, the 9:13–21 episode has an overall *occasion-OUTCOME* paragraph pattern, the *OUTCOME* being occasioned by the blowing of the trumpet. This in itself shows that God's sovereignty is at work, that he has overall control of the events taking place and their timing.

Within the *OUTCOME* itself there is also *occasion–OUTCOME* patterning with the killing of one third of rebellious earth people (9:18) as the prominent *OUTCOME*, followed by a *NEGATIVE OUTCOME* (9:20–21). This is marked as unexpected, and thus has marked prominence in the episode. Instead of repenting of their idolatry and sin as would be expected, the rebellious people continued right on doing the awful things listed.

NOTES

9:13b a voice from the four corners of the golden altar Some manuscripts do not have τεσσάρων 'four' modifying κεράτων 'horns'. The text of Hodges and Farstad accepts it, and the UBS Committee has bracketed it, giving it a "C" rating. Some versions translate τῶν κεράτων here as 'horns' (its literal meaning) and some as 'corners'. The reason for this is that there was a horn-like projection on each of the four corners of the altar. Translating more generically as 'corners' may give a clearer idea of the position from which the voice came. For languages where it is difficult to collocate one voice with four positions of origin, a rendering of 'a voice coming from between the four corners of the golden altar' (cf. NEB) may be appropriate.

9:14b the four angels who are bound at the great river Euphrates These angels are generally considered to be Satan's on the basis of their having been restrained until God's chosen time. The connection they have with the destructive cavalry is not clear, but their release is the occasion of the attack which kills one third of the rebels. However, within the Roman Empire, and among the Jews in particular, the land beyond the Euphrates was regularly feared as the source of barbarian attacks on the civilized world. This is clearly the background to this part of John's vision.

9:15a held ready *by God* for that *exact* hour of that day, of that month, of that year The exactness of the hour of release shows God's control. Note that while God's control is so pervasively in focus in the Revelation that he may be seen as the agent keeping ready these four "angels" who may well be angels of Satan, it is still highly important and relevant to the message of the book to clearly maintain the distinction between good and evil, between God and Satan. It is necessary to keep this in mind in determining agency and verbs to be used in translation into other languages.

9:16a *Then I saw an army come from beyond the Euphrates* Superficially there seems to be a gap in the narrative between 9:15, the release of the angels of destruction at the Euphrates, and 9:16, John being told the number of the soldiers. However, this can be explained by the fact that for John's readers the unleashing of murderous forces at the Euphrates would inevitably imply the appearance of a terrible invading force. See the note on 9:14b. This is confirmed by the use of the article in τῶν στρατευμάτων 'the soldiers'. Aune says, "the author intends us to understand that these angels have been restraining the armies of various nations from devastating the civilized world".

9:16b twice ten thousand times ten thousand (*or*, 200,000,000) John's remark that he heard the number of the cavalry is like that in 7:4, where the symbolic number is usually interpreted as all inclusive. BDAG comments, "An indefinite number of incalculable immensity is indicated". The alternate rendering 'two hundred million' occurs in the display. Note, however, that exact numbers are not in focus.

9:17a those who rode them The beings mounted on the horses do not seem to participate directly in the slaughter. Since this is a demonic attack the riders are probably not humans.

They wore breastplates which were *red* like fire, dusky blue *like smoke,* and *yellow* like sulphur It is not completely clear whether both the horses and the riders wore breastplates, or just the riders. Instead of telling what the breastplates are made of, the description gives their colour, which may be a reflection on metal of the fire, smoke, and sulphur from the horses' mouths.

For ὑακίνθινος Moulton and Milligan in the *The Vocabulary of the Greek New Testament* give a "dusky blue colour". Swete says, "Here ὑακίνθινος is doubtless meant to describe the blue smoke of a sulphurous flame".

The third word used in describing the breastplates is θειώδης, which BDAG glosses as 'sulphurous', and so the display rendering of '*yellow* like sulphur'.

9:17c From their mouths fire, smoke and *burning* sulphur were coming out Here attention switches from the horses' heads to what was coming out of their mouths. Obviously it was the fumes and flames of burning sulphur. Ladd says, "Their terror-inspiring appearance is emphasized by the sulphurous, fiery smoke that poured from the mouths of these beasts".

9:18 The structure of the Greek sentence, with asyndeton and fronting of the phrase 'from these three…' shows that the writer is here switching from the description of the cavalry back to the main events of the narrative.

From these three terrible afflictions The term πληγή, sometimes translated as "plague", occurs several times in the book. Its first and literal meaning is 'a blow', but it also has the figurative sense 'a blow of fate, misfortune', often in both secular and biblical literature with the idea that it is from God.

9:19a power In this context 'power' is used as an abstract noun. To clarify it in a language which does not have an equivalent an alternate rendering for the display could be as follows: 'The way the horses harm *people* is by means of their using their mouths and their tails'.

9:19b their tails have heads like snakes by which they harm *people* It is said that the tails with heads of snakes are a means of harming people. As already specified in 9:18, it was the fire, smoke, and sulphur that killed a third of the rebels. Some commentators emphasize a distinction between the harm of the tails and the slaughter from the horses' mouths. The 'harm' if seen as distinct could be that inflicted on the two thirds of people who were not killed.

9:20 The rest ... did not repent even then Although a NEGATIVE OUTCOME would usually not have prominence, here it is unexpected and prominent. It is marked as such in the Greek by the word order (preposed subject), by the repetition of the subject ('the rest ..., those who...'), and by οὐδέ 'not even then' (as in Matt. 21:32, Luke 23:40).

the things which they had made with their hands This is taken to refer to the idols in terms often used in the Old Testament in irony (Deut. 4:28; Ps. 115:4–8). Many take the immoral acts listed in 9:21 to have resulted from the false worship.

9:21 occult powers The word φάρμακον occurs in several related forms in the New Testament. Generally it refers to a use of occult powers. Abbott-Smith gives a first meaning as the use of medicines, drugs, or spells. Mounce says that φάρμακον "refers to witchcraft and the use of magic potions which were a part of heathen idolatry".

BOUNDARIES AND COHERENCE

The 9:13–21 episode begins, as others in the scene, with the announcement that the angel in sequence blew his trumpet. This is the sixth angel. It closes with the detail of the negative outcome of the trial to which the rebellious earth people were subjected at the blowing of the sixth trumpet. A new setting and new characters are introduced immediately in the chapter which follows: an angel other than the seven trumpet angels appears, and the events centre around him and his announcement rather than direct reference to judgment as in this episode.

Coherence is evident in the unit on the basis of an *occasion*-OUTCOME sequence and by the fact that one group of people are being dealt with. The action is all described in terms of its effect on the rebellious earth people, even though the usual longer descriptive phrase is not used of them here.

PROMINENCE AND THEME

The *occasion* which begins the sequence of events in the episode is the sounding of the trumpet by the sixth angel. This angel is commanded to release the agents of the judgment which is to come on the rebellious people in order to show whether or not they will accept the opportunity to repent. The OUTCOME, 9:18, the death of one third of the people, is given marked prominence by the lengthy description of the cavalry (9:16–17), which slows down the narrative before it. The redundant repetitions in the wording of 9:18–19 then build up the tension before the unexpected outcome of 9:20–21, the refusal of the survivors to repent, which has marked prominence (see the note). The theme gives the episode's overall *occasion*, the OUTCOME in 9:18 and the NEGATIVE OUTCOME.

SCENE CONSTITUENT 10:1–11:13 (Episode cluster: Interlude of 8:6–11:19)

THEME: A mighty angel holding a small open scroll shouted and the thunders responded. Then he swore that God would no longer delay in completing his secret purpose. When I took and ate the scroll as I was instructed, I was commanded to prophesy again about all people. Christ told me to mark out his worshipers from the nations and he appointed two witnesses to prophesy to the nations. Afterwards the beast from the underworld killed them and the nations rejoiced over their dead bodies, but God resurrected them and took them to heaven. At the same time a great earthquake occurred, causing those who survived it to become afraid and acknowledge God as awesome.

MACROSTRUCTURE	CONTENTS
NUCLEUS₁	10:1–11 A mighty angel holding a small open scroll shouted and the thunders responded, but a voice from heaven prohibited me from recording what they said. The angel swore that the living Creator of the universe would no longer delay in completing his secret purpose. When I was ordered by the heavenly voice, I took the open scroll from the angel. When I had eaten it as I was instructed, I was commanded to prophesy again about all people.
NUCLEUS₂	11:1–13 Christ told me to mark out his worshipers from the nations and he appointed two witnesses to prophesy to the nations during a limited time. Then the beast from the underworld killed them and the nations rejoiced over their dead bodies. But God resurrected his witnesses and took them to heaven, and at the same time a great earthquake occurred, causing those who survived it to become afraid and acknowledge God as awesome.

INTENT AND MACROSTRUCTURE

Both the structure and the focus of this interlude are parallel to those of the interlude 7:1–17. It is a two-part narrative focusing on God's people and providing encouragement for them. Also, as in that previous interlude, John himself plays a part in the narrative.

BOUNDARIES AND COHERENCE

The boundaries of this interlude are clearly marked by its being sandwiched between the events of the sixth and seventh trumpets. At 10:1 new participants are introduced, a mighty angel and John himself. The end of the unit is followed by the third 'woe' and a switch of scene from earth back to events in heaven.

Coherence within the unit is provided by John's participation in both, and by the repeated references to prophesying (10:7, 11; 11:6, 10).

PROMINENCE AND THEME

The two elements of the unit are equally prominent, and so the theme consists of a summary of them.

EPISODE CLUSTER CONSTITUENT 10:1–11 (Episode cluster: Nucleus₁ of 10:1–11:13)

THEME: A mighty angel holding a small open scroll shouted and the thunders responded, but a voice from heaven prohibited me from recording what they said. The angel swore that the living Creator of the universe would no longer delay in completing his secret purpose. When I was ordered by the heavenly voice, I took the open scroll from the angel. When I had eaten it as I was instructed, I was commanded to prophesy again about all people.

MACROSTRUCTURE	CONTENTS
NUCLEUS₁	10:1–7 A mighty angel holding a small open scroll shouted and the thunders responded, but a voice from heaven prohibited me from recording what they said. The angel swore that the living Creator of the universe would no longer delay in completing his secret purpose.
NUCLEUS₂	10:8–11 When I was ordered by the heavenly voice, I took the open scroll from the angel. When I had eaten it as I was instructed, I was commanded to prophesy again about all people.

INTENT AND MACROSTRUCTURE

The components of the 10:1–11 episode cluster are in a conjoined relationship, as is shown by the use of πάλιν 'again' in 10:8 to link them.

There are two significant related points in the episode cluster. Both answer critical questions raised either explicitly or implicitly in the discourse. The first question was asked overtly by the martyred saints in 6:10: "How long will it be until you judge those who live on the earth?" In 6:11 another group is mentioned for whom the martyred saints must wait, so a second question not actually asked but certainly in the minds of John's readers is: "What is to be the activity of the second group?" The oath of the angel gives the answer to the first question by proclaiming that there shall be no further delay in final judgment (10:6b). John as representative of the second group (1:9) shows that they provide the answer to the second question in being witnesses (10:11b), as he eats and assimilates the little scroll. These answers are presented respectively in the first and second episodes of this cluster.

BOUNDARIES AND COHERENCE

All of chapter 10 revolves around the scroll which the mighty angel carries: βιβλαρίδιον in 10:2, 9, and 10, βιβλίον in 10:8. The mighty angel is introduced in 10:1 and is last mentioned in 10:10. A voice from heaven speaks in 10:4, 8 and (probably) 11. Chapter 11 begins with a new object, the measuring rod.

PROMINENCE AND THEME

Since the two episodes in the episode cluster are in a conjoined relationship they are equally naturally prominent and so the theme of the cluster is taken from them both.

EPISODE CLUSTER CONSTITUENT 10:1–7 (Episode: Nucleus₁ of 10:1–11)

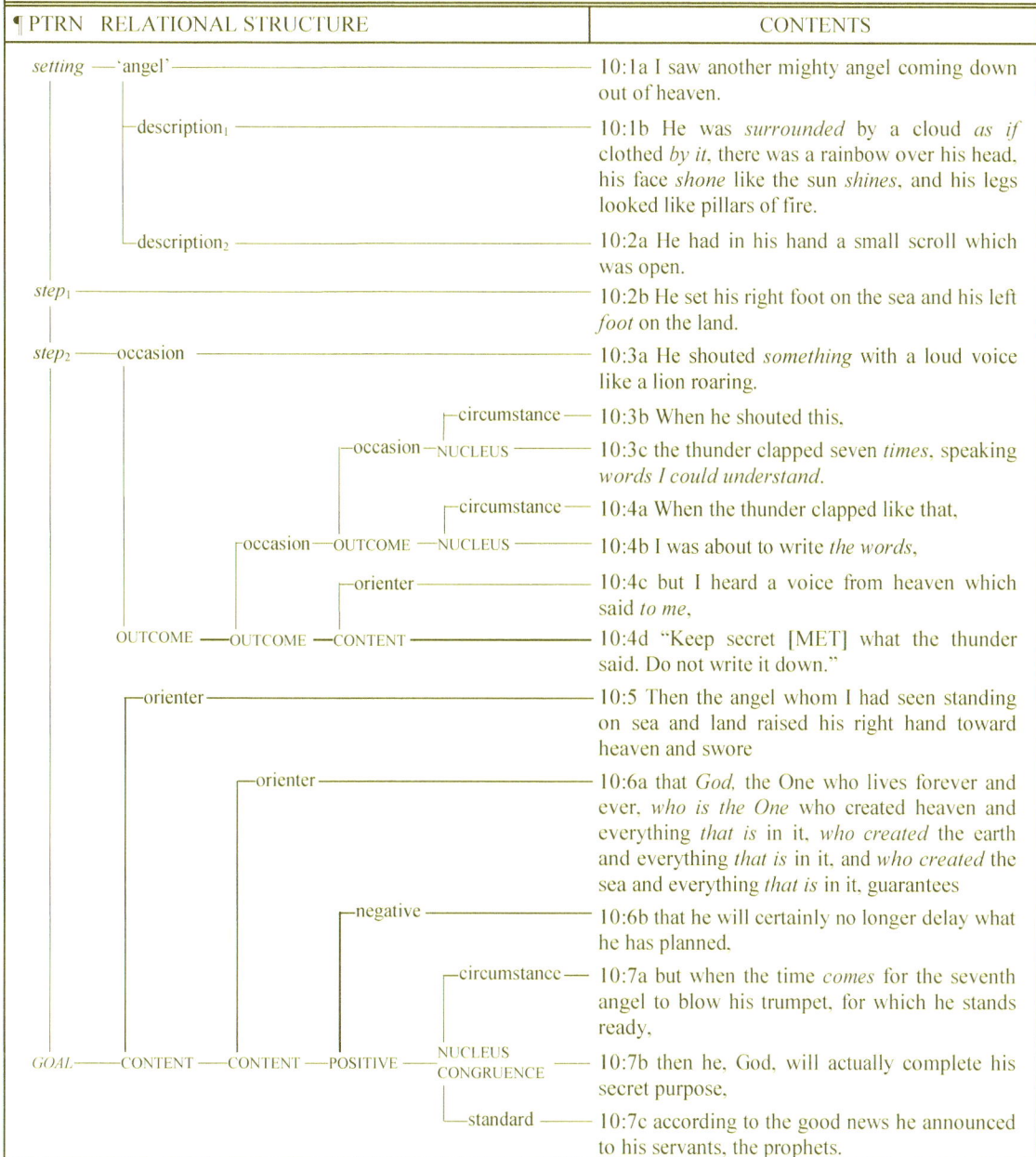

INTENT AND PARAGRAPH PATTERN

The 10:1–7 episode has a *step-GOAL* pattern as the mighty angel, who John sees coming down from heaven, sets his right foot on the sea and his left on the land, and makes two announcements, the second of which reveals that God will no longer delay the fulfilling of his purposes.

Note that there are two timelines in this episode. One is the *step-GOAL* action of the mighty angel. The other is the occasion-OUTCOME interaction between the thunder, John, and the voice from heaven in 10:3b–4d, occasioned by the shout of the angel in 10:3a.

NOTES

10:1a another mighty angel The adjective is in the predicate position without the article, presenting an additional statement about the angel and emphasizing his strength. Some have identified the angel with Christ because of this description. But there are several reasons against this idea. He is called "another," whereas Christ is unique, and in Revelation Christ is never called an angel. Also, the oath of the angel would not be appropriate from a divine being.

10:1b He was *surrounded* by a cloud *as if clothed by it* The angel's description indicates his having come from the presence of God. The cloud around him and the comparison with fiery pillars call to mind God's protection and guidance of his people in the wilderness (Exod. 13:21–22). The rainbow was also a symbol of God's goodness.

10:2a He had in his hand The use of the verb marks this as the most important part of the description.

a small scroll which was open The perfect participle ἠνεῳγμένον 'having been opened' seems to emphasize the aspect of openness, which is in contrast to the sealed message of the thunders.

10:2b He set his right foot on the sea and his left *foot* on the land Some have called attention to the size of the angel necessary for this position. But in a symbolic composition it is hardly necessary to stress this point. In the first place, his position accords well with the majesty of his description. Also, it is in harmony with his swearing by the Creator of the universe (10:6a) and with the universal application of John's prophecy (10:11).

10:3a The angel's shout is an event on the main timeline of the episode, but it occasions a subsidiary timeline of actions by secondary participants. These actions have an essentially negative conclusion, in that John is told not to write what he hears. For these reasons the occasion is here equally prominent with its outcome.

10:3c the thunder clapped seven *times*, speaking *words I could understand* Thunder is mentioned several times in the book (4:5; 8:5; 10:3–4; 11:19; 16:18; there are other references where a sound is said to be like thunder). The first occurrence is in the setting of Act 2 where the heavenly throne is described. The three others outside those here in chapter 10 are clearly in connection with the administration of judgment. Because of these other contexts we expect the occurrences here to have to do with judgment, though the command to seal their utterance restrains speculation. It is evident that they spoke articulately because John was about to write what was said. The sealing of their response shows a reserve in the mind and purpose of God regarding further revelation. In 10:8 the voice that commanded John to take the scroll is the same voice from heaven that prohibited the recording of the voices of the thunders. Both incidents have to do with a direct command to John, which in this context must be from God.

The rendering in the display seeks to maintain a balance between the figurative imagery and how it might be described in more natural, and thus more easily transferable, terms. An alternate would be 'The thunder clapped/roared seven *times*. The sound of the thunder was *like a person* speaking'.

10:4d Keep secret The Greek is σφράγισον 'seal up', but if taken literally this could imply that something was written down and had to be sealed. However, in view of the following command it is clearly a metaphor for keeping something secret (see BDAG, and CEV, NLT).

10:5 the angel whom I had seen standing The fact that the subject comes first in the Greek sentence shows that at this point narration returns to the angel, who now gives the detail of the main purpose for which he had come.

10:6a-b and he swore that *God*, the One who lives forever and ever . . . guarantees that *he* will *certainly* no longer delay Swearing by God here may well have the sense that God is the one in whom lies the certainty of the acts implied in 'There will be no more delay' and 'the mystery of God will be accomplished'. This is more in focus here than 'swearing by God' in the sense of 'God knows that I am telling the truth'. The description of God as eternally existing and as the Creator of the universe argues for this sense of 'swear'.

he* will *certainly* no longer delay *what he has planned Clearly the meaning of χρόνος 'time' is 'delay' rather than 'time in contrast to eternity'. The conjunction ἀλλά 'but' immediately following and the statement it introduces confirm this point. Heb. 10:37 uses the verbal form χρονίζω as meaning 'to delay.' Here and in Rev. 2:21 the idea of a time of waiting is in mind. The connection with the rest period of 6:11 is important.

There is a question as to what event or events are no longer to be delayed. Two clues to the answer follow:

1. The most common use of ἀλλά in the New Testament is to mark the POSITIVE side of a negative-POSITIVE construction, a construction in which the two sides are in some sense equivalent. In this case, then, it is the consummating of the secret purposes of God that is to be delayed no longer.
2. The delay is to end 'in the days when the seventh angel sounds his trumpet'. It would seem appropriate to consider the message announced at the blowing of the seventh trumpet (11:15–18) to reveal what the consummation will consist of. It includes God taking his mighty power and reigning, his judging of the rebels, and his rewarding of God's servants (see Beasley-Murray).

10:7a when the time *comes* for the seventh angel to blow his trumpet The Greek text uses 'in the days of,' a phrase frequently used in the New Testament, which may refer to a period of time as in Luke 17:26.

10:7b then ... actually This translates καί at the beginning of the clause, which serves to confirm, or emphasise, the action of the verb.

his secret purpose The phrase τὸ μυστήριον τοῦ θεοῦ 'the mystery of God' is interpreted to be God's plan for his creation throughout all time. It is a secret gradually unfolded by God's revelation in prophecy and its fulfilment.

10:7c the good news he announced to his servants The word translated 'good news announced' is of interest because it is the word used of the Gospel, that is, εὐαγγελίζω 'to announce good news.' This points not only to the judgment but to the triumph as well.

BOUNDARIES AND COHERENCE

The episode begins with John's seeing another mighty angel coming down from heaven carrying an open scroll. While all of chapter 10 has to do with the scroll, 10:1–7 are in a *step-GOAL* pattern as the angel comes with the purpose of making an announcement to the whole world, not just to John himself. The unit 10:8–11 has an *occasion-OUTCOME* pattern as the angel interacts with John.

PROMINENCE AND THEME

In 10:3b and 10:4a the use of 'tail-head' linkages slows down the narration of the events, as does the non-event of 10:4b. This gives marked prominence to the second *step*. In 10:5–6 the descriptions of the angel and of God again slow down the narrative and give added prominence to the GOAL that follows, the contents of the angel's affirmation. The theme therefore consists of the second *step*, including the OUTCOME occasioned by it, and the GOAL.

EPISODE CLUSTER CONSTITUENT 10:8–11 (Episode: Nucleus₂ of 10:1–11)

THEME: When I was ordered by the heavenly voice, I took the open scroll from the angel. When I had eaten it as I was instructed, I was commanded to prophesy again about all people.

¶ PTRN RELATIONAL STRUCTURE	CONTENTS
┌─ orienter ───	10:8a The voice I had heard from heaven spoke to me again and said:
┌─ proposal ── CONTENT ───	10:8b "Go and take the scroll which is open in the hand of the angel who is standing on the sea and the land."
occasion ── EXECUTION ───	10:9a I went to the angel and asked him to give me the small scroll.
┌─ orienter ───	10:9b He said to me,
┌─ proposal ── CONTENT ───	10:9c "Take it and eat it up. It will make your stomach bitter/sour, but in your mouth it will taste sweet like honey *tastes*."
OUTCOME ── EXECUTION ───	10:10 I took the small scroll from the hand of the angel and ate it up. In my mouth it *did indeed taste* sweet like honey *tastes*, and when I had eaten it, it made my stomach bitter.
┌─ orienter ───	10:11a I was told *by the voice from heaven*,
SEQUEL ── CONTENT ───	10:11b "You must prophesy again about many people *groups*, many nations, *speakers of* many languages, and many kings."

INTENT AND PARAGRAPH PATTERN

In the 10:8–11 episode, the interaction between the voice from heaven, John, and the mighty angel produces an *occasion-OUTCOME* paragraph pattern in which proposal-EXECUTION stimulus-response activity is significant. 10:11 is labelled SEQUEL since it reveals the meaning of the action of eating the little scroll which is both sweet and bitter.

NOTES

10:8a The voice I had heard from heaven This is the voice that spoke in 10:4c.

10:9a asked him to give me the small scroll Even though John had been told to go and get the scroll, he had to use his initiative in asking for it. The importance of this point is that John is acting volitionally even in his trance.

10:9b He said The historical present λέγει 'he says' is used in the Greek in order to highlight the execution of this command in 10:10.

10:9c eat it up In both references (10:9c, 10) the intensive verb κατεσθίω 'eat up/devour' is used, indicating that the scroll is to be completely consumed. The contrast between the sweet and the bitter shows that the messenger rejoices in God's promise but reacts in compassion for those who do not accept God's deliverance. Ezek. 2:8–3:3 relates a similar vision of eating a scroll containing a message from God.

10:10 In my mouth it *did indeed taste* … made my stomach bitter The order of reference here, 'mouth … stomach' is switched from that in 10:9c 'stomach … mouth.' This probably shows John is affirming that things did indeed turn out as the angel had said. This is also confirmed by the use of καί 'and/indeed' three times in this verse.

when I had eaten it This redundant repetition of reference to the eating serves to emphasise the bitter reaction.

10:11a I was told *by the voice from heaven* The verb used in the Greek text is an indefinite plural, λέγουσιν 'they say', similar to the English expression "it was said". Though the commission is not unambiguously attributed to the voice from heaven which spoke in 10:4 and 8, it cannot be denied that God is the source of the command. It would seem that since the voice from heaven is the originator of the action regarding the consuming of the scroll, it is this voice that would be the most logical to be used if an agent of the speaking must be supplied in translation. It is not because the speaker is unimportant that the indefinite form λέγουσιν 'they say' is used.

10:11b You must prophesy again BDAG gives the primary sense of προφητεύω as 'prophesy', meaning 'to proclaim a divine revelation'. The nature and content of the prophecy are not specified here. This shows that this episode is designed to point forward to the events that follow.

about This is the usual translation of the preposition ἐπί here, although some commentators (Aune, Beale) think it means 'against'. BDAG classifies it as introducing those to whom something happens. This is understandable because it gives the inclusive list of rebellious earth people for whom judgment is imminent.

many people *groups*, **many nations,** *speakers of* **many languages, and many kings** The fourfold classification of people also occurs in 5:9; 7:9; 11:9; 13:7; 14:6; 17:15, with various modifications. The list here is the only one which includes kings. It may be looking ahead to the political aspect of the judgment which deals with kings in chapter 17.

BOUNDARIES AND COHERENCE

The opening boundary of the 10:8–11 episode has been discussed under the preceding episode (10:1–7), while the closing boundary has been discussed under the episode cluster (10:1–11). Its coherence is indicated by the *occasion-OUTCOME-SEQUEL* paragraph pattern structure and the focus on the small scroll.

PROMINENCE AND THEME

Most naturally prominent in this episode are the OUTCOME and SEQUEL. However, the first proposal, which is a type of occasion, is prominent in that it is a command and is from God. The second proposal is less prominent since it repeats the command of taking the scroll, and other features of it are repeated in the EXECUTION in 10:10

Several devices in 10:8-9 serve to slow down the narrative and give marked prominence to the OUTCOME in 10:10. These include the description of the angel in 10:8b, repeated from 10:2b, the two proposal-EXECUTION structures, where each EXECUTION repeats the information from the proposal, and the historical present tense in 10:9b.

EPISODE CLUSTER CONSTITUENT 11:1–13 (Episode: Nucleus₂ of 10:1–11:13)

THEME: Christ told me to mark out his worshipers from the nations and he appointed two witnesses to prophesy to the nations during a limited time. Then the beast from the underworld killed them and the nations rejoiced over their dead bodies. But God resurrected his witnesses and took them to heaven, and at the same time a great earthquake occurred, causing those who survived it to become afraid and acknowledge God as awesome.

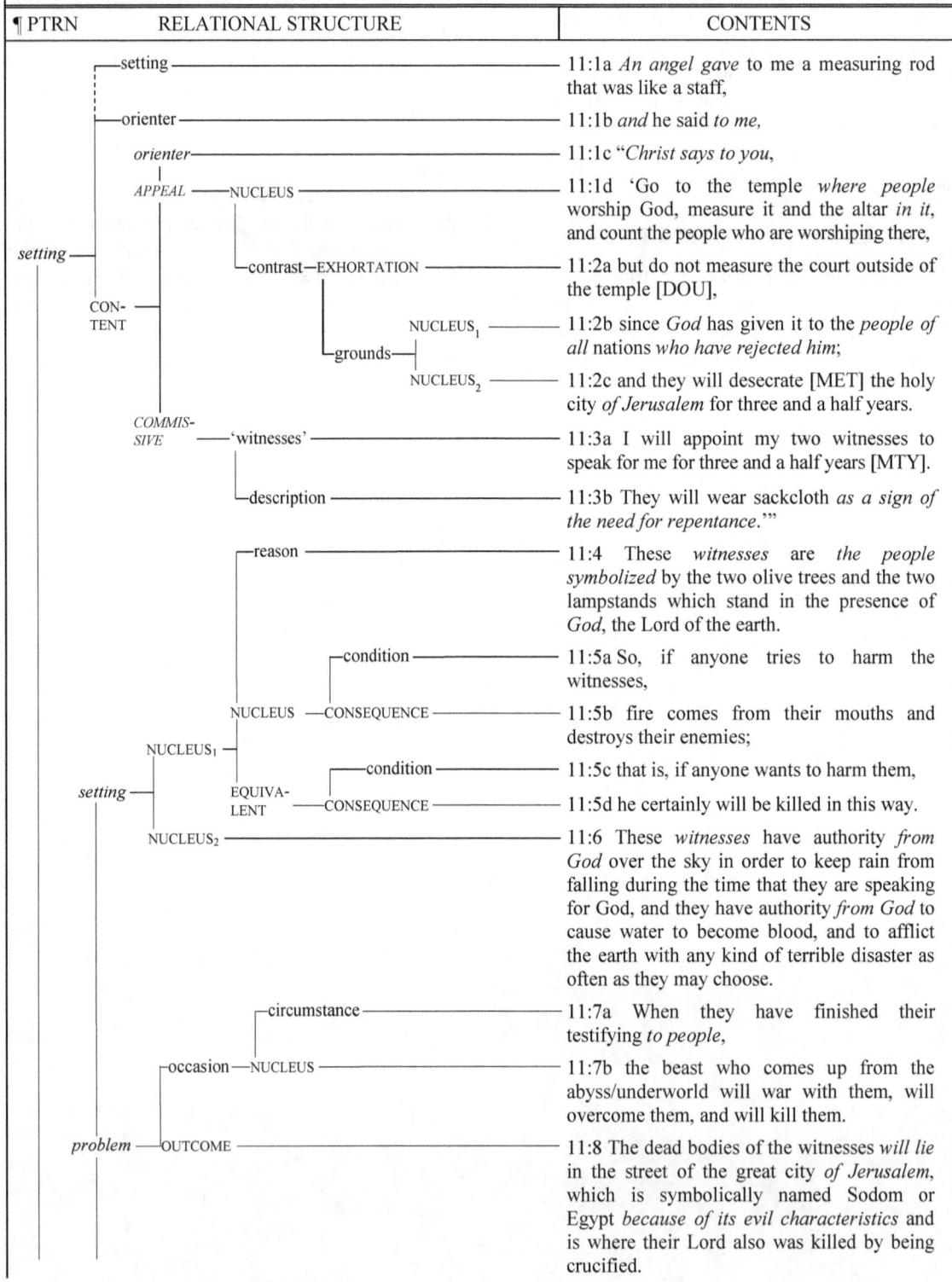

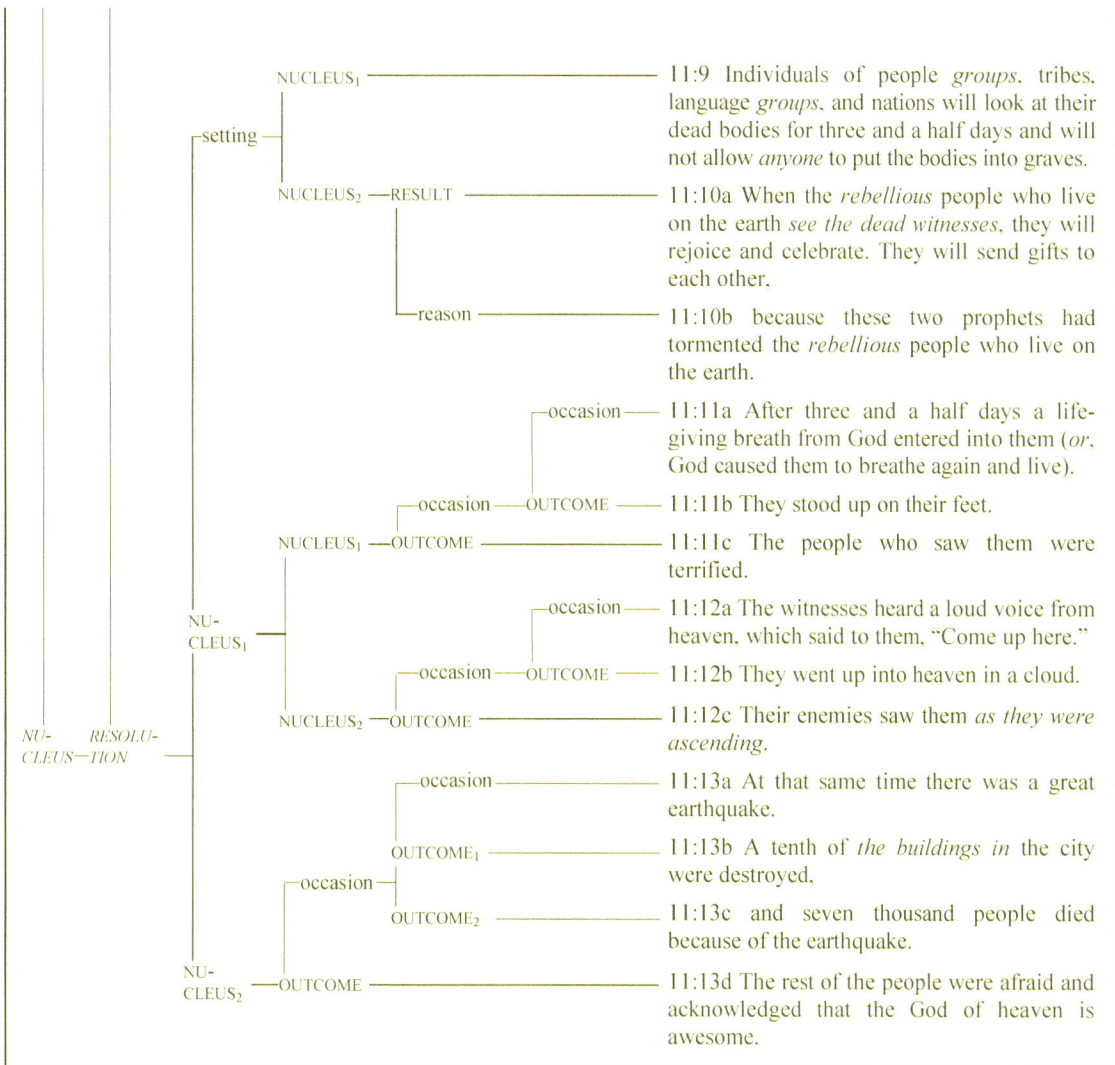

INTENT AND PARAGRAPH PATTERN

Since the quote begun in 11:1c continues through to the end of 11:3, the 11:1–13 episode begins with Christ's *APPEAL* to John to measure the temple and count the worshipers (symbolizing God's protection of his people) and a *COMMISSIVE* in which Christ commits himself to sending forth his two witnesses. This is then followed by a *problem-RESOLUTION* paragraph pattern describing the future experience of the two witnesses as they are attacked by evil forces and are rescued by God. Not only the *COMMISSIVE* but also the *APPEAL* may have a prophecy-fulfilment relationship with 11:4–13.

A view of this episode as an epitome of the whole book helps in understanding it. It occurs almost in the middle of the book and presents God's servants separated from rebellious earth people (11:1–4), their rejected witness (11:5–6), the intervention of evil power resulting in its temporary victory (11:7–10), and God's final deliverance and triumph (11:11–13).

NOTES

11:1a-c *An angel* **gave to me a measuring rod that was like a staff** *and* **he said** *to me: Christ says to you* The Greek has Καὶ ἐδόθη μοι κάλαμος ὅμοιος ῥάβδῳ, λέγων 'And was given to me a reed like a staff, saying,' so there is the possibility of confusing the identity of speakers and actors. The one who gave John the measuring rod is assumed to have been an angel on the basis that the text of the whole book shows no clear instance in which an object is given directly to John by a divine person. Grammatically the speaker here would be the same person who had given the rod to John. But if the same quote continues through the end of 11:3, we must deal with the fact that the speaker is clearly either God or Christ. No one else could make a statement such as 11:3a–b. One solution is to assume that the one speaking directly to John is the angel and that he is quoting the words of Christ. This solution is chosen for the display.

a measuring rod that was like a staff The term κάλαμος means either a reed which is used as a measuring stick or any kind of measuring stick/rod (cf. 21:15). As for ῥάβδος, it is a staff or rod, presumably made out of wood.

11:1d Go to the temple The term for 'temple' here, ναός, normally refers to the sanctuary within the temple area (the ἱερόν). It contained the 'Holy Place' and the 'Holy of Holies.' Only the priests on duty were allowed to enter this building, but there is no problem in this verse with the saints being in this area because they have been made "priests to God" (1:6; 5:10).

count the people who are worshiping there To measure worshipers means to count or to quantify them. Note that John's execution of this command is not mentioned here. Alford's best explanation of this is that "the result of it is found in the subsequent prophecies: in the minute and careful distinctions between the servants of God and those who receive the mark of the wild-beast..." If the measuring of the temple and God's people is fulfilled in the rest of the episode, it is seen in the way that God protects his servants, here especially the two witnesses. This solution would explain why some surface factors seem to suggest that 11:1–13 is two episodes, most notably the two seemingly different topics of measuring the temple and the experience of the two witnesses, but at the same time there are other surface factors, like the quotation, which suggest that 11:1–13 is all one episode.

11:2a do not measure the court outside of the temple, Since 'leave ... out' and 'don't measure it' mean the same thing in this context, they have been collapsed into one proposition here. Both τὴν αὐλὴν τὴν ἔξωθεν 'the court outside' in the first clause and αὐτήν 'it' in the second clause are forefronted to show the contrast with 11:1d.

11:2b since *God* has given it to the *people of all nations who have rejected him* In New Testament times the outer court was called the court of the Gentiles because they were not allowed to pass beyond it into the other courts. The term τὰ ἔθνη 'the nations' usually means 'Gentiles, those who are not God's people', or, in Revelation, 'rebellious earth people'. The prediction that they will trample the holy city along with their actions in 11:9–12 favour this secondary meaning, that is, 'the people of the earth not in subjection to God'.

11:2c and they will desecrate the holy city *of Jerusalem* for three and a half years This gives the second grounds for the exhortation to exclude the outer courtyard from the measuring and from God's protection. The object of the sentence, 'the holy city', comes first in the Greek, indicating a switch of focus from the temple in 11:1d-2b.

The verb πατέω 'trample' here has the idea of mistreatment and abuse of a holy place.

for three and a half years The Greek has 'forty-two months' which is the same period of time as the 'thousand two hundred and sixty days' in 11:3b. This is undoubtedly intended to echo the oppression of God's people for three and a half years in Dan.7:25; 12:7 and indicates a definite time which is under God's control.

11:3a I will appoint my two witnesses to speak for me The Greek is καὶ δώσω τοῖς δυσὶν μάρτυσίν μου καὶ προφητεύσουσιν 'And I will give to my two witnesses and they will prophesy'. The use of 'give' with no direct object may mean that "power/authority" is implied, as in the many cases in Revelation where the Greek has 'give' followed by an infinitive (e.g., 2:7). RSV has "I will grant my two witnesses power." A verbal causative could also be used here: 'I will cause my two witnesses to prophesy' as in 3:9 (see note). JB and TEV use 'send'.

my two witnesses The use of the definite article in this phrase τοῖς δυσὶν μάρτυσίν μου indicates that these are not new characters to John's readers. Verse 11:4 shows that they are the witnesses known from Zech.4:3, 11–14. Since the function is witnessing, the number two conforms to the requirement for settling an issue (Deut. 17:6; 19:15; John 8:17). Later in this episode (11:10) the two witnesses are referred to as "the two prophets."

to speak for me It is best to understand 'prophesy' in the sense of 'speak for God' here.

11:3b They will wear sackcloth *as a sign of the need for repentance* Sackcloth, a very rough cloth made from the hair of goats or camels, was worn as a sign of mourning or repentance, or by prophets preaching repentance.

11:4 These *witnesses* are *the people symbolized by* The fact that οὗτοι 'these' comes first in the sentence shows that setting or background information about the witnesses (11:4–6) begins here.

the two olive trees and the two lampstands This echoes the vision of Zech.4:3–4, 11–14. There the two olive trees are the two men chosen and anointed to serve the Lord of all the earth (Zech. 4:14). The phrase "the Lord of the earth" is found only here in Revelation. It is particularly appropriate for the witnesses who face the rebellious earth people, and it connects with the Old Testament passage.

11:5a So, if anyone tries to harm the witnesses This sentence starts with καί, which is interpreted as 'so', indicating the active result of who the witnesses are, as stated in the previous verse. Because they are God's special witnesses they can destroy anyone who tries to harm them.

11:5c-d The use of an Equivalence unit here gives a strong emphasis to the fate of any who oppose the witnesses.

11:6 authority *from God* It is clear from the very introduction of the witnesses that their authority is delegated and directed by the divine source (11:4). The specific demonstrations of authority link the witnesses with Elijah (1 Kings 17:1) and Moses (Exod. 7:17).

11:7a When they have finished their testifying *to people* The time has been set in 11:3a, and the witnesses are kept from harm until it is completed. The verb τελέω is used to express the completion because it carries the idea of reaching a goal and accomplishing a purpose.

11:7b the beast who comes up from the abyss/underworld Here the beast is referred to with the definite article either as one already known or because the abyss/underworld has already been mentioned (9:1), and terrible beasts were commonly associated with it. Some commentators (Beasley-Murray, Ladd, Mounce, Swete) suggest the possibility that the use of the definite article may point back to the beasts coming from the sea in Dan. 7:3, especially the fourth of these beasts (Dan. 7:7–11). In Hebrew the concepts of 'the abyss' and 'the ocean deeps' were closely connected. In 9:2–6 the evil forces that come from the underworld caused suffering for earth people, and their king, the angel of the underworld, was introduced in 9:11 as "The Destroyer". Moffatt therefore grants the possibility of the connection of the "supernatural fiend and foe" of 9:11 with the beast.

11:8 The dead bodies of the witnesses *will lie* The word for dead bodies in the Greek text is collective singular. The plural form is used in 11:9.

in the street πλατεῖα 'wide road, street' is used here in order to indicate that the bodies would be left unburied in a place clearly visible to all.

the great city *of Jerusalem* Although Jerusalem is never called "the great city" elsewhere in scripture, it must be intended here because of the statement at the end of this verse referring to the crucifixion. The term 'the great city' is usually reserved for cities of renowned evil, such as Nineveh (Jonah 1:2), Babylon (Rev. 17:18, etc.), and Rome.

which is symbolically named Sodom or Egypt *because of its evil characteristics* The idea is that God sees a likeness in the great city to the notoriously evil Sodom and to the great instance of slavery and oppression in Egypt. If an agent is needed for the 'naming' in translation, 'which is symbolically named *by God*', or 'which *we(inc)* might name symbolically' might be possibilities.

where their Lord also was killed by being crucified This draws a parallel between the death of the witnesses and the death of Christ himself.

11:9 Individuals of people *groups*, tribes, language *groups*, and nations will look at their dead bodies for three and a half days and will not allow *anyone* to put the bodies into graves The subject of the verbal phrase is the earth people referred to in a way similar to the fourfold listing in 10:11 and in other citations. In the construction ἐκ τῶν λαῶν καὶ φυλῶν καὶ γλωσσῶν καὶ ἐθνῶν 'out of peoples and tribes and languages and nations' the preposition ἐκ 'from, out of' is recognized as partitive, that is, not all of the people of these groups but some part of each are indicated.

The refusal of burial was a distinct expression of heaping shame on the witnesses. The period of time in days is like the years of suffering during their prophesying, but it does not accord with the period of Christ's experience in the grave.

The tense of the verbs in this verse is changed to the historic present. This points forward to the future tense δῶρα πέμψουσιν 'they will send gifts' in the next verse.

11:10a they will rejoice and celebrate. They will send gifts to each other The first two finite verbs are still in the historic present in the Greek, but the third is in the future with its object coming before the verb. This shows that the people's pleasure at the witnesses' death was so great that they *even* celebrated it with gifts to each other!

11:10b these two prophets had tormented The rejoicing of the people because they were no longer tormented confirms their unrepentant attitude. An inclusio emphasizes this description since the verse begins and ends with the phrase 'the dwellers on the earth' frequently used for those who rejected God (3:10; 6:10; 8:13; 11:10; 13:8, 12; 17:2). In 13:8 these are the worshipers of the beast who are distinguished from those whose names are written in the Lamb's book of life.

In the Greek the subject of this clause comes before the verb, which indicates that the focus of the discourse is switched back to the two prophets.

11:11a a life-giving breath from God entered into them (*or*, **God caused them to breathe again and live**) From here to the end of the episode the Greek narrative uses past tenses. It is difficult in English translation to continue with the future tense and at the same time appropriately reflect the aspects communicated in the Greek text. In other languages it may be possible to continue in the future or make other adjustments, such as using past tense earlier in the narrative.

The use of the past tense shows that the main event-line has been resumed here, and that the RESOLUTION (11:11-13) is more prominent than the preceding material. It also shows the writer's certainty that the events would happen.

11:11c The people who saw them were terrified The noun phrase φόβος μέγας 'great fear' comes first in the sentence, indicating how greatly the people were afraid.

11:12a The witnesses heard a loud voice from heaven The subject of ἤκουσαν 'they heard' is not overtly specified, but it must be the two witnesses, not those who saw them stand up (11:11b), since they are the thematic participants throughout this passage.

Some manuscripts have ἤκουσα 'I heard' rather than ἤκουσαν 'they heard'. The UBSGNT text has ἤκουσαν with a "B" rating, though the text of Hodges and Farstad has ἤκουσα.

11:12b They went up into heaven in a cloud The definite article with "cloud" in the Greek is not generally taken to mean it was a special cloud, but may be used because clouds are traditionally associated with an ascension (Acts 1:9). It seems to be more a veil than a vehicle for the witnesses. There is less emphasis on the clouds than on the fact that the enemies saw them go up. The sight convinced them that God was at work and that the witnesses belonged to him (3:9).

11:13b–c A tenth of *the buildings in* the city were destroyed, and seven thousand people died because of the earthquake In the first of these clauses in the Greek the subject (τὸ δέκατον τῆς πόλεως 'the tenth[part] of the city') is put first, and in the second the subject (ὀνόματα ἀνθρώπων 'names of people') is put last. This emphasises that the catastrophe is limited in the amount of damage done and by the number of those who were killed. The Greek text's ὀνόματα ἀνθρώπων 'names of people' is a phrase which is understood to apply to humanity in general, not one particular group of people.

11:13d acknowledged that the God of heaven is awesome The attitude of the people goes beyond that recorded of survivors in 6:15–17. There, fear and cry for shelter from God's wrath seemed to be the main reaction. Here, it is recognition that God is powerful. The Greek is ἔδωκαν δόξαν τῷ θεῷ τοῦ οὐρανοῦ 'gave glory to the God of heaven.'

BOUNDARIES AND COHERENCE

The initial boundary is clear as John's attention is switched from the little book to a measuring rod and the temple in Jerusalem. Since 11:14 is another reference to the woes, concluding the second woe and announcing the third, it definitely marks a boundary and should be handled as an independent unit in itself. Coherence is maintained in 11:1–13 with the introduction of characters interacting with each other in a single episode. Humanity is divided into two groups (11:1d–2c). The interaction between the two begins in 11:2c with the nations trampling the holy city. Satan and God both intervene as the conflict develops and the episode takes on aspects that seem to make it an epitome of Revelation.

It is true that some major participants in 11:1–2 and 11:3–13 are different: John with the measuring rod in 11:1–2 and the two witnesses in 11:3–13. However, there are strong ties between 11:2 and 3: the same time period of three and a half years, and the fact that the quotation initiated in 11:1c continues through 11:3 without interruption. In fact there is a good case for seeing the actions of 11:2b–c and 11:3 as simultaneous, and 11:4–13 as detailing the action summarized in 11:3.

PROMINENCE AND THEME

The naturally prominent parts of both 11:1–3 and 4–13 are thematic. The victory of God's people through his intervention is the naturally prominent event toward which the episode moves. This is also given marked prominence by various linguistic devices, such as those noted at 11:10b and 11a and the phrase 'at the same time' in

11:13a. The apparent victory of evil forces is completely reversed by this deliverance, God's judgment, and the acknowledgement by rebels that God has vindicated his sovereignty.

SCENE CONSTITUENT 11:14 (Propositional Cluster: Prominence orienter for 8:6–11:19)

THEME: *The second tragic event has occurred, and the third is coming soon.*	
RELATIONAL STRUCTURE	CONTENTS
┌─ occasion	11:14a The second tragic event is past.
└─ OUTCOME	11:14b Be aware that the third tragic event is coming soon.

INTENT

As with the 8:13 propositional cluster and the one in 9:12, the 11:14 propositional cluster functions as a prominence orienter signaling the tragic event that is about to take place.

BOUNDARIES AND COHERENCE

To begin, the propositional cluster announces that the second tragic event has past, and in closing it warns that the third will come soon. Coherence is shown by the topic of a sequence of tragic events.

It has significance on a higher level than that of the episode and so does not belong in the same paragraph as the episode before it or after it.

PROMINENCE AND THEME

The OUTCOME of this unit is marked for prominence both by the emphasis marker ἰδού and by the historic present tense of the verb 'is coming.' The occasion is also included in the theme since it marks the place of this unit in the section 8:6–11:19.

SCENE CONSTITUENT 11:15–19 (Episode: Goal of 8:6–11:19)

THEME: When the seventh angel sounded his trumpet, voices in heaven declared that the Lord God and his Messiah now rule over the world, and the elders declared that the time had come for God's final judgment. Then the heavenly sanctuary became open to view and cosmic manifestations of judgment occurred on earth.

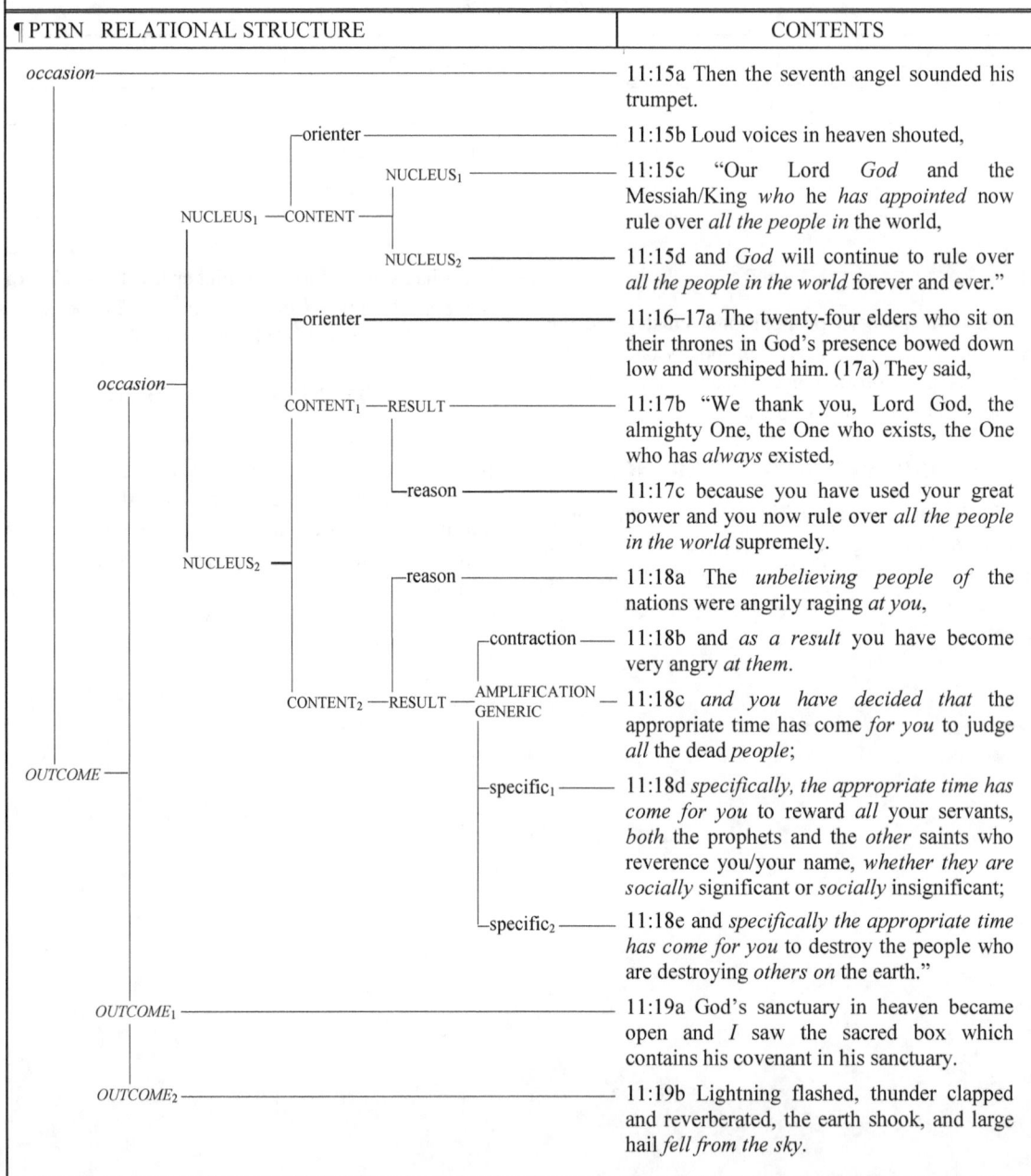

INTENT AND PARAGRAPH PATTERN

The 11:15–19 episode has an *occasion-OUTCOME* paragraph pattern as other seal and trumpet episodes do. Within this OUTCOME there is also an *occasion-OUTCOME* pattern: the announcement of our Lord and his Christ's rule over all the world and of the time for judgment occasion the opening of the heavenly sanctuary to view and physical manifestations on earth (Mounce, 1998, p. 228).

NOTES

11:15a Then the seventh angel sounded his trumpet In contrast to the opening of the seventh seal which brought silence in heaven, the blowing of the seventh trumpet calls forth loud shouts in heaven announcing God's victory.

11:15c Our Lord *God* **and the Messiah/King** *who* **he** *has appointed* The meaning of the genitive 'his Christ' is explicated in the display.

now rule over The shout is proleptic because there is still conflict necessary to complete the victory. This has been the pattern of the vision, understood as intended to encourage those who are in the great tribulation.

Since βασιλεία 'kingdom' is an abstract noun here, focusing more on the reign of God and Christ than on a physical kingdom, it is translated 'rule over.'

11:15d *God* **will continue to rule** The clause βασιλεύσει εἰς τοὺς αἰῶνας τῶν αἰώνων 'he will rule forever and ever' does not specify whether the subject is God or his Messiah. Although 'his Messiah' is the nearest noun, there is no other reference to Christ in this unit and the focus throughout is on God, making him the more likely subject of the verb.

11:17b the One who exists, the One who has *always* **existed** Some manuscripts include the phrase ὁ ἐρχόμενος 'the one who is coming'. This is not included by the UBS committee because it seems to be an addition by a copyist to conform to 1:4.

11:17c you have used your great power and you now rule over *all the people in the world* **supremely** 'You have taken your great power' is somewhat idiomatic. TEV translates as "you have used your great power". Mounce says, " 'Great power' does not indicate omnipotence as a divine attribute in a general sense, but points to the final conflict in which God overpowers all his enemies". It is possible that 'taken your great power' is a metonymy in which the means stands for the result, that is, the overcoming of all enemies. For this reason 'supremely' is included in the Display text.

11:18a–b *The unbelieving people of* **the nations were angrily raging** *at you*, **and** *as a result* **you have become very angry** *at them* The wrath of the nations is met by God's wrath. The rebellious earth people rage because their self-seeking ego is thwarted. God's anger is rooted in his holy reaction to every evil force.

11:18c the appropriate time has come *for you* **to judge** *all* **the dead** *people* The Greek verb κρίνω may be glossed as 'judge, administer justice' or 'condemn, punish'. While God's anger leads to condemnation and punishment, the use of κρίνω here would appear to have the sense of 'judge, administer justice' since the rewarding of God's servants immediately follows. The time to judge the dead is described in 20:11–15 as the final judgment. A comparison with that passage shows several terms in common, such as: 'the dead', 'the great and the small', and judgment according to deeds, using the passive form of the verb.

11:18d to reward *all* **your servants,** *both* **the prophets and the** *other* **saints who reverence you/your name,** *whether they are socially* **significant or** *socially* **insignificant** This part of the pronouncement is emphasized by the use of various terms by which God's servants are known. In order to show which terms are differentiating and which are synonymous, adjustments are made in the display. It seems evident that all are servants and all are saints who reverence the name of the Lord, but some only are prophets; and taken as a whole, some are socially significant and some are not.

11:18e destroy the people who are destroying *others on* **the earth** The appropriateness of requiting destruction for those who destroy is significant.

11:19a God's sanctuary in heaven became open The episode just before the sounding of the seventh trumpet begins with the measuring of the temple on earth (11:1–2), the temple being interpreted as symbolic of God's people. The word used there and in this verse is ναός, which may mean the whole temple area but is used particularly for the sanctuary devoted to priestly worship. This was considered to be the location of God's actual presence among his people. Here it serves to indicate that God in heaven is about to act in accordance with his covenant promises, represented by the ark.

I **saw the sacred box** The Greek text says 'the ark of his covenant was seen in his sanctuary'. Whereas 'the sacred box was visible' is a very appropriate translation in languages where such a translation is possible, in the display this is rendered as '*I* saw the sacred box' since in some languages the case frame for 'see' must be fully satisfied.

11:19b Lightning flashed, thunder clapped and reverberated, the earth shook, and large hail *fell from the sky* These cosmic manifestations represent judgment and show the natural creation in harmony with what God is doing (cf. 8:5; 16:18–21).

BOUNDARIES AND COHERENCE

After the announcement of the third woe, this unit is introduced by the sounding of the seventh trumpet. It closes with the cosmic manifestations. These are judged to belong to the unit in the same way that they do at the close of the series giving the opening of the seals (8:5).

Coherence is found in the declaration of the consummation of the divine kingdom and the immediate responses made to that announcement. 12:1 begins a new episode with new participants: the woman, her son, the dragon.

PROMINENCE AND THEME

The trumpet blast is the initiating *occasion* for the declaration of the kingdom and the beginning of judgment, topics which are thematic within the book. The opening of the heavenly sanctuary and the display of cosmic power on earth are OUTCOMES of this declaration. All these are therefore included in the theme.

ACT CONSTITUENT 12:1–14:20 (Scene: Step₃ of 4:1–16:21)

THEME: Satan, as a powerful dragon, attacked God's Messiah but was defeated. Then his agents, two terrible beasts, attacked and defeated God's people. They caused all earth people to submit to them. But then I saw the Lamb on Mount Zion with all God's faithful people, and angels announced God's judgment on those who did not worship him. The Son of Man harvested the grain of the earth and the grapes of the earth were crushed in the winepress of God's anger against evil people.

MACROSTRUCTURE	CONTENTS
problem	12:1–13:18 Satan, as a powerful dragon, tried to attack a royal woman and her newborn son, but God saved them and the dragon was defeated in a heavenly battle. A voice from heaven celebrated God's sovereignty and warned the people on earth of the tragic struggle coming to them. Then I saw a terrible beast rise from the sea. It insulted God and physically defeated his people, so that all earth people worshiped it. Then I saw another beast come from the earth. It caused earth people to make an image of the first beast and to worship it and to be marked with the beast's name. These events require God's people to remain steadfast and faithful to him and to think wisely.
RESOLUTION	14:1–20 I saw the Lamb on Mount Zion with all God's faithful people. Three angels came announcing aspects of God's judgment on those who do not worship him. Someone like a Son of Man harvested the grain of the earth, and an angel harvested the grapes of the earth, which were thrown into the winepress of God's anger against evil people. They were crushed in the winepress and the blood flowed out.

INTENT AND MACROSTRUCTURE

While we may analyse the overall macrostructure of Revelation as *step-GOAL*, in which God is taking the steps necessary to judge the world and bring in his kingdom, it also has the nature of *problem-RESOLUTION*. And it is the conflict between good and evil in this scene that brings out the *problem-RESOLUTION* nature of the book most forcefully. Chapters 12–13 present the *problem* of Satan attacking God's Messiah and attempting to destroy the saints by setting his agents in command of the world and its entire economy. Chapter 14 then gives the RESOLUTION, which shows the saints kept safe by the Lamb and the judgment, first proclaimed (14:6–13) and then implemented (14:14–20), on all the earth.

BOUNDARIES AND COHERENCE

The scene is analysed as covering the narration from a point immediately following the episode in which the seventh trumpet is sounded to the end of the episode immediately preceding the one in which the series of judgments involving the bowls of God's wrath are introduced. Verses 12:1 and 3 introduce Christ and Satan, the protagonists of this scene, and 15:1 introduces the angels with the bowls, the central characters of the next scene.

At first sight it may appear that there is no coherence between chapters 12–13 and chapter 14.

The characters in chapters 12–13, the woman, the child, the dragon, the two beasts, are different from the characters of chapter 14, the Lamb, the saints, the angels and the Son of Man. Moreover the main locations of the two parts are different, earth and heaven. However, both Aune (p. 795) and Pattemore (5.2.1) show that there are numerous links between the two parts of the scene:

1. The worship of the beast and the marking of his followers on the hand or the forehead (13:11–18) are echoed in 14:1–5 where the saints who worship God bear his name and that of the Lamb on their foreheads.
2. Those who worship the beast in chapter 13 are condemned to eternal punishment in 14:9–11.
3. In 13:17 the saints cannot buy anything, but in 14:3–4 they are described as "bought".
4. The call for endurance in 14:12 is very similar to that in 13:10 and echoes the content of 12:17.
5. The beast of chapter 13 and its activities are described in terms that are clearly drawn from Daniel 7, and would inevitably put the reader of Revelation in mind of that passage. In Dan. 7 the fate of God's people is resolved by the appearance of "one like a son of man" who comes in the clouds. Then Rev.14:14–16 shows "one like a son of man" seated on the clouds bringing judgment and the vindication of the saints.

PROMINENCE AND THEME

In a *problem-RESOLUTION* unit the second part has natural prominence, but the theme also requires a summary of the *problem*. The *RESOLUTION* also has marked prominence in that it contains the third of three appeals within the scene (13:10, 13:18, 14:12), and this last one is followed by a promise.

SCENE CONSTITUENT 12:1–13:18 (Episode Cluster: Problem of 12:1—14:20)

THEME: Satan, as a powerful dragon, tried to attack a royal woman and her newborn son, but God saved them and the dragon was defeated in a heavenly battle. A voice from heaven celebrated God's sovereignty and warned the people on earth of the tragic struggle coming to them. Then I saw a terrible beast rise from the sea. It insulted God and physically defeated his people, so that all earth people worshiped it. Then I saw another beast come from the earth. It caused earth people to make an image of the first beast and to worship it and to be marked with the beast's name. These events require God's people to remain steadfast and faithful to him and to think wisely.

MACROSTRUCTURE	CONTENTS
occasion	12:1–18 A royal woman gave birth to a son, who was saved by God when a powerful dragon sought to devour him. There was a battle in heaven in which Michael and his angels defeated the dragon, Satan, and his angels and threw them out of heaven. A voice from heaven celebrated the victory and the sovereignty of God and warned of the tragic struggle coming to people on earth. When the dragon pursued the woman, God helped her to safety. This made the dragon very angry and he prepared to fight against her other offspring.
OUTCOME$_1$	13:1–10 I saw a terrible beast rising from the sea, and earth people worshiped the dragon and the beast. God allowed the beast to insult him and to fight and physically defeat his own people, so all earth people worshiped it, that is, all people not recorded in the book of life. God's people themselves will suffer captivity and death, so they must remain steadfast and faithful to God.
OUTCOME$_2$	13:11–18 I saw another beast coming up from the earth. It exercised the authority of the first beast and it caused earth people to worship the first beast. It performed miracles and caused people to make an image of the first beast. Everyone who refused to worship the image was ordered to be killed. It caused all people to be marked with the name of the first beast. Anyone who thinks wisely should understand this mark since it is the number 666.

INTENT AND MACROSTRUCTURE

This unit is the longest sustained piece of narrative in the whole book. It is therefore natural that it should have an *occasion-OUTCOME* structure. It presents the story of a series of attacks by first Satan and then two of his followers on God's Messiah and God's people. However, it is noticeable that whereas the attacks of Satan himself, in the form of the dragon, on the Messiah are each immediately thwarted, those by his followers on God's people are shown as unresolved. This fits with the overall didactic purpose of the book, which is addressed to Christians undergoing persecution. The resolution of the attacks on them is shown in the next unit as occurring at a heavenly rather than earthly level.

BOUNDARIES AND COHERENCE

The initial boundary of the unit coincides with that of the Scene. Coherence within it is provided by the continuing thread of the narrative, developing from attacks on God's Messiah and his mother to attacks on God's people. Coherence is also provided by the topic of worship. In 12:10–12 God is worshiped for his defeat of the dragon, and on the other hand worship of the dragon, the beast and its image is mentioned at 13:4, 8, 12, 15. At the end of chapter 13 the story of the dragon and the beasts comes to an end (albeit unsatisfactorily for God's people) and they are only mentioned in passing thereafter. Chapter 14 begins with a change of setting and new characters.

PROMINENCE AND THEME

Although chapter 12 focuses on the more spiritually significant characters, God, the child Messiah, and Satan, the unresolved attacks on God's people in chapter 13 show that these outcomes are more prominent. Both 13:1–10 and 13:11–18 culminate in appeals, which give them added prominence. The theme consists of a summary of the narrative.

EPISODE CLUSTER CONSTITUENT 12:1–18 (Episode Cluster: Occasion of 12:1–13:18)

THEME: A royal woman gave birth to a son, who was saved by God when a powerful dragon sought to devour him. There was a battle in heaven in which Michael and his angels defeated the dragon, Satan, and his angels and threw them out of heaven. A voice from heaven celebrated the victory and the sovereignty of God and warned of the tragic struggle coming to people on earth. When the dragon pursued the woman, God helped her to safety. This made the dragon very angry and he prepared to fight against her other offspring.

MACROSTRUCTURE	CONTENTS
occasion	12:1–6 A royal woman gave birth in great pain to a son, who was destined to rule all nations. Instead of being destroyed by the powerful dragon which sought to devour him, he was caught up to God. Then the woman fled to be cared for in the wilderness for a limited time.
OUTCOME₁	12:7–12 There was a battle in heaven in which Michael and his angels defeated the dragon, Satan, and his angels and threw them out of heaven. A voice from heaven celebrated the victory and the sovereignty of God and warned of the tragic struggle coming to people on earth.
OUTCOME₂	12:13–18 When the dragon pursued the woman who had borne the male child, God helped her to safety. This made the dragon very angry and he prepared to fight against her other offspring.

INTENT AND MACROSTRUCTURE

This is the first part of the narrative of the attacks on God's Messiah and his people, and it has a simple *occasion-OUTCOME* structure. The birth of the Messiah child is the *occasion* for the heavenly battle in which Satan is defeated and for the beginning of his subsequent campaign on earth against God's people, starting with the woman who bore the Messiah. In 12:1–6 the frequent use of the historical present tense in the verbs (12:2b 'cries', 12:4a 'drags', 12:4b 'has set', 12:5b 'is destined to', 12:6b 'has') shows that this part is setting the scene for the rest of the unit.

BOUNDARIES AND COHERENCE

The beginning of the unit coincides with that of the Scene and it introduces the characters of the narrative, the woman, God who protects her, and her enemy the dragon. 12:18 clearly rounds off this part of the story and provides a transition to the next unit where the conflict is between the dragon's representative, the beast, and the woman's offspring, God's people.

PROMINENCE AND THEME

The first *OUTCOME* appears to be more prominent, in that it details the heavenly defeat of Satan and warns the saints on earth of the resulting struggle they will face. The second *OUTCOME* is of a more transitional nature. However, the *occasion* provides the characters for the narrative of this unit, so all three parts are represented in the theme.

EPISODE CLUSTER CONSTITUENT 12:1–6 (Episode: Occasion of 12:1–18)

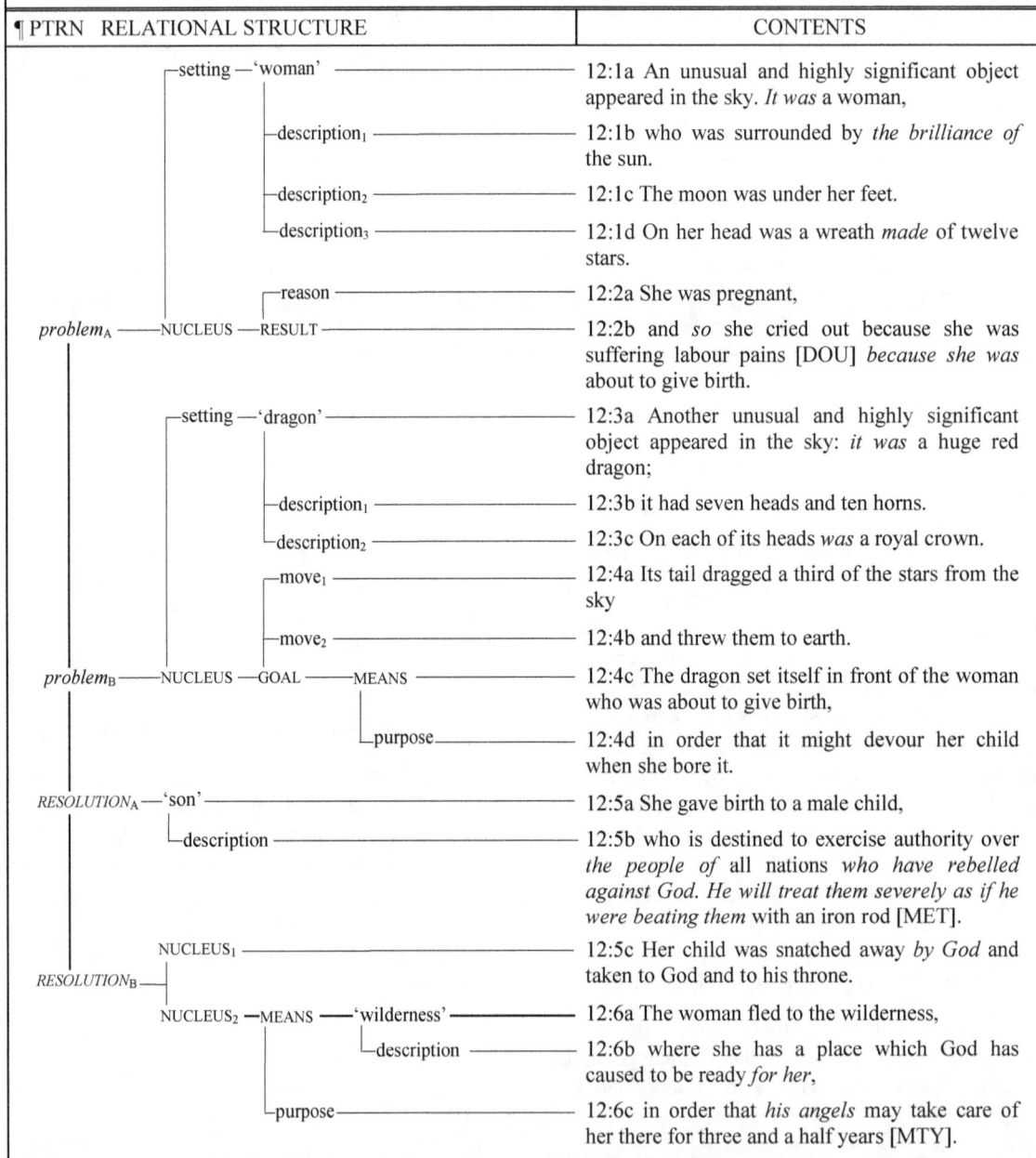

INTENT AND PARAGRAPH PATTERN

The 12:1–6 episode has a *problem-RESOLUTION* paragraph pattern. It is analysed as having two problems, *problem_A* is the woman's suffering pain because she is about to bear a child, *problem_B* is the dragon's intent to devour the child. *Problem_A* is resolved with the birth of the child (*RESOLUTION_A*) and *problem_B* is resolved by the child being snatched away to God and with the woman's flight to the place prepared for her by God (*RESOLUTION_B*).

NOTES

12:1a An unusual and highly significant object The Greek word σημεῖον 'sign' refers to an object or event that is not only unusual but carries spiritual significance.

12:1b who was surrounded by *the brilliance of the sun* The primary sense of the verb περιβάλλω is 'to put something round something/someone.' Reference to 'clothing', as in the English versions, is only secondary, and in this instance is difficult or impossible to envision. Therefore in the display text, 'a woman clothed with the sun' is adjusted to 'a woman who was surrounded by *the brilliance of the sun*'.

12:1c under her feet The preposition simply means 'under', but the use of the phrase 'under the feet' in Matt. 22:44 and Heb. 2:8 suggests that it implies dominion. However, some take it to mean simply a seated position for the woman, with the moon as a footstool.

12:1d a wreath The noun στέφανος 'wreath' is used frequently for an award or ceremonial headgear, often symbolising victory. But there are instances of its meaning a royal crown (2 Sam. 12:30). BDAG recognizes that in this instance it may have royal significance. Certainly the combined effect of 12:1b–d is to picture the woman as royalty.

12:2b she cried out The Greek uses the historical present tense here, indicating that this event points forward to a later one, the birth of the son in 12:5. This is a justification for the *problem-RESOLUTION* analysis.

suffering labour pains In the Greek text there are two terms meaning suffering: ὠδίνουσα 'suffering birth-pains' and βασανιζομένη, a more general term for suffering. Moore (p. 66) lists these words as a near-synonymous doublet and they are rendered only as 'suffering labour pains' in the display since there is only one concept being communicated.

12:3a *it was* a huge red dragon Here ἰδού immediately preceding the introduction of a character highlights the importance of the character in the following narrative.

a huge red dragon The dragon has been used in most ancient western and middle eastern literature, as well as in the Old Testament, to symbolize evil power. The serpent of Gen. 3:14 has probably influenced the symbolism in biblical literature. Foerster (TDNT, vol. 2, p. 281) says, "Δράκων ... means 'serpent,' esp. 'dragon' or 'sea-monster.' " Our modern western concept of the shape of the dragon may be quite different from that of Biblical times. However, in using 'dragon' to translate δράκων here it is not the exact form of the monster that is important, but its denotation of an evil monster of great size, and also its potentiality of being classified as being somewhat serpent-like.

In Revelation the dragon is clearly symbolic of Satan (12:9) and in 12:13–14 it is referred to as 'the serpent'. The colour red may emphasize his murderous character.

In those cultures where the serpent or dragon generally has a good connotation, the translation will need to be done in such a manner that the evil nature of the monster here in Rev. 12 is communicated.

12:3c royal crown The term for crown here, διάδημα, particularly signifies royalty. The royal power of Satan is in contrast to that of Christ (19:12) in that it has been usurped.

12:4a Its tail dragged a third of the stars from the sky The historic present tense in σύρει 'drags' highlights the next event, in 12:4b. This establishes the formidable power of the dragon and the threat he poses to the child who is about to be born.

12:4c-d There are several redundant phrases here ('who was about to give birth', 'when she bore it', '*her* child'). These serve to slow down the narrative, build up the tension, and give more prominence to what follows.

12:4c the dragon set itself in front of the woman In the Greek the full noun subject ὁ δράκων 'the dragon' preceding the verb, together with the use of the perfect tense in the verb, indicates that this is backgrounded with respect to the following events.

12:5a a male child In the Greek the neuter ἄρσεν 'a male' after υἱόν 'son' indicates that this is a reference to Isaiah 66:7 and therefore refers to the Messiah. A literal translation 'male son' in English would be an unnaturally redundant expression. In some other languages it may be necessary to say simply 'a son.'

12:5b to exercise authority over *the people of* all nations *who have rebelled against God. He will treat them severely as if he were beating them with an iron rod* See the notes on 2:26–27. This is a quote from Psalm 2:9 and confirms that the child is the Messiah.

12:5c snatched away *by God* and taken to God The verb used is ἁρπάζω, which has the idea of a sudden taking away. In the present passage the woman's child is rescued from imminent danger. In other New Testament usage the word has been translated 'caught up', as in Paul's vision (2 Cor. 12:2) or the rapture of the church (1 Thess. 4:17).

12:6c in order that *his angels* may take care of her The Greek word τρέφω 'to nourish' may be broadened to mean child rearing. For this reason we interpret the provision of God to include more than meeting the need for food.

three and a half years This is literally 'a thousand two hundred and sixty days' as in 11:3. The specific time places the picture in its eschatological perspective under God's control. It is repeated in 12:14 and it coincides with periods of time prophesied for persecution of the church (11:2; 13:5).

BOUNDARIES AND COHERENCE

The royal woman is introduced in 12:1 and temporarily leaves the stage in 12:6, Michael and his angels and the war in heaven coming on stage at that point.

Coherence in the unit is also evidenced by the structure in which two *problems* are followed by two appropriate RESOLUTIONS. The pregnant woman is threatened by the dragon, delivers her child, and after his rescue she flees to safety. Only those characters participating in this event are introduced.

PROMINENCE AND THEME

In a *problem-RESOLUTION* unit, both the *problem* and RESOLUTION are central to the theme and each of these is mentioned in the theme statement for this unit. At the nucleus of each *problem* (12:2a–b, 12:4c–d) there is a verb in the historic present or perfect tense and a piling up of redundant phrases. Both these features give added prominence to the RESOLUTIONS. The historic present tenses used in 12:5 and 12:6 point forward to two significant themes that will be developed later: the child ruling the nations with a rod of iron, and the sheltering of the woman in a safe place.

EPISODE CLUSTER CONSTITUENT 12:7–12 (Episode: Outcome₁ of 12:1–18)

THEME: There was a battle in heaven in which Michael and his angels defeated the dragon, Satan, and his angels and threw them out of heaven. A voice from heaven celebrated the victory and the sovereignty of God and warned of the tragic struggle coming to people on earth.

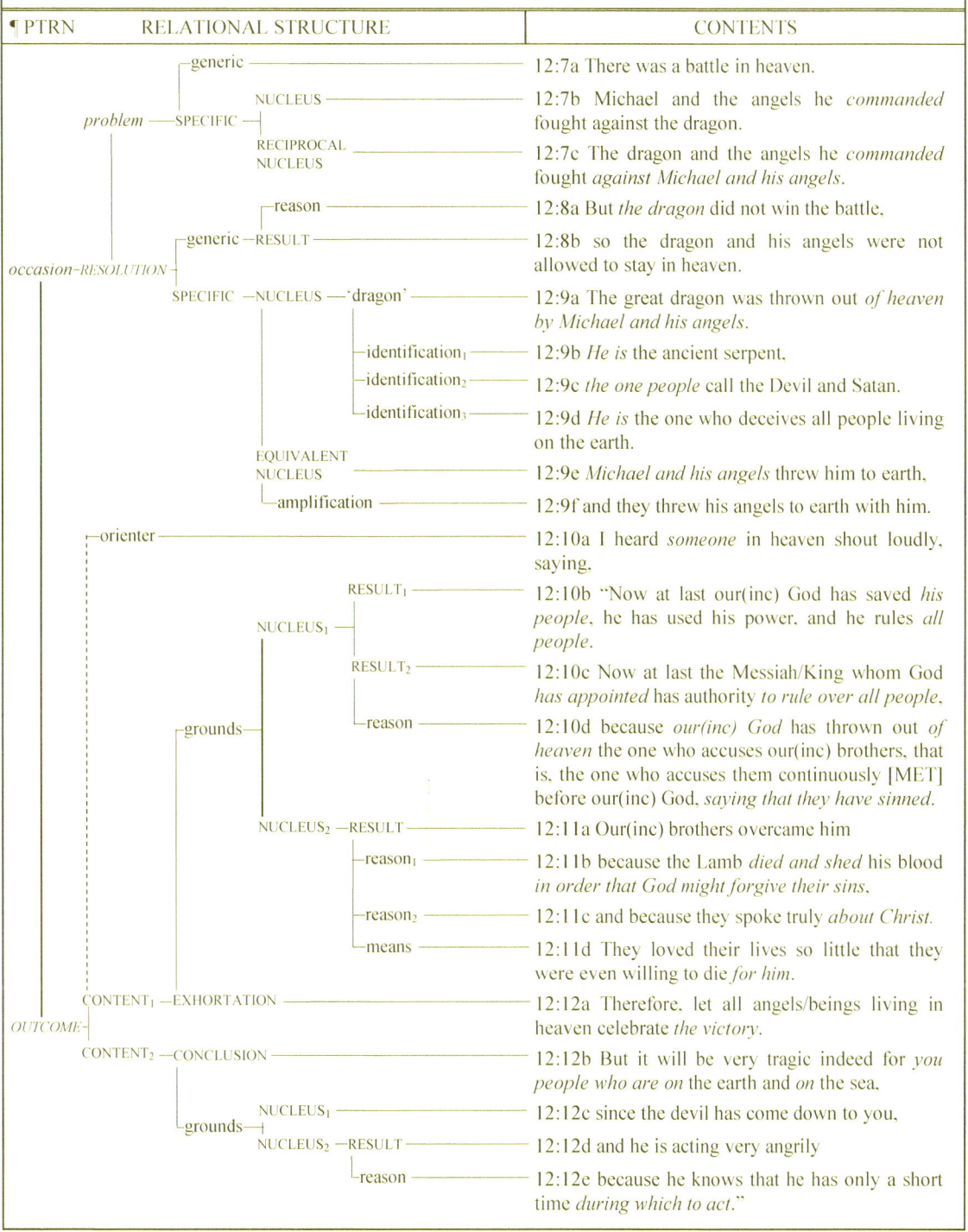

INTENT AND PARAGRAPH PATTERN

This episode begins with a *problem-RESOLUTION* paragraph pattern in which the *problem* of battle in heaven between Michael and his army and the dragon and his forces is resolved by the dragon and his angels being thrown out of heaven. This *RESOLUTION* occasions a declaration from heaven of the great victory of God and his Christ; and it also occasions a warning to the people on earth that the dragon (the Devil) has come down to them with great anger. The narrative reinforced by heavenly declaration is meant to encourage the readers that the battle on earth, and the consequent sufferings in which they are involved, are taking place in the context of a heavenly victory that has already been won.

NOTES

12:7a There was a battle in heaven Here 'heaven' has to do with the authority of God and his Christ. To translate here as 'in the sky' (the meaning of ἐν τῷ οὐρανῷ in 12:1) would not carry the significance as well as 'in heaven'. It is recognized, however, that in many languages one word serves to represent both 'sky' and 'heaven', even as in Greek.

12:7b Michael and the angels he *commanded* fought Whereas an indicative form of the verb might be expected, the construction τοῦ πολεμῆσαι is the infinitive of "to fight" used with the genitive article. It is recognized as unusual and discussed by several grammarians. Robertson (pp. 1066, 1093) calls the phrase an explanatory apposition—which would be appropriate for a generic–SPECIFIC relationship.

12:7c The dragon and the angels he *commanded* fought The statement pictures Satan as the leader in charge of angelic followers. In Revelation the term "angel" is used for evil beings as well as for those who serve God.

12:8a But *the dragon* did not win the battle The verb ἴσχυσεν 'be powerful' has a secondary meaning of 'to win out, prevail'. It is used in this sense in Acts 19:16.

12:9 This verse states in a positive form, and in more detail, what was said negatively in 12:8.

12:9a was thrown out Often in the New Testament βάλλω 'throw' is used in a strong sense, as in the casting out of demons by Christ's power. Here the expulsion of Satan is emphasized by repetition in a sandwich construction (12:9a, 9e) with the description of Satan in between.

by Michael and his angels To fill out the case frame, the phrase 'Michael and his angels' has been supplied to indicate the agents of the expulsion from heaven. Since Michael and his angels have fought with and gained victory over the dragon and his angels, they appear to be the direct agents of the expulsion (Lenski).

12:9b the ancient serpent This item of the description refers back to the story of Gen. 3 and shows him as the tempter.

12:9c the one people call the Devil and Satan The word διάβολος 'devil' comes from διαβάλλω 'to bring charges with hostile intent', as in slander. The word 'Satan' had a Semitic origin, literally meaning 'adversary', but had become a name. Certainly it would retain the idea of adversary but would have taken on all the components of meaning and connotations that Satan's person, actions, and characteristics communicate.

12:9e *Michael and his angels* threw him to earth In Luke 10:18 Jesus spoke of Satan's falling from heaven.

12:10a I heard *someone* in heaven shout loudly The identity of the speaker or speakers is not explicit in the text, and various suggestions are made by commentators. It may be an angel, or one of the elders, or one of the martyrs (see 6:10).

12:10b Now at last our(inc) God has saved *his people*, he has used his power, and he rules *all people* Three nouns are used in the text, each with the article indicating reference to the salvation, power, and rule that had been expected. Ἄρτι 'now' occurring as first word in the sentence shows that these expected events have at last taken place.

12:10c the Messiah/King whom God *has appointed* has authority *to rule over all people* See the note on 11:15c.

12:10d our(inc) God has thrown out *of heaven* Here it is more natural to understand God as the agent of the expulsion since he is the explicit agent of most of the actions expressed in the abstract nouns in the immediate context and he is the primary agent of the expulsion anyway.

accuses them continuously The Greek has ἡμέρας καὶ νυκτός 'day and night' which is a standard metaphor but has no literal relevance in the context of heaven.

saying that they have sinned 'Accuse' is a type of orienter and whenever it is used in specific situations, even though its content may not be made explicit, it is always implicitly present. To clarify the implicit content it is made explicit in the display. Morris says that Satan "urged the sins of the *brethren* in the very highest court".

12:11a-b Our(inc) brothers overcame him because the Lamb *died and shed* **his blood** The preposition διά with the accusative does not indicate an instrumental relationship. Alford says, "by virtue of that blood having been shed: not as in the English versions, '*by* the blood,' as if διά had been with the genitive. The meaning is far more significant; their victory over Satan was grounded in, was a consequence of, his having shed his precious blood: without that, the adversary's charges against them would have been unanswerable." In fact, the 'means' by which the saints achieved this victory is expressed in 12:11d.

in order that God might forgive their sins This is the purpose of Christ's shedding his blood and it fills out the significance of the highly abbreviated 'blood of the Lamb'. The purpose is very important here since it shows how Satan's accusation is repudiated: The brothers are not liable to accusation as sinners since their sins have been forgiven on the basis of Christ's death on their behalf.

12:11c because they spoke truly *about Christ* 'Their testimony' is understood as a subjective genitive here ('they spoke truly') and in most of its occurrences in Revelation.

'Witness' is an orienter and is semantically incomplete without some representation of its content, and so 'about Christ' is supplied as content.

12:11d They loved their lives so little that they were even willing to die *for him* The relationship of this proposition to what precedes it is not entirely clear. However Bratcher and Hatton say, "It seems better to interpret (this) ... as the underlying attitude that enabled them to defeat Satan." Thus their attitude to their lives was a 'means' to the RESULT of their overcoming Satan (12:11a) as in the display.

12:12b *people who are on* **the earth and** *on* **the sea** Earth and sea make a comprehensive reference to those who will experience the tragic outcome of Satan's being expelled from heaven.

12:12e he knows that he has only a short time *during which to act* The knowledge is recognition of his defeat. The time is mentioned specifically in 12:14.

In the Greek ὀλίγον καιρόν 'short time' is emphasised by coming before the verb. However, it does not specify whether this is a time for actions of which Satan is the agent (he 'acts/works') or in which he is the patient ('before he will be finally/eternally punished'). The former seems more appropriate to the immediate narrative.

BOUNDARIES AND COHERENCE

The unit begins at 12:7, where a different event, the battle in heaven, is introduced. New participants are also introduced: Michael and his angels and the angels of the dragon. At 12:13 the woman is introduced again. Coherence is evident from the one event described and celebrated. What happened would not be complete without the praise song which celebrates and states the consequences of the event.

PROMINENCE AND THEME

The result of the battle, the RESOLUTION, is naturally prominent within 12:7–9. The OUTCOME of the devil's defeat, which calls for celebration in heaven and means tragedy for earth, is naturally prominent for the whole paragraph. The two aspects of the OUTCOME are judged to be of equal importance.

EPISODE CLUSTER CONSTITUENT 12:13–18 (Episode: Outcome₂ of 12:1–18)

THEME: When the dragon pursued the woman who had borne the male child, God helped her to safety. This made the dragon very angry and he prepared to fight against her other offspring.

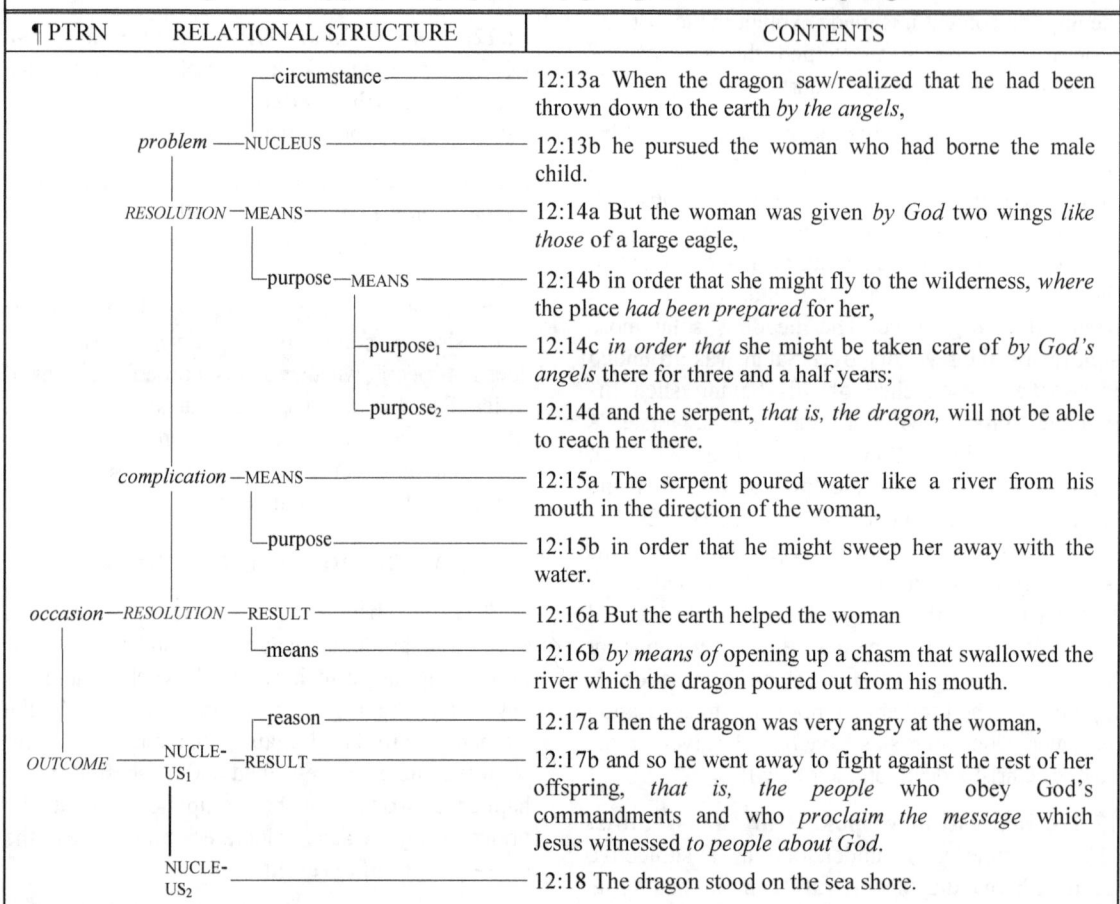

INTENT AND PARAGRAPH PATTERN

The intent of the 12:13–18 episode is to show through narrative God's protection of his people against Satan's attacks. Verses 12:13–16 have a *problem-RESOLUTION* paragraph pattern including a *complication* (12:15) which is resolved in 12:16 with the deliverance of the woman. This deliverance occasions anger in the dragon which leads to his going off to fight the rest of the woman's offspring, God's people. This OUTCOME provides a transition to the episodes of chapter 13, which detail the conflict between Satan and God's people.

NOTES

12:13a When the dragon saw/realized that he had been thrown down to earth The expression 'saw/realised' may be more or less a formula for bringing a main participant into a new setting, especially after a long interruption (the declaration by the voice from heaven, 12:10–12).

by the angels This information supplies the agent of the expulsion, which is not in focus at this point.

12:14a But the woman was given *by God* Here again the frequently occurring verb expressing permission or aid from a higher authority (ἐδόθησαν 'were given') is used. God is the nonfigurative agent of the giving and so the primary agent as far as the narrative is concerned.

two wings *like those* of a large eagle The eagle is noted for swiftness and strength. Old Testament references to it often show God's protection and care for his people (Exod. 19:4; Deut. 32:11; Isa. 40:31).

12:14b–c where the place *had been prepared* for her, *in order that* she might be taken care of The text specifies that it is her place, as in 12:6, which says that she has a place in the wilderness. The time during which she will be nourished by God is the same as that shown in 11:2 and 12:6. (See note at 11:2.)

12:14d the serpent, *that is, the dragon,* **will not be able to reach her there** The change from 'dragon' to 'serpent/snake' here and in the following verse calls attention to the description of the dragon in 12:9b. The choice of words here may be for the purpose of bringing to mind the enmity pronounced between the woman and the serpent in Gen 3:15.

12:15–16 The action in these verses does not follow the three and a half years of 12:14c; it is contemporary with the dragon's pursuit of the woman in 12:13.

12:16b opening up a chasm that swallowed the river Here the earth is personified by the use of the words 'helped', 'opened its mouth', and 'swallowed'. Such personification is not unusual for apocalyptic drama. In the display the personification 'its mouth' is adjusted to 'a chasm' to minimize the conception that the earth is being represented in actual human form.

There is double redundancy in the Greek text here: the repetition of the subject ἡ γῆ 'the earth' with the second verb, and the repeated description of the river as coming from the dragon/serpent's mouth. This slows down the narrative and makes the reader wonder what will happen next.

12:17b the rest of her offspring, *that is, the people* **who obey God's commandments and who** *proclaim the message* **which Jesus witnessed** *to people about God* The rest of her offspring are identified in Rom. 8:29 and Heb. 2:11 by being called brethren of Jesus. They are interpreted to be Christians in general (Beckwith, Ladd, Mounce, Swete), described as obedient and holding the witness of Jesus. Here again, the witness is that which Jesus bore (1:9; 6:9; 20:4).

12:18 The dragon stood A textual problem occurs here in that some manuscripts read ἐστάθην 'I stood' rather than ἐστάθη 'he stood'. UBSGNT has ἐστάθη in the text with a B rating. The other form is judged by the UBS Editorial Committee and many commentators to be a scribal correction of an earlier manuscript in order to adjust the verb to εἶδον 'I saw' in 13:1.

In the display 'the dragon' is used instead of 'he' to clearly identify him.

BOUNDARIES AND COHERENCE

The unit begins with a new location for the dragon as a result of his having been thrown to earth. This is the setting for the *problem-RESOLUTION* paragraph pattern in 12:13–16. As mentioned in Intent and paragraph pattern, 12:17–18 forms a transition to the following episodes. Chapter 13 seems to be the unfolding of 12:17–18 as it describes the 'making of war with the rest of the offspring' of the woman. Except for mention of the dragon giving 'his power and his throne and his great authority' to the beast in 13:2 the dragon's active participation on the timeline ends with his standing on the seashore, and the beast takes over as main participant in 13:1.

The continuous narrative of the pursuit of the woman by the dragon provides the coherence of the unit.

PROMINENCE AND THEME

In a *problem-RESOLUTION* paragraph pattern both the *problem* and the *RESOLUTION* are thematic. The *OUTCOME* (12:17) is given additional prominence by the slowing down of the narrative in 12:16b. The theme thus includes the thwarting of the dragon's pursuit of the woman, and his moving to a different type of attack.

EPISODE CLUSTER CONSTITUENT 13:1–10 (Episode: Outcome₁ of 12:1–13:18)

THEME: I saw a terrible beast rising from the sea, and earth people worshiped the dragon and the beast. God allowed the beast to insult him and to fight and physically defeat his own people, so all earth people worshiped it, that is, all people not recorded in the book of life. God's people themselves will suffer captivity and death, so they must remain steadfast and faithful to God.

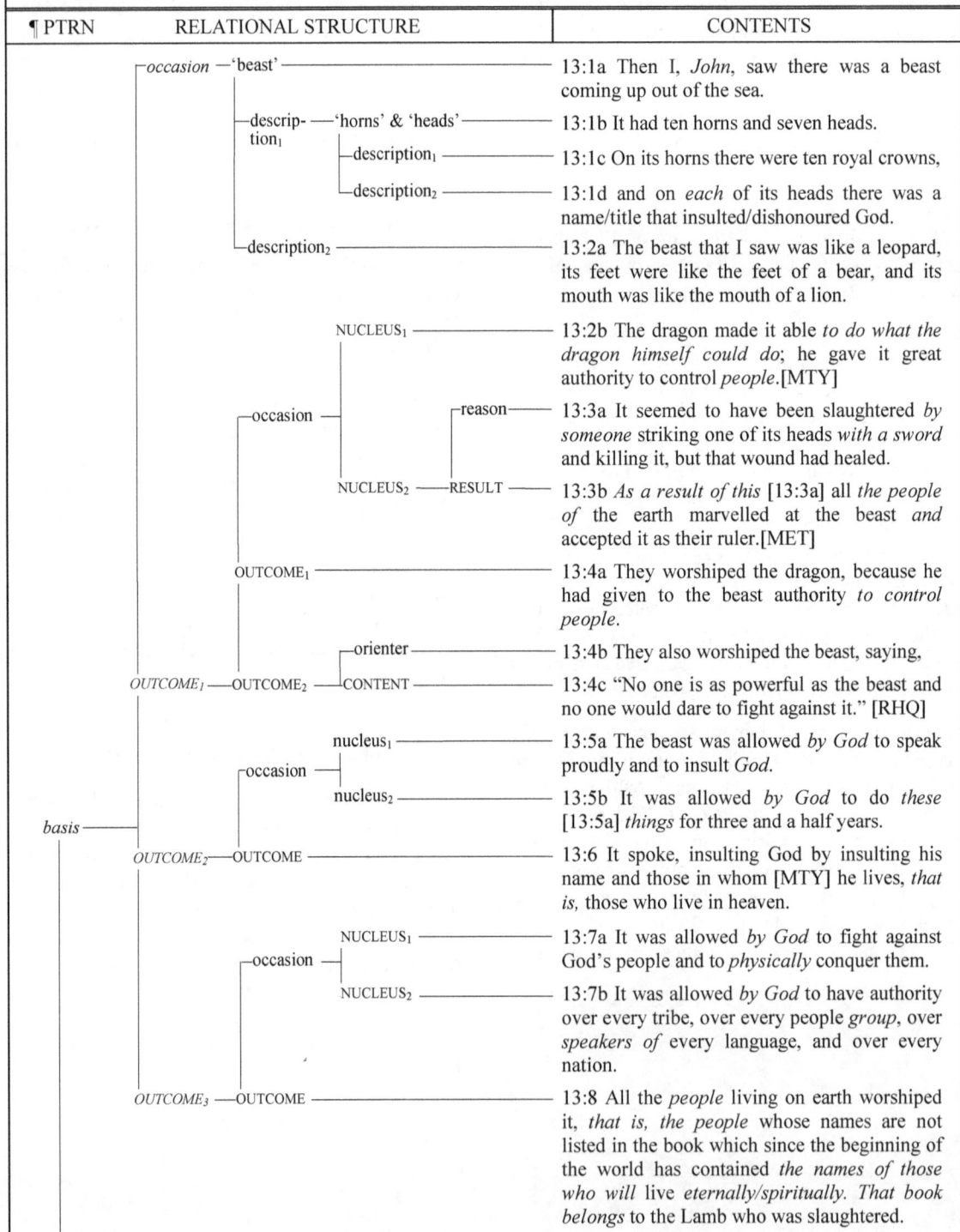

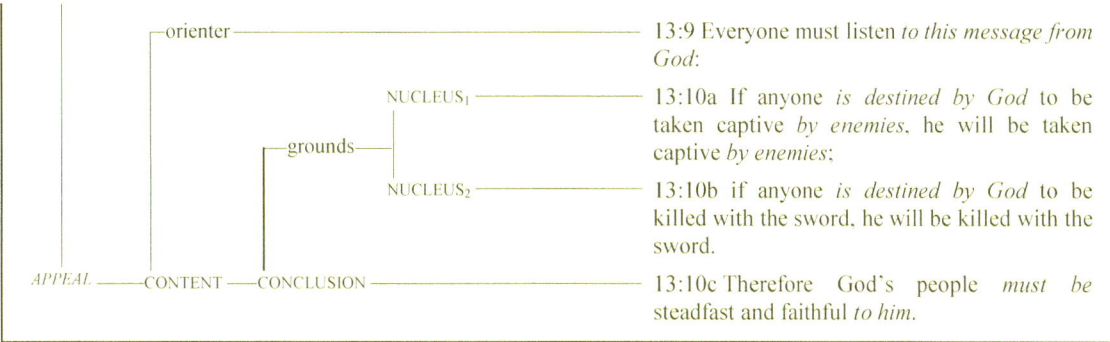

INTENT AND PARAGRAPH PATTERN

Clearly, 13:10c represents an *APPEAL* (see the notes for that proposition). In fact, it would appear to be a very thematic *APPEAL* since it represents one of the main hortatory intents of the book (i.e. to encourage the saints to endurance and faithfulness) and it occurs at a point in the book where the *need* for such endurance is given great emphasis. However, as has been mentioned above (12:1–13:18), the section in which this unit occurs is a sustained narrative, and thus the narrative structure of *occasion–OUTCOME* comprises the *basis* (13:1–8) of the *APPEAL*. This narrative provides a warning of the appearance of the beast from the sea, his attacks on God and God's people, and the way that all the people of the earth will worship him and the dragon.

NOTES

13:1a Then I, *John*, saw there was a beast coming up out of the sea. The strong narrative link between 12:18 and 13:1 is shown by the marked word order of the Greek sentence (Aune). The phrase 'from the sea' comes immediately after the verb, showing that it is known information (from 12:18). The object of the clause, 'a beast', is also postposed, as new participants often are in narrative sentences.

13:1b–c It had ten horns and seven heads. On its horns there were ten royal crowns The beast resembles the dragon as he appeared in 12:3. In Dan. 7 and Rev. 17:12 the horns of the beast represent different rulers. Here the beast as portrayed may be the epitome of evil rule concentrated in one ruler, the ten horns, each with a royal crown, symbolizing his very great power and authority.

13:1d and on *each* of its heads there was a name/title that insulted/dishonoured God The word ὄνομα 'name' appears in both singular and plural form in major manuscripts. With the plural reading, the most likely sense would be that each head had a blasphemous name. With the singular reading it could be understood as distributive, also meaning that each head had a blasphemous name (Alford), though probably the focus is on the blasphemy itself rather than on any sense that plurality would express.

13:2a like a leopard ... a bear ... a lion The combination of the terrifying characteristics of these three strong and fierce animals presents a powerful, frightening beast indeed.

13:2b The dragon made it able *to do what the dragon himself could do* The Greek uses the term δύναμις 'power' which is an abstract noun and is propositionalized here according to the context. The beast is presented as having no power of its own, being fully under the control of the dragon. In translation it would be important to avoid indicating that Satan was powerless after endowing the beast with his power. It was a matter of sharing his power, throne, and authority, or, more exactly, of working through an agent.

great authority to control *people* The Greek is τὸν θρόνον αὐτοῦ καὶ ἐξουσίαν μεγάλην 'his throne and great authority.' As in 2:13a (see the note), 'the throne' is here used by metonymy for what is done from the throne – 'controlling people'.

13:3a It seemed to have been slaughtered *by someone* striking one of its heads *with a sword* and killing it The ὡς 'as, as though' does not mean that the wound was not really a mortal one, since ὡς ἐσφαγμένον 'as having been slain' is also used in the description of the slaughtered Lamb in 5:6. That the wound resulted in the (temporary) death of the beast is also verified by the statement of the effect its healing had on the people (13:3b, 14; 17:8). 13:14 also confirms that the weapon with which the beast had been struck was a sword.

13:3b all *the people of* the earth 'The whole earth' is hyperbole to some extent since the faithful saints at least would not be included. An alternate for the display would be '*people over* the whole earth'.

marvelled at the beast *and* accepted it as their ruler The Greek text is ἐθαυμάσθη ὅλη ἡ γῆ ὀπίσω τοῦ θηρίου 'the whole earth was amazed after the beast'. It is difficult to know the exact meaning of this clause. BDF takes it as a pregnant (i.e. elliptical) construction for ἐθαύμασεν ἐπὶ τῷ θηρίῳ καὶ ἐπορεύθη ὀπίσω αὐτοῦ 'wondered at the beast and went after it'. Many English versions basically follow such a rendering (JB, NEB, NIV, NRSV, REB, RSV, TEV). If this is the basic meaning, 'went after' or 'followed' means 'declare allegiance to' and is functioning as a dead metaphor.

13:4c "No one is as powerful as the beast..." These statements made in worship of the beast are parodies on Old Testament worship of God as in Exod. 15:11 and Ps. 35:10.

The figure of rhetorical question is reduced to a statement in the display. The greatness implied in 'who is like the beast' is defined by 13:2b and includes power, regency, and authority.

13:5a The beast was allowed *by God* to speak proudly In verses 13:5 and 7, which are parallel in structure, ἐδόθη 'was given,' is used four times. In Revelation the word has been found to refer to something which God allows to happen for his own purpose (see note on 6:2).

Note that the speaking proudly is most likely further defined by 'blasphemies', and so TEV translates as "The beast was allowed to make proud claims which were insulting to God".

insult *God* In 13:5–6, as in 13:1, βλασφημία, or its cognate verb, is to be understood as insulting God in the sense of the beast saying that he himself is God. Beyer (TDNT, vol. 1, p. 622) says, "In the NT the concept of blasphemy is controlled throughout by the thought of violation of the power and majesty of God". Note, then, that this is a special sense of 'insult' and this sense might be made clearer with a phrase such as 'insult God by saying that he himself was God'.

13:5b It was allowed *by God* to do *these things* The Greek has ἐδόθη αὐτῷ ἐξουσία ποιῆσαι 'was given to him authority to do,' so it appears that this proposition is merely indicating the time frame of the beast's activity (Aune, Mounce). In a similar way the parallel proposition 13:7b indicates the extent of that activity.

13:6 insulting his name God's name in scripture represents his character, who he is. It would seem that the use of God's name here also has reference to the fact that the beast used God's name as his own title, thus inferring that he had the characteristics of God.

and those in whom he lives, *that is,* those who live in heaven The meaning of τὴν σκηνὴν αὐτοῦ, literally, 'his tent/dwelling' will depend on whether one follows the Greek text which has a καί 'and' before τοὺς ἐν τῷ οὐρανῷ σκηνοῦντας 'those in heaven dwelling' or the one which does not have it. The καί is omitted in several important manuscripts. The UBS committee supports the omission, attributing the καί to copyists trying to adjust the syntax (Metzger, p. 674), and gives the text with its omission a B rating. Because of John's style in Revelation, it would be highly plausible that the omission marks the phrase as appositional. As apposition, τοὺς ἐν τῷ οὐρανῷ σκηνοῦντας 'those in heaven dwelling' identifies τὴν σκηνὴν αὐτοῦ 'his dwelling' and thus RSV translates as "his dwelling, that is, those who dwell in heaven". If this is what was intended by the author, then we are apparently to understand metonymy in τὴν σκηνὴν αὐτοῦ 'his tent/dwelling': the dwelling of God being put for individuals with whom, or in whom, God dwells (Hughes, Mounce, Aune).

On the other hand, it is also possible to understand 'those dwelling in heaven' as a further object of the insults, either on the basis of a rare construction in John's syntax or on the basis of the Greek text containing καί 'and'. This is apparently the conclusion of some of the modern versions such as NIV, TEV, TNT, though a majority of commentators and English versions take the appositional interpretation.

13:7a It was allowed *by God* to fight against God's people and to *physically* conquer them This is the outworking of 12:17 where the dragon set out to make war on God's people.

This is not a spiritual defeat but a physical conquering, whether by death, imprisonment, or other types of domination. 13:10 makes this clear.

13:8 All the *people* living on earth worshiped it, *that is, the people* whose names are not listed in the book ... The worship is restricted to those whose names have not been written in the Lamb's book of life. The book is mentioned in 3:5 and in 17:8; 20:12, 15; 21:27.

since the beginning of the world Grammatically it is possible to take ἀπὸ καταβολῆς κόσμου 'from the foundation of the world' as modifying either γέγραπται 'written' or the participle ἐσφαγμένου 'slaughtered,' referring to the Lamb. The latter connection, being much closer, is more probable grammatically and its doctrinal correctness is verified by 1 Pet. 1:19–20. However, in Rev. 17:8, in a very similar context to this, ἀπὸ καταβολῆς κόσμου 'from the foundation of the world' is unambiguously connected to γέγραπται 'written.' Thus either connection is valid, and each interpretation is supported by many commentators.

13:9 Everyone must listen to *this message from God* This is like the message given to the seven churches at the close of each letter in chs.2–3. Here it is attributed to God because he is understood to be ultimately in control of the activity of the beast.

13:10a–b If anyone *is destined by God* to be taken captive The focus here is on the declaration that the destinies of the believers are in God's control. This is highlighted by the marked word order in the Greek, with the postposing of ὑπάγει 'he goes' in 13:10a and the preposing of ἐν μαχαίρῃ 'with a sword' in 3:10b. While those taken captive and those killed by the sword are in God's hands and have been promised that the second death will not harm them (2:11b), they must remain steadfast in their faith. The Old Testament reference that forms a background for this saying is Jer. 15:2.

13:10c Therefore God's people *must be steadfast and faithful to him.* The Greek text is ῟Ωδέ ἐστιν ἡ ὑπομονὴ καὶ ἡ πίστις τῶν ἁγίων 'Here is the endurance and the faith of the saints'. This is a mitigated appeal calling the saints to steadfastness and faithfulness. Caird says in his comment on 13:9, "In each of the seven letters to the churches these words accompanied the promise to the Conqueror. By their solemn repetition here at the heart of his book John indicates that he is turning once again to give the church its marching orders".

The teaching is that the saints may have to endure martyrdom with steadfastness and faithfulness, but they will have everlasting life.

BOUNDARIES AND COHERENCE

The unit begins as John sees a beast rising from the sea—a new character coming on to the scene—and it closes with the appeal to the saints. The next unit introduces the beast from the earth in 13:11. The tendency in Revelation of καὶ εἶδον 'and I saw' to occur at the beginning of a unit supports these boundaries since it occurs in 13:1 and 13:11.

Coherence is shown by discussion of the activity allowed the beast from the sea. Because of the nature of his activity, blasphemy is mentioned four times (13:1d, 5a, 6 two times). His universal authority is mentioned three times (13:2b, 4a, 7b). Verse 13:7a (see the note) provides a link both to 12:17, the dragon's intention to attack God's people (and therefore the appearance of the beast in 13:1a) and to the hortatory peak of the unit in 13:10.

PROMINENCE AND THEME

Natural prominence is on the *APPEAL*, marked prominence also being signalled on it by the command to listen. The *basis* for the *APPEAL* is also included in the theme, as a summary of the *occasion* and the three *OUTCOMES*.

EPISODE CLUSTER CONSTITUENT 13:11–18 (Episode: Outcome₂ of 12:1–13:18)

THEME: I saw another beast coming up from the earth. It exercised the authority of the first beast and it caused earth people to worship the first beast. It performed miracles and caused people to make an image of the first beast. Everyone who refused to worship the image was ordered to be killed. It caused all people to be marked with the name of the first beast. Anyone who thinks wisely should understand this mark since it is the number 666.

¶PTRN	RELATIONAL STRUCTURE	CONTENTS
basis	setting — 'beast'	13:11a Then I *John* saw another beast,
	—description₁	13:11b which was coming up from the earth.
	—description₂	13:11c It had two horns *on its head* like a sheep has.
	—description₃	13:11d But its way of speaking was like a dragon's.
	NUCLEUS₁	13:12a It exercised all the authority of *the first beast to rule people* on behalf of the first beast.
	NUCLEUS₂ — 'first beast'	13:12b It made all [MTY] the people who live on the earth to worship the first beast,
	—identification	13:12c that is, the one which *someone* had struck *with a sword* and killed but its wound had healed.
	NUCLEUS₃	13:13 The second beast performed great miracles, even causing fire from the sky to fall to earth while people watched.
	NUCLEUS₄ — GENERIC	13:14a By means of the miracles which *God* allowed it to perform on behalf of the *first* beast it deceived the *unbelieving* people on earth *into believing that the first beast was worthy to be worshiped.*
	—specific — move	13:14b It told the *people* living on earth to make an image of the beast which *someone* had struck with a sword *and killed and yet* it had come back to life *again.*
	GOAL — means	13:15a Then *God* allowed it to give life to the image of the beast,
	PURPOSE	13:15b in order that the image of the beast might actually speak and might order that *people* should kill all those who did not worship the image of the beast.
	NUCLEUS₅ — NUCLEUS₁	13:16 The second beast required that everyone, those of little *social importance* and of great *social importance*, the rich and the poor, the free *people* and the slaves, must be marked *by its agents* on the right hand or on the forehead *with the first beast's name,*
	NUCLEUS₂	13:17 and it required that no one might buy *anything* or sell *anything* if he did not have the mark, which is the name of the beast or the number which represents its name.
APPEAL	NUCLEUS₁	13:18a A person must think wisely *to understand the meaning of the mark.*
	NUCLEUS₂ — 'number' — EXHORTATION	13:18b Anyone who thinks wisely should decipher the number *which represents the name* of the beast,

|—grounds ——————— 13:18c for it is a man's number;
|—identification ——————— 13:18d Its number is six hundred and sixty-six.

INTENT AND PARAGRAPH PATTERN

In parallel with 13:1–10 the episode 13:11–18 is hortatory and consists of a *basis* and an *APPEAL* marked by the Greek conjunction ὧδε 'here is.' However, in the *basis* (13:11–17) the present tense is used in the Greek, rather than the aorist tense. This indicates that the material is not so much a narrative as a description. The *setting* in 13:11 is backgrounded by the use of the imperfect tense.

NOTES

13:11a–b another beast, which was coming up from the earth Though this beast comes from the earth rather than the sea its basic origin is evil. It is only in this verse that it is referred to as a beast; in other passages it is called the "false prophet" (16:13; 19:20; 20:10).

13:11e two horns *on its head* like a sheep has The mention of horns shows that ἀρνίον, although traditionally translated as 'lamb', is here used in its more generic sense of 'sheep' (Aune, BDAG).

13:12a It exercised all the authority of the first beast *to rule people* on behalf of the first beast There is a question as to whether ἐνώπιον αὐτοῦ 'before him' should be understood primarily as a location, or as an indicator of relationship between the two beasts. It seems that its primary function is to show that the second beast acts on behalf of and in support of the first beast, since in this unit the first beast never performs any actions itself.

13:12b all the people who live on the earth While the Greek says, 'makes the earth and the people dwelling in it worship the first beast', it is obvious that 'the earth' is a metonymy for its inhabitants. The purpose of the metonymy plus literal representation may be to indicate all-inclusiveness. On this basis Bratcher and Hatton suggest the alternate rendering "it forces all the people in the world to worship the first beast".

13:14a By means of the miracles which *God* allowed it to perform on behalf of the *first* beast it deceived the *unbelieving* people on earth *into believing that the first beast was worthy to be worshiped* If we understand God as the agent of the action represented by ἐδόθη 'was given', then it is best to understand the participants of this verse as follows: the second beast is the actor (agent) performing the 'signs', and it is its intention along with the intention of the first beast to deceive the people into believing that the first beast is divine so that they would worship it (see also 2 Thess.2:9–11).

13:14b which *someone* had struck with a sword and killed The Greek has ὃς ἔχει τὴν πληγὴν τῆς μαχαίρης 'which received the blow of the sword,' but this is obviously a direct reference to 13:3 and 13:12, so the proposition is filled out accordingly.

13:15b might order that *people* should kill all those who did not worship the image of the beast Grammatically it would be the image which pronounced the sentence of death. However, the text is not clear at this point, so some consider that it is the second beast who orders the executions.

13:16 The second beast required that everyone ... must be marked The list used as specifics for 'all' is given to emphasize that the command was all-inclusive. In 7:3–8 another wording is used to bring out the inclusive sealing of God's servants. The surface structure here does not show strongly the connection between the worship and the marking, but in other passages they are closely linked (14:9, 11; 15:2; 16:2; 19:20; and 20:4).

with the first beast's name The name is that of the first beast. See 15:2.

13:17 the name of the beast or the number which represents its name The easiest, though not necessarily correct, explanation of the meaning of 'the number of the name' would be that it stands for the name through the common contemporary method known as gematria, in which the letters of the Greek alphabet also had numerical value.

13:18b–c Anyone who thinks wisely should decipher the number *which represents the name of the beast*, for it is a man's number The text may be translated not only as 'the number of a man' but also as 'a human number'. However, this still implies that the number refers to a specific man who was known to John and his original audience, possibly a Roman emperor such as Nero or Domitian.

BOUNDARIES AND COHERENCE

The unit begins with John's seeing another beast, this one coming up from the earth. It closes with the declaration regarding the meaning of the mark of the first beast. Beginning at 14:1 there is another paragraph-introducing καὶ εἶδον 'and I saw' and the principal participants of chapter 13, the dragon and the two beasts are no longer on stage. Coherence in the unit is based on the presentation in detail of the second beast's activities in relation to that of the first beast. The relationship of the two is significant and adds to the importance of the first beast. Earth dwellers are mentioned four times (13:12b, 14a, 14b, 16).

That 13:18 is in the same semantic paragraph as 13:11–17 can be seen from the fact that 18 completes the paragraph pattern and that τὸν ἀριθμὸν τοῦ θηρίου 'the number of the beast' in 18 refers to τὸν ἀριθμὸν τοῦ ὀνόματος 'the number of the name' in 17.

PROMINENCE AND THEME

The appeal to think wisely in order to understand the meaning of the beast's name is naturally prominent. The unit is construed as having five main statements of the activity of the second beast, which form the *basis* for the *APPEAL*. Because the *basis* is formed of conjoined descriptions of the second beast and its activity, a summary of these descriptions is included in the theme statement.

SCENE CONSTITUENT 14:1–20 (Episode Cluster: Resolution of 12:1–14:20)

THEME: I saw the Lamb on Mount Zion with all God's faithful people. Three angels came announcing aspects of God's judgment on those who do not worship him. Someone like a Son of Man harvested the grain of the earth, and an angel harvested the grapes of the earth, which were thrown into the winepress of God's anger against evil people. They were crushed in the winepress and the blood flowed out.

MACROSTRUCTURE	CONTENTS
setting	14:1–5 I saw the Lamb standing on Mount Zion with the complete company of the redeemed, who were marked with God's seal. They were singing a new song. Only they can learn the song because they are pure and faithful to God and have been redeemed for an offering to him.
step	14:6–13 I saw an angel come to tell all people to worship God. A second angel announced that God had destroyed the great city symbolized as Babylon. A third angel declared that all worshipers of the beast would experience God's furious anger. Therefore God's people must be steadfast, since God will bless them.
GOAL	14:14–20 I saw someone like a Son of Man harvest the grain of the earth. Then an angel from the sanctuary harvested the grapes of the earth. He threw them into the winepress which symbolises God's anger against the wicked people of earth. They were trodden in the winepress and a stream of blood flowed out.

INTENT AND MACROSTRUCTURE

Although the three parts of this unit do not form an obvious narrative progression, on closer consideration it can be seen that the judgment of God on those who have rejected him is first announced in 14:6–13 and then effected in 14:14–20. These therefore stand in a *step–GOAL* relationship. The opening subunit 14:1–5 functions as *setting*, in which the focus is switched to the heavenly viewpoint after the scenes of evil on earth in chapters 12–13.

BOUNDARIES AND COHERENCE

The opening boundary of the unit is established by the end of the narrative of Satan and the two beasts at 13:18, and the change of scene and participants at 14:1. The end of the unit is marked by the reference to ἄλλο σημεῖον 'another sign' in 15:1, parallel to 'a great sign' in 12:1, and the change of participants.

Coherence within the unit is provided by the focus on the themes of judgment and the contrast between those who received the mark of the name of the beast, who will be judged, and God's people who are marked with his name. The phrase ἦλθεν ἡ ὥρα 'the time has come', referring to the hour of judgment, occurs in both the second and third subunits (14:7, 15), as does reference to the wrath of God (14:10, 19). In addition to the contrast of those marked with the name of the Lamb (14:1) and those who bear the name of the beast (14:11), there may also be a contrast between the purity of God's people (14:4) and the fornication of Babylon (14:8). In 14:3 it is noted that God's people are redeemed 'from the earth', whereas in 14:6 judgment is announced against all who dwell 'on earth'.

PROMINENCE AND THEME

The GOAL is naturally prominent, but summaries of the *setting* and the *step* are included in the theme, since the contrast between the fate of God's people and that of the people of earth is part of the higher level hortatory purpose of the book.

EPISODE CLUSTER CONSTITUENT 14:1–5 (Episode: Setting of 14:1–20)

THEME: I saw the Lamb standing on Mount Zion with the complete company of the redeemed, who were marked with God's seal. They were singing a new song. Only they can learn the song because they are pure and faithful to God and have been redeemed for an offering to him.

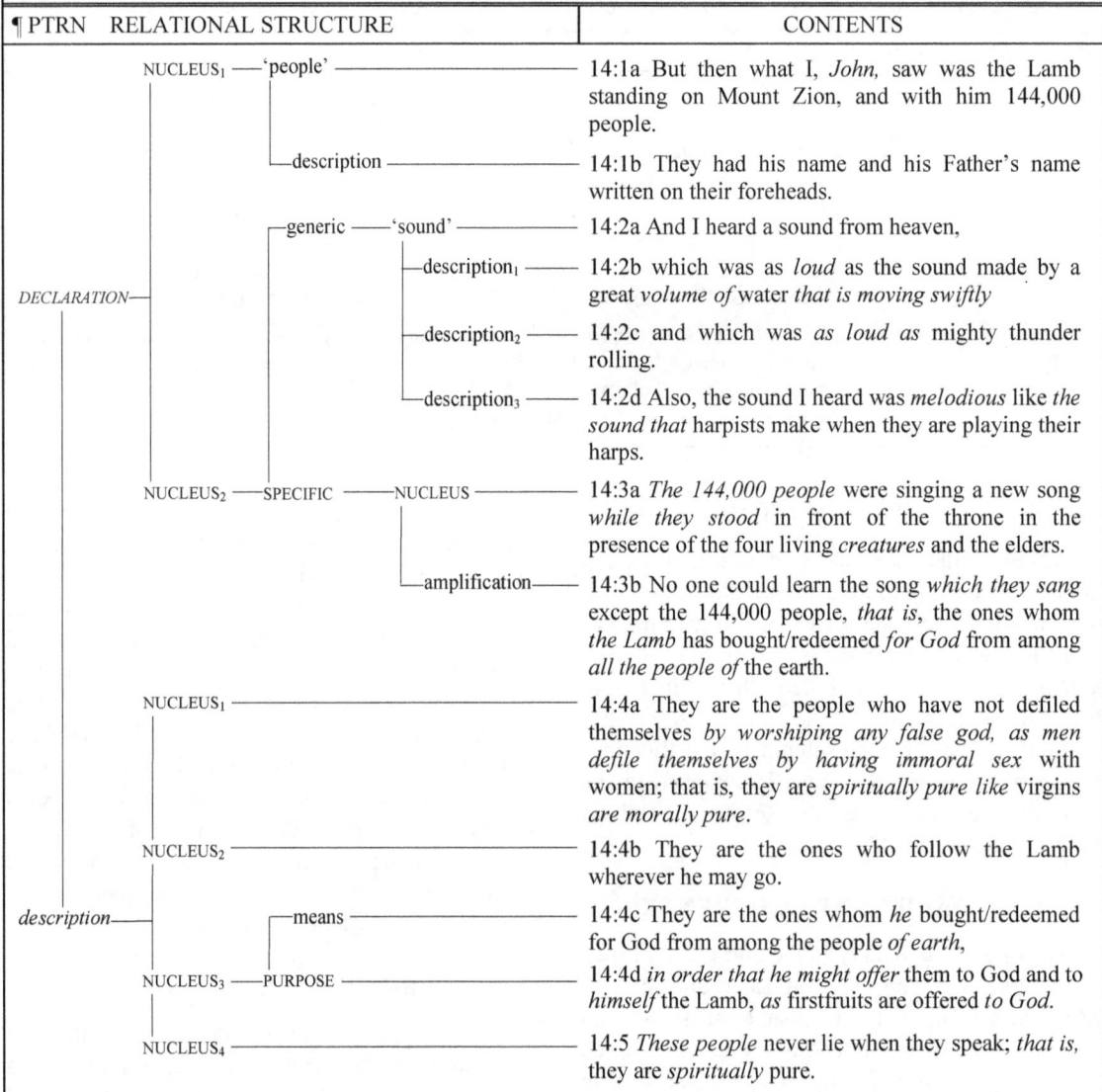

INTENT AND PARAGRAPH PATTERN

It is appropriate that this unit, which gives the setting for the resolution to the problem of the apparent triumph of evil in 12:1–13:18, should be descriptive, consisting of a DECLARATION that the Lamb stands triumphant and the company of God's people are celebrating their redemption. This is supported by a *description* of the saints, which shows their fitness to be God's people. The descriptive nature of the unit is indicated by the repeated use of the present tense and verbless clauses in the Greek.

NOTES

14:1a But then what I, *John*, saw was the Lamb, standing on Mount Zion, and with him 144,000 people The addition of καὶ ἰδού 'and behold' to καὶ εἶδον 'and I saw' (see note on 6:2) calls attention first to the Lamb and also to the 144,000 with him. Thus it emphasizes the encouragement intended by this picture of the triumph of the Lamb and God's people.

on Mount Zion In the Old Testament Zion stands for deliverance (Joel 2:32; Mic. 4:7). It is the highest of the Jerusalem hills and was the site of the

Temple. Evidently this verse speaks of its heavenly counterpart, or simply uses the name symbolically, because the action is described as before the heavenly throne (14:3a).

144,000 people This identifies those who join the Lamb in his triumph with the complete people of God, who were marked with his seal in 7:3–4.

14:1b They had his name and his Father's name written on their foreheads The divine name is in contrast to the name and number of the beast. To the victors of 3:12 Christ has promised that he will write on them God's name and his own name. Placing the divine names on them means God owns and protects them. It is the seal of 7:3.

14:2a And I heard a sound from heaven It is not necessary to understand a change in scene from an earthly mount Zion to heaven. It is John who hears the sound 'from heaven' and the position of the 144,000 cannot be determined from his position as though they were one and the same.

14:2b the sound made by a great volume of water *that is moving swiftly* The text for 14:2b is literally 'like the sound of many waters' as in 1:15b.

14:2d Also, the sound I heard was *melodious* **like** *the sound that* **harpists make when they are playing their harps** The series of three occurrences of the comparative particle ὡς 'like, as', one in each description of the sound, signals a string of similes. The element in the comparisons not made explicit is the point of comparison in each case. It is quite evident for the first two that the point of comparison is the loudness of the sound. But the third description with its comparison to the sound of harpists playing on their harps has no evident indication that loudness is the point of comparison. It would appear that it has more to do with the musical quality of the sound. Mounce says, "it is like the swelling refrain of an ensemble of harpists". Morris says, "The voice was not only loud, but melodious and attractive".

Two devices are used here to slow down the description and thus highlight the main point in 14:3. Firstly, the topic of the comparison is repeated with a relative clause 'the sound which I heard,' and secondly, the last comparison employs a redundant string of cognate terms, literally 'harpists harping on their harps.'

14:3a *The 144,000 people* **were singing a new song** *while they stood* **in front of the throne, in the presence of the four living** *creatures* **and the elders** The Greek is simply ᾄδουσιν 'they sing', so there is division of opinion among commentators as to who is singing—an angelic choir or the 144,000. However, the 144,000 appear to be the topic of this unit, and no other actors are mentioned in it. Moreover, since 14:3b is a comment on 3a (see the note) the fact that there is no overt marking of different subjects would indicate that the same subject is meant.

14:3b No one could learn the song *which they sang* **except the 144,000 people** The use of the Greek imperfect tense here shows that this is a background comment on 14:3a.

whom *the Lamb* **has bought/redeemed** *for God* **from** *among all the people of* **the earth** To satisfy the case frame 'the Lamb' is made explicit in the display as agent of the redemption and 'God' is made explicit as the beneficiary.

The phrase 'redeemed from the earth' is echoed in 14:4c as 'redeemed from the people' and so it clearly has the same meaning as 5:9 'redeemed from every tribe and tongue and people and nation' (Aune).

14:4a They are the people who have not defiled themselves *by worshiping any false god, as men defile themselves by having immoral sex* **with women; that is, they are** *spiritually pure like* **virgins** *are morally pure* The implicit parts of the metaphor need to be made explicit here in order to avoid the consequence of a literal interpretation of the words 'who have not defiled themselves with women, for they are virgins.' Such a literal interpretation would imply an unscriptural view of marriage (Matt. 19:4–6; Eph. 5:31–32; Heb. 13:4) and would even imply that the 144,000 were all men. To take the text literally ignores the symbolism used in the Old Testament of unfaithful Israel as God's virgin defiled by her idolatry (Jer. 18:13–15, Amos 5:2). A literal interpretation also fails to do justice to the symbol of the church as the chaste bride of Christ in the New Testament (2 Cor. 11:2).

14:4d *in order that he might offer* **them to God and to** *himself* **the Lamb,** *as* **firstfruits are offered** *to God* Since the redemption has already been mentioned (in 14:3a) the PURPOSE is here more prominent than the means. The primary Old Testament description of firstfruits is the gathering made before the full harvest and offered to God with thanksgiving (Lev. 23:9–14; Deut. 26:1–11). The term often applies literally to that which is gathered or done first, but it often just means an offering. Charles shows that the word ἀπαρχή 'firstfruits' is used about sixty-six times in the Septuagint, of which only nineteen are translated from the Hebrew word for 'firstfruits'. In 41 instances it is a translation of Hebrew words for 'offering'. On this basis, even if we translate here as 'firstfruits', the significance of the firstfruits will be that they are an offering to God and not necessarily that they are the first of many such offerings to God.

14:5b they are *spiritually* pure The term ἄμωμος 'unblemished' indicates something that is pure and perfect, without any faults, and therefore fit to be an offering to God.

BOUNDARIES AND COHERENCE

The opening of this unit coincides with the beginning of the larger unit 14:1–20. The unit closes with the end of the presentation of the main characters in 14:5. The next unit begins with καὶ εἶδον 'and I saw' and a change of setting. The setting in this paragraph is in heaven (14:2–3). The Lamb is mentioned overtly three times (14:1a, 4b, 4d) and twice by his redemptive act (3b, 4c). God is referred to in 14:1 as 'the Father', in 14:3 by 'the throne' and in 14:4 by name.

PROMINENCE AND THEME

Within the *DECLARATION–description* paragraph pattern, 14:1–3 are naturally prominent. Within the *DECLARATION* itself added prominence is given to the second NUCLEUS (14:3) by the repetitive descriptions which slow down the discourse in 14:2. Since both constituents of the paragraph pattern are thematic, and especially since the *description* constituent potentially has motivational elements, 14:4–5 are also represented in the theme statement.

EPISODE CLUSTER CONSTITUENT 14:6–13 (Episode: Step of 14:1–20)

THEME: I saw an angel come to tell all people to worship God. A second angel announced that God had destroyed the great city symbolized as Babylon. A third angel declared that all worshipers of the beast would experience God's furious anger. Therefore God's people must be steadfast, since God will bless them.

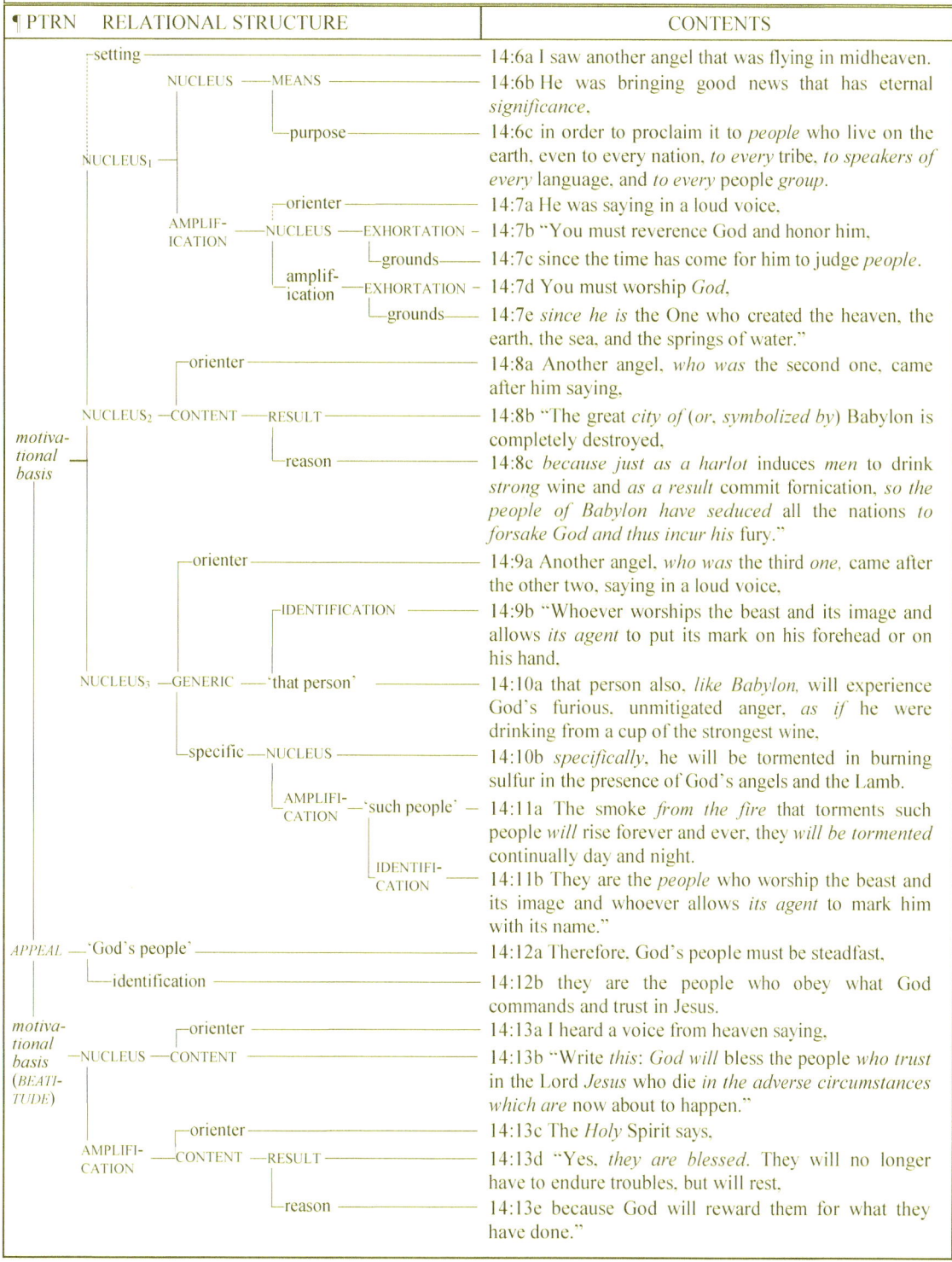

INTENT AND PARAGRAPH PATTERN

Although at first sight 14:6–7, 8, and 9–11 might be seen as three separate narrative paragraphs, more careful study reveals that 14:6–13 is one unit. Subunits 14:6–7, 8, 9–11 are all acting as a *motivational basis* for the APPEAL in 14:12 (see Boundaries and Coherence). The three nuclei of this *motivational basis* form a progression from a general announcement of judgment in 14:6–7, to the judgment on evil human society in 14:8, and the specific judgment on individuals in 14:9–11.

While 14:12 is not in imperative form, it is a construction that in Revelation appears to act as an APPEAL, and the contents of these APPEALS appear to be highly prominent (cf. 13:10, 18).

14:13 is one of the seven beatitudes of the Revelation (1:3; 16:15; 19:9; 20:6; 22:7, 14). As an encouragement to the saints who may have to suffer death for their faith, this beatitude also acts as a *motivational basis* for the appeal to endurance in 14:12.

NOTES

14:6a another angel Although no angel has been mentioned in the immediately preceding context, this one is the first in a series of six angels in 14:6–20. Three are mentioned in this unit, in 14:6, 8, and 9. Then three more in 14:15, 17, and 18. Each of these six angels are said to be ἄλλος 'another.' This seems to be a literary pattern, used not only for coherence but also for distinctiveness and prominence of the message or work of each.

Some manuscripts omit ἄλλον in 14:6, but this could well be a scribal error. It could be by accident because of the similarity of the first two words after καί, or by deliberate change because of the referent problem (see Metzger, p. 678). UBSGNT has ἄλλον in the text with a B rating.

14:6b good news that has eternal *significance* This is the only place in the N.T. where εὐαγγέλιον 'gospel' is used without the article 'the'. It is therefore unlikely to refer to the good news of Jesus Christ. It seems to be simply referring to the specific message of 14:7.

The point of 'eternal' here may well be that the eternal significance of the message makes it more important for mankind to obey than the message of the temporary world power that is about to be completely destroyed.

14:7b "You must reverence God and honour him The proclamation here is basic and universal (14:6c), calling for all to reverence God in view of immediate judgment. That he is Creator is the basis on which worship is demanded.

REB renders δότε αὐτῷ δόξαν 'give him glory' as "pay him homage". One of the meanings given for δόξα 'glory' in Louw and Nida (87.4) is "honour as an element in the assignment of status to a person". To give glory to God here means to acknowledge that God is all he says he is and shows himself to be and honour him as such.

14:7c since the time has come for him to judge *people* The focus of 7c is motivational grounds for the EXHORTATION of 7b. The grounds on which such a command can be demanded are given in 7e, most directly related to 7d.

14:8a *who was* the second one The numeral does not occur in some manuscripts, but because of the pattern of the context in which the next angel is called "third", Metzger suggests its non-occurrence is probably an error.

14:8b "The great *city of* (*or, symbolized by*) Babylon In its most basic or generic sense Babylon represents man in community opposing God, foreshadowed by the account in Gen. 11:3–9. Babylon had also been used as a name for Rome, as 1 Pet. 5:13 apparently shows.

completely destroyed The repetition of the verb is interpreted as emphasis with the meaning of complete destruction. Chapters 17 and 18 elaborate on this brief announcement.

14:8c *because just as a harlot* induces *men* to drink *strong* wine and *as a result* commit fornication, *so the people of Babylon have seduced* all the nations *to forsake God and thus incur his* fury There is a question here as to whether θυμός means 'passion' or 'anger'. While 'passion' might appear to be more appropriate in the context of wine and fornication, there is a potential lexical problem with it. Büchsel (TDNT, vol. 3, p. 167) says of θυμός, "Everywhere in the NT it means wrath". A majority of commentators therefore take it to mean 'anger, wrath' here in Rev. 14:8. In the other occurrences of οἶνος 'wine' with θυμός in Revelation (14:10; 16:19; 19:15), θυμός means 'anger', and so the phrase τοῦ οἴνου τοῦ θυμοῦ 'the wine of the anger' is potentially a set phrase in which the combination would always be understood as 'the wine of the anger' no matter what the context.

If θυμός is understood to mean 'anger' here in 14:8, then it will refer to the fury of God which comes upon Babylon for her sin of morally and/or spiritually seducing all the nations.

This, therefore, raises the question of whether the figure of 'fornication' is intended to focus on the general immorality of the world power or on its seducing the people of the world to worship itself rather than God. In the context of the worship of the beast in chapters 13–14 the latter is most likely, since 'fornication' was regularly used in the O.T. as a figure of Israel's worship of false gods (e.g. Jer. 3:6–10).

οἶνος 'Wine' may be a figure both for that which the harlot gives to the nations to seduce them and also for the wine of the anger of God.

If the interpretation is taken that θυμός means 'passion' here, then we might propositionalize 14:8c as '*because* it *zealously seduced* all the nations *to forsake God just as a harlot* passionately induces *men* to drink *strong* wine and *as a result* commit adultery'.

While 8c is formally a descriptive relative clause, it functions semantically as a reason for the destruction of the city it describes. In 17:3-4 the city is described as a seducing prostitute.

14:9b Whoever worships the beast and its image This worship is in contrast to that called for in 14:7d, and it epitomizes the rebellion and disobedience of the people of the earth. The verb προσκυνεῖ 'worship' is in the present tense, which reinforces the warning of 14:12 for any who might be inclined to start to worship the beast. This judgment is pronounced on an individual basis. All have been called to worship God, and all will be judged on whether they rebel or obey.

Note that the identification of those who worship the beast and receive its mark and thus are the objects of God's wrath is emphasized by occurring at both the beginning and the end of the angel's message (14:9b and 11b). This indicates marked prominence on the identification propositions, as in the display diagram. The emphasis on the identification could be seen as having mitigated hortatory intent and feeds into the APPEAL for endurance.

14:10a that person also, *like Babylon* The use of καὶ αὐτός at the beginning of the apodosis indicates the parallel with Babylon, which also drank the wine of God's wrath.

will experience God's furious, unmitigated anger, *as if* he were drinking from a cup of the strongest wine. The cup of God's furious anger answers to the cup of seduction in 14:8c. The figure of God's cup of wrath is mentioned in the Old Testament (Job 21:20; Ps. 75:8; Isa. 51:17; Jer. 25:15–38), largely as a prophetic warning. Here the strong language used describes a draught prepared to the fullest strength. There are two words used here of God's anger, θυμός and ὀργή. Though in many contexts it is difficult to distinguish a difference, ὀργή might be seen as the steady attitude of God's displeasure with sin as expressed in 11:18. The devil is said to have great fury (θυμός) in 12:12c, emphasizing the emotion of his anger. Here it is the wine of God's fury which is poured out in full strength. It could be called his "hot anger". In the display θυμός is handled as an adjective, 'furious', while ὀργή is translated as 'anger'.

14:10b in burning sulphur The punishment is specified literally as 'in/with fire and sulphur'. If we conceptualize this according to natural phenomenon, the best understanding would probably be 'burning sulphur', and this is the way NIV translates it. Bratcher and Hatton comment, "Sulphur burns with great heat and produces an unpleasant smell".

in the presence of God's angels and the Lamb If this picture can be freed from the human concept of space, it may mean that the angels and the Lamb concur in the justice of the punishment.

In the display, the term 'holy angels' is represented by 'God's angels' since this is the basic meaning of 'holy.'

14:11a The smoke *from the fire* that torments such people *will* rise forever and ever; they *will be tormented* continually day and night Present tense is used in the Greek text to give prominence to this proposition. The ceaseless torment is emphasised by the time phrase being brought forward before the verb in the Greek sentence.

14:12a Therefore, God's people must be steadfast The word ὧδε 'here, this' marks a relationship between what has come before and what follows. The whole force of the messages of the three angels, which has built up in a terrifying crescendo, is the utter seriousness of giving in to the secular world power, whether in worship or identification. The mention of 'endurance' thus comes across with directive force. Beasley-Murray says,

> Eternal issues are at stake in the struggle between the Devil's 'lamb' and the followers of God's Lamb. Let them not yield in the final hour of crisis. Accordingly verse 12 is intended not to provide a satisfactory prospect of judgment on the

impenitent, but a spur for Christians not to join their number.

14:12b trust in Jesus It is best to understand 'the faith of Jesus' as believing in him, trusting in him (Alford; Ladd), or being faithful to him (NIV, REB, TEV).

14:13a–b I heard a voice from heaven saying, "Write *this:*..." As a voice from heaven the declaration has divine authority (Morris, Mounce). The fact that John is specifically told to write this declaration also marks it as prominent.

14:13b *God will* bless the people *who trust* in the Lord *Jesus* who die *in the adverse circumstances which are* now about to happen The blessing pronounced is one of the seven beatitudes in the book (1:3; 14:13; 16:15; 19:9; 20:6; 22:7, 14). The basis of their blessing is not legalistic merit but love that demonstrates their devotion to Christ. They have been faithful unto death (2:10). As noted in 1:3a, it is possible to translate μακάριος as a state, 'blessed, happy, fortunate', or with the transitive verb 'bless', showing how that state is occasioned: 'God will bless'.

now Opinions differ on the relationship of ἀπ' ἄρτι 'from now (on).' Some are concerned to connect it with ἀποθνῄσκοντες 'dying', since that is the most likely connection grammatically. Others fear that would require making a difference with those who have died previously by adding a special blessing for those who die after this blessing. So some accept the shorter reading of the Greek text which omits ναί 'yes', and connects 'from now on' with the following clause, as NEB: "Henceforth, says the Spirit, they may rest from their labours". This makes good sense, but it is not possible if we follow the text having the strongest manuscript support. It may well be that the purpose of 'from now on' is to focus on those of John's audience who are about to face possible death because of their faith (cf. Ladd, Swete). As motivational support the beatitude is intended to encourage these saints to be faithful.

14:13d because they will no longer have to endure troubles, but will rest Commentators understand the ἵνα as meaning 'in that', as in 22:14. The toil is understood as steadfast resistance to the demands of all that is against Christ and embodied in the Antichrist.

Though ἀναπαύω has the primary meaning of 'rest' as a state, in a context like this it has the possibility of indicating the cessation of an action/event rather than focusing on the state of rest. That is, we might translate as 'they will cease to toil' or 'they will no longer toil' with no other mention of 'rest'. But for this context in which a sharp contrast is intended between the saints' difficult time on earth and the wonderful rest that awaits them it seems best to propositionalize not only from the cessation aspect but also as a state of rest.

14:13e because *God* will reward them for what they have done 'Their works follow them' in the sense that the result of their works is realized in the eternal world. But what are these 'works', and how and on what basis are they rewarded? Mounce says that "their deeds are acts of steadfast resistance to the demands of Antichrist" and that "the faithfulness of the martyrs unto death is not a legalistic work which merits eternal bliss, but a manifestation of their devotion to Christ".

BOUNDARIES AND COHERENCE

The opening boundary of this unit in 14:6, as of many others, consists of John's words καὶ εἶδον 'and I saw.' The unit closes at the end of 14:13 with the confirming voice from heaven. The next unit begins at 14:14 with a repetition of the words καὶ εἶδον. The ὧδε 'here, this' of 14:12 indicates its link with 14:6–11, which is reinforced by the parallelism of clause structure between 14:11b οἱ προσκυνοῦντες τὸ θηρίον 'those worshiping the beast' and 14:12b οἱ τηροῦντες τὰς ἐντολὰς τοῦ θεοῦ 'those obeying God's commands.'

There may be a question as to whether 14:13 forms part of this unit or is a separate unit in itself, functioning at a higher level. However, it has the same hortatory theme as 14:12, encouraging the saints to remain steadfast 'in the Lord' even to death.

PROMINENCE AND THEME

In a hortatory paragraph not only the *APPEAL* but also the *bases* are thematic. In this case the *APPEAL* is given additional prominence by the *motivational basis* that follows it. The speech of the third angel (14:9–11) is given marked prominence by the use of present tense verbs and by its clear sandwich structure (repetition of the content of 14:9b in 14:11b).

EPISODE CLUSTER CONSTITUENT 14:14–20 (Episode: Goal of 14:1–20)

THEME: I saw someone like a Son of Man harvest the grain of the earth. Then an angel from the sanctuary harvested the grapes of the earth. He threw them into the winepress which symbolises God's anger against the wicked people of earth. They were trodden in the winepress and a stream of blood flowed out.

¶PTRN RELATIONAL STRUCTURE	CONTENTS
nucleus₁	14:14a Then I, *John,* saw a white cloud,
setting — NUCLEUS₂ — 'person'	14:14b and on the cloud *someone* who looked like a man (*or,* like a Son of Man) was sitting *as king of the whole world.*
description₁	14:14c He was wearing a golden victor's wreath on his head.
description₂	14:14d In his hand he held a sharp sickle.
orienter	14:15a Another angel came out of the sanctuary, and in a loud voice he said to the One who was sitting on the cloud,
occasion — CONTENT — EXHORTATION	14:15b "Use your sickle to reap *the grain* harvest,
grounds — RESULT	14:15c since the time to reap the harvest has come,
reason	14:15d because the grain on earth is ripe."
NUCLEUS₁ — OUTCOME	14:16 The One who was sitting on the cloud swung his sickle across the earth and reaped its harvest of grain.
NUCLEUS₁	14:17 Another angel came out of the sanctuary that is in heaven, and he also held a sharp sickle.
setting	
NUCLEUS₂	14:18a And another angel *who is* the one who has the authority over the fire *of the altar* came from the altar.
orienter	14:18b He said in a loud voice to the angel who held the sharp sickle,
occasion — CONTENT — EXHORTATION	14:18c "Use your sharp sickle to reap the harvest of grapes in the vineyard of earth,
grounds	14:18d since its grapes are ripe."
move	14:19a The angel swung his sickle across the earth and reaped its harvest of grapes,
OUTCOME occasion — GOAL	14:19b and then he threw them into the huge winepress which *symbolizes* God's angry punishing *of the wicked people of earth.*
occasion	14:20a *The contents of* the winepress were trodden *by God's agents* outside the city.
NUCLEUS₂ — OUTCOME — OUTCOME	14:20b Then blood flowed out from the winepress *in a stream as deep* as the height of horses' bridles *from the ground, and extended* 1600 stadia (*or,* 300 kilometres).

INTENT AND PARAGRAPH PATTERN

The 14:14–20 episode is narrative, relating in summary form God's final judgment of the evil people of earth. The structure is seen as two parallel nuclei, either sequential or equivalent, relating the judgment in terms of a grain harvest and a harvest of grapes, both based on the imagery of Joel 3:13. The two nuclei each have an *occasion–OUTCOME* structure.

NOTES

14:14a–b Then I, *John*, saw a white cloud, and on the cloud *someone* who looked like a man (*or*, like a Son of Man) was sitting *as king of the whole world* The association of a cloud and 'a Son of Man' in 1:7 clearly links this description with Dan. 7:13, "with the clouds of heaven there came one like a son of man" (RSV). Although the identity of the personage here as Christ is questioned by some commentators, further evidence for its validity is the reference in 1:13 where the same phrase, ὅμοιον υἱὸν ἀνθρώπου '(one) like a son of man' is used and followed by a self-identification as Christ. (See the note on 1:13.) Some object that it is not theologically correct for an angel to command the Son of God. But this needs to be considered in the light of Mark 13:32 and the fact that the angel in 14:15 is acting as an intermediary communicating God's message to his Son.

as king of the whole world See the note on 1:7a.

14:14c a golden victor's wreath on his head The crown here is the στέφανος, which primarily relates to victory. The use of στέφανος is appropriate here in a context which refers to complete triumph over the evil forces described in chapters 12–13.

14:14d a sharp sickle Sickle in English is usually more restricted than the Greek δρέπανον, which could be any sharp, curved knife, whether used for harvesting grain or fruit, or for pruning, or even as a sword.

14:15a Another angel The angel is said to be "another" with reference to the three mentioned in the previous unit. As in 14:17 "the sanctuary" refers to the heavenly sanctuary, the presence of God, which fits with the command that the angel brings.

14:15b–d Use your sickle to reap *the grain harvest* since the time to reap the harvest has come, because the grain on earth is ripe In the Greek, θέρισον 'reap, harvest' is used without an object in this verse, but it always refers to reaping grain, not other crops. This speech is echoing the first part of Joel 3:13, an OT prophecy of God's final defeat and judgment of his enemies.

14:16 The One who was sitting on the cloud swung his sickle across the earth and reaped its harvest As in Joel 3:13, this symbolizes judgment, here judgment of all the people of earth who have rebelled against God. However, it would be wrong to make this explicit in translation, since what John says he saw here was *not* people being judged but someone in the sky swinging a sickle across the surface of the earth and harvesting grain from it.

14:17 Another angel came out of the sanctuary that is in heaven Emphasis is placed on the fact that the sanctuary is in heaven, drawing attention to the angel's having come from God's presence.

14:18a another angel *who is* the one who has the authority over the fire *of the altar* came from the altar This angel is introduced in a way exactly parallel to the one in 14:17, indicating that the two are of equal status.

The altar stands in the sanctuary, that is, in the presence of God. It is probably best to take 'the fire' here to refer to the fire of the altar (Lenski, Mounce, Swete) rather than fire in general. Both the altar and the fire refer back to the last episode in the series of the opening of the seals (8:1–5), in which fire taken from the altar was thrown to earth. The thought is traced from the cry for justice made by the saints under the altar (6:10), linking the prayers of saints to the commands for judgment.

14:19a The angel swung his sickle across the earth and reaped its harvest of grapes This is parallel to 14:16, but here the picture of judgment is extended to show what happens to the grapes when they have been harvested. They are trampled and crushed in the winepress (14:19b). This is a further echo of Joel 3:13, with possible hints of Isaiah 63:3.

14:19b and then he threw them into the huge winepress which *symbolizes* God's angry punishing *of the wicked people of earth* The symbolic description takes on more explicit figurative meaning with the use of 'the winepress of the anger of God'. Since the genitive in 'the winepress of the anger' is indicating function, and that function needs to be made explicit, the meaning of the symbolism is necessarily indicated in the display text.

The phrase τὸν μέγαν 'the great' agrees in its case (accusative) with τὴν ληνόν 'the winepress' but not in its gender. In its gender (masculine), though not in its case, it agrees with τοῦ θυμοῦ 'the anger', which represents the nonfigurative meaning of 'the winepress' (see Beckwith, p. 664).

14:20a *The contents of* **the winepress were trodden** *by God's agents* **outside the city** The text is not explicit here as to what was trodden. A possible translation would be the 'The grapes of the winepress were trodden', but since the latter part of the verse states that it was blood that flowed from the winepress it may be better to use a more generic object of the treading.

The phrase 'God's agents' is used here because the actual person is not specified in the text. 19:15 says that the rider of the white horse will tread the winepress, but it would be inappropriate to anticipate that information here.

outside the city The city is not identified here, but commentators suggest that Jerusalem may be intended, as a parallel to Christ's crucifixion outside Jerusalem (Heb. 13:12), where he suffered God's anger and punishment for the sins of God's people.

14:20b Then blood flowed out from the winepress The mention of the blood shows that the symbolism of wine for blood has been dropped (see the note on 14:19b). It may also indicate a further reference to Isaiah 63:3.

in a stream as deep as **the height of horses' bridles** *from the ground* The Greek is literally 'as far as the bridles of the horses', but this is a metaphor in which the point of comparison is implicit. It has therefore been made explicit in the display.

BOUNDARIES AND COHERENCE

The boundaries of the unit are clear. It begins with καὶ εἶδον 'and I saw', the common marker used for a new paragraph or higher-level unit in Revelation. The next occurrence of καὶ εἶδον occurs at the beginning of 15:1. The closing of the paragraph coincides with the end of the scene.

The topic of the harvesting of earth gives coherence to the unit. The noun phrase ἡ γῆ 'the earth' is mentioned six times, and δρέπανον 'sickle' seven times, and each of these occurs in both the field harvest and the vintage subunits (14:14–16, 17–20). Ripeness of the crop is affirmed for the field harvest and for the vintage, and in both cases the orders for the harvest to take place come from within the heavenly Temple (14:15, 18).

PROMINENCE AND THEME

The unit is charted as having two subunits of equal natural prominence to describe the complete harvest of earth. It might seem that the second subunit, which gives the more graphic description and provides information about the result, would have greater prominence. But this is balanced by the marked prominence which the description of the One like a Son of Man (14:14) gives to the first subunit. The theme gives the main points of both parts of the unit.

ACT CONSTITUENT 15:1–16:21 (Scene: Goal of 4:1–16:21)

> *THEME: Those who had overcome the beast praised God and seven angels were given the seven bowls of God's anger. As these were poured out the people who had worshipped the beast suffered terrible afflictions and then the rulers of earth united for the final battle against God, but Jesus called on his people to be ready for him. When the last bowl was emptied God's punishment of people was complete, but they continued to curse him.*

MACROSTRUCTURE	CONTENTS
setting	15:1 I saw in heaven the seven angels whose duty it was to inflict the seven last terrible afflictions upon rebellious earth people.
interlude	15:2–4 I saw the people who had overcome the beast standing by the sea of glass and singing God's praise for his mighty deliverance and just judgment.
step	15:5–8 I saw the angels being given the seven bowls of God's anger in the heavenly sanctuary, which became filled with the smoke that signified God's glory.
GOAL	16:1–21 The pouring out of the first five bowls brought judgment in the form of terrible afflictions on the people of earth who had worshipped the beast. When the sixth bowl was poured out the rulers of earth began to unite for the final battle against God, but Jesus called on his people to be ready for him. When the seventh bowl was emptied God announced that his punishing of people was complete. Cosmic manifestations and wide destruction followed, but the people cursed God.

INTENT AND MACROSTRUCTURE

Like the other scenes containing series of seven events (the seals, 5:1–8:5, and the trumpets, 8:6–11:19) this scene with its seven bowls has a narrative *step-GOAL* structure. However, being the culmination of these other series (as the GOAL of 4:1–16:21) it is not surprising that its structure is more elaborate. Thus it has not only a *step-GOAL* framework, with an interlude (15:2–4) reminiscent of that in 7:1–17, but also a GOAL (16:1–21) which itself has a *step-GOAL* structure.

BOUNDARIES AND COHERENCE

The coherence of this unit is seen in the seven angels and their bowls containing seven plagues. The angels with their plagues are introduced in 15:1; the angels are prepared for their task in 15:5–8, and carry out that task in 16:1–21. While one of the seven angels is mentioned in 17:1, this angel is now performing a different role, showing to John the major participant of the next scene, the harlot Babylon.

Further coherence is provided by repeated mentions of the wrath of God (15:1, 7; 16:1, 19).

PROMINENCE AND THEME

The GOAL in this *step-GOAL* unit is naturally prominent, but the *step* is also thematic. The *interlude* has a hortatory function in encouraging the readers, by showing their participation in the final judgment, so it also is included in the theme.

SCENE CONSTITUENT 15:1 (Propositional cluster: setting of 15:1–16:21)

THEME: *I saw in heaven the seven angels whose duty it was to inflict the seven last terrible afflictions upon rebellious earth people.*		
RELATIONAL STRUCTURE		CONTENTS
NUCLEUS – 'sign'		15:1a I, *John*, saw another great and marvelous sign in heaven.
└ identification — 'terrible afflictions'		15:1b *It was* seven angels, whose duty it was *to inflict* seven terrible afflictions *upon rebellious earth people.*
└ identification — RESULT		15:1c *These are* the last *terrible afflictions that God will inflict upon them*
└ reason		15:1d because they will accomplish God's *purpose in becoming* angry.

INTENT

The 15:1 propositional cluster serves as a *setting* for the scene (15:1–16:21) since it introduces the new participants, the seven angels. However, it also serves as a summary or superscription (Aune) for the scene, as it identifies the task which the angels are going to carry out, the final series of punishments of rebellious earth people in this phase of God's dealing with them.

NOTES

15:1a in heaven The Greek ἐν τῷ οὐρανῷ can be translated either as 'in the sky' or 'in heaven', but here no doubt heaven is intended since John uses the same phrase to refer to the sanctuary in heaven in 15:5 and the seven angels come from there.

15:1b whose duty it was *to inflict* seven terrible afflictions These words are a rendering of the Greek words ἔχοντας πληγὰς ἑπτά 'having seven plagues'. Since in the narrative the angels only receive the bowls containing the plagues at 15:7, the words here must refer to their task (cf. Bratcher and Hatton). But since "duty" is an abstract noun, an alternate propositionalization would be '*It was* seven angels whom *God* had appointed *to inflict…*'.

seven terrible afflictions See the note on 9:18.

15:1d because they will accomplish God's *purpose in becoming* angry In the display text ἐτελέσθη ὁ θυμὸς τοῦ θεοῦ 'the wrath of God is finished/completed' is taken in the sense of fulfilling the aim of God's anger, namely to bring the rebellious people of earth to repentance. God will no longer punish them with that aim—only the final everlasting punishment awaits them.

BOUNDARIES AND COHERENCE

Although 15:1 itself forms the start of a new scene (see under 15:1–16:21), it is immediately followed by a repetition of καὶ εἶδον 'and I saw' in 15:2, indicating another new unit. Unit 15:2–4 then deals with different participants from those introduced in 15:1, thus confirming that 15:1 functions as a setting or superscription for the whole scene 15:1–16:21.

PROMINENCE AND THEME

Since both the introduction of the seven angels and their purpose are the functions of this propositional cluster, they both must be represented in the theme statement.

SCENE CONSTITUENT 15:2–4 (Paragraph: Interlude of 15:1–16:21)

THEME: I saw the people who had overcome the beast standing by the sea of glass and singing God's praise for his mighty deliverance and just judgment.

¶ PTRN RELATIONAL STRUCTURE	CONTENTS
description₁	15:2a I saw what looked like a sea *made of* glass and mixed with fire.
NUCLEUS₁	15:2b And I saw the people who had overcome the beast *by means of their not worshiping it* or its image and by their not *allowing its agent to mark them with* the number which corresponds to the beast's name. They were standing by the sea *that looked like it was made* of glass.
description₂	
NUCLEUS₂	15:2c They had in their hands harps *which are for praising* God.
orienter	15:3a They were singing a song *like* God's servant Moses *sang*; in their song *they praised God for delivering his people by means of* the Lamb, saying,
DECLARATION NUCLEUS₁	15:3b "Whatever you do is powerful and marvellous, Lord God almighty.
NUCLEUS₂	15:3c You *always* act righteously and truthfully, *you who are* king *over all* nations.
EQUIV-ALENT — RESULT	15:4a Everyone will fear *you* and glorify you [RHQ], Lord,
NUCLEUS₃ — reason	15:4b because you alone are holy.
EQUIV-ALENT — RESULT	15:4c All nations will come and worship before you,
reason	15:4d because you show everyone that you have righteously judged *rebellious earth people*."

INTENT AND PARAGRAPH PATTERN

The 15:2–4 paragraph has only one verb which could indicate action on a timeline, ᾄδουσιν 'they sing'. However, in descriptive units present tense is used for foreground elements, so description is much more likely to be the character of this paragraph than narrative. Note that the *description*-DECLARATION structure here is somewhat different from the *description*-DECLARATION structure which occurs when an author describes something and then makes a declaration based upon that description. Here the structure can be seen as one in which the author describes a scenario and its participants and then has the participants themselves make a declaration.

As an interlude this unit functions as delaying the narrative of the scene and thus heightening the tension before its goal is related. At another level the unit also functions as an encouragement to the readers by showing the triumph of those who refused to worship the beast. It shows them standing before the throne of God, witnessing the final judgment and praising God for it.

NOTES

15:2a I saw what looked like a sea *made of* glass and mixed with fire The sea is that of 4:6, before the throne of God. Here it is combined with the idea of the river of fire flowing from the throne, as in Dan.7:10. For translation, it would seem that 'mixed' or 'mingled' needs only to be taken in the sense that fire was somehow connected with the sea of glass.

15:2b the people who had overcome the beast *by means of their not worshiping it* or its image and by their not *allowing its agent to mark them with* the number which corresponds to the beast's name The Greek text for this segment is complex semantically, referring to overcoming "the beast and its image and the number." Yet there were not three things that were overcome, only one, the beast. The image and the number were representations of the beast, by the rejection of which the saints achieved their victory.

were standing by the sea Greek ἐπί may mean 'on' or 'by'. Both of these have been used in English versions and neither would be wrong. That these people are 'by/on the sea' means they are in the presence of God (4:6).

15:2c They had in their hands harps *which are for praising* God The genitive form of τοῦ θεοῦ 'of God' could be understood as possessive, because it was God who gave them the harps. However, their use in praising God is more in focus.

15:3a a song *like* God's servant Moses *sang*; *in their* song *they praised God for delivering his people by means of* the Lamb The 'song of Moses' and 'the song of the Lamb' are genitive phrases and since they do not indicate possession here they are propositionalized according to their meaning. The song of Moses is understood to be the praise for the deliverance from Egypt, celebrated at the Red Sea (Exod. 15). The 'song of the Lamb' means a song about the Lamb's deliverance of God's people. The article and the repetition of ᾠδή 'song' could suggest two songs. But they are actually one song because the deliverance of the children of Israel is a type of the great deliverance through the Lamb. The song has one theme, proclaiming the mighty works of God in judgment and victory.

An alternate form of the propositions might be:

> They were singing a song like Moses *sang when he praised God for delivering his [God's] people from Egypt; in their* song *they praised God for delivering his people by means of* the Lamb.

15:3b–c "Whatever you do is powerful and marvellous, Lord God almighty. You *always* act righteously and truthfully, *you who are* king *over all* nations The parallel lines are typical of Hebrew poetry.

There are several vocatives referring to God in the song of the victors. Vocatives here are another method for emphasising the divine character and greatness of God. But in many languages vocatives are only used for the purpose of gaining the attention of the one(s) to whom one is speaking. Therefore in some languages vocatives may need to be changed into a full clause.

There is textual uncertainty about the word ἐθνῶν 'nations' used in the UBS text. The main variant reading is αἰώνων 'ages'. According to Metzger (pp. 679–680) the external evidence for ἐθνῶν and αἰώνων is nearly the same, but the UBS committee felt that "(a) αἰώνων was introduced by copyists who recollected 1 Tim. 1.17 . . . and (b) the reading ἐθνῶν is more in accord with the context (v. 4)."

15:4a Everyone will fear *you* and glorify you The rhetorical question 'Who will not fear and glorify your name?' is adjusted to a statement. The verb could be translated "to fear" or "to reverence," but the display uses "fear" because of the context of judgment and the balance of thought provided by δοξάσει 'glorify.' As in other passages, 'your name' really means God, himself.

15:4b–d because you alone are holy. All nations will come and worship before you, because you show everyone that you have righteously judged rebellious earth people." Although there are three clauses here introduced with ὅτι 'for, because,' the verse actually exhibits the parallel structure of Hebrew poetry. The first ὅτι (4b) gives the reason for 4a by referring to God's holiness, using a term the New Testament reserves for the divine attribute. The second ὅτι (4c) parallels the RESULT in 4a, restating it in a declarative sentence rather than as a rhetorical question. This second use of ὅτι is that of amplification, one of its functions. The third ὅτι (4d) gives the reason for the universal recognition (4c). This recognition, or worship, is not taken to mean an act of repentance, but of acknowledging that God has vindicated his righteous acts. It is like the fearing and giving glory of 11:13. The song celebrates victory, but judgment makes a way for victory.

you have righteously judged *rebellious earth people* BDAG classifies this occurrence of δικαίωμα under 'righteous deed' but says it also might be translated here as 'sentence of condemnation'. In this context of judgment of the unbelievers, the supplying of the obligatory object of the transitive verb as 'rebellious earth people' seems appropriate.

BOUNDARIES AND COHERENCE

For the opening boundary see Boundaries and Coherence for 15:1. This unit is the only place in the scene where the victorious saints are mentioned, and the description of them and their song gives 15:2–4 its coherence. At 15:5 attention switches back to the seven angels.

PROMINENCE AND THEME

In a *description-DECLARATION* paragraph pattern the DECLARATION is more naturally prominent, but the *description* is also thematic. Within the DECLARATION, the fact that the victors have conquered and sing the song of Moses, which was a song of deliverance, plus the fact that they praise God for his great and wonderful deeds, point to a focus on deliverance here. The words 'just and true ways' and 'righteous judgments' show a focus on God's judging in a completely just manner.

SCENE CONSTITUENT 15:5–8 (Paragraph: Step of 15:1–16:21)

THEME: I saw the angels being given the seven bowls of God's anger in the heavenly sanctuary, which became filled with the smoke that signified God's glory.

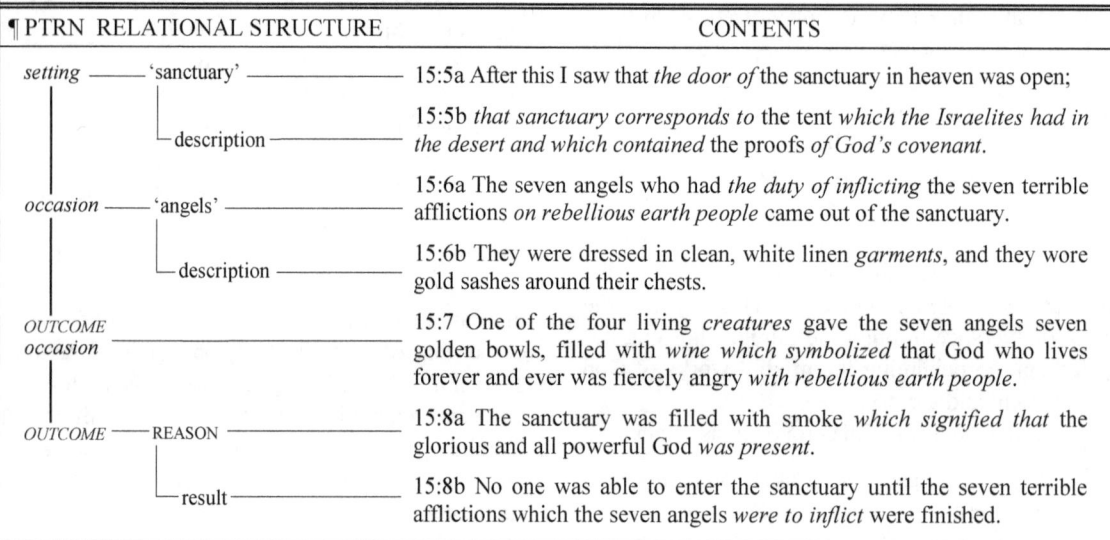

¶ PTRN RELATIONAL STRUCTURE	CONTENTS
setting — 'sanctuary'	15:5a After this I saw that *the door of* the sanctuary in heaven was open;
└ description	15:5b *that sanctuary corresponds to* the tent *which the Israelites had in the desert and which contained* the proofs *of God's covenant.*
occasion — 'angels'	15:6a The seven angels who had *the duty of inflicting* the seven terrible afflictions *on rebellious earth people* came out of the sanctuary.
└ description	15:6b They were dressed in clean, white linen *garments*, and they wore gold sashes around their chests.
OUTCOME occasion	15:7 One of the four living *creatures* gave the seven angels seven golden bowls, filled with *wine which symbolized* that God who lives forever and ever was fiercely angry *with rebellious earth people.*
OUTCOME — REASON	15:8a The sanctuary was filled with smoke *which signified that* the glorious and all powerful God *was present.*
└ result	15:8b No one was able to enter the sanctuary until the seven terrible afflictions which the seven angels *were to inflict* were finished.

INTENT AND PARAGRAPH PATTERN

In the 15:5–8 paragraph, the seven angels are made ready for their mission of pouring the seven bowls of God's judgment on rebellious earth people.

There are three aorist verbs that indicate action on a timeline, ἐξῆλθον 'they came out,' ἔδωκεν 'he gave,' and ἐγεμίσθη 'was filled (with smoke)'. The paragraph thus has a narrative timeline with a stimulus-response chain, so it is of the *occasion-OUTCOME* paragraph pattern type. This is confirmed by the narrative introducer 'after these things' in 15:5.

NOTES

15:5a–b After this I saw that *the door of* the sanctuary in heaven was open; *that sanctuary corresponds to* the tent *which the Israelites had in the desert and which contained* the proofs *of God's covenant* The phrase ἡ σκηνή τοῦ μαρτυρίου 'the tent of the witness' is one of the names given to the tent constructed in the wilderness (Num. 9:15). It was so called because it contained the ark of the covenant. In the ark were the stone tablets of the ten commandments, which were the proofs, or witness, of God's covenant with his people.

Several commentators point out that the whole phrase 'the sanctuary of the tent (of witness in heaven)' contains an apposition and means 'the sanctuary in heaven, that is (or, which corresponds to) the tent.' It is notable that at this point, when God is about to answer the prayers of his people for justice, the action is shown as flowing from the place that signifies his covenant with them.

15:6b clean, white linen *garments* The linen is specified as being clean and white, both terms frequently associated with heaven. The word for 'white' may also be translated 'bright, shining'.

they wore gold sashes around their chests The gold of the sashes symbolizes both royalty and a divine relationship. The position of the sashes suggests they wore long priestly robes (1:13).

15:7 One of the four living *creatures* Participation of one of the living creatures adds importance to the event. They are introduced in 4:6–8 and mentioned several times in the book.

bowls The Greek φιάλη refers to a type of large shallow bowl that usually contained wine or other liquid offerings that were to be poured out in worship. In 5:8 it is the type of bowl containing the burning incense.

filled with *wine which symbolized* that God who lives forever and ever was fiercely angry *with rebellious earth people* Here the golden bowl represents by metonymy the liquid within the bowl. Thus it also represents the wrath of God. But in a full proposition the liquid also needs to be mentioned since the word 'filled' is used in the text. Bratcher and Hatton suggest using wine for the liquid in view of the "wine of the wrath of God" in 14:10.

15:8a The sanctuary was filled with smoke *which signified that* **the glorious and all powerful God** *was present* Smoke is often used in scripture to indicate the active presence of God (Exod. 19:18; Isa. 6:4; see Alford, Mounce, Swete). Swete says, "On this occasion the smoke proceeds from (ἐκ) the Divine glory and power, i.e., from the personal character and attributes of God and His boundless resources." Note that since smoke here is a manifestation of that essence or attribute of God which is elsewhere often manifested by radiant light it is probably better not to translate 'glory' here as 'radiance', 'light', etc., but by some word that indicates the awesome divine character. This is the intention in the use of 'glorious' in the display.

15:8b No one was able to enter the sanctuary until the seven terrible afflictions which the seven angels *were to inflict* **were finished** The finality of this ending refers back to 15:1, where the same word τελέω 'to finish' is used to express it. This emphasizes the completeness of the judgment. Although it is the result of 15:8a it is inherently less prominent since it is irrealis, and it is not referred to again.

BOUNDARIES AND COHERENCE

Its narrative timeline sets 15:5–8 off from 15:2–4. It is set off from the timeline action in 16:1–21 by the narrative introducer 'and I heard' at 16:1, and by the fact that that unit deals with the ordered action of the pouring out of the seven bowls.

Coherence is provided by the references to 'the sanctuary' in 15:5a, 8a and 8b.

PROMINENCE AND THEME

In an *occasion-OUTCOME* paragraph pattern, the final OUTCOME is usually the most naturally prominent component, but the *occasions* are also thematic. Here the first outcome (15:7), which is the second occasion, is highlighted by having a transitive verb, in contrast to the passive of 15:8a.

SCENE CONSTITUENT 16:1–21 (Episode: Goal of 15:1–16:21)

THEME: The pouring out of the first five bowls brought judgment in the form of terrible afflictions on the people of earth who had worshipped the beast. When the sixth bowl was poured out the rulers of earth began to unite for the final battle against God, but Jesus called on his people to be ready for him. When the seventh bowl was emptied God announced that his punishing of people was complete. Cosmic manifestations and wide destruction followed, but the people cursed God.

MACROSTRUCTURE	CONTENTS
setting	16:1 I heard a voice from the sanctuary tell the seven angels to pour out on earth the bowls that represent the anger of God.
step₁	16:2–9 When the first angel poured out his bowl it caused severe sores on the worshipers of the beast. The second turned sea water to blood and all sea creatures died. The third turned all fresh water to blood and the rebellious people got the punishment they deserved by having to drink it. When the fourth bowl was poured out it caused the sun's heat to scorch people very badly and they cursed God.
step₂	16:10–11 When the fifth angel poured out his bowl it brought complete darkness on the beast's followers and they cursed God.
step₃	16:12–16 When the sixth angel poured out his bowl the River Euphrates dried up, providing a way for the rulers of earth to unite against God. Evil spirits gathered them for battle at Harmagedon. But Jesus called on his people to be ready for his coming.
GOAL	16:17–21 When the seventh bowl was emptied, God announced that his punishing of rebellious people was complete. Cosmic manifestations and wide destruction also followed, but the people cursed God.

INTENT AND MACROSTRUCTURE

As with the seven seals (5:1–8:5) and the seven trumpets (8:6–11:19) this unit has a narrative *step-GOAL* structure, with the first four bowls forming one sub-unit. 16:1 forms a *setting*, linking the unit to 15:5. It is sometimes considered that 16:12–16 form an interlude between the last *step* and the *GOAL*, as in the other series, but there are reasons to reject such an analysis (see below, 16:12–16 Boundaries and Coherence).

BOUNDARIES AND COHERENCE

The opening boundary of the unit is marked by Καὶ ἤκουσα 'Then I heard,' which introduces a new stage in the action. The end of the unit also forms the end of the second act of the body of the book. Although one of the bowl angels reappears in 17:1 the break is marked by a change of scene, with the narrator, John, coming to the forefront of the narrative, and by a lack of further reference to the bowls.

Coherence within the unit is provided primarily by reference throughout to the seven bowls, but also by references to the beast and his followers (16:2, 10, 13) and by references to the 'terrible afflictions (plagues)' and 'intense pain' suffered by the earth people as a result of the judgments (16:9, 10, 11, 21).

PROMINENCE AND THEME

In a *step-GOAL* pattern both the *steps* and the *GOAL* are considered thematic and the *GOAL* to which the *steps* lead is most prominent. In this case the pouring out of the sixth bowl (16:12–16) is given added prominence by its introduction of a new theme, the final battle on 'the great day of God' and by the beatitude, from Christ himself, that is occasioned by this reference.

EPISODE CONSTITUENT 16:1 (Propositional cluster: setting of 16:1–21)

THEME: *I heard a voice from the sanctuary tell the seven angels to pour out on earth the bowls that represent the anger of God.*		
RELATIONAL STRUCTURE		CONTENTS
┌─orienter │ │ └─CONTENT		16:1a I *John* heard a loud voice, *which came* from the sanctuary *in heaven*, say to the seven angels *who had the seven bowls*.
		16:1b "Go from here and pour out on the earth *the liquid/wine in* the seven bowls, *which represents* God's being angry with *rebellious people*."

INTENT

This short unit provides the setting for the whole of 16:1–21. It shows that all the plagues which are inflicted on the earth happen at the command of the voice from the heavenly sanctuary, presumably the voice of God.

NOTES

16:1a a loud voice The descriptive adjective μεγάλης 'loud' stands before the noun φωνῆς 'voice', emphasizing its loudness. Its coming from the sanctuary is generally taken to mean it is God's voice, since it has just been said (15:8) that no one could enter the sanctuary during the seven plagues.

16:1b Go from here The compound verb ὑπάγετε 'go away' may be interpreted as a command to the angels to go from the heavenly sanctuary, which in 16:2a they do (ἀπῆλθεν 'he went away'). This ties them to the sanctuary, just as ἐξῆλθον 'went out' does in 15:6, authenticating the judgments. However, since ὑπάγετε and ἀπῆλθεν can be understood in other contexts as having the sense of 'go' or 'went' without focus on the point of departure, another potential translation here would be 'Go' by itself.

pour out No limit is expressed for the pouring out of God's wrath as in earlier judgments (8:7–12; 9:15), and since the implication is that the bowls were completely poured out or emptied, unlimited judgment is no doubt meant. Full and final expression of God's wrath is the characteristic mark of this scene.

the liquid/wine in* the seven bowls, *which represents* God's being angry with *rebellious people See the note on 15:7.

BOUNDARIES AND COHERENCE

In 16:1 the introductory phrase 'and I heard' and the switch of main participant (from one of the living creatures to the unnamed loud voice) indicates that this is the start of a new unit. At 16:2 the focus again switches, to the actions on earth of the seven angels.

PROMINENCE AND THEME

The theme is comprised of the main points of the orienter and the content.

EPISODE CONSTITUENT 16:2–9 (Paragraph Cluster: Step$_1$ of 16:1–21)

THEME: When the first angel poured out his bowl it caused severe sores on the worshipers of the beast. The second turned sea water to blood and all sea creatures died. The third turned all fresh water to blood and the rebellious people got the punishment they deserved by having to drink it. When the fourth bowl was poured out it caused the sun's heat to scorch people very badly and they cursed God.

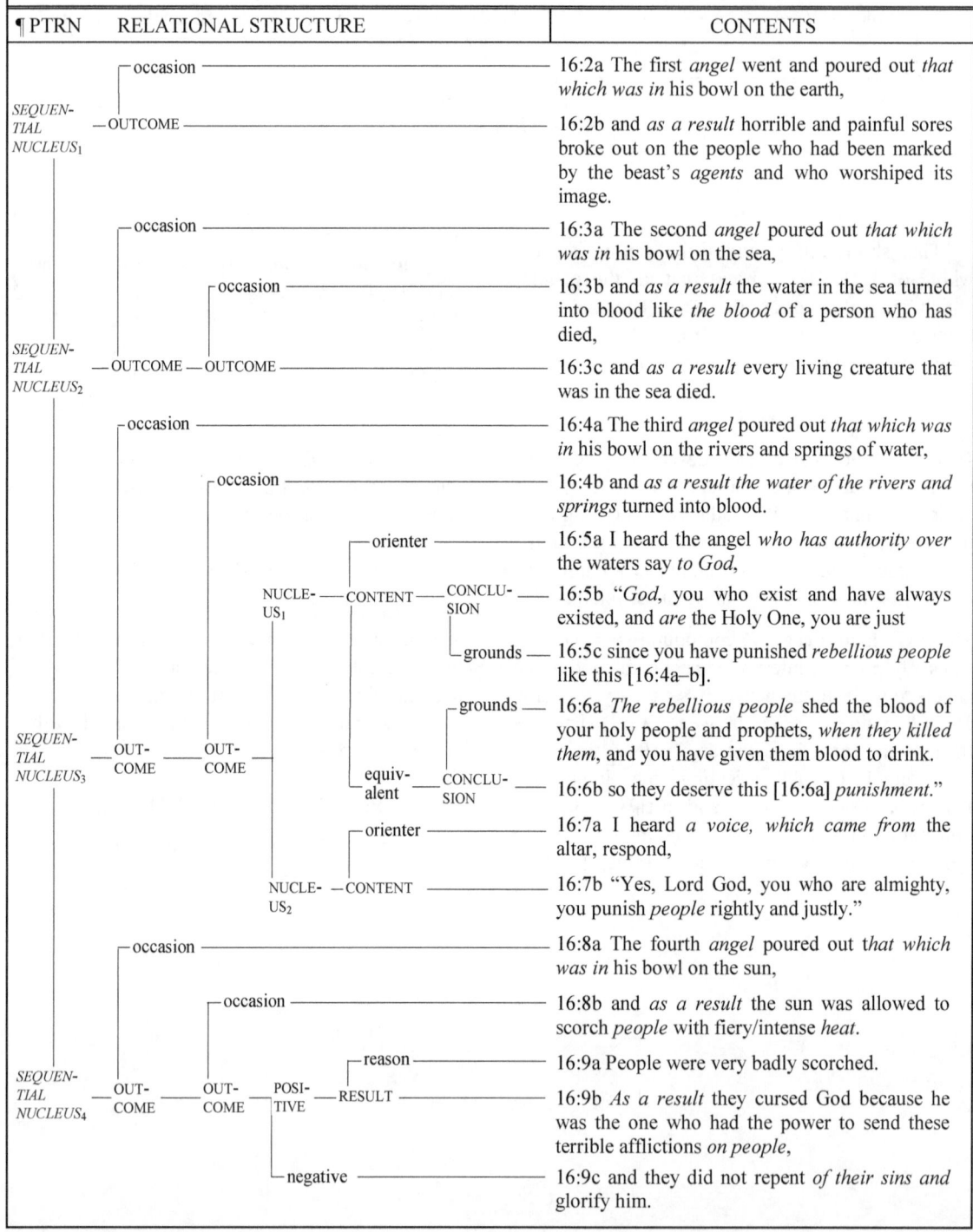

¶PTRN	RELATIONAL STRUCTURE	CONTENTS
SEQUENTIAL NUCLEUS$_1$	┌ occasion ─────────── └ OUTCOME ───────────	16:2a The first *angel* went and poured out *that which was in* his bowl on the earth,
		16:2b and *as a result* horrible and painful sores broke out on the people who had been marked by the beast's *agents* and who worshiped its image.
SEQUENTIAL NUCLEUS$_2$	┌ occasion ─────────────── │ ┌ occasion ── └ OUTCOME ─ OUTCOME ── └	16:3a The second *angel* poured out *that which was in* his bowl on the sea,
		16:3b and *as a result* the water in the sea turned into blood like *the blood* of a person who has died,
		16:3c and *as a result* every living creature that was in the sea died.
SEQUENTIAL NUCLEUS$_3$	┌ occasion ─────────────── │ ┌ occasion ──────── │ │ ┌ orienter ── │ │ │ │ │ NUCLE- ─ CONTENT ─ CONCLU- │ │ US$_1$ SION │ │ └ grounds ── │ │ ┌ grounds ── │ │ equiv- ─ CONCLU- │ │ alent SION ── └ OUT- ─ OUT- ┌ orienter ── COME COME NUCLE- ─ CONTENT ── US$_2$	16:4a The third *angel* poured out *that which was in* his bowl on the rivers and springs of water,
		16:4b and *as a result the water of the rivers and springs* turned into blood.
		16:5a I heard the angel *who has authority over the waters* say *to God,*
		16:5b "God, you who exist and have always existed, and *are* the Holy One, you are just
		16:5c since you have punished *rebellious people* like this [16:4a–b].
		16:6a *The rebellious people* shed the blood of your holy people and prophets, *when they killed them,* and you have given them blood to drink.
		16:6b so they deserve this [16:6a] *punishment*."
		16:7a I heard *a voice, which came from* the altar, respond,
		16:7b "Yes, Lord God, you who are almighty, you punish *people* rightly and justly."
SEQUENTIAL NUCLEUS$_4$	┌ occasion ─────────────── │ ┌ occasion ──────── │ │ ┌ reason ── └ OUT- ─ OUT- ─ POSI- ─ RESULT ── COME COME TIVE └ negative ──	16:8a The fourth *angel* poured out *that which was in* his bowl on the sun,
		16:8b and *as a result* the sun was allowed to scorch *people* with fiery/intense *heat.*
		16:9a People were very badly scorched.
		16:9b *As a result* they cursed God because he was the one who had the power to send these terrible afflictions *on people,*
		16:9c and they did not repent *of their sins* and glorify him.

INTENT AND PARAGRAPH PATTERN

In common with the first parts of the series of seven seals (6:1–8) and seven trumpets (8:6–12), this unit has a tightly knit narrative structure of four sequential actions. However, in this case the parallelisms between the sub-units are not as close as in the other series.

NOTES

16:2b horrible and painful sores According to BDAG the meaning of ἕλκος is 'sore, abscess, ulcer'. It is used in the LXX for the plague of boils (Exod. 9:9) and Job's boils (Job 2:7). The two Greek words used to describe the sores (κακός and πονηρός) are generic words for 'bad' and 'evil', and used together in a physical context like this could be translated as 'very bad sores.'

the people who had been marked by the beast's *agents* An alternate propositionalization would be 'the people who had been marked *by the beast's agents as* belonging to the beast'.

16:3b the water in the sea turned into blood like *the blood* of a person who has died Commentators agree that the water was turned into coagulated and corrupt blood.

16:5a the angel *who has authority over* the waters In 7:1–2 there is a reference to angels 'who control the four winds,' and in 14:18 there is mention of the angel 'who has authority over the fire,' so the Greek term here, ὁ ἄγγελος τῶν ὑδάτων 'the angel of the waters,' must refer to one with authority over the waters. Commentators say that in view of 16:3 and 4 this will be both the waters of the sea and the fresh water, but in fact 16:4a and 6a show that it is the fresh waters that are in focus here.

16:5b–6b The angel's speech forms a couplet in which the second part, 16:6a–b, mirrors the first, 16:5b–c, in both structure and meaning. The first part states that God has justly punished the sinners, and the second part states that they deserved the punishment they received.

16:6a shed the blood of your holy people and prophets, *when they killed them* Shedding blood would normally be a metaphor for killing, but here it is obviously literal, in view of the next reference to drinking blood. However, the act of killing is nevertheless implied, so it is supplied in the display.

your holy people and prophets 'Saints' refers to God's people and includes 'prophets'. While in other contexts ἅγιοι 'holy ones, saints' is translated as 'God's people', here it seems best translated as 'your holy people'.

16:7a *a voice, which came from* the altar There is a question about the source of the voice, whether it is that of an angel associated with the altar in some way or of the martyrs under the altar (6:9–11) or of the saints whose prayers are offered on the altar (8:3–4). Swete says, "The Altar or its Angel represents the sacrifices and prayers of the Church...." Morris says, "The altar is especially connected with the prayers of the saints (8:3) which introduced judgments of God (8:5)". The surface structure is personification but the important thought may be that saints and angels agree in their response to God's justice.

16:8a–b The fourth *angel* poured out *that which was in* his bowl on the sun, and *as a result* the sun was allowed to scorch *people* with fiery/intense *heat*. Here again ἐδόθη 'it was given/allowed' is used. No doubt it has the function of emphasizing the control God has over his judgments as it does elsewhere in Revelation.

It is best to translate καυματίσαι τοὺς ἀνθρώπους ἐν πυρί 'to burn people with fire' so that it communicates the idea that the type of burn intended is that which would come from intense heat of the sun rather than actual fire.

16:9a very badly scorched The use of the cognate accusative in the Greek ἐκαυματίσθησαν ... καῦμα μέγα 'scorched a great scorching' indicates the intensity of the punishment.

16:9b–c The outcome of the suffering is given in a positive-negative form: positive in the sense that it was an action (however evil) that was taken; negative in the sense that it was unrealized action, action that should have been taken.

16:9b cursed God The reaction to the heat is blasphemy, which confirms the settled rebellion against God and against the acknowledgement of his control. The verb βλασφημέω has the general meaning of 'insult, defame'. Many translations (NIV, NLT, RSV, TEV) use 'cursed' here.

Note that here the participial construction 'the one having the power over these plagues' actually functions semantically as reason.

16:9c they did not repent *of their sins and* glorify him The unrepentant attitude is like that of 9:20–21. Robertson (pp. 998–999) understands the infinitive δοῦναι 'to give' as an infinitive of result. This might be translated as 'They refused to repent and as a result give glory to God'.

BOUNDARIES AND COHERENCE

The unit begins with a switch of scene from the action in heaven to the actions of the first four angels on earth. However, it is debatable whether the unit ends with the pouring out of the fourth bowl or the fifth or the sixth. To some extent the actions of all seven angels form a continuous series, but it is also true to say that there is more parallelism between the first four. The fact that the first four bowls are poured out on the land, the sea, the fresh waters and the sun, while the fifth angel pours his bowl out on the throne of the beast, would give coherence to verses 1–9. Another factor indicating that 16:9 may be the close of the unit is the reference to the blasphemy of the unrepentant people, which also comes at the close of other units in 16:11 and 21.

PROMINENCE AND THEME

The four sequential nuclei are equally prominent and comprise the theme.

EPISODE CONSTITUENT 16:10–11 (Paragraph: Step₂ of 16:1–21)

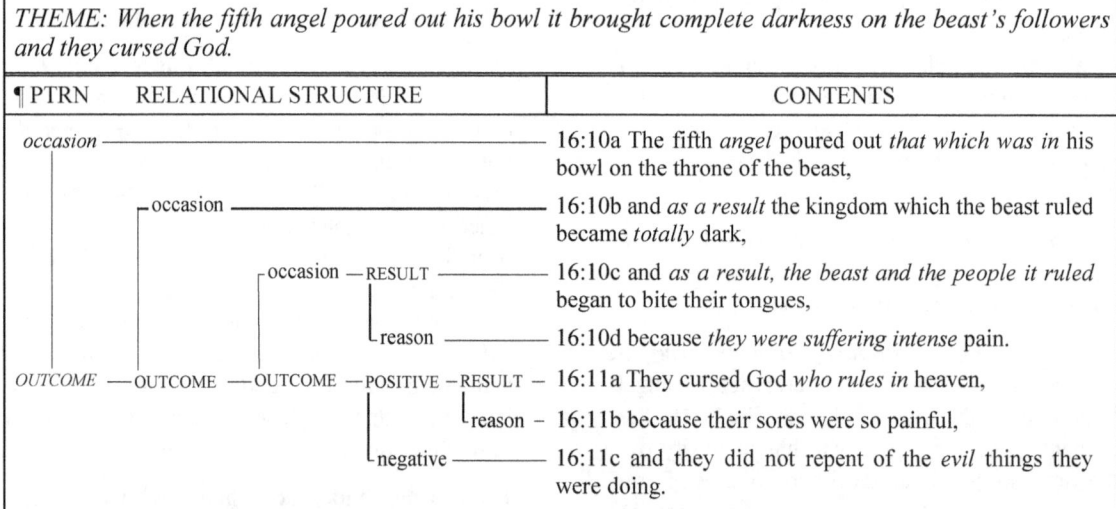

INTENT AND PARAGRAPH PATTERN

This unit has a narrative *occasion–OUTCOME* structure, in which the *occasion* is the pouring out of the fifth bowl and the *OUTCOME* is the utter darkness that descends on the followers of the beast (who by this stage of the narrative are synonymous with the rebellious people of earth), and their reaction to their sufferings.

NOTES

16:10c *the beast and the people it ruled* began to bite their tongues, The verb ἐμασῶντο 'began to bite' has a plural subject, which must refer to the beast and its subjects in view of the previous reference to the kingdom of the beast.

16:10d because *they were suffering intense* pain The pain was so intense that it caused them to bite, or gnaw, their tongues, but the pain's source is not specified here. The word for pain could also be translated 'suffering' or 'distress', but since there is a reference to sores in 16:11c and the sores would be more likely to produce intense pain than the darkness, the sores are probably the source of the pain. The darkness would make the pain all the more oppressive.

16:11a They cursed God *who rules in* heaven Since the phrase τὸν θεὸν τοῦ οὐρανοῦ 'the God of heaven' is a genitive construction, we need to ask its meaning or function. The choice would seem to be between 'God (*or*, the God) who lives in heaven' and 'God (*or*, the God) who rules in/from heaven'. The latter is more meaningful and fits the context.

16:11b because their sores were so painful An option suggested by Bratcher and Hatton for rendering 'for their pains and sores' is 'for their painful sores'. This would seem exegetically correct since it is most logical that the pain would have come from their sores.

16:11c they did not repent of the *evil* things they were doing. The relationship in 16:11a-c between blaspheming and lack of repentance is the same as that in 16:9b–c.

BOUNDARIES AND COHERENCE

The initial boundary for this paragraph was discussed in the Boundaries and Coherence for 16:2–9. The final boundary is marked by reference to people reacting to judgment by cursing God, as at the end of the other units 16:2–9 and 17–21. It is true that there is reference to the beast in 16:10 and in 16:13, but in 16:10 he is a king on a throne whereas in 13 he is merely a location for the emergence of the evil spirits.

PROMINENCE AND THEME

As an *occasion–OUTCOME* paragraph both components are essential to the theme.

EPISODE CONSTITUENT 16:12–16 (Paragraph Cluster: Step₃ of 16:1–21)

THEME: When the sixth angel poured out his bowl the River Euphrates dried up, providing a way for the rulers of earth to unite against God. Evil spirits gathered them for battle at Harmagedon. But Jesus called on his people to be ready for his coming.

¶ PTRN	RELATIONAL STRUCTURE	CONTENTS
occasion		16:12a The sixth *angel* poured out *that which was in* his bowl on the great river Euphrates
OUTCOME₁	occasion	16:12b and *as a result* its water/flow dried up,
	OUTCOME	16:12c so that a path was ready for the rulers of the eastern *countries to cross the river with their armies*.
	move₁ — 'spirits'	16:13 Then I saw three evil spirits, which *looked* like frogs, *come out* from the mouth of the dragon, from the mouth of the beast, and from the mouth of the false prophet.
	description	16:14a These were demonic spirits that perform miracles.
	move₂ — MEANS	16:14b They went everywhere to all the rulers of the whole world,
	purpose — 'the great day'	16:14c in order to gather them together to the battle *which will be fought* on the great day *when* Almighty God *destroys his enemies*.
	orienter	16:15a *I heard the Lord Jesus say*,
	grounds	16:15b "**Listen to me**. I will come *unexpectedly*, like a thief *comes in the night*.
	PAREN-THESIS — EXHOR-TATION	16:15c *God* will bless anyone who *is ready for me by staying alert and living righteously*, like someone who stays awake at night with his clothes on so that he will not be ashamed because *people* see him going around naked *if a thief comes*." [MET]
OUTCOME₂ — GOAL		16:16 *The evil spirits* [16:13] gathered the rulers [16:14b] together at a place which is called in the Hebrew *language* Harmagedon.

INTENT AND PARAGRAPH PATTERN

Like the other bowl judgments this unit has a narrative *occasion–OUTCOME* structure. However, it is noticeable that as the narrative approaches the goal of the scene, and of the act, the structure becomes more complex, with two *OUTCOMES*. The first is the direct result of the pouring of the angel's bowl in the River Euphrates, and the second is the beginning of preparations for the final battle between the power of God and the forces of evil.

In 16:15 there is the third beatitude in the book. Coming from Christ himself, it might seem to break the timeline of the unit, but structurally it can also be seen as a parenthetical comment on the concept of 'the great day of God' in 16:14c (see the Note). It has a hortatory function as a warning to the believers that they must remain alert and faithful during the great battle with evil which is to come. It thus fulfils one of the purposes of the whole prophetic discourse, that of encouraging spiritual readiness for Christ's return.

NOTES

16:12a–c The sixth *angel* **poured out** *that which was in* **his bowl on the great river Euphrates, and** *as a result* **its water/flow dried up, so that a path was ready for the rulers of the eastern** *countries to cross the river with their armies* For both Jews and Romans the River Euphrates represented the ultimate Eastern boundary of their territory, beyond which were the lands of fierce nations such as the Parthians and the Medes who would from time to time invade them and bring terrible destruction. As a very large river the Euphrates was never known to dry up, so in the present symbolical context of the vision its drying up would mean that every barrier was removed for the final conflict of God with the powers of evil.

16:13 Then I saw three evil spirits, which *looked* **like frogs,** *come out* **from the mouth of the dragon, from the mouth of the beast, and from the mouth of the false prophet** The spirits are called ἀκάθαρτα 'unclean', referring to their evil character. The word is used of demons in the Gospels (Matt. 12:43–45). An alternate for 'which looked like frogs' would be 'in the form of frogs'.

the false prophet The false prophet is identified as the beast from the land (13:11–18), who acted on behalf of the first beast, worked miracles and deceived the people of earth. It completes the triad of evil beings, a mocking imitation of the holy trinity. It is called a prophet as it speaks on the behalf of the dragon and the first beast, as a prophet speaks on behalf of God. It is called 'false' because it uses lies and deception.

16:14a These were demonic spirits The Greek text has a genitive phrase πνεύματα δαιμονίων 'spirits of demons' in which the noun in the genitive case functions as an adjective.

16:14b They went everywhere The historic present tense used here points forward to the main event in 16:16.

to all the rulers of the whole world These demonic spirits go to all the kings (i.e. rulers) of the whole world. Their purpose was to bring all earthly power to conflict with the Almighty God.

16:14c the battle *which will be fought* **on the great day** *when* **Almighty God** *destroys his enemies* As elsewhere in scripture where "the day of the Lord", "the day of Christ", etc. is used, 'the great day of God the Almighty' is metonymy for the time "when the total redemptive purpose of God will be consummated, both for salvation and judgment, both for individuals, the church, and the whole creation" (Ladd).

16:15a–b *I heard the Lord Jesus say,* "**Listen to me**. **I will come** *unexpectedly* ..." See Intent and paragraph pattern for the function and relationship of this verse. The parenthesis seems to be occasioned by the mention of 'the great day of God' in 16:14c. Christ himself warned his disciples that they must always be ready because that day, when he would return in triumph, would come upon them as unexpectedly as a burglar in the night-time (Matt. 24:43–44). The warning must have been regarded as very significant by the early church since it was repeated by Paul (1 Thess. 5:2) and Peter (2 Pet. 3:10) and in Revelation (3:3). So it is appropriate that it is interjected at this point, just as the preparations for the battle of that day are begun.

Even though the warning is presented here without an orienter in the surface structure, exegetically it is obvious that it is from Christ. The term ἰδού 'lo, behold' can be taken in this context as a command to listen (TEV) and is a marker of emphasis (as in 1:7, 2:22, 3:8 etc.). It is followed by ἔρχομαι 'I come, I am coming' in the present tense, which is used to foreground the most important point, as is usual in non-narrative material. These elements, the use of ἰδού and the foregrounding, together with the fact that the words come from Christ himself (echoing 3:3) combine to give the parenthesis marked prominence.

16:15c *God* **will bless anyone who** *is ready for me by staying alert and living righteously like someone who* **stays awake at night with his clothes on** This beatitude is the third of the seven found in the book. See note on 1:3. It is a mitigated command to be faithful to the end and remain alert, guarding against sin. The literal meaning of γρηγορέω is "to remain awake". This instance is listed in BDAG as figurative, meaning 'to be on the alert'.

with his clothes on The participial phrase τηρῶν τὰ ἱμάτια αὐτοῦ 'keeping his garments' is used figuratively in that the garments represent the conduct and character of God's people. Some have interpreted the charge concerning the garments to mean they should be kept at hand so that one could dress quickly, but this does not seem as appropriate for representing the nonfigurative meaning as actually keeping the garments on all the time. The thought in focus is that when Christ arrives there will not be time to make preparation; the Christian must be ready and continually watching. Metaphorically this is likened to someone having to jump up suddenly in the middle of the night to deal with an unexpected event like a burglary.

16:16 *The evil spirits* **[16:13] gathered the rulers [16:14b] together at a place which is called in the Hebrew** *language* **Harmagedon** The demons were successful in gathering the political leaders of the whole world and their armies to the designated place. The name of the place is given in the GNT as Ἁρμαγεδών 'Harmagedon'. This is presumed to represent the Hebrew for 'mountains of Megiddo.' But although Megiddo was the site of many historic battles between God's people of Israel and their enemies, it is in a plain, not in the mountains. The name may therefore be a reference to Ezek. 38–39, where the final battle with the forces of evil takes place in 'the mountains of Israel.'

BOUNDARIES AND COHERENCE

The initial boundary for this unit was discussed in the Boundaries and Coherence for 16:10–11. Its final boundary at 16:16 is established by the appearance of the seventh angel in 16:17 and the switch of scene from earth to heaven.

However, the internal coherence of 6:12–16 can be questioned, since 16:13 begins with Καὶ εἶδον 'And I saw,' which normally introduces a new unit. Mounce says, "Verses 13–16 are sometimes taken as a brief interlude between the sixth and seventh bowls similar in structure to the break between the sixth and seventh seals (chap. 7) and the sixth and seventh trumpets (10:1–11:14)". But he then asserts that these verses "should be viewed as a topical expansion of v.12 (with v.15 serving as a summons to readiness). …preparation for war is the common theme". This is especially true if one takes the 'kings from the east' in 16:12 as part of, or representative of, the 'kings of the whole world' in 16:14.

The interjection of the beatitude in 16:15 might also be considered as compromising the coherence of the unit, but once its connection to 16:14c is recognized (see Intent and Paragraph Structure above) it can be seen as consistent with the theme of preparation for the final battle.

PROMINENCE AND THEME

The *occasion* and both the OUTCOMES are represented in the theme statement. The interjected warning (16:15) also has prominence as a mitigated exhortation. It is one of the seven beatitudes of the book and is spoken by Christ himself to encourage his people to faithfulness.

EPISODE CONSTITUENT 16:17–21 (Paragraph Cluster: Goal of 16:1–21)

THEME: When the seventh bowl was emptied, God announced that his punishing of rebellious people was complete. Cosmic manifestations and wide destruction also followed, but the people cursed God.

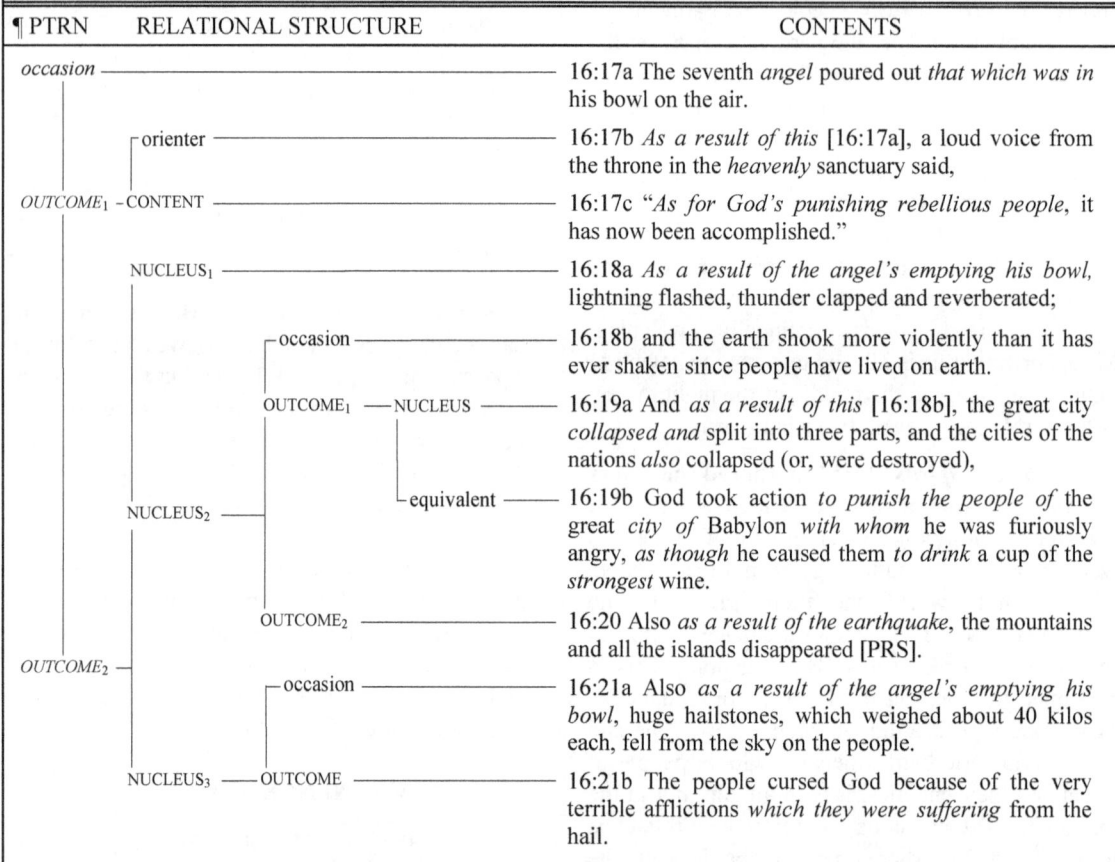

INTENT AND PARAGRAPH PATTERN

The 16:17–21 episode ends the bowl judgments with the outpouring of the seventh bowl. There are two OUTCOMES of this outpouring. The first is the announcement of the completion of the punishment of rebellious people (γέγονεν 'it has happened', 16:17). This is highly significant since it applies not only to the seven bowls, but to the whole judgment action of the three series presented in the second act. The second OUTCOME is the mighty earthquake that destroys Babylon and the cities of the nations and the devastating hailstorm. With this final punishment the reaction of the rebellious people of earth is not repentance but insulting God.

NOTES

16:17b a loud voice from the throne in the *heavenly* sanctuary said The voice comes from God's presence. Lenski says, "…there rings out a great voice 'out of the Sanctuary from the throne,' out of the symbol of God's holiness, from the symbol of his power, rule and dominion…". However some commentators hold that nowhere in Revelation does the text state explicitly that God speaks. He has given the revelation to his Son (1:1).

16:17c "*As for God's punishing rebellious people*, it has now been accomplished." The Greek has simply γέγονεν 'it has happened, come to pass'. This may apply first to the command of 16:1, but it more likely applies to the whole series of judgments described in the second act (4:1–16:21). These may be what are referred to in 4:1 as ἃ δεῖ γενέσθαι 'the things which must happen'. However, although some English versions translate it as 'it is finished/over' it should be noted that the verb γίνομαι is not listed in BDAG or other lexicons with the meaning 'be finished' and no other examples of its use with this meaning are adduced by commentators. J. B. Phillips translates it as "The end has come", which may indicate that it refers to the 'great day of God' (16:14) rather than to the series of judgments. See also the note on the almost identical verb γέγοναν at 21:6.

16:18a lightning flashed, thunder clapped and reverberated The cosmic manifestations which followed the emptying of the seventh bowl have occurred in 4:5 in the description of the throne and at the close of the other two series of judgments (8:5; 11:19). The repetition and the context show that these words should be translated in an emphatic way.

16:18b and the earth shook more violently than it has ever shaken since people have lived on earth Strong emphasis is on the violence of the earthquake: 'great, such as never had occurred since people lived on the earth, so great was that earthquake'. The emphasis is indicated in the Greek by the preposing of the subject noun before the verb, σεισμὸς ἐγένετο μέγας 'an earthquake happened great.'

16:19a the great city *collapsed and* **split into three parts, and the cities of the nations** *also* **collapsed (*or*, were destroyed)** The fall of the great city and the cities of the nations is complete. In 11:8 'the great city' was identified as Jerusalem and was equated with Sodom and Egypt, but in ch.18 Babylon is 'the great city.' It is therefore clear that the term does not stand for any specific city on earth, but prophetically it stands for "civilized man in organized community" (Morris). There is therefore no difference of reference here between 'the great city,' 'the cities of the nations' and 'Babylon' in 16:19b.

Literally the Greek says 'the great city became three parts,' but all the commentators understand this to mean that the whole city experienced devastation and destruction.

16:19b God took action *to punish the people of* **the great** *city of* **Babylon** This is a restatement of 16:19a since 'Babylon' is synonymous with 'the great city' (see previous note). The Greek says 'Babylon the great was remembered before God' but the "remembering" of God can mean blessing and protection for his own, or punishment for his enemies. The meaning in this passage is punishment. It does not imply that God has been forgetting, but it highlights the fact that the time for action has come, as an angel declared in 10:6 and another angel elaborated in 14:8.

with whom **he was furiously angry,** *as though* **he caused them** *to drink* **a cup of the** *strongest* **wine** See the notes on 14:8c and 14:10a. 'Anger' and 'wrath' in a context like this refer not only to God's emotions but also to the carrying out of his will in just punishment. The function of the repetition of synonyms in 'the anger of his wrath' is to indicate the great intensity of the anger and may be translated as a hendiadys such as 'furious anger' (TEV). The intensity of the anger implies intensity of the wine: '*strongest* wine'.

16:20 Also *as a result of the earthquake*, **the mountains and all the islands disappeared** The verbs used in the Greek with reference to the islands and the mountains, 'fled' and 'were not found', are personifications and are metaphorically synonymous, signifying disappearance. This disappearance is the result of the terrible earthquake (Alford, Morris, Mounce). In 6:14 the islands and mountains are shaken from their places and in this verse they disappear entirely. This may imply that in 6:14 the appearance of the earth was starting to change and here the change is completed.

16:21a Also *as a result of the angel's emptying his bowl*, **huge hailstones, which weighed about 40 kilos each, fell from the sky on the people** The hail is not seen as caused by the earthquake but as another direct result of the seventh bowl. The verb "fell" is in the historic present tense, highlighting the OUTCOME in 16:21b.

16:21b The people cursed God because of the very terrible afflictions *which they were suffering* **from the hail** For 'curse' see the note on 16:9b. The intensifier σφόδρα 'very, extremely' is separated from the adjective it modifies and, being placed at the end of this part of the discourse, it highlights the climax of the judgment.

BOUNDARIES AND COHERENCE

The unit begins at 16:17 with the emptying of the last bowl of the last series of judgments in the fifth scene of the second act. The final boundary comes at the end of the punishment resulting from the last bowl and is coincident with the end of the act. It has some transitional features. An obvious feature indicating that chapter 17 belongs to another higher level unit is the introduction of the harlot in 17:1. She is the major antagonist in all of chapters 17 and 18. The beginning of the third act is also marked by a change of scene for the narrator in 17:3.

Coherence within 16:17–21 is evident from the fact that the activities described are the physical manifestations on earth that ensue from the emptying of the seventh bowl of God's wrath.

PROMINENCE AND THEME

Both *OUTCOMES* (16:17 and 16:18–21) are thematic. The announcement of completion of judgment certainly contains marked prominence in the sense that it applies not only to the seventh bowl, but to the whole judgment action of the three series presented in the second act. But the second *OUTCOME* is also prominent as the carrying out of the final punishment. The final nucleus of this outcome (16:21b) is given marked prominence by the historic present tense in 16:21a.

The theme gives the divine statement of justice satisfied and the immediate results of the emptying of the seventh bowl, including the cosmic response and the negative reaction of rebellious people.

PART CONSTITUENT 17:1–20:15 (Act: Step$_3$ of Body)

THEME: I saw the great prostitute, Babylon, who was drunk with the blood of God's people. When she was destroyed I heard the inhabitants of heaven praising God and God's people rejoicing that the time had come for the marriage of the Lamb. Then I saw the King of kings going out to destroy the rebellious people of the nations. The beast and the false prophet led the people to fight against God's people but they were all destroyed, Satan was imprisoned, and God's people reigned as kings for a thousand years. After Satan led another rebellion against God, God had him thrown in the lake of fire. Then God judged all people by their deeds and all whose names were not in the book of life were thrown into the lake of fire.

MACROSTRUCTURE	CONTENTS
step	17:1–19:10 I saw the great prostitute, Babylon, who was drunk with the blood of God's people. When she was destroyed the people of earth lamented and God's people rejoiced. Then I heard the inhabitants of heaven praising God for destroying her and I heard God's people rejoicing that the time had come for the marriage of the Lamb. I was told that those whom God invites to the Lamb's wedding are blessed.
GOAL	19:11–20:15 I saw the King of kings going out to destroy the rebellious people of the nations. The beast and the false prophet led the people to fight against God's people but they were all destroyed, Satan was imprisoned and God's people reigned as kings for a thousand years. After Satan led another rebellion against God, God had him thrown in the lake of fire. Then God judged all people by their deeds and all whose names were not in the book of life were thrown into the lake of fire.

INTENT AND MACROSTRUCTURE

Just as the overall structure of Revelation shows a progression towards the complete destruction of evil and God's establishment of his perfect kingdom, so this Act also has a progressive narrative structure. Since 19:11–20:15 reveals the final destruction of the devil and all who follow him, while the destruction in 17:1–19:10 is limited to that of the evil world system represented by Babylon, there is certainly progression between these two units in the Act. The structure is therefore that of *step-GOAL*.

BOUNDARIES AND COHERENCE

The beginning boundary of this Act is discussed under the Boundaries and Coherence for Part Constituent 4:1–16:21. The Act deals with the destruction of all that is evil in the world, and it closes at 20:15 with the elimination of the final evil, death itself, and of the evil and rebellious people of earth, those who are not registered in the Lamb's Book of Life. Chapter 21 begins a new Act with the description of the new heaven and new earth free from all evil, and after an introductory scene it has John called and transported by an angel to a new location (21:9–10), just as at the start of this Act (17:1–3).

The coherence of 17:1–22:15 lies in the repeated focus on God's actions against the forces of evil defeating and destroying them. Yet throughout there are also encouraging references to God's people, showing them that they are separate from the evil that is being destroyed and that they will triumph over it through Christ (17:14, 18:4, 20, 19:5–9, 14, 20:4–6).

PROMINENCE AND THEME

In a *step-GOAL* structure like this both the *step* and *GOAL* are thematic enough to be included in the theme statement. Thus, the theme shows the details of God's progressive judgment and destruction of all that is evil.

ACT CONSTITUENT 17:1–19:10 (Scene: Step of 17:1–20:15)

THEME: I saw the great prostitute, Babylon, who was drunk with the blood of God's people. When she was destroyed the people of earth lamented and God's people rejoiced. Then I heard the inhabitants of heaven praising God for destroying her and I heard God's people rejoicing that the time had come for the marriage of the Lamb. I was told that those whom God invites to the Lamb's wedding are blessed.

MACROSTRUCTURE	CONTENTS
setting	17:1–2 One of the angels of the bowls offered to show me how God will punish the great prostitute who has seduced the earth people to act immorally.
situation	17:3–18:24 I was bewildered when I saw a prostitute sitting on a red beast and I saw that she was drunk with the blood of God's people. But an angel showed me that the beast represented the rulers of earth and the woman was the great city that dominated earth people and they would be destroyed by God and the Lamb. Then I heard voices from heaven declare that the great city of Babylon is destroyed, that the people of earth will bewail their loss, but God's people must flee from the city and rejoice.
REACTION	19:1–8 I heard a great crowd in heaven, led by the twenty-four elders and the four living creatures praising God for punishing and destroying the great prostitute. Then a great crowd of God's people praised his sovereignty and rejoiced that the time had come for the marriage of the Lamb and his bride.
CODA (BEATITUDE)	19:9–10 An angel told me that God will bless the people who have been invited to celebrate the marriage of the Lamb. I was then cautioned not to worship the angel, but only God.

INTENT AND MACROSTRUCTURE

The reaction to the destruction of Babylon as expressed in the victory cry of the great multitude in 19:1–8 is certainly emotive in nature, so the main relationship in this unit is considered as *situation-REACTION*. The use of 'after these things' in 19:1 confirms that it is a sequential unit. Since the beatitudes of Revelation do not always have clear-cut relationships with surrounding units, though there is always some thread of correspondence, it seems best to understand the beatitude in 19:9–10 as a *CODA* loosely connected with what comes before it in 17:1–19:8, and especially with 19:1–8. The beatitude has significance on a higher, mitigated hortatory level.

BOUNDARIES AND COHERENCE

Chapters 17 and 18 clearly deal with the destruction of Babylon. This leads to the triumphal shout of the great multitude in the *REACTION*, including references to Babylon's corrupting the earth with her fornication (linking back to 17:2), and to the blood of God's servants being avenged on her (linking back to 17:6). In 19:6 the focus begins to turn to the marriage of the Lamb. The beatitude in 19:9–10 also focuses on the marriage of the Lamb. However, 19:11 introduces the mighty warrior on the white horse, so it can be seen as beginning a new major unit dealing with the final destruction of the forces of evil. It seems best to see all of 17:1–19:10 as one major unit, with the references to the marriage of the Lamb as occasioned by the destruction of Babylon, the symbol of all that is evil in human society. Yet these references are also transitional to the last Act (21:1–22:5), where in contrast to the prostitute, the focus is on the bride, the wife of the Lamb (see 21:2, 9). As elsewhere in Revelation, a transitional preview comes at a point quite far removed from the actual presentation, (see, for instance, 14:8 foreshadowing this unit).

PROMINENCE AND THEME

In this descriptive unit the REACTION is naturally prominent. It is thus significant in terms of the overall message of Revelation that it does not present the destruction of evil human society as focal, but rather its focus is on the liberating effect this has on God's people. The CODA has marked prominence by being introduced with the command for John to write it and because it includes a special endorsement of its validity. By its connection to the other beatitudes in the discourse it has higher-level significance. The theme therefore gives the *situation* and the REACTION to it, and also includes the beatitude.

SCENE CONSTITUENT 17:1–2 (Paragraph: Setting of 17:1–19:10)

THEME: *One of the angels of the bowls offered to show me how God will punish the great prostitute who has seduced the earth people to act immorally.*

¶PTRN RELATIONAL STRUCTURE	CONTENTS
orienter	17:1a One of the seven angels who had the seven bowls came to me, John, and said to me,
APPEAL — 'prostitute'	17:1b "Come *with me* and I will show you how *God* will condemn and punish the great prostitute, who sits *as ruler* over *the place with* many *streams of* water.
description₁	17:2a With her the rulers of earth *people* have acted immorally,
description₂	17:2b and she *has seduced* the people who live on the earth to become drunk from the *strong* wine *she gives them and* to commit fornication with her."

INTENT AND STRUCTURE

This unit provides a setting for the scene, and to some extent for the whole act, by stating that the final judgment is now taking place and by bringing the one who actually saw the vision, John, back into the narrative. It also introduces the participant in focus throughout the scene—the great prostitute, who turns out to be Babylon, symbolizing all human society organized in rebellion against God.

NOTES

17:1a and said to me To introduce the quotation, the preposition μετά 'with' is used with ἐλάλησεν 'spoke', giving the idea of friendly conversation (Lenski).

17:1b condemn and punish The Greek for this is κρίμα 'judgment', which may mean simply a decision, but for which the present context demands the sense listed in BDAG, a sentence of condemnation including the punishment to follow it, as in 2 Pet. 2:3.

the great prostitute An alternate for the display text might be 'condemn and punish the great city which is symbolized by a prostitute' (see TEV). This could simplify the interpretation of the following clause, which would be translated as 'which is situated by many streams of water.' However, it involves bringing forward part of the interpretation of the vision from 17:18 into the depiction of the vision itself, which may not be regarded as legitimate.

Some versions have translated μεγάλης 'great' as 'famous' (JB) or 'Notorious' (LB), probably because 'great' does not collocate so well with 'prostitute'.

who sits *as ruler* over *the place with* many *streams of* water The term 'many waters' means 'many rivers' or 'many streams of water,' and is drawn from the prophecy against Babylon in Jer.51:13, "You who live by many waters and are rich in treasure, your end has come".

Aune and other commentators show that the sense communicated by 'sitting' is enthronement as ruler. This agrees with 17:18. According to 17:15 the waters symbolise 'peoples and multitudes and nations and languages' over whom the prostitute has dominion.

17:2a With her the rulers of earth *people* **have acted immorally** The prostitute is said to have led the rulers of the world into sexual immorality. In the Old Testament, adultery is a common metaphor for idolatry and unfaithfulness to God. But while this symbolism may well be intended here (as many commentators state) the focus of the picture given by the angel is on the great prostitute's sin of enticing the rulers and people of the world into immorality.

17:2b and she *has seduced* **the people who live on the earth to become drunk from the** *strong* **wine** *she gives them and* **to commit fornication with her** Unlike in 14:8c 'the wine' here simply indicates the seductiveness of the prostitute, the evil power that entices the people of the earth to rebel against God.

BOUNDARIES AND COHERENCE

The opening of the unit coincides with the beginning of the act. The unit ends with the close of the angel's first speech since the action in 17:3 initiates the actual vision of judgment. The unit coheres as consisting of an orienter-CONTENT construction only, the CONTENT being an *APPEAL*.

PROMINENCE AND THEME

In this *orienter-APPEAL* construction not only the *APPEAL* but also the orienter is prominent enough to be thematic, since the identification of the speaker is important.

SCENE CONSTITUENT 17:3–18:24 (Episode cluster: Situation of 17:1–19:10)

THEME: I was bewildered when I saw a prostitute sitting on a red beast and I saw that she was drunk with the blood of God's people. But an angel showed me that the beast represented the rulers of earth and the woman was the great city that dominated earth people and they would be destroyed by God and the Lamb. Then I heard voices from heaven declare that the great city of Babylon is destroyed, that the people of earth will bewail their loss, but God's people must flee from the city and rejoice.

MACROSTRUCTURE	CONTENTS
problem	17:3–6 I saw a prostitute sitting on a red beast and I saw that she was drunk with the blood of God's holy people. I was very bewildered by this.
resolving incident	17:7–18 The angel revealed that the beast and its seven heads and ten horns represented rulers who would be overcome by the Lamb and destroyed. He identified the woman as the great city dominating earth people, and declared that it would be destroyed.
RESOLUTION	18:1–24 I heard voices from heaven declare that the great city of Babylon is destroyed, that the people of earth will bewail their loss, but God's people must flee from the city and rejoice.

INTENT AND STRUCTURE

As with most of the higher level units in Revelation, this one has a basic narrative structure in which the narrator plays the role of an observer. Here he is shown a powerful immoral woman, drunk with the blood of God's people. His puzzlement at the significance of this leads to an explanation by an angel, and then he sees the terrible destruction of the woman, who is revealed as Babylon, the symbol of human society in rebellion against God. The unit thus has a solutionality nature. John's puzzlement at the power of the evil woman is the *problem*, the angel's explanation is a *resolving incident* that begins to solve the problem, and the final destruction of Babylon is the RESOLUTION.

BOUNDARIES AND COHERENCE

The main coherence of this unit is provided by its focus throughout on the great prostitute, the city of Babylon. Its opening boundary is the movement of John to a position where he can see Babylon, and the next unit begins at 19:1 with a switch of scene to heaven. Although the focal character is variously referred to as "the prostitute", "Babylon", and "the great city", there are references throughout to its filthy immorality (17:4–5, 18:2–3, 9), its power (17:3, 9, 18, 18:7, 10, 12–16, 18–19), and its responsibility for the death of many of God's people (17:6, 18:6, 20, 24).

PROMINENCE AND THEME

In this *problem-RESOLUTION* unit each of the elements is prominent and included in the theme.

EPISODE CLUSTER CONSTITUENT 17:3–6 (Paragraph: Problem of 17:3–18:24)

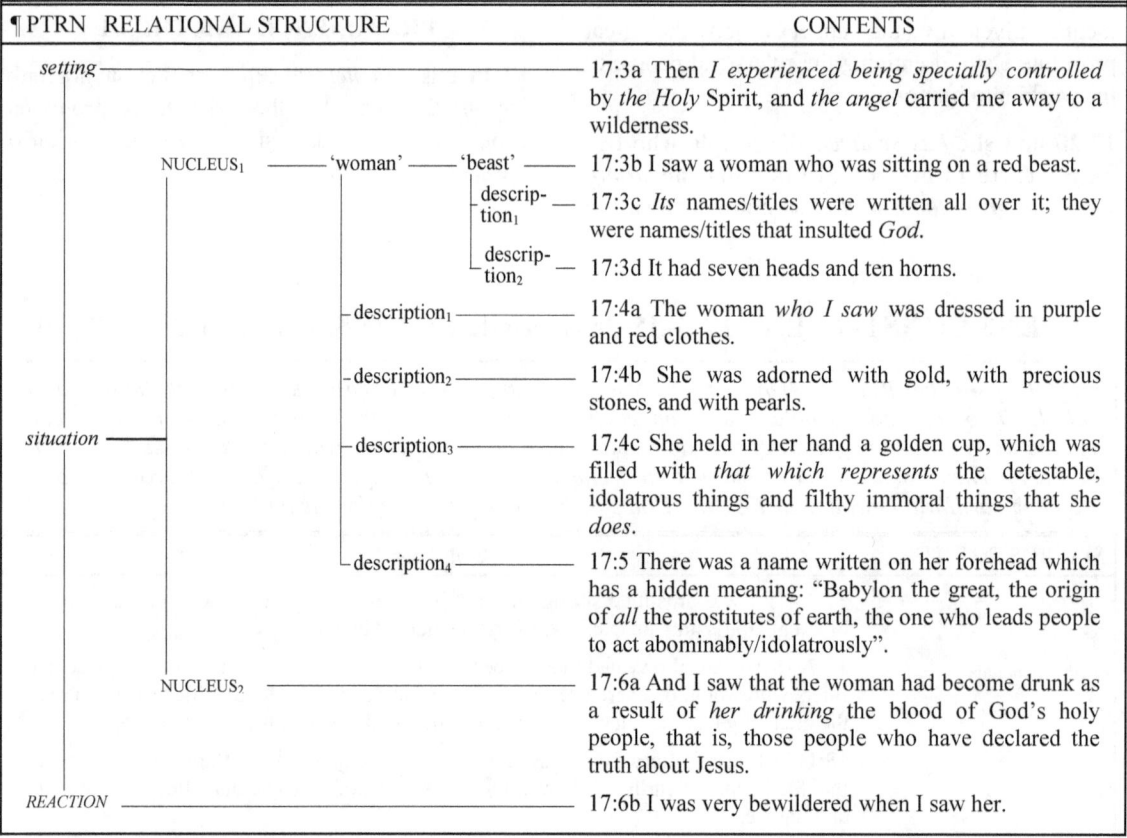

THEME: *I saw a prostitute sitting on a red beast and I saw that she was drunk with the blood of God's holy people. I was very bewildered by this.*

¶PTRN RELATIONAL STRUCTURE	CONTENTS
setting	17:3a Then *I experienced being specially controlled* by *the Holy* Spirit, and *the angel* carried me away to a wilderness.
NUCLEUS₁ — 'woman' — 'beast'	17:3b I saw a woman who was sitting on a red beast.
description₁	17:3c *Its* names/titles were written all over it; they were names/titles that insulted *God*.
description₂	17:3d It had seven heads and ten horns.
description₁	17:4a The woman *who I saw* was dressed in purple and red clothes.
description₂	17:4b She was adorned with gold, with precious stones, and with pearls.
description₃	17:4c She held in her hand a golden cup, which was filled with *that which represents* the detestable, idolatrous things and filthy immoral things that she *does*.
description₄	17:5 There was a name written on her forehead which has a hidden meaning: "Babylon the great, the origin of *all* the prostitutes of earth, the one who leads people to act abominably/idolatrously".
NUCLEUS₂	17:6a And I saw that the woman had become drunk as a result of *her drinking* the blood of God's holy people, that is, those people who have declared the truth about Jesus.
REACTION	17:6b I was very bewildered when I saw her.

INTENT AND PARAGRAPH PATTERN

This paragraph consists of John's vision of a woman sitting on a beast and his bewildered reaction to the sight. The focus of the description is on the woman, who is referred to by a noun phrase in 17:3b, 17:4a and 17:6a. John's reaction to the scene he describes is presented as a cause-effect reaction, rather than as a volitional statement, so the paragraph pattern is descriptive *situation-REACTION*.

NOTES

17:3a *I experienced being specially controlled* by the *Holy* Spirit See the note on 1:10a.

17:3b I saw a woman who was sitting on a red beast This statement shows a close association between the woman and the beast. The woman is in a position of power, but dependent on the beast.

This beast might be identified by its seven heads and ten horns as that described in 13:1. However, Aune points out that there is nothing else in the text to indicate that John considered it to be a reappearance of the beast from the sea. In 13:1 each head has a blasphemous name, but here the beast is covered with such names.

17:3c *Its* names/titles were written all over it; they were names/titles that insulted *God* The implication is that the beast had written on his body names or titles that belong to God alone. Mounce says, "The reference is to the blasphemous claims to deity made by Roman emperors who employed such titles as *theios* (divine), *sōtēr* (savior), and *kyrios* (Lord)".

17:4a The woman *whom I saw* was dressed in purple and red clothes The woman's clothing symbolized luxury and seduction, as did her adornments. The purple may stand for royalty, though colours in the New Testament are not always clearly identified symbolically.

17:4c She held in her hand a golden cup, which was filled with *that which represents* the detestable, idolatrous things and filthy immoral things that she *does* The cup and its contents are particularly suited to seduction. Both descriptions of the contents are strong. The noun βδέλυγμα 'abomination, detestable thing' is specified as "anything that must not be brought before God because it arouses his wrath" (BDAG) and even more specifically "as in the OT ... of everything connected with idolatry" (ibid).

The second description of the contents of the golden cup is τὰ ἀκάθαρτα τῆς πορνείας αὐτῆς 'the unclean things of her fornication'. Moore (p. 66) classifies this as a near-synonymous doublet with 'abominations'. As we have seen earlier, 'fornication' alludes to idolatry. Thus, there is a heavy stress on idolatry in this doublet, though the idolatry probably carries with it the idea of all kinds of immoral practices.

17:5 There was a name written on her forehead which has a hidden meaning: "Babylon the Great ..." Some versions and commentators attach the word 'mystery' to the name as if it were part of the name, which is grammatically possible. But a common interpretation (Charles, Düsterdieck, Ladd, Morris, Mounce) is that the word is not part of the name but indicates the name should not be taken literally. This is more like the use of 'mystery' in other references in the book. (See note on 1:20.) The puzzling name is intended to be understood by revelation.

the origin of *all* the prostitutes of earth, *the one who leads people to act* abominably/idolatrously 'The mother of the prostitutes' is figurative, carrying the idea that the woman is the source of all who follow her way of life (cf. 2:23).

17:6a And I saw that the woman had become drunk as a result of *her drinking* the blood of God's holy people, that is, those people who have declared the truth about Jesus The expression 'was drunk with the blood' refers particularly to the extent of her murderous persecution of God's people and to her enjoyment of it. Charles calls it a familiar phrase in ancient literature (Isa. 49:26). The καί 'and' does not signal that there are two different groups of people but conjoins two different descriptions of the same people.

17:6b I was very bewildered when I saw her The use of the word 'mystery' in 17:5 in regard to the prostitute and the fact that the angel says in 17:7, 'I will tell you the mystery of the woman...' in response to John's statement ἐθαύμασα, suggests that here ἐθαύμασα means 'I wondered' in the sense of 'I was bewildered'. JB has "I was completely mystified."

BOUNDARIES AND COHERENCE

The initial boundary is marked by John's being moved to a new setting, and by the introduction of new participants. There are differing opinions as to where the final boundary of this paragraph comes, since the Greek does not indicate significant discontinuity between 17:6 and 7. Several versions (NIV, RSV, TEV) begin the next paragraph with "And seeing her I was greatly astonished." However, this sentence is pivotal as the most prominent semantic constituent (REACTION) of 17:3–6 and it marks the function of the unit as the *problem* for which the next unit is the *resolving incident*.

The unit 17:3–6 draws its coherence from its being a single extended description of the woman whom John saw.

PROMINENCE AND THEME

John's bewilderment is the most naturally prominent feature of the unit, being his REACTION to the *situation* he was shown by the angel. But the REACTION is incomprehensible without a statement of the situation and so both must appear in the theme statement.

EPISODE CLUSTER CONSTITUENT 17:7–18 (Episode: Resolving incident of 17:3–18:24)

THEME: The angel revealed that the beast and its seven heads and ten horns represented rulers who would be overcome by the Lamb and destroyed. He identified the woman as the great city dominating earth people, and declared that it would be destroyed.

¶ PTRN RELATIONAL STRUCTURE	CONTENTS
orienter	17:7a The angel said to me,
orienter — EXHORTATION	17:7b "You should not be bewildered [RHQ],
grounds	17:7c *since* I will tell you the secret of *what is represented by* the woman and the beast which carries her, the beast which has the seven heads and the ten horns.
DECLARATION₁ — REASON	17:8a The beast which you saw lived *before now*, then did not live, is about to come up from the abyss/underworld, and will be destroyed *by God*.
result	17:8b People who live on the earth and whose names are not listed in the book which since the beginning of the world *has contained the names of those who* live *spiritually/eternally* will be amazed when they see that the beast lived, then did not live, but reappeared.
mitigated appeal	17:9a The one who thinks wisely *can understand* this [17:7c–8].
NUCLEUS₁ — NUCLEUS₁	17:9b The seven heads *of the beast* represent seven hills on which the woman sits.
NUCLEUS₁ — NUCLEUS₂	17:9c They also represent seven rulers, 17:10 five *of whom* have perished [MET], one is alive, *and* the other *one* has not yet come; and when this last one comes, he is destined to remain for *only* a short *time*.
NUCLEUS₁ — CONTENT — DECLARATION₂ — NUCLEUS₁	17:11a The beast who lived *before now* and then did not live is *like* an eighth *ruler in that he comes after the other seven,* and he is of the same type as the seven *rulers*.
NUCLEUS₂ — NUCLEUS₂	17:11b He will be destroyed *by God*.
NUCLEUS₁	17:12 The ten horns which you saw represent ten rulers, who have not yet begun to rule *people,* but they will receive authority in order to rule *people* together with the beast *for a short time, as if just* for one hour.
DECLARATION₃ — NUCLEUS₂	17:13 These rulers will have one common purpose to give to the beast their right and authority *to rule people* [DOU].
occasion	17:14a These rulers will fight against the Lamb.
NUCLEUS₃ — OUTCOME — RESULT	17:14b The Lamb will overcome them,
reason	17:14c because he is Lord ruling over all other lords and King ruling over all other kings, and the people who are with him are the ones whom *God* has called, whom *he* has chosen, and who remain faithful *to him*."

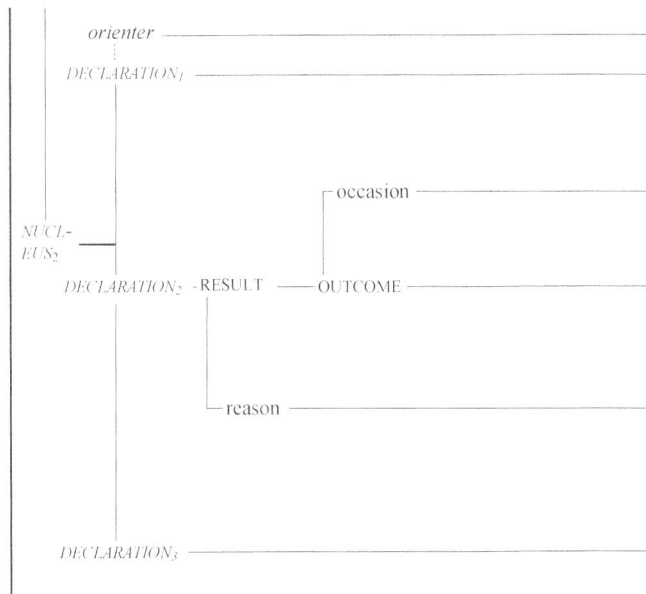

INTENT AND PARAGRAPH PATTERN

The angel's address to John is given in two parts. The first, 17:7–14, consists of a series of DECLARATIONS which identify the beast and its seven heads and ten horns with evil powers and show that they will soon come to an end. These DECLARATIONS are introduced by a mitigated EXHORTATION (in the form of a rhetorical question). The second part of the address, 17:15–18, consists of further DECLARATIONS giving the identity of the woman and the waters where she sits, and showing how she will be destroyed. The whole unit is thus descriptive in nature.

NOTES

17:7a The angel said to me "You should not be bewildered The angel's question "Why are you surprised?" would be a real one if the angel were truly puzzled by John's perplexity. Instead, it serves as a mitigated command, the grounds of which are an elaborate interpretation of the mystery.

17:8a-b Although the second part of this verse is the result of the first part, the switch from present tenses in the Greek, 'was ..., is ..., is about to ...' to the future 'will be amazed' indicates that the first part is the nucleus and the second is a subsidiary comment or response.

17:8a The beast which you saw lived *before now*, then did not live, is about to come up from the abyss/underworld, and will be destroyed *by God*. The beast is identified and described as ἦν καὶ οὐκ ἔστιν καὶ μέλλει ἀναβαίνειν ἐκ τῆς ἀβύσσου καὶ εἰς ἀπώλειαν ὑπάγει 'was, and is not, and is about to come up out of the abyss and is going to destruction'. This description is meant to parody both the expression used of God in 1:4, ὁ ὢν καὶ ὁ ἦν καὶ ὁ ἐρχόμενος 'the One who is, the One who was, and the One who is coming', and the description of the Lamb in 1:18: ἐγώ ... ὁ ζῶν, καὶ ἐγενόμην νεκρὸς καὶ ἰδοὺ ζῶν εἰμι εἰς τοὺς αἰῶνας τῶν αἰώνων 'I ... am the living one, and I became dead and behold I am alive forever'.

'God' is supplied as agent of the beast's destruction to fill out the case frame. However, the focus of this sentence is not on God's action, but on the fact that the beast will not live for ever, as the Lamb will.

17:8b whose names are not listed in the book which since the beginning of the world *has contained the names of those who* live *spiritually/eternally* This is almost exactly the same as the description of those who worshipped the beast in 13:8.

will be amazed when they see that the beast lived, then did not live, but reappeared While the Greek word translated as 'amazed' in the display here was translated as 'bewildered' in 17:6b and 7b in John's case, the difference in translation seems justified since the context in his case suggests that the sense of θαυμάζω as 'be bewildered' is more in focus than a gullible, beguiled sense of being amazed, as here.

17:9a The one who thinks wisely *can understand* this [17:7c–8] For the fourth time in Revelation, ὧδε 'here, this' is used to call attention to the need for patience or wisdom (13:10, 18; 14:12). These uses of ὧδε are similar to the beatitudes in that they act as mitigated APPEALS. However, in this paragraph the mitigated appeal is probably not the most prominent constituent of the paragraph.

Some commentators think ὧδε 'this' refers to 17:9b and what follows, but it is more likely that, as in the previous references cited, it refers to what precedes. Aune says:

> The parallel sayings in 13:18 and 17:9 *conclude* a riddle and function to emphasize that a mysterious set of apocalyptic symbols requires interpretation. An important parallel outside Revelation is found in the apocalyptic discourse in Mark 13:14, where the author breaks in and directly addresses the reader with a parenthetical comment, "Let the reader understand," a saying that *follows* the apocalyptic symbol of the "desolating sacrilege."

17:9b The seven heads *of the beast* represent seven hills on which the woman sits At the time when Revelation was written Rome was widely known as a city built on seven hills. So this reference would have immediately identified the beast as Rome.

17:9c They also represent seven rulers Commentators have had numerous different ways of identifying these seven rulers with seven specific Roman emperors. The huge variety of these identifications indicates that this is an unsatisfactory interpretation. It is much more likely that the number seven is symbolic of completeness as elsewhere in the Bible. This would indicate to John's readers that the power which was persecuting them would not last indefinitely. Moreover, since the sixth of the seven rulers was said to be currently ruling, they could be sure that the end would not be far in the future.

17:10 five *of whom* have perished The term ἔπεσαν 'have fallen' is here used metaphorically of dying. Significantly it is also used in 18:12 of Babylon being destroyed.

when this last one comes, he is destined to remain for *only* a short *time* This part of the sentence is highlighted by the temporal clause, 'when he comes.'

The use of δεῖ 'must' here indicates some type of constraint. Bratcher and Hatton say, "As often in the New Testament, the word translated must refers to God's control of human affairs".

The shortness of the time is emphasised by ὀλίγον 'short' occurring first in the clause in the Greek, indicating 'only a short time'.

17:11a The subject of this sentence, 'the beast who … did not live' is moved to the beginning in the Greek, indicating that this is a second nucleus for the declaration, not a continuation of the series of seven rulers from 17:10.

he is of the same type as the seven *rulers* The Greek text is ἐκ τῶν ἑπτά ἐστιν 'he is from/of the seven'. This may mean that he follows their pattern and is of the same type as them. Some commentators understand the Greek text to mean 'he is *one* of the seven', but this would have been better communicated as εἷς ἐκ τῶν ἑπτά ἐστιν 'he is one of the seven' (Mounce).

17:12 but they will receive authority in order to rule *people* together with the beast The conjunction ἀλλά 'but' shows that this is an amplification (negative-positive) of the previous statement. On the one hand, since the horns were part of the description of the beast, it might be assumed that the beast was the source of their delegated authority. On the other hand, the limited period of their authority would seem to indicate that it was given by God, and this is confirmed by 17:16. Barnes makes the comment, "It is not said from what source this power is received, but it is simply implied that it would in fact be conferred on them".

***for a short time*, as if just for one hour** As commonly in Revelation the hour means just a short time (cf. Rev.18:10, 17, 19) rather than a fixed period of time.

17:13 These rulers will have one common purpose: The subject pronoun 'these', coming at the start of the Greek sentence, shows that this is a further comment about the horns/kings.

to give to the beast their right and authority to rule people. Literally 'and they give their power and authority to the beast'. This states the content of their common purpose.

Moore (p. 66) classifies 'their power and authority' here as a near-synonymous doublet. 'Power/right' and 'authority' are both abstract nouns. A possible verbal rendering is 'they will give/allow the beast to rule what they have been ruling'.

17:14a These rulers will fight against the Lamb In Greek the subject is οὗτοι 'these', as at the start of 17:13, so it probably refers again to the rulers. According to 16:14–16, the propaganda of evil spirits has served to bring this consensus of decision to fight against the Lamb.

17:14c he is Lord ruling over all other lords and King ruling over all other kings The first noun in each genitive construction, 'lord of lords, king of kings,' encodes not only the title but also the event or state which that title represents in relationship to the others involved. This might be 'rules over' or 'is greater than'.

are the ones whom *God* has called, whom *he* has chosen, and who remain faithful *to him* As for filling out the case frame, some commentators maintain that God is always referred to as the one who does the calling, though Rom. 1:6 could be used for arguing for Christ as agent also. Here, if God is supplied as agent, then it is also natural to supply 'God' as the one to whom the followers were faithful.

17:16a *The rulers represented by* the ten horns This adjustment is made in the display since the ten horns have already been identified as 'rulers' in 17:12, and it is more collocationally appropriate to say 'the rulers represented by the ten horns will hate the harlot' than to say 'the ten horns will hate the harlot'.

17:16b as a result Here καί introduces the result of their hating the prostitute.

they will take away everything that she has The Greek word translated 'desolate' in the RSV is often used in scripture in reference to a city or kingdom. At the same time, it would be best to translate it with a word that can refer both to a person and to a city. The primary meaning of 'desolate' is to be deprived or emptied of anything that is of value, especially that which is in focus in the context (see TEV).

they will leave her naked, they will devour her flesh, and they will burn *the rest of* her up with fire. Various commentators point out that the woman is here treated as a shamed prostitute (left naked), as the victim of a wild beast (her flesh eaten), and as a conquered city (burned).

they will burn *the rest of* her up with fire. Since the object pronoun 'her' occurs first in the Greek clause, there is probably an intended contrast between 'her flesh' and '*the rest of* her.'

17:17 until all that God has said should happen In the Greek text this is literally 'the words of God'. 'God has said' is the verbal form of 'the words of God'.

BOUNDARIES AND COHERENCE

There are differences of opinion on the opening boundary of the unit. Some include 17:6b, but this analysis considers 17:6b as the head of the previous unit. It expresses the problem which the angel begins to resolve in this unit by interpreting the vision of the woman and the beast.

Opinions also differ on whether this is one unit or two units, since there is a second orienter for the angel's speech at 17:15a. However, the lack of an overt subject in the Greek of this second orienter indicates that it belongs to the same unit as 17:7–14. Also, the next unit begins with the typical introductory phrase μετὰ ταῦτα εἶδον 'after this I saw'.

The coherence of 17:7–18 is indicated by the references throughout to the beast, with its heads and its horns, and to the woman, and by the identifications of each of these with evil powers that will soon disappear.

PROMINENCE AND THEME

In a descriptive paragraph pattern it is the DECLARATION that is most prominent. In this unit the series of DECLARATIONS is especially thematic since they begin to solve John's bewilderment about the vision he has seen of the prostitute and beast. The theme therefore consists of a summary of the DECLARATIONS.

EPISODE CLUSTER CONSTITUENT 18:1–24 (Episode: Resolution of 17:3–18:24)

THEME: I heard voices from heaven declare that the great city of Babylon is destroyed, that the people of earth will bewail their loss, but God's people must flee from the city and rejoice.

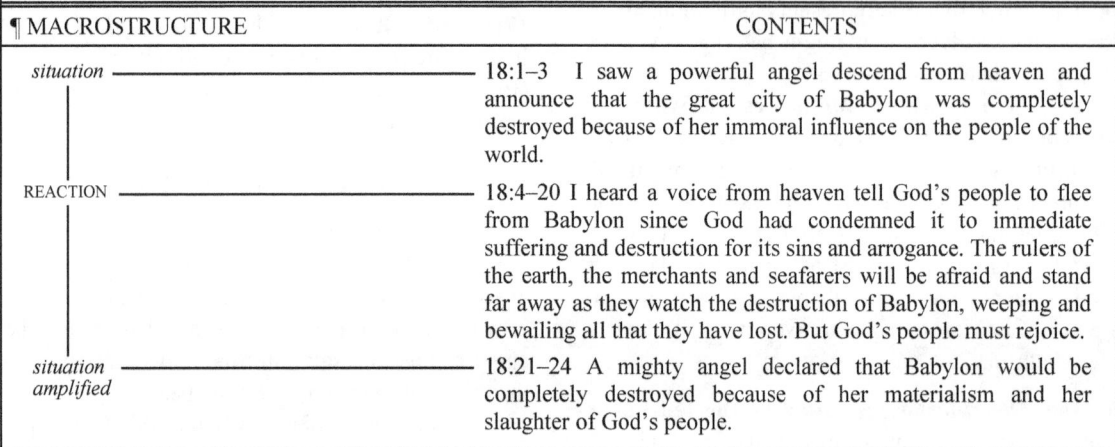

¶ MACROSTRUCTURE	CONTENTS
situation	18:1–3 I saw a powerful angel descend from heaven and announce that the great city of Babylon was completely destroyed because of her immoral influence on the people of the world.
REACTION	18:4–20 I heard a voice from heaven tell God's people to flee from Babylon since God had condemned it to immediate suffering and destruction for its sins and arrogance. The rulers of the earth, the merchants and seafarers will be afraid and stand far away as they watch the destruction of Babylon, weeping and bewailing all that they have lost. But God's people must rejoice.
situation amplified	18:21–24 A mighty angel declared that Babylon would be completely destroyed because of her materialism and her slaughter of God's people.

INTENT AND MACROSTRUCTURE

The major problem in analysing the structure of 18:1–24 is the question of where each of its speech units ends. Although it is clear that the speech of the angel introduced in 18:1 ends with 18:3c, there is very little agreement about the end of the speech that begins at 18:4b. Some commentators have that speech ending at 18:5, many versions and commentators end it at 18:8c, and others continue it through 18:19 or 18:20. Even within that speech there are other disagreements, such as whether 18:20 is spoken by the mariners (as 18:19), or by the voice of 18:4, or by the narrator, John. However, the analysis adopted here takes the whole of 18:4a–20 as the words of the heavenly voice introduced in 18:4a, for the following reasons:

1. A break in the speech at the end of 18:5 is required by some commentators (e.g. Bratcher and Hatton, p. 259; Morris, p. 210) to allow a new addressee, since they do not consider it appropriate that the people of God (addressees in 18:4–5) be instructed to exact vengeance on Babylon. However, in the Greek there is no indication whatsoever of a change of addressee, and in these verses what is envisaged is judgment, not vengeance. Moreover, in 2:26–27, 5:10, 20:4 God's people are told that they will be kings and judges of the nations, and Aune (p. 994) points out that in 1 Cor. 6:2–3 "Paul expects Christians to play an active role in judgment". In addition this same theme may be what is referred to by 'your judgment' in 18:20 (see the note).

2. Ending the speech with 18:8 (as NRSV, NCV, TEV, CEV, NLT) makes 18:9–19 the words of the narrator. But these verses, with their extended detail and future tenses are unlike John's first-person narrative style elsewhere in Revelation. On the other hand, continuing the speech through 18:20, as suggested by many commentators (e.g. Alford, p. 715; Düsterdieck, pp. 443, 447; Swete, p. 234), provides an overt speaker for that verse (the voice of 18:4a) and avoids many of the difficulties of the transition from the mariners' speech of 18:19.

If this analysis is accepted, the unit can be seen as a descriptive one, with the announcement of Babylon's destruction forming the *situation*, followed by a REACTION in the form of a speech by the heavenly voice. This is then followed by an amplification of the *situation*.

BOUNDARIES AND COHERENCE

The 18:1–24 paragraph cluster begins with the boundary marker μετὰ ταῦτα εἶδον 'after these things I saw' and the introduction of 'another angel coming down out of heaven'. The next μετὰ ταῦτα occurs at the beginning of 19:1. The whole of chapter 18 deals with the destruction of Babylon. Although 19:1–8 also consists of a reaction, it is not so much a reaction to Babylon's destruction as to the solution of the problem of Babylon's sin.

PROMINENCE AND THEME

This is a *situation-REACTION* unit so both *situation* and REACTION form the theme.

EPISODE CONSTITUENT 18:1–3 (Paragraph: Situation of 18:1–24)

THEME: I saw a powerful angel descend from heaven and announce that the great city of Babylon was completely destroyed because of her immoral influence on the people of the world.		
¶ PTRN	RELATIONAL STRUCTURE	CONTENTS
	setting — 'angel'	18:1a After this I, *John*, saw another angel, coming down from heaven, who was very powerful.
	└ description	18:1b The earth became bright because he was shining so intensely.
	┌ *orienter*	18:2a He shouted with a mighty voice,
NUCLEUS	*CLAIM* — REASON	18:2b "The great *city of* (*or*, *symbolized by*) Babylon has been completely destroyed,
	└ RESULT	18:2c as a result all *kinds of* evil spirits now live there, and all *kinds of* foul and detestable birds now live there.
	*justification*₁	18:3a *Babylon has been destroyed* because, *just as a prostitute seduces men to* drink *strong* wine and commit fornication with her, *so Babylon has seduced the people of* all nations *to forsake God and thus incur his* fury,
	*justification*₂	18:3b and the rulers of the earth have acted immorally *and idolatrously* with her,
	*justification*₃	18:3c and the merchants of the earth have become rich because of her excessive consumption of the luxuries *of the world*."

INTENT AND PARAGRAPH PATTERN

The *NUCLEUS* of the 18:1–3 paragraph is the *CLAIM* by the angel that the great city of Babylon has fallen. The angel is introduced in a *setting* that emphasises his fitness for this momentous announcement by referring to his great authority, his glory and his mighty voice. The intent of the paragraph is thus expository, with three *justifications* being given for the sentence of destruction that has been passed on Babylon.

NOTES

18:1a After this I, *John*, saw another angel coming down from heaven, who was very powerful The Greek word ἐξουσία may mean 'power' or 'authority'. The latter is favoured by the versions. However, BDAG lists this reference under the gloss "*ability* to do something, *capability*, *might*, *power*". The context shows that both 'power' and 'authority' are appropriate.

18:1b The earth became bright because he was shining so intensely The preposing of the subject of the Greek sentence shows that this is a background comment.

As Bratcher and Hatton (p. 256) point out, "δόξα here has the physical sense of the brilliant light that marks the angel as God's messenger".

18:2 In a *reason*–RESULT relationship the RESULT has natural prominence, and that is reinforced here by its tripartite structure: 'dwelling of demons, haunt of evil spirits, haunt of … birds.' However, in this case the *reason* (18:2b) is also given marked prominence by the repetition of its verb ἔπεσεν 'fallen' (see note 18:2b).

18:2a He shouted with a mighty voice The adjective used is ἰσχυρᾷ 'strong', in contrast to other angels who have spoken in a φωνῇ μεγάλῃ 'great' or 'loud voice' (5:2; 10:3). The difference may not be very significant, but is not ignored.

18:2b The great *city of* (*or*, *symbolized by*) Babylon has been completely destroyed The expression is the same as in 14:8, and the repetition of the verb gives emphasis, as in that passage. This is expressed in English as complete destruction. See the note on 14:8b.

18:2c all *kinds of* evil spirits ... foul ... birds The words 'evil' and 'foul' here both represent the same Greek word ἀκάθαρτος 'unclean'. As Babylon has played the shameless harlot with the rulers of the earth, so her habitation is taken over by those things that are disgustingly foul.

'Every foul spirit' seems to mean 'all kinds of foul spirits', and since 'demon' and 'unclean spirit' are basically synonymous (see Moore, p. 66), they are rendered with the one phrase 'all kinds of foul spirits'.

now live there 'Live' is used in the display text as a translation of both κατοικητήριον 'dwelling-place' and φυλακή 'guardpost, watching-place'. The main idea is that of a forsaken place, and that various undesirable creatures are present because people are no longer there.

and all *kinds of* foul and detestable birds now live there Some texts include a phrase found in a few manuscripts: 'the guardpost of all unclean beasts'. The UBS committee includes this phrase in the text, feeling that it probably was in the original text of Revelation and was deleted by accidental omission. However, it is in brackets since it is not found in some very important manuscripts (Metzger, pp. 682–683). KJV and modern English versions omit it. On this basis we also omit it.

foul and detestable birds This seems to be an echo of the prophecies of Babylon's fall in Isaiah 13:19–22 and Jeremiah 50:39, and of the destruction of Edom in Isaiah 34:11. Various birds such as the owl and the raven were unclean animals according to the Mosaic law, so for a place to become their roost would be the ultimate degradation.

18:3a Babylon *has been destroyed* This is supplied at the beginning of the verse in order to communicate its proper relationship with 18:2b.

drink *strong* wine There is considerable manuscript confusion about πέπωκαν 'have drunk'. The form πέπτωκαν 'have fallen' has very good support, but the metaphorical makeup and sense of the verse with its background in the Old Testament and similarity to Rev. 14:8 and 17:2 seem to demand the sense of 'to drink' (Metzger, p. 683). The word appearing in the UBS text, πέπωκαν 'have drunk', is given a D rating showing that the UBS committee had great difficulty in reaching a decision. Many modern English versions accept this choice, RSV gives "fallen by" in a footnote.

***so Babylon has seduced the people of* all nations** Although the Greek here is almost identical to 14:8c, the personification of the city of Babylon has been kept in the display here because of the extended figure of Babylon as a prostitute throughout chapters 17–18.

***and thus incur his* fury** See the note on 14:8c.

18:3b have acted immorally *and idolatrously* with her As was mentioned in the note on 14:8c, fornication and sexual immorality are common O.T. metaphors for Israel's worship of false gods. This is therefore represented in the display.

18:3c the merchants of the earth have become rich because of her excessive consumption of the luxuries *of the world* There is a question here as to the meaning of δύναμις 'power' and στρῆνος. The noun στρῆνος may mean either 'luxury' or 'sensuality', probably the type of sensuality concerned with a self-indulgent demand for riches. The translation of these two words must reflect an activity or state through which the merchants 'became rich'. Note also that it is the merchants' economic loss that they mourn as they contemplate Babylon's destruction in 18:11–17a. The self-indulgence of Babylon demanded every sort of luxury. Supplying these luxuries enhanced the merchants' profits. BDAG glosses the collocation of the two words as 'excessive wealth'. Barclay (1969, p. 267) translates: "the demands of her wanton luxury have made the world's merchants rich".

BOUNDARIES AND COHERENCE

John's sight of the strong angel descending from heaven begins the unit at 18:1 and it closes at 18:3, the end of the angel's message. In 18:4 another voice begins to speak so there is a new participant. Thus coherence is evident within 18:1–3 in that there is only one direct speech discourse.

PROMINENCE AND THEME

The angel's CLAIM is naturally prominent and it receives added prominence from the repetitions it contains. The *setting* and a summary of the *justifications* are also vital to the theme.

EPISODE CONSTITUENT 18:4–20 (Paragraph Cluster: Reaction of 18:1–24)

THEME: I heard a voice from heaven tell God's people to flee from Babylon since God had condemned it to immediate suffering and destruction for its sins and arrogance. The rulers of the earth, the merchants and seafarers will be afraid and stand far away as they watch the destruction of Babylon, weeping and bewailing all that they have lost. But God's people must rejoice.

MACROSTRUCTURE	CONTENTS
orienter	18:4a I heard another voice speak *to God's people* from heaven, which said,
situation	18:4b–8 God's people must flee out of Babylon since God will now punish it for its sins. Babylon must be caused to suffer for the suffering it has caused to others, for its self-glorification, and for its self-indulgent life-style, because the mighty Lord God has condemned it to immediate destruction for its arrogance.
NEGATIVE REACTION	18:9–19 The rulers of the earth, the merchants and the seafarers will watch the destruction of Babylon standing far away out of fear. They will weep and bewail all that they have lost.
POSITIVE REACTION	18:20 God's people must rejoice since God has condemned and punished Babylon.

INTENT AND MACROSTRUCTURE

The 18:4–20 paragraph cluster gives the speech of a heavenly voice describing to God's people God's judgment against Babylon and the reaction to it. It is noticeable that the subunit concerned with the judgment itself (18:4b–8) is not a description or narrative but a hortatory paragraph, yet in terms of the unit as a whole it functions as a *situation* to which the rest of the unit gives the REACTION. The reaction is thus seen to be in response to the judgment and destruction of Babylon, not to the role of God's people in it. The major part of the reaction is a NEGATIVE REACTION on the part of the kings, rich merchants, and maritime traders. This may have been intended as an encouragement to John's readers, in that those who they saw prospering from the evil of the world will be totally devastated in the end.

NOTES

18:4a I heard another voice speak *to God's people* from heaven, which said Commentators are divided over whether this is the voice of God (Bratcher and Hatton, p. 258), Christ (Charles, p. 97), or an angel speaking on God's behalf (Alford, p. 715; Düsterdieck, p. 443; Morris, p. 210; Mounce, p. 324; Swete, p. 225). In 18:4b the speaker says 'my people,' which would imply that it is God or Christ speaking. In 18:5 God is referred to in third person, which some take to be proof that this second voice is that of another angel speaking on the behalf of God. However, it is possible in Greek for a speaker to refer to himself in the third person. But since John does not specify who the speaker is, it is best not to try to make it explicit in translation.

BOUNDARIES AND COHERENCE

The unit opens with John narrating the next incident in his vision using the common formula Καὶ ἤκουσα 'and I heard…'. This introduces the speech of the heavenly voice. There is then no indication in the Greek of a change of speaker until the resumption of John's narrative in 18:21. (See Intent and Macrostructure for 18:1–24.) In fact the structure of the Greek in 18:9 (see Note) argues for continuity at this point. The coherence of the unit is shown by the focus throughout on Babylon and its destruction. There are also repeated references to Babylon's pride and luxurious living (18:7a, 7d, 10d, 12–13, 14, 16, 18d).

PROMINENCE AND THEME

The tripartite structure of the NEGATIVE REACTION (rulers, merchants, seafarers) gives it more marked prominence than its negative nature would otherwise merit. The theme therefore consists of both REACTIONs with a summary of the *situation*.

PARAGRAPH CLUSTER CONSTITUENT 18:4b–8 (Paragraph: Situation of 18:4–20)

THEME: God's people must flee out of Babylon since God will now punish it for its sins. Babylon must be caused to suffer for the suffering it has caused to others, for its self-glorification, and for its self-indulgent life-style, because the mighty Lord God has condemned it to immediate destruction for its arrogance.

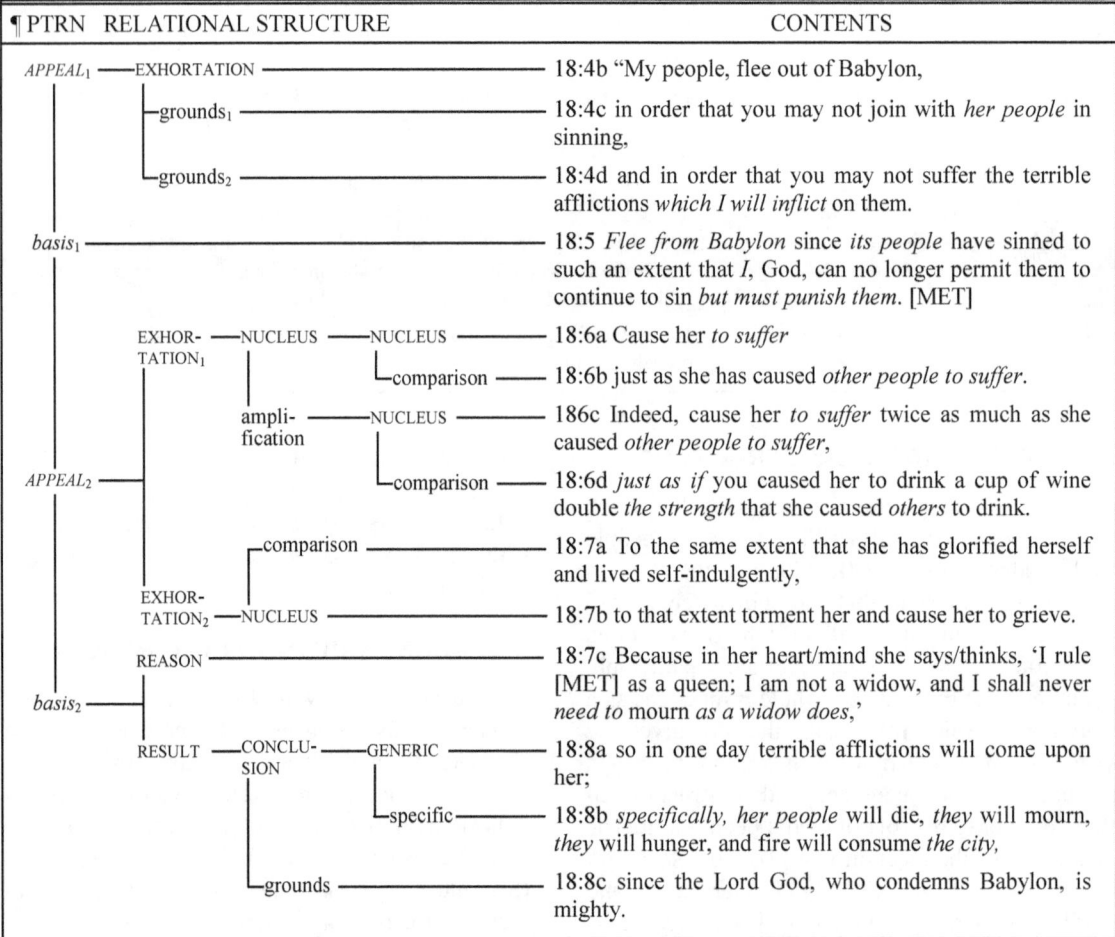

INTENT AND PARAGRAPH PATTERN

As noted above (18:4–20, Intent and Macrostructure), although this 18:4b–8 unit has a descriptive function it has a hortatory paragraph pattern. There are two APPEALs, each with a justifying basis. Firstly, God's people are commanded to leave Babylon on the basis that God is now going to take action against her because of her sins. Then, secondly, the execution of judgment on Babylon is commanded on the basis that in her pride she regards herself as immune from punishment and so she must be peremptorily destroyed.

Whilst many commentators feel that the second APPEAL must have a different addressee than the first (see above, 18:1–24, Intent and Macrostructure), there is no indication whatsoever in the Greek of a change of speaker or addressee at the beginning of 18:6. All the English versions mark the speech as continuing without change at this point. Aune (p. 994) points out that the main argument against 18:5–8 being addressed to God's people is that it would violate NT teaching on love for enemies and non-retaliation. He comments that this is not an exegetical argument but a theological one. Yet what is commanded in 18:5–8 is not, in fact, retaliation but retribution for Babylon's sins against God. God's people are told to pay Babylon back for what she has done to other people (and thus against God), not for anything she has done to them.

NOTES

18:4b–c My people, flee out of Babylon in order that you may not join with *her people* in sinning Several commentators stress the relevance of this to one of the themes of Revelation: that God's people must separate themselves from the evil way of life of those they live among. However, here in the vision of Babylon's destruction it is a very literal exit from the city, not a metaphorical separation, that the heavenly voice is commanding.

18:4d the terrible afflictions *which I will inflict on them* The Greek is ἐκ τῶν πληγῶν αὐτῆς 'from her blows/plagues'. For the word πληγή referring to sufferings inflicted by God, see the note on 9:18.

18:5 *Flee from Babylon* The APPEAL is repeated in order to show clearly that this verse is the *basis* for 18:4b (Thomas, p. 321; Lenski, p. 518), not the reason for 18:4d.

since *its people* have sinned to such an extent that *I*, God, can no longer permit them to continue to sin *but must punish them* Structurally this verse is a couplet in the Greek, with two parallel statements having the same meaning: 'her sins are piled up to heaven' and 'God has remembered her misdeeds.' This gives it added prominence. Both refer to the scale of Babylon's sins and the impossibility of God's ignoring them. The καί 'and' which introduces the second clause is therefore to be understood as signalling simple coordination rather than result.

Metaphorically ἐκολλήθησαν 'piled up' describes the magnitude of Babylon's sins. The phrase ἄχρι τοῦ οὐρανοῦ 'as high as the heaven/sky' is also probably best seen as indicating the vast amount of sin. It does not mean that since the sins have reached as far as heaven they have come into God's sight. The anthropomorphic figure of God's not forgetting their sin is also reduced in the display.

18:6 Special literary features are used in the Greek here for emotive force, particularly alliteration and repetition. The alliteration is produced in a large part by the repetition of the roots of ἀποδίδωμι 'to repay,' of διπλ- 'double, to double,' and of κεράννυμι 'to mix.'

18:6a–b Cause her *to suffer* just as she herself caused *other people to suffer*. Indeed, cause her *to suffer* twice as much as she caused *other people to suffer* These commands are not contradicting each other but are a literary feature emphasizing the severity of Babylon's sentence. What is in focus is not so much a carefully measured double recompense as emphasis on severity of recompense.

The verb ἀποδίδωμι 'to repay' here has no expressed object, but suffering is obviously intended in view of the context of judgment and afflictions.

18:6d *just as if* Since 18:6d is a restatement of 18:6c in figurative language, it is represented as a comparison in the display text, rather than as a direct imperative.

you caused her to drink a cup of wine Instead of translating κεράσατε literally as 'mix' it is translated as 'caused to drink' in the display. BDAG glosses this reference first as 'mix' but then says that perhaps its meaning is 'pour (in)' as in 14:10. TEV has 'fill her cup'. An alternate would be '*just as if* you filled her a cup with wine double *the strength* that she gave *others and caused her to drink it*'.

double *the strength* As in 14:8, 10 it is the destructive nature of strong, or undiluted, wine that is in focus here.

18:7a she has glorified herself Her sin is more specific here. Since it shows her pride, it anticipates the second indictment which follows in 7c, which quotes her arrogant boast.

and lived self-indulgently This represents the verb στρηνιάω, which echoes the noun στρῆνος 'luxury' in 18:3c, emphasising the sinful extravagance which resulted from Babylon's pride.

18:7b torment her and cause her to grieve βασανισμός 'torment, torture' has the sense of excruciating pain, as when someone is tortured to extract information from them, or as caused by a scorpion sting (see 9:5).

18:7c in her heart/mind she says/thinks Literally this is 'in her heart she says'. But 'heart' as the place where inward thoughts about oneself are made is language specific. It may be that the most appropriate translation is 'she thinks' with no reference to the heart or mind etc. In the Greek this charge against Babylon is given extra force by the use of the present tense, 'she says', and by the fact that 'in her heart' is moved to the beginning of the clause.

'I rule as a queen The Greek for this is literally 'I sit a queen'. This might be translated as 'I sit on the throne as a queen' or 'I sit on the throne, I am a queen'.

I am not a widow, and I shall never *need to* mourn *as a widow does*,' Literally this is 'a widow I am not and sorrow I do not see'. In the Greek the use of the double negative οὐ μή with the aorist subjunctive tense of the verb, plus the moving of the verb to final position, shows that this is a very definite, emphatic statement, typifying Babylon's haughty pride. In Isaiah 47:8 Babylon says, "I shall not sit as a widow or know the loss of children" (RSV).

18:8a so in one day terrible afflictions will come upon her The fiery judgment of her pride will be complete destruction. The "one day" has reference to the definiteness and swiftness of her judgment. It is given emphasis by its position before the verb in the Greek.

18:8b *her people* will die This translates θάνατος, the common word for 'death'. However, in lists of disasters (as 6:8b) θάνατος can also mean specifically death by disease or in an epidemic.

***they* will mourn** Again πένθος is used, having occurred in 18:7c in connection with widowhood. Here it can be translated in a more generic sense of sorrow, though the mourning for loss of loved ones would also be appropriate.

18:8c since the Lord God, who condemns Babylon, is mighty The word for mighty is ἰσχυρός, emphasized by its being forefronted. God is fully capable of carrying out the sentence he has pronounced.

BOUNDARIES AND COHERENCE

The opening boundary of the unit is the beginning of the speech of the heavenly voice. At the end of 18:8 the hortatory part of the speech closes (until 18:20) and the voice begins a descriptive passage in 18:9. Although there have been some attempts to divide the passage at 18:6 (see above, Intent and paragraph pattern) this is unnecessary and not supported by the Greek text. From 18:4b to 8 the unit coheres as being hortatory in nature, with imperative verbs all apparently addressed to God's people. There is also a focus throughout on Babylon's sins and the 'terrible afflictions' that will be visited upon her (18:4d, 8a).

PROMINENCE AND THEME

Since this is a hortatory unit the *APPEAL*s have natural prominence. However, each *basis* also has stylistic features (18:5, 7c) that give marked prominence. The theme therefore gives the main points of the *APPEAL*s and *bases*.

PARAGRAPH CLUSTER CONSTITUENT 18:9–19 (Paragraph: Negative Reaction of 18:4–20)

THEME: The rulers of the earth, the merchants and the seafarers will watch the destruction of Babylon standing far away out of fear. They will weep and bewail all that they have lost.

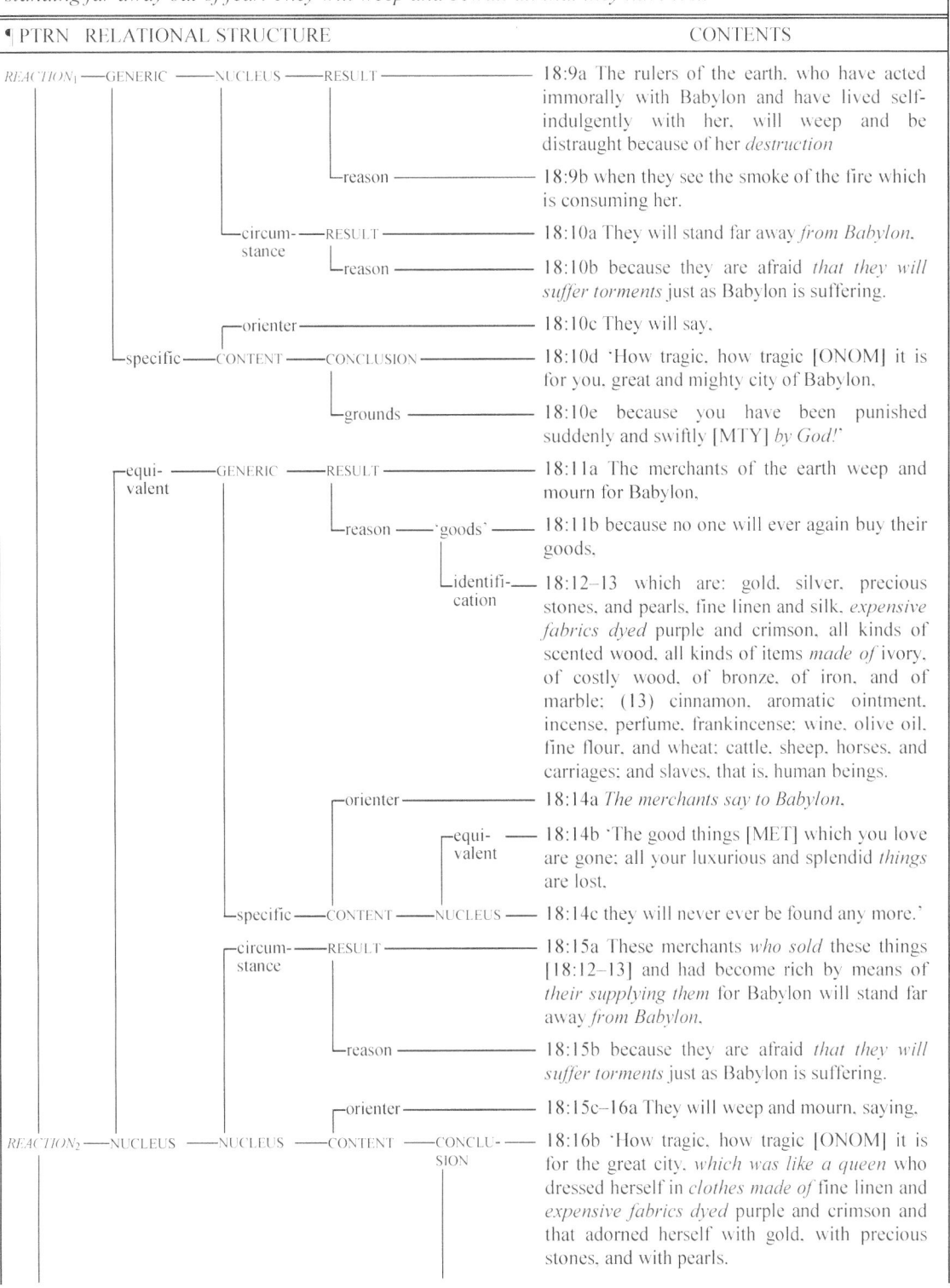

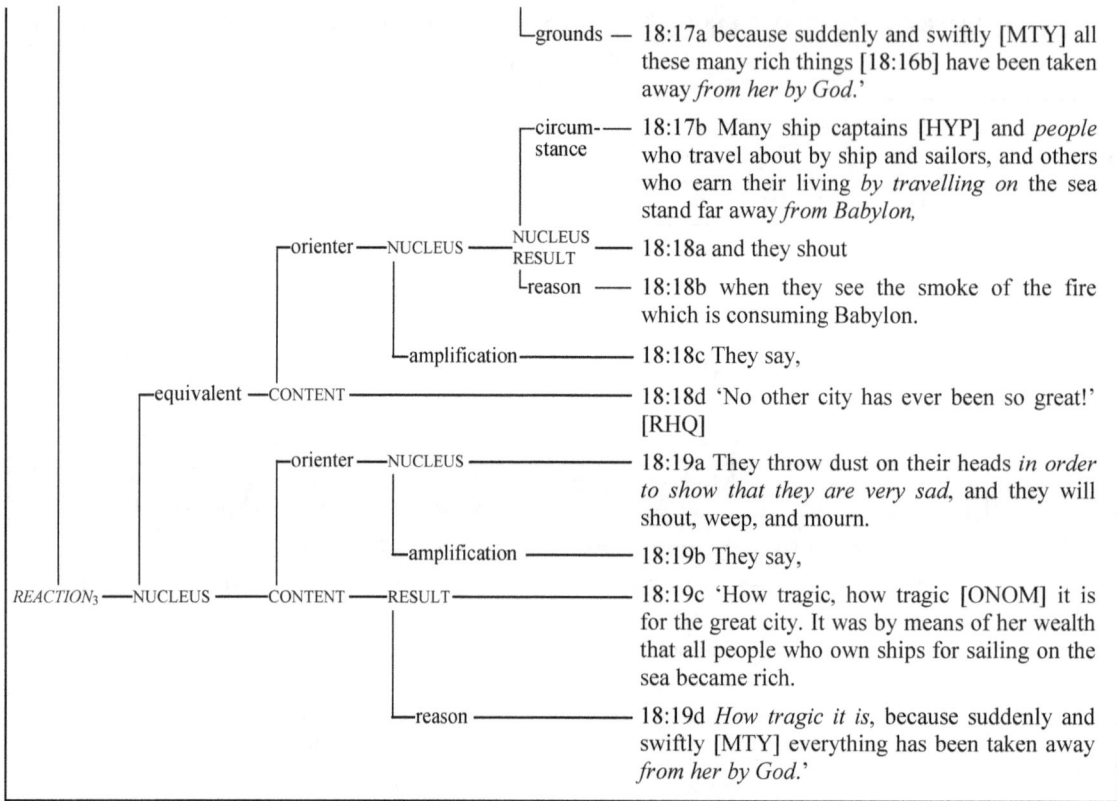

INTENT AND PARAGRAPH PATTERN

The unit 18:9–19 consists of *the* REACTIONS of the three groups, kings, merchants, and seafarers, as they react with distress at the destruction of the great city that had brought privileges and riches to them. There are many similarities between the structures of the three REACTIONS, and each group is shown standing at a distance, mourning, and uttering a dirge.

The poetic form of these dirges is much like that of the Old Testament prophets' dirges, and there is particular background for many details of this chapter in Ezek. 27 and 28. The intent of the unit is either a warning to the addressees of Revelation not to participate in the things these groups do, or an encouragement to them that in the final outcome it is they who will rejoice and not those who seem to have so many reasons for rejoicing now. The latter seems to be the primary intent here.

NOTES

18:9 In the Greek this verse begins with the main clause "The rulers of the earth ... will weep", and not with the subordinate time clause "when they see the smoke ...." This emphasises continuity of theme with the judgments of the previous unit and thus supports the idea that there is no change of speaker between 18:8 and 9 (see Intent and Macrostructure for 18:1–24).

18:9a The rulers of the earth, who have acted immorally with Babylon and have lived self-indulgently with her These kings are identified as those referred to in 17:2 and 18:3, who were seduced by her splendour and the wine of her harlotry. They are not the ten kings of 17:12 and 16, since those rulers belong to a different description of the destruction of Babylon.

will weep The verb κλαίω 'weep' in various forms occurs four times, in 18:9, 11, 15, and 19. It refers more to the physical expression of sorrow than to deep emotion. The latter is shown by the addition in 11, 15, and 19 of πενθέω 'to mourn/grieve'. The mourners are showing sadness and concern for their own loss.

In the Greek text 18:9–10 and 15–17a are in the future tense, which views the event as a whole. However, 11–14 is in the present tense and 17b–19 is mainly in the imperfect, both of which portray the event as ongoing.

be distraught because of her *destruction* The verb κόψονται 'will lament' refers to people mourning not so much for a dead friend but because of what they will suffer since that friend can no longer help them. See the note on 1:7b–d.

18:10a They will stand far away *from Babylon* The distance is cited in 18:10, 15, and 17. In each case the adverbial phrase is given extra prominence by coming before the verb.

18:10b they are afraid *that they will suffer torments* **just as Babylon is suffering** Bratcher and Hatton say, "these kings will be afraid that they will be punished with Babylon".

18:10d How tragic, how tragic it is for you, great and mighty city of Babylon Here οὐαί 'woe' is an exclamation, a reaction to the tragedy of Babylon's destruction. It is the onomatopoeic form of the wail, repeated for emphasis, and placed first in the quotation. The form occurs in 18:10d, 16b, and 19c.

you, great and mighty city of Babylon This is apostrophe, in which a thing, such as a city, is personalised and addressed. Some English versions (GW, CEV, NLT96) remove the figure of speech and translate in the third person, 'that great city …, it has been punished'.

18:10e punished The Greek word is κρίσις 'judgment,' which is inclusive enough to cover the whole process of investigation, decision, and the execution of the sentence passed. Here the verdict has already been given and the carrying out of the sentence is in focus. There is a potential problem as to who is the assumed agent of the 'judgment/punishment'. Would the kings of the earth recognize that the destruction was from God? However, the fact that the word used is κρίσις 'judgment', which is often associated with the judgment of God, argues that this is indeed what is referred to here.

suddenly and swiftly The 'one hour' of the text means "a short time" (Aune, p. 997). This is emphasised by its coming before the verb in the Greek.

18:11a–b The merchants of the earth weep and mourn for Babylon, because no one will ever again buy their goods As merchants, the loss of their market is the cause of their sorrow. The categorisation of their merchandise in 18:12–13 is a list of luxuries ending with human slaves.

18:12–13 *expensive fabrics dyed* **purple** 'Purple' refers to cloth dyed with an expensive dye extracted from a type of shellfish called the murex (Mounce, p. 330). '*Expensive fabrics*' in the display maintains the focus on the costliness of all the materials mentioned in the list.

and crimson According to BDAG the cloth called κόκκινος was dyed with a purple-red dye made from the dried bodies of a scale insect (similar to the cochineal) which clings to the leaves of an oak tree.

all kinds of scented wood The phrase ξύλον θύϊνον refers to wood from a North African tree (*callistris quadrivalvis*) of the cedar family, sometimes known as the sandarac tree. The wood is both fragrant and highly polishable and so used for costly furniture and ornamental work. Thus RSV's 'scented wood' and TEV's 'rare woods' describe the wood from slightly different aspects. The wood is sometimes referred to as citron wood, but is different from the wood of the citron fruit tree.

In the list, 'every' occurs before 'sandarac wood', before 'article of ivory' and 'article of costly wood'; 'every article' also modifies 'bronze', 'iron', and 'marble'. While the use of 'every' or 'all' may be hyperbolic to a certain extent, it is probably communicating the great variety of the items being discussed. There is a problem, however, in that 'every' modifies 'sandarac wood' directly. It may be that this specific was also used as a generic for high quality, rare, scented wood.

cinnamon Cinnamon is a sweet-smelling spice made from the bark of certain trees. It was used as perfume, medicine, incense and flavouring for food. It may well be that we are to understand its use here as for perfume rather than for flavouring food.

aromatic ointment The Greek word ἄμωμον refers to an aromatic shrub or the oil derived from it. It possibly came from India (BDAG) or Armenia (Swete, p. 231).

perfume BDAG glosses μύρον as 'ointment, perfume'. Although most English versions translate it as 'myrrh' in this verse, it is not the usual Greek word for myrrh. Thomas (p. 334) states that it refers here to perfume in general.

frankincense Frankincense is from the resinous gum of a certain tree in Arabia. BDAG says it was used for both medicinal and cult purposes. It was burned as incense. As with the other items in the list it was very valuable.

fine flour BDAG glosses σεμίδαλις as "*fine flour*, the finest grade of wheat flour".

wheat The term σῖτος referred specifically to wheat, but also more generally to other types of grain. Wheat was a major source of merchants' wealth in the Roman empire, because the city of Rome imported vast quantities of it from Egypt since bread was the staple food of its population.

carriages These are four-wheeled carriages, such as the rich and high-status people would use.

slaves, that is, human beings Following the material commodities, slaves are designated by the noun σωμάτων 'bodies', a term often used to refer to them. Some take the connective καί to be ascensive, 'even', which would express John's reaction to their being demeaned in this way. Phillips translates as "slaves, the very souls of men". Another meaning of καί in some contexts is 'that is', and this is how RSV takes it here.

18:14a *The merchants say to Babylon* Lenski (p. 526) says that in this verse the prostitute is dramatically addressed by God. This may be true in some sense, but in the form of the text it would seem that the verse acts as a specific CONTENT of the 'weeping and mourning' of 18:11 (Alford, p. 719). Some versions do supply the orienter here, as in the display: NIV, NLT, REB, TEV.

18:14b–c The good things which you loved are gone; all your luxurious and splendid *things* are lost, they will never ever be found any more If Babylon is regarded as a city, this is personification. But, in fact, throughout this chapter Babylon is portrayed primarily as a female prostitute.

good things The word ὀπώρα can refer to the late summer when fruit would be harvested, or it can be used of the fruit itself. Louw and Nida (3.34) say that here ὀπώρα "is to be understood in a figurative sense of 'good things'" (cf. Bratcher and Hatton, p. 265; NLT, and TEV). This is almost certainly true since the other two items mentioned in the verse, luxurious and splendid things, are generic, while literal fruit would be specific.

they will never ever be found any more That such things will never be found again emphasizes the finality of the loss. This clause is heavily emphasized with three forms of the negative. The Greek is 'they will never find them any more'. This is probably an impersonal third person plural substituting for the passive.

18:15b The Greek text of this is identical with that of 18:10b.

18:16b How tragic, how tragic it is for the great city, *which was like a queen* who dressed herself in *clothes made of* fine linen and *expensive fabrics dyed* purple and crimson and that adorned herself with gold, with precious stones, and with pearls The personification of the city in the Greek text is changed into a simile in the display, likening the city to a queen. A queen is more contextually appropriate here than a prostitute since it is the great wealth that is in focus. This is also in accord with the description of Babylon in 18:7.

Here in the Greek text the city is referred to in the third person, whereas in 18:10 the second person is used.

18:17a suddenly and swiftly The display uses 'suddenly and swiftly' again to express the 'one hour' of the catastrophe.

taken away *from her by God* The same verb is used in the Greek here as in 17:16b. See the note at 17:16b.

18:17b Many ship captains and people who travel about by ship and sailors, and others who earn their living *by travelling on* the sea The Greek here has 'Every ship captain, everyone who sails to a place and sailors and all others who earn their living on the sea'. This is clearly hyperbole, indicating the huge number of lesser people who were affected by Babylon's downfall. Bratcher and Hatton say "this list intends to include all people who make their living in maritime trade".

***people* who travel about by ship** The Greek text is literally 'everyone who sails to a place'. There are many suggestions about how this text may be corrupt, or what it might mean. Most likely it refers to small-scale traders who travelled from place to place along the coast (Aune, pp. 105–106) on other people's ships.

others who earn their living *by travelling on* the sea Literally this is 'whoever works the sea'. This would seem to be an all-inclusive statement, covering all maritime traders not already mentioned. It does not refer to fishermen.

18:18c–d They say, 'No other city has ever been so great!' The display changes the rhetorical question to an exclamation of the strong emotion of these mourners.

18:19a They throw dust on their heads *in order to show that they are very sad* The action of throwing dust on one's head is a cultural form having its own cultural function and meaning and so the function is made explicit in the display. This act was used widely in the culture of John's day as a sign of extreme distress.

18:19c by means of her wealth The Greek term τιμιότης means "great value, high cost". BDAG glosses it here as "*abundance of costly things*". Most versions translate this as "wealth".

18:19d has been taken away *from her by God* This is the same as in 18:17a. See the note on 17:16b.

BOUNDARIES AND COHERENCE

After the previous hortatory unit, 18:9 begins a description of the negative reaction of earth people to the destruction of Babylon. The following unit, 18:20 is again hortatory – a call to God's people to celebrate God's justice. Coherence of the unit is clear from the similarity of the three reactions, with each of the groups standing in fear at a distance, mourning and uttering a dirge. Compare especially 18:10 with 15–17a and 17b–19. Words referring to weeping and mourning occur in 18:9, 11, 15, 19. The strong contrast of rejoicing comes in the next unit.

An alternate analysis would be to treat each of the units dealing with separate participants (i.e. the kings, merchants, and maritime traders) as separate paragraphs.

PROMINENCE AND THEME

The three *REACTIONS* are co-ordinate and since they share so many parallel features they are equally prominent. The theme therefore comprises a summary of all three.

PARAGRAPH CLUSTER CONSTITUENT 18:20 (Paragraph: Positive Reaction of 18:4–20)

RELATIONAL STRUCTURE	CONTENTS
THEME: *God's people must rejoice since God has condemned and punished Babylon.*	
EXHORTATION	18:20a Rejoice over *the destruction of* Babylon, *you who belong to* heaven, God's people, *including* the apostles and prophets.
grounds	18:20b because God has condemned and punished Babylon for what *she did* to you."

INTENT AND STRUCTURE

The call to God's people to rejoice is in the imperative, but the verb is expressive and the unit functions in the expressive higher-level unit 18:4–20. The intent is to affect the emotions of the saints, encouraging them to rejoice that God has acted. Whereas the people of the world lamented what the fall of Babylon meant for them, the reaction of God's people should be the opposite – celebration.

NOTES

18:20a Rejoice over *the destruction of* Babylon God's people are called to rejoice at what has happened to Babylon.

***you who belong to* heaven, God's people, *including* the apostles and prophets** The address is to 'heaven' in the vocative singular with 'saints, apostles, and prophets' following in the nominative plural. It is normal for the second (and following) vocatives to be in nominative form according to Robertson (p. 464.e). It is debatable whether 'heaven' refers to the angels, or to the saints, apostles, and prophets who belong there, or to believers who have died. However, in the reason given for the rejoicing (20b) it is those who are addressed in the vocatives whose judgment is being vindicated. This would tend to suggest that only humans are being addressed (Chilton, pp. 458–459; Lenski, pp. 528–529), particularly those who have suffered at the hands of Babylon (see 18:6 and 24). Mounce (p. 332) also defends this identification on the grounds of the parallel in 12:12.

***including* the apostles and prophets** The apostles and prophets are also God's people.

18:20b because God has condemned and punished Babylon for what *she did* to you The Greek says literally that 'God has judged your judgment (τὸ κρίμα ὑμῶν) on her', which may well be an echo of 17:1, where John is invited to view the judgment (τὸ κρίμα) of Babylon. See the note on 17:1b.

BDAG gives two translations: "*God has pronounced judgment for you against her*" and "*God has pronounced on her the judgment she wished to impose on you*". The first of these takes τὸ κρίμα ὑμῶν as 'your case/lawsuit' referring to the claims of the martyrs as in 6:10. The second translation takes τὸ κρίμα ὑμῶν as an objective genitive '(her) judgment/punishment of you.' Caird

(p. 230), Aune (p. 1008), and Bratcher and Hatton (p. 268) support this second rendering. Bratcher and Hatton (ibid.) also give a simpler version, 'God has condemned Babylon for the things that she has done to you,' and this is followed in the display.

BOUNDARIES AND COHERENCE

The 18:20 paragraph is coherent as a single call for God's people to rejoice.

PROMINENCE AND THEME

Both the EXHORTATION and its grounds are thematic.

EPISODE CONSTITUENT 18:21–24 (Paragraph: Situation of 18:1–24 amplified)

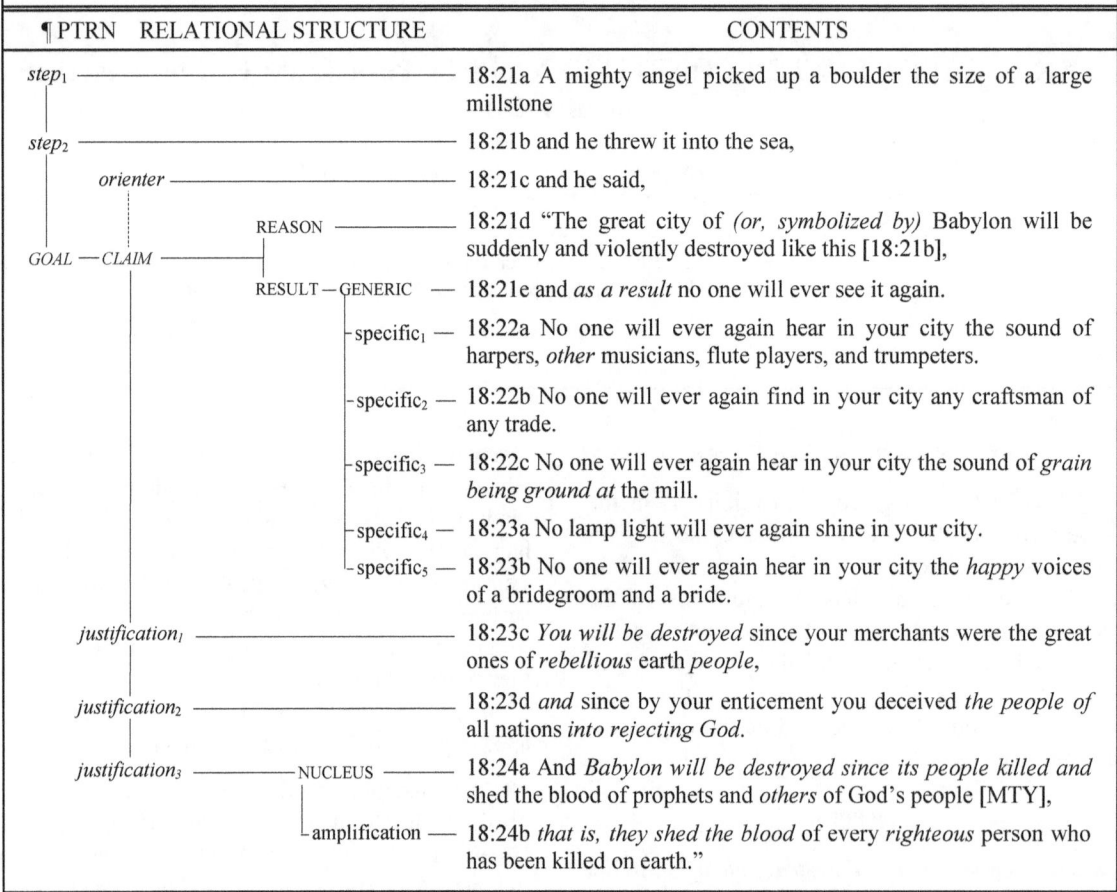

INTENT AND PARAGRAPH PATTERN

In this unit there is a mixture of narrative and expository elements. Most of the paragraph is the speech of the mighty angel declaring the sure destruction of Babylon. However, this occurs in an overall *step-GOAL* framework, with the mighty angel first picking up the large stone, then throwing it into the sea and finally explaining how his action illustrates the destruction of the city.

There are many similarities between this unit and 18:1–3, of which it is an amplification or résumé. The structure is parallel to the structure of that unit, with a speech containing a CLAIM and three *justifications* that refer to the arrogance of Babylon's merchants and its corruption of the nations of the world.

NOTES

18:21a–b A mighty angel picked up a boulder the size of a large millstone and he threw it into the sea The angel showed symbolically the destruction of Babylon in the very way it had been prophesied in Jer. 50–51, see especially 51:63–64. The act served to emphasize the decisive and final significance of God's judgment.

the size of To represent ὡς 'like,' the display uses "the size of" (NIV, TEV) since that is the basis of the comparison.

18:21d The great city of *(or, symbolized by)* Babylon will be suddenly and violently destroyed like this This is referring to the same thing as 18:2b. As in 18:2b–c there is here a reason-result relationship in which the reason has marked prominence. In this case the prominence comes from οὕτως 'thus' referring to the preceding dramatic action.

will be suddenly and violently destroyed like this The verb is βάλλω 'throw' as in 18:21b, but here it is used in the figurative sense of 'overthrow, throw down.' The manner of the overthrow, like the throwing of the boulder into the sea, is described as a ὅρμημα 'rush, sudden violent movement.'

18:21e and *as a result* The connector καί is used with the sense of result here.

no one will ever see it again As the boulder is thrown into the sea it sinks to the bottom, never to be seen again. This symbolizes the complete and final destruction of Babylon. The use of ἔτι 'any more' in the text reinforces the strong οὐ μή 'not.' The words are repeated five more times in 18:22–23 to express finality.

18:22a–23b This is a list of specific common sights and sounds of Babylon, which have all come to an end with the destruction of the city. It is drawn from the words of Ezekiel 26:13, a prophecy of the destruction of Tyre, and Jeremiah 25:10, a prophecy of the destruction of Jerusalem. In each Greek clause the focus is on the subject: harpists etc., craftsmen, milling, lamplight, weddings.

18:22a in your city The Greek here switches from referring to Babylon in the third person to the second person, 'in you.' This may be because it is quoting from Ezek. 26:13 which used the second person. The display gives 'in your city' to adjust the personification.

***other* musicians** The word μουσικοί is translated 'singers' by several English versions and commentators, but in all the references given in the Greek lexicons its meaning is 'musicians.'

18:22b any craftsman of any trade The word τεχνίτης refers to a skilled workman rather than an ordinary worker.

18:22c No one will ever again hear in your city the sound of *grain being ground at* the mill An alternate would be 'no one will ever again grind grain at the mills in your city'.

18:23b No one will ever again hear in your city the *happy* voices of a bridegroom and a bride The Greek word φωνή is a generic word that refers not only to the voice but to sound in general. So here it is not limited to the voices of the bridegroom and bride, but potentially refers to all the sounds of a wedding. 'Happy' in the display helps to indicate the significance of the mention of the voice of bridegroom and bride here.

18:23c *You will be destroyed* since your merchants were the great ones of *rebellious* earth *people* While it is difficult to understand at first sight that one of the major *justifications* for the destruction of Babylon was the fact that the merchants of Babylon were the great ones of earth, most commentators maintain that the ὅτι at the beginning of 23c does act as introducing the first reason for Babylon's destruction. It is probable that 'the earth' here as elsewhere in Revelation means 'rebellious earth people'.

18:23d since by your enticement The word φαρμακεία is glossed as 'sorcery, witchcraft'; it can also refer to the drugs and spells used in such things. Here it is probably to be taken figuratively. The wealth and power of Babylon bewitched the nations into obeying its wishes (cf. Swete p. 237; Beasley-Murray). In the Greek this phrase is preposed for extra prominence.

you deceived *the people of* all nations *into rejecting God* Words like 'deceive' are not complete in their contextual sense unless the content of the deception is understood. Throughout Revelation πλανάω 'to deceive' is used of those who deceive people into disobeying or rejecting God.

18:24a and *Babylon will be destroyed since* Although there is not a third ὅτι 'since' at the beginning of this verse it is obviously a third *justification* for the destruction of Babylon (Alford, p. 722; Düsterdieck, p. 448; Ladd, Mounce, p. 335; Swete p. 238). The alternative interpretation would be that the change of pronoun reference (see the next note) indicates that the speech of the angel has ended with 18:23 and these are the words of the narrator. However, this sort of comment is unlike the role that John plays elsewhere in Revelation.

its people killed and shed the blood There is a switch here in the Greek from second person singular to feminine third person singular referring to Babylon. This mirrors the earlier switch from third person to second person in 18:22. In this case the switch may again be due to the use of an Old Testament quotation, since 18:24 is a conflation of Ezekiel 24:7 and Jeremiah 51:49. Both of these verses refer to the condemned city in the third person, whereas 18:23d was quoting Isaiah 47:9, which is in the second person. Düsterdieck (p. 448) says that the discourse change from the direct address of apostrophe to a "judgment of firm objectivity" specially emphasizes the most important reason for Babylon's guilt.

killed and shed the blood of prophets and others of God's people This is the prime accusation brought against Babylon. It is repeated from 17:6 and referred to again in 19:2. The Greek text 'In her was found the blood of prophets and saints…' is a metonymy in which 'blood' is substituted for what caused the blood to flow out: murder.

18:24b ***that is, they shed the blood*** **of every** ***righteous*** **person who has been killed on earth** Jesus brought out the same principle in Matt. 23:34–36. The accumulated guilt confirms the view that Babylon here represents all human rebellion in all ages.

The question is whether it is still the martyred people of God who are being referred to in 18:24b (Alford, p. 722; Charles, p. 112; Düsterdieck, p. 448; Ladd; NLT) or whether all innocent murder victims are included (Bratcher and Hatton, p. 271; Mounce, p. 335; Hughes; Beale, p. 923).

BOUNDARIES AND COHERENCE

The 18:21–24 unit begins with the introduction of the mighty angel, following the end of the speech of the heavenly voice. The mighty angel's speech ends at 18:24b and at 19:1 there is a typical introducer of a higher-level unit, μετὰ ταῦτα ἤκουσα 'after these things I heard'. Coherence is clear from the action and speech of the one angel. The switches of pronoun reference at 18:22a and 24a might be considered to argue against the coherence of the unit, but see the notes for an explanation of that phenomenon.

PROMINENCE AND THEME

The declaration of Babylon's complete and final destruction which functions as the CLAIM within the GOAL is most naturally prominent. In a CLAIM-*justification* paragraph pattern the *justification* is integral to the theme and so is included in the theme statement.

SCENE CONSTITUENT 19:1–8 (Paragraph: Reaction of 17:1–19:10)

THEME: I heard a great crowd in heaven, led by the twenty-four elders and the four living creatures praising God for punishing and destroying the great prostitute. Then a great crowd of God's people praised his sovereignty and rejoiced that the time had come for the marriage of the Lamb and his bride.

¶ PTRN	RELATIONAL STRUCTURE	CONTENTS
NUCLEUS₁	SITUATION₁ — CONCLUSION — orienter	19:1a After these things I heard *what sounded* like a great crowd in heaven who were saying,
		19:1b "Hallelujah. God is great! Our(inc) God has saved *his people*! He *is* glorious and mighty,
	grounds — CONCLUSION	19:2a for he punishes *people* rightly,
	grounds₁ — RESULT	19:2b *since* he has punished the great prostitute (OR, the great *city which is like a* prostitute)
	reason	19:2c *because* she used to seduce the *people of* earth to act immorally like herself,
	grounds₂	19:2d and *since* he has made her pay the just penalty for *killing and* shedding the blood of his servants."
	SITUATION₂ — CONCLUSION — orienter	19:3a The crowd spoke a second time saying,
		19:3b "Hallelujah. God is great!
	grounds	19:3c For *the great prostitute (or, the city)* has *been completely destroyed for ever, so* the smoke of the fire *that consumes* her/it will rise forever and ever."
	REACTION — CONTENT — orienter	19:4a Then the twenty-four elders and the four living *creatures* prostrated themselves and worshiped God, who sits on the throne, and they said,
		19:4b "This is true. Hallelujah. God is great!"
	situation — CONTENT — orienter	19:5a A voice from the throne said,
		19:5b "Praise our(inc) God, all his servants, *that is*, all *people* who reverence him, *whether* they *are of* little *social importance* or of great *social importance*."
NUCLEUS₂ — REACTION	NUCLEUS₁ — CONCLUSION — orienter	19:6a Then I heard what sounded like a great crowd *of people*, like the sound of a great volume of water *that is moving swiftly*, and like the sound of loud thunder, saying,
		19:6b "Hallelujah. God is Great!
	grounds	19:6c For the Lord God, the almighty *One*, now rules over *all the people in the world*.
	NUCLEUS₂ — CONCLUSION	19:7a Let us(inc) rejoice, let us be extremely glad, and let us glorify him,
	grounds₁	19:7b since *the time* has come for the Lamb to marry *his bride*,
	grounds₂ — NUCLEUS	19:7c and *since* his bride has prepared herself.
	amplification	19:8a *God* has granted to her that she should dress in fine linen which is bright and clean."
	parenthesis	19:8b The fine linen represents the righteous acts which God's holy people do.

INTENT AND PARAGRAPH PATTERN

The expressive nature of this unit is clear from the songs of praise to God and of joy in anticipation of the marriage of the Lamb. The intent is to affect the emotions of the addressees by encouraging them to rejoice in God's great victory over the evil forces of this world and in the glorious union of Christ and his church. The unit consists of two *situation-REACTION* paragraphs. The first gives the response of the heavenly beings to the destruction of Babylon and the second gives the response of God's people.

NOTES

19:1a a great crowd in heaven It is specified that the praise comes from a heavenly crowd, which many interpret to be comprised of angels, as in 5:11 (Bratcher and Hatton, Charles, Ladd, Morris, Swete). However, some take it to be in answer to the call of 18:20, and in that case the redeemed would also be included. The term σωτηρία 'salvation' may also point to this. The term is also used in 7:10, in the mouths of a great crowd of the redeemed. Mounce says that the voice is likely that of the church triumphant as in 7:9–10, 13–17.

19:1b Hallelujah, God is great! The expression ἀλληλουϊά is the Greek transliteration of a Hebrew phrase that means "praise God". However, it is not used as an imperative commanding others to praise God, but as a personal expression of praise by the speaker. In the display it is both transliterated and translated so that the emotional effect will be communicated.

Our(inc) God has saved *his people*! He *is* glorious and mighty There is no verb in the Greek text of this clause but its subject 'salvation and glory and power' is preposed in the Greek for extra prominence. In the doxologies of Revelation, attributes of God (such as his power and wisdom) occur in conjoined form with other abstract nouns such as 'blessing', 'honour', and 'thanks', representing events in which the actors are those doing the praising and thanking (see especially 7:12).

19:2a for he punishes *people* rightly In Greek this starts with ὅτι 'since, because' signalling the logical reason/grounds for 19:1b. In 16:7 the same wording is also used with reference to a judgment that has just been enacted. Swete says about 19:2, "A definite reason is given for the present psalm of praise—the execution of judgment upon Babylon" (cf. Morris, Charles, Mounce).

19:2b since he has punished the great prostitute (*or*, the great *city which is like a* prostitute) There is a second ὅτι 'because, since' at the beginning of 2b. Some commentators understand it as a logical argument for the truth of 2a: '*We know this* [2a] *is true* since God has punished the great prostitute'. Swete says, "That the Divine judgments are true and just has been shown anew by His sentence on the Great Harlot" (cf. Charles, Morris). However, other commentators understand this ὅτι construction as a restatement of the first one in more specific terms. Mounce says, "The second ὅτι clause does not justify the first ὅτι clause—the righteousness of divine judgment needs no justification or human approval—but is parallel to it and supplies a specific example of the more general truth" (cf. Düsterdieck, Lenski).

19:2c *because* she used to seduce the *people of earth* to act immorally like herself Fairly often a relative clause in Greek will function semantically as indicating reason. This is the case here.

Bratcher and Hatton say that ἔφθειρεν 'corrupted' here has the idea of leading into sin. BDAG classifies this reference as "in the realm of morals and religion—*ruin* or *corrupt someone* in his inner life, by erroneous teaching or immorality".

19:2d and *since* he has made her pay the just penalty for *killing and* shedding the blood of his servants Literally this is 'he has avenged the blood of his servants from her hand.' The concept of avenging is more specific than that of punishing, as it links the scale or form of the penalty to that of the crime. Here the judgment is a direct answer to the prayers of the saints as in 5:8, 6:10, and 8:3. It is given as further grounds for 19:2a.

19:3b–c Hallelujah, God is great! For *the great prostitute* (*or, the city*) *has been completely destroyed for ever, so* the smoke *of the fire that consumes* her/it will rise forever and ever This utterance repeats the praise and the reason for it (Alford, Charles, Mounce), this time with an emphasis on the eternal completeness of the destruction, strengthened by use of the historic present tense. The eternal burning may be a subtle way of likening Babylon to Sodom and Gomorrah, as in Jude 7. The complete meaning of the statement that her smoke rises forever is made explicit in the display.

19:4a Then the twenty-four elders and the four living *creatures* prostrated themselves and worshiped God The introductory καί 'then' and the responsive 'amen' of 4b show that 4a–b is a result or reaction to 19:1-3.

19:4b This is true. Hallelujah, God is great! The meaning of the ἀμήν 'amen' is that the elders and living creatures are in total agreement with what has been said in the doxology of 19:1–3. Their "amen" gives the seal of approval as in 5:14. This is the last time the elders and living creatures are mentioned in the text.

19:5a A voice from the throne said The voice can hardly be that of God who is on the throne, because of the third person reference to 'our God' in the quotation. In 3:12 Christ speaks of "my God" four times, but the plural possessive pronoun here is significant. The voice may be that of the four living creatures that are described as near the throne (4:6b), or it may be an angel.

19:5b Praise our(inc) God, all his servants, *that is,* **all** *people* **who reverence him,** *whether* **they** *are of* **little** *social importance* **or of great** *social importance.* The voice calls for universal praise from all God's servants, with two appositional phrases, indicating that no one is excluded of all those who belong to him.

19:6a Then I heard what sounded like a great crowd *of people* Some of the commentators who maintain that the voice in 19:1 was that of angels say that this voice is that of the universal church (Swete, Bratcher and Hatton), or of the martyr host (Charles), but Ladd says it is the same voice of the angels as in 19:1. The use of the first person plural pronoun functioning as an inclusive ("Let us rejoice and exult and give him glory") sounds more like an appeal to mankind than to angels. Also the fact that φωνή 'voice, sound' is anarthrous here suggests a different group from 19:1.

19:6c For the Lord God, the almighty One, now rules over *all the people in the world* The form of the verb is aorist and is generally taken to be an inceptive aorist. God's rule has begun to take its final, complete form, since the destruction of Babylon marks the end of evil in the world. This makes possible the final union of Christ and his people, as in the next verse.

the almighty *One* The word παντοκράτωρ is used nine times in Revelation and only one other time in the rest of the New Testament. The term describes the One who holds all things in his control. See note on 1:8d.

19:7a Let us(inc) rejoice, let us be extremely glad, and let us glorify him The verbs used for this happy celebration give a superlative aspect. The subjunctive form of the verbs in the Greek has an expressive force which could be translated as 'We delight in rejoicing and being extremely glad and glorifying him.'

19:8a *God* **has granted to her** God is the agent for the passive verb ἐδόθη 'it was given' here. This is significant since the righteous acts which the fine linen represents are only possible through God's empowerment. The passive form of this verb occurs twenty-one times in Revelation. See the note on 6:2a.

19:8b The fine linen represents the righteous acts which God's holy people do This explanation is understood by many to come from John. It is difficult to know the exact meaning of δικαιώματα since elsewhere it usually means 'ordinances', which is not appropriate here. Some commentators take it to mean 'sentence of justification' (Morris), or the saints' own inherent righteousness by virtue of being washed in Christ's blood, not imputed "but their own by their part in and union to Him" (Alford); but many take it to mean 'righteous acts' (BDAG, Düsterdieck, Ladd, Lenski, Mounce, Swete; cf. Rom. 5:18).

represents The Greek text has 'is', but the more specific meaning is 'represents' or 'symbolizes'.

BOUNDARIES AND COHERENCE

The 19:1–8 unit is introduced at 19:1 with the characteristic higher-level unit introducer μετὰ ταῦτα ἤκουσα 'after these things I heard'. There are many opinions about its close, but this analysis accepts 9:8 because it ends the call to praise God for victory over Babylon and for the result of that victory. All of 19:1–8 consists of songs of praise to God. Although the last song moves on to a new topic, the marriage of the Lamb, in 19:7a–8a, its beginning in 19:6b–c is clearly parallel to 19:1b–2d and 3b–c. The four hallelujahs in 19:1b, 3b, 4b and 6b tie the unit together; they occur nowhere else in the New Testament. There is no doubt that 19:1–8 looks both backward and forward, but there is no typical higher-level unit introducer at the beginning of 19:6 that would signal a major break. The command in 19:9 by the angel to John to write a special message certainly begins a new unit.

PROMINENCE AND THEME

As far as natural prominence is concerned the two REACTIONS, that of heaven in 19:4 and of earth in 19:6–8, are equal. The first two SITUATIONS, 19:1–2 and 3 are given marked prominence since they also are introduced with the hallelujah exclamations. The theme affirms the destruction of Babylon and God's supreme reign, which will bring the wedding of the Lamb and his bride.

SCENE CONSTITUENT 19:9–10 (Episode: Coda of 17:1–19:10)

THEME: An angel told me that God will bless the people who have been invited to celebrate the marriage of the Lamb. I was then cautioned not to worship the angel, but only God.

¶PTRN RELATIONAL STRUCTURE	CONTENTS
OCCASION — NUCLEUS ┬ orienter ───────	19:9a Then *the angel* said to me,
└ CONTENT ───────	19:9b "Write *this*: *God will* bless the people who have been invited *by him* to the feast *which celebrates* the Lamb's marrying *his wife*."
prominence orienter ┬ orienter ───────	19:9c He also said to me,
└ CONTENT ───────	19:9d "These words [19:9b] are truly *what* God *declares*."
OUTCOME occasion	19:10a I prostrated myself at his feet in order to worship him.
┬ orienter ───────	19:10b But he said to me,
├ negative ── EXHORTATION ──	19:10c "Do not *worship me*
└ grounds ───────	19:10d since I am your(sg) fellow servant and the fellow servant of your(sg) fellow believers who proclaim *the message which* Jesus witnessed *to people about God*.
OUTCOME — POSITIVE ── EXHORTATION ──	19:10e *Instead,* worship God,
└ grounds ───────	19:10f since *everyone who* proclaims *the message which* Jesus witnessed *to people about God is truly* speaking forth the words of God *as the Holy* Spirit *causes me to do*."

INTENT AND PARAGRAPH PATTERN

This episode presents a beatitude declared by the guiding angel and John's reaction to it. The *occasion-OUTCOME* framework of the paragraph identifies it as narrative in form. However, the intent of the beatitude is emotive—to encourage the saints.

NOTES

19:9a Then *the angel* said to me In the Greek text the only subject reference is the third person form on the verb λέγει 'he says'. However, it is obvious that the reference must be to an angel. The most probable reference would be the angel who began to guide John at the beginning of this scene in 17:1, one of the seven bowl angels.

19:9b Write *this*: *God will* bless The beatitude here is the fourth of seven in the book (1:3; 14:13; 16:15; 19:9; 20:6; 22:7, 14). This one is specially emphasized by the comment that it is truly what God declares.

have been invited *by him* The Greek verb is in the perfect tense-aspect, which may be interpreted as referring to the permanent call of God (Rom. 11:29).

feast *which celebrates* 'Which celebrates' is the necessary propositionalization of the relationship between 'feast' and 'marriage' in the genitive noun phrase.

19:9d These words The fact that the angel says in 19:9b "Write!" strongly suggests that the immediate reference of 'These words' in 9d is to the beatitude in 9b.

are truly *what* God *declares* The genitive 'of God' indicates God as the originator of the words, the One who declares them.

19:10a I prostrated myself at his feet in order to worship him The worship John had just seen

(19:1–8) and the awesome hope must have overwhelmed him. For the position he took before the angel, see the note on 4:10. In an effort to explain why John worshiped the angel many commentators presume he was so impressed that he mistook the angel for Christ. The text does not give this information, but it is hard to understand any other reason for John's making this mistake.

19:10c Do not *worship me* The angel's response was quick and emphatic. The prohibition is generic, Ὅρα μή 'see that not', with the specific act not made explicit. So 'worship me' is made explicit in the display.

19:10d fellow believers See the note on 1:9b.

who proclaim *the message which* Jesus witnessed *to people about God* As elsewhere in Revelation 'the witness of Jesus' is here taken as a subjective genitive, referring to the witness that Jesus bore about God (Caird, Lenski, Mounce). The angel serves God in the same way as God's human servants who bear the witness that Jesus bore.

However, a good number of commentators understand 'the witness of Jesus', especially in 19:10f, as an objective genitive meaning the witness that is borne about Jesus. Yet, in view of the conjunction γάρ 'for' in 19:10f the genitive phrase must surely have the same meaning there as in 10d.

19:10e *Instead*, worship God The negative-POSITIVE relation may be appropriately signalled here with 'instead'. In the Greek text there is no formal marker but 'God' is preposed to indicate the contrastive focus.

19:10f since The normal rule is to understand γάρ 'for, since' as relating to the closest clause it can support. Here this would be 'worship God', which comes immediately before it. Some commentators take this conjunction as introducing an explanation by the narrator, John. But that is not necessary, since the angel could just as easily give the grounds for his own injunction to worship God alone.

everyone who **proclaims *the message which* Jesus witnessed *to people about God* is *truly* speaking forth the words of God *as the Holy Spirit causes me to do*** The text is literally 'the witness of Jesus is the spirit of prophecy'. The term 'spirit' is variously interpreted by commentators. Some interpret it as the 'essence' of prophecy, so that faithful witness to God's words is the spirit/essence of all true prophecy. Others take 'prophecy' as modifying 'spirit' here, so that the prophetic spirit is what empowers those who witness. However, neither of these interpretations gives adequate grounds for the angel's direction of worship to God rather than to himself. It is therefore better to follow Hughes, who shows that both angels and believers are merely servants entrusted with God's messages.

BOUNDARIES AND COHERENCE

The unit begins at 19:9 with the reintroduction of the narrator as a participant rather than simply as an observer/auditor. Verses 9–10 are tied together by an *occasion-OUTCOME* chain: the beatitude spoken by the angel, John's reaction to the angel's speech and the resulting rebuke from the angel. At the beginning of 19:11 there is the higher-level marker καὶ εἶδον 'and I saw'. The main character of the next unit is the rider on the white horse.

PROMINENCE AND THEME

The beatitude 19:9a–b is given marked prominence by the angel's second speech, in 9c–d, which functions as a prominence orienter. In fact, the three uses of the historic present, λέγει 'he says' in 9a, 9c and 10b, give prominence to all the speeches within this unit. As the unit itself is an aside from the main narrative they point forward to the resumption of the main narrative in 19:11. The three speeches are therefore all thematic.

ACT CONSTITUENT 19:11–20:15 (Scene: Goal of 17:1–20:15)

THEME: I saw the King of kings going out to destroy the rebellious people of the nations. The beast and the false prophet led the people to fight against God's people but they were all destroyed, Satan was imprisoned and God's people reigned as kings for a thousand years. After Satan led another rebellion against God, God had him thrown in the lake of fire. Then God judged all people by their deeds and all whose names were not in the book of life were thrown into the lake of fire.

MACROSTRUCTURE	CONTENTS
setting	19:11–16 I saw One mounted on a white horse, who is Trustworthy and Genuine, and who judges and makes war according to what is right. He was going out to strike down and destroy the rebellious people of the nations. He is the King of kings and Lord of lords.
step₁	19:17–21 An angel announced that God was going to destroy all rebellious earth people. Then the beast and its false prophet gathered earth kings with their armies against the rider and his army, but they were destroyed, and the birds gorged themselves on the dead bodies of the rebellious earth people.
step₂	20:1–3 I saw an angel who seized, bound, and imprisoned Satan for a thousand years.
step₃	20:4–6 I saw that those who had been faithful to God received authority and reigned as kings with Christ for a thousand years. God will bless those who are in this first group that he has caused to live again.
step₄	20:7–10 When Satan was released, he deceived the nations into fighting against God's people. But God sent fire that destroyed them and Satan was thrown into the lake of fire.
GOAL	20:11–15 I saw God's throne with the people who had died standing in front of it. Record books and the book of life were opened. God judged each person by his deeds. Death itself and all whose names were not in the book of life were thrown into the lake of fire.

INTENT AND MACROSTRUCTURE

The unit 19:11–20:15 consists of a series of events that cover the final destruction of the devil and all who follow him. The main actors include the rider on the white horse (Christ), an angel, and God's people. But it is clear that the volitionality throughout is God's (see 19:17b, 20:3e, 4c, 9c–10a, 11). The unit thus has a *step–GOAL* structure in keeping with the general narrative pattern of the book.

BOUNDARIES AND COHERENCE

19:11 marks the beginning of this unit with a switch of characters. Instead of Babylon and the heavenly host who rejoice in its downfall there is the rider on the white horse, Satan and his followers, and the faithful people of God. The closing boundary of this unit coincides with that of Part Constituent 17:1–20:15 and is discussed under the Boundaries and Coherence of that unit.

The repeated references to judgment (19:11, 20:4, 10, 11–15) give coherence to the unit, as do the references to the destruction of all that is evil: the enemies of God on earth (19:15, 18, 21), the beast and the false prophet (19:20), Satan (20:10), and finally all those who were not God's people, and even death itself (20:14–15).

PROMINENCE AND THEME

The GOAL is clearly the most prominent part, since it covers the final destruction of all who are not God's people. Yet the *steps* have also to be included in the Theme since they give the details of the destruction of the powers of evil and the part that God's people play in this triumph.

SCENE CONSTITUENT 19:11–16 (Descriptive Paragraph: setting of 19:11–20:15)

THEME: I saw One mounted on a white horse, who is Trustworthy and Genuine, and who judges and makes war according to what is right. He was going out to strike down and destroy the rebellious people of the nations. He is the King of kings and Lord of lords.

¶PTRN RELATIONAL STRUCTURE	CONTENTS
setting	19:11a I saw that heaven was open, and there was a white horse.
DESCRIPTION₁ — 'One' — NUCLEUS₁	19:11b The name of the One who was mounted on the horse is "Trustworthy and Genuine."
NUCLEUS₂	19:11c It is according to what is right that he judges *all beings* and makes war *against his enemies*.
description₁	19:12a His eyes *were shining* like a flame of fire *shines*.
description₂	19:12b On his head there were many royal crowns.
description₃	19:12c There was a name written *on him* of which only he knows *the meaning*.
description₄	19:13a The cloak he was wearing was drenched with blood.
description₅	19:13b His name is *also* "The Word of God."
description₂ — 'armies'	19:14a The armies of heaven were following him *mounted* on white horses.
description	19:14b They were wearing clean *garments made of* white linen.
DESCRIPTION₃ — NUCLEUS₁ — means	19:15a From his mouth a sharp sword went out,
PURPOSE	19:15b in order to strike down *the rebellious people of* the nations.
NUCLEUS₂	19:15c He himself will exercise authority over them *severely as if beating them* with an iron rod,
NUCLEUS₃	19:15d and he will *destroy them just as a person* crushes *grapes in a* winepress; *he will do this on behalf of* God almighty, who is furiously angry *at them*.
DECLARATION — orienter	19:16a On his cloak *at the position of* his thigh, a name was written, which is
CONTENT	19:16b "King ruling over *all other* kings and Lord ruling over *all other* lords."

INTENT AND PARAGRAPH PATTERN

This paragraph is a typical descriptive paragraph, describing the rider on the white horse, the victorious King of kings and Lord of lords going out against the rebellious people of the nations. It consists of three *descriptions* leading up to the final DECLARATION. The first *description* (19:11b–c) is supported by several subsidiary descriptions (19:12–13).

NOTES

19:11a heaven was open The Greek perfect passive participle presents the situation as a state (reflected in the NIV as "standing open"). It does not mention the act by which the door had been opened.

and there was a white horse The main purpose of ἰδού is to introduce Christ, the major participant (see Levinsohn, p. 113–115). But here ἰδού comes immediately before ἵππος λευκός 'horse white' rather than the rider itself. As in 14:14, another instance where ἰδού introduces a lesser participant, it is followed by a participial phrase, so it may be seen as a device to slow down the introduction of the main character and give him added prominence.

Some English versions use 'there was' (TEV) or 'there before me' (NEB, NIV) as a focus marker or topic introducer to translate the function of ἰδού.

19:11b The name of the One who was mounted on the horse is "Trustworthy and Genuine" The Greek text is literally 'and the one sitting upon it is called faithful and true'. 'Faithful' and 'true', of course, describe the rider's character, and in one sense it would be proper to translate as Phillips: "whose rider is called faithful and true". However, this is no doubt intended as a name, and by far the majority of versions translate it as such. The same Greek words are used to describe Christ in 3:14.

19:11c It is according to what is right that he judges *all beings* and makes war *against his enemies* In the Greek there is prominent focus on ἐν δικαιοσύνῃ 'in righteousness,' which applies to both the judging and the making war.

Aune says that the Greek verb κρίνειν 'to judge' is used here in the sense of 'to rule'. This is reasonable since the context is that of a king going out to war, not that of a judge. Aune compares this use of κρίνειν to that in Luke 22:30.

19:12a His eyes *were shining* like a flame of fire *shines* The same image is used of Christ in 1:14 and 2:18.

The use of δέ at the beginning of the verse along with οἱ ὀφθαλμοὶ αὐτοῦ as a point of departure indicate the switch from the introduction of the rider to a backgrounded description of him.

19:12b On his head there were many royal crowns In 14:14 the one generally interpreted as Christ coming to harvest the earth wears a golden στέφανος 'crown (of victory)' and in Matt. 27:29 the thorns made a στέφανος for him. But here it is many διάδημα 'royal crowns' that he wears. Though victory is in the context, it is a supreme victory which leads to reigning in total sovereignty. For this reason it is appropriate that the crowns be specified as 'royal'. In the New Testament period, it is noted that a conquering king wore his own crown along with that of the monarch he had conquered. Now for the final battle Christ wears many crowns because he overcomes all kings.

19:12c a name written *on him* This is a case where the agent of the writing is completely backgrounded. Different languages have different methods of handling this. The only appropriate way to handle it in English is by no mention of the agent whatsoever. The same is true in 19:16.

of which only he knows *the meaning* It was the meaning of the name that was unknown, not the form of the name, since John saw it. The Greek verb οἶδα is therefore to be taken in the sense of 'to understand'. The idea is that humans cannot fully fathom the divine nature.

19:13a The cloak he was wearing The word ἱμάτιον is a term that can have either a general meaning of 'garment' or a specific meaning of 'cloak' or 'robe'.

was drenched with blood Concerning the word translated here as 'drenched', there are other variant readings found in the manuscripts. The display rendering follows the reading of the fourth edition of the UBS text, βεβαμμένον 'dipped, soaked' which is given a B rating. One variant is ἐρραντισμένον 'sprinkled'. Many commentators accept this reading.

The question of whose blood has drenched the rider's cloak is a matter of interpretation. Some limit it to that of his slain enemies, though he is understood to be going out to battle rather than returning from it. Of course, in apocalyptic literature the question of timing is not a serious one, as seen by the many proleptic scenes. The main difference is that some insist that it is his own blood, because it is through his sacrifice that he has become the conqueror (5:5–6). Since victory is the focus of this paragraph, it seems somewhat more probable that the blood is that of his enemies (Alford, Bratcher and Hatton, Charles, Ladd, Mounce, Walvoord), rather than his own blood (Lenski, Morris).

19:13b His name is *also* "The Word of God" Just as God gave life to the world when he spoke his word (Genesis 1), so Christ came into the world and is "The Word of God" which he spoke to the world. He not only brought life to his new creation, but also, by the sword of his mouth, he brought judgment and destruction to those who refuse his provision of life.

19:14a–b The armies of heaven were following him.... They were wearing clean *garments made of* white linen The question arises as to the identity of these armies. In 17:14 those who are with the Lamb when he is engaged in battle with kings of the earth are those who are called, chosen, and faithful, which certainly may be said of the saints. But in 12:7 it is Michael and the angels of heaven who defeat Satan and his angels. Since no particular group is specified here, some take the followers to include both angels and saints (Alford, Düsterdieck).

The use of the imperfect tense ἠκολούθει 'were following' suggests that the information about the armies is of secondary importance compared with that about the rider.

19:15a From his mouth a sharp sword went out Like many other expressions in this unit this one is also found in the early chapters of the book (1:16; 2:12, 16). It is a symbol of the mighty power of his spoken word.

19:15b in order to strike down The inclusion of ἐν αὐτῇ 'by/with it' in the ἵνα purpose clause of 15b, plus the fact that 'with it' is fronted before the verb, gives prominence to this proposition.

19:15c will exercise authority over them *severely as if beating them* **with an iron rod** See the note on 2:27 for this idiom. The sense of the full construction here shows that it either means to rule with complete sovereignty (Swete, Walvoord), or to destroy (BDAG, Lenski, Mounce). Versions translate as "rule" here but the clauses coming immediately before and after refer to destruction.

The use of the future tense in the Greek (whereas the other verbs in this verse are in the present tense) may be carried over from the original in the Septuagint Psalm 2:9.

19:15d and he will *destroy them just as a person crushes* **grapes** *in a* **winepress** The multiple-genitive phrase here, which includes metaphors and abstract nouns, is very complex. Since this is so and since treading the winepress is not formally presented as a part of what John sees, the metaphor is spelled out in the display text.

he will do this on behalf of **God almighty** Since it is Christ who is carrying out the punishment but God is also described as being involved ('the fury of the wrath of God'), an appropriate means must be determined to maintain the relation between God and Christ in this context.

who is furiously angry *at them* As in 16:19, the function of the repetition of synonyms in 'the anger of the wrath' is to indicate the great intensity of the anger and may be translated as a hendiadys such as 'furiously angry', or in any way in which the anger may be intensified.

19:16a On his cloak *at the position of* **his thigh, a name was written** The text says literally that the name is on his garment and on his thigh, which is potentially ambiguous. It is questionable that it would be written twice, though some commentators understand it that way (Barnes, Morris). Others take καί as epexegetical, in which case it might be understood as 'specifically', thus locating the name on the cloak at the position of the thigh (Ladd, Mounce, Swete). Probably the point is that the name was written where all could see it.

The highlighting of this declaration is shown both by the postposing of the focal constituent 'a name written,' and by the use of καὶ ἔχει 'and he had' rather than ἔχων 'having' as in 12c.

BOUNDARIES AND COHERENCE

In 19:11 there is a new setting, heaven, and one of the main characters of Revelation, Christ, is reintroduced, this time as a rider on a white horse. 19:16 ends the description and 19:17 begins a new unit with the paragraph (or higher-level) marker καὶ εἶδον 'and I saw' and the introduction of a new character, an angel standing in the sun.

In this unit the focus on the one character and the four names (19:11b, 12c, 13b, 16b) are significant coherence factors.

PROMINENCE AND THEME

The first DESCRIPTION (19:11b–c) is given prominence by the use of ἰδού 'behold' in 19:11a. The third DESCRIPTION (19:15) is highlighted by features of its structure (note 19:15b). Therefore the theme statement is composed of these three elements.

SCENE CONSTITUENT 19:17–21 (Episode: Step₁ of 19:11–20:15)

THEME: *An angel announced that God was going to destroy all rebellious earth people. Then the beast and its false prophet gathered earth kings with their armies against the rider and his army, but they were destroyed, and the birds gorged themselves on the dead bodies of the rebellious earth people.*

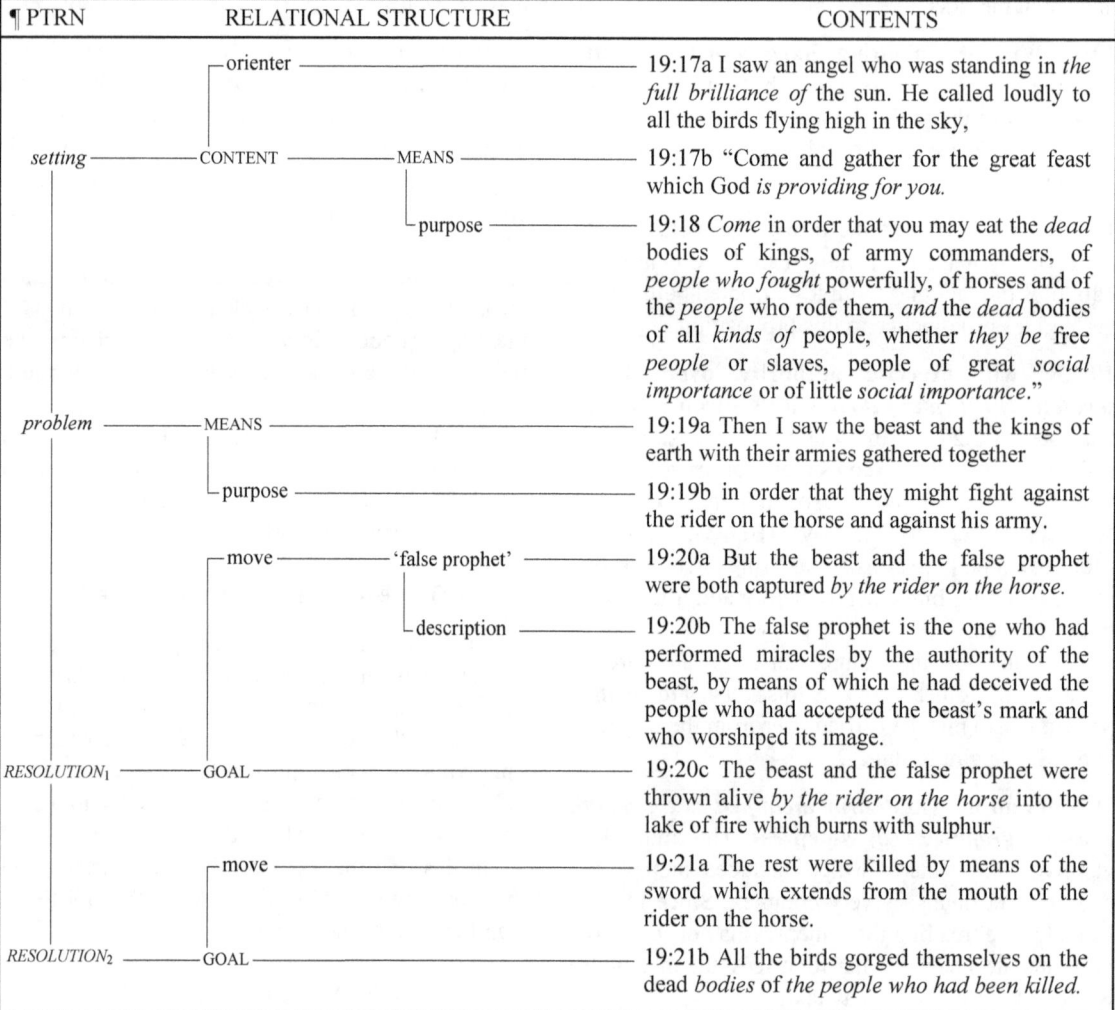

INTENT AND PARAGRAPH PATTERN

The intent of the 19:17–21 paragraph is to encourage the saints by showing them the final and complete destruction of the beast and the false prophet along with all their followers who bear the mark of the beast.

Seen as narrative, this paragraph has a *problem-RESOLUTION* structure. The invitation to the birds (19:17b–18) is a narrative *setting* that functions as a means of delaying and highlighting the narration of the battle. The mention of the birds again at the end of the unit (19:21b) may be regarded as an inclusio. Alternatively the unit could be seen as having a chiastic structure: introduction of the birds (19:17-18), introduction of the evil forces (19:19), outcome for the evil forces (19:20–21a), outcome for the birds (19:21b).

NOTES

19:17a I saw an angel who was standing in *the full brilliance of* the sun A majority of English versions use the locative phrase 'in the sun' (JB, NEB, NIV, RSV) as in the Greek text: ἐν τῷ ἡλίῳ. The question is whether this is intended to mean in the body of the sun itself or in the full light of the sun as Phillips: "in the blazing light of the sun". Goodspeed, TEV, and Twentieth Century translate as 'on the sun'. It would appear that the sense is that the angel is surrounded by the sun's rays, though he must be high in the sky, probably with the sun at its zenith.

all the birds A prediction that birds will devour the carcasses of God's enemies is made frequently in the Old Testament (Deut. 28: 26; 1 Sam. 17:44, 46; Jer. 7:33; 16:4). However, most of the imagery in 19:17–18 is drawn from Ezek. 39:17–20.

flying high in the sky The Greek word μεσουράνημα is literally 'midheaven', indicating a position high in the sky.

19:17b the great feast which God *is providing for you* This feast may be meant to contrast with the feast which celebrates the marriage of the Lamb. It is called 'the feast of God' because God provides it for the birds, with the implication that the judgment here portrayed is the action of God.

19:18 the *dead* bodies It was a great dishonour for dead bodies not to be buried, but to be eaten by birds would be even worse.

***people who fought* powerfully** The text uses ἰσχυρῶν 'strong/powerful'. Since this word may be used in many contexts in which there would be different shades of meaning, it seems best to interpret and present it in this context as referring to military strength. Some versions also translate it contextually: "heroes" (JB), "soldiers" (TEV), "fighting men" NEB, "warriors" (REB).

the *dead* bodies of all *kinds of* people In the Greek text the words 'fleshes of all' occur followed by 'both free people and slaves, both small and great', showing that this refers to all kinds of people (Beasley-Murray). The implication is that this refers to all those who had the mark of the beast (Düsterdieck, Ladd, Lenski, Morris).

19:19a gathered together In 16:14 after the emptying of the sixth bowl the demonic spirits went throughout the whole world to gather the kings to the battle on the great day of God Almighty. They are together in 16:16. Then John takes up other events until at this point he gives the outcome of the battle.

19:19b in order that they might fight The Greek text has ποιῆσαι τὸν πόλεμον 'to make war' as the predicate of the infinitive clause denoting purpose. They intended armed conflict, probably expecting to defeat the rider of the horse. But there is no record or description of a battle. Similarly in 17:14 the text says πολεμήσουσιν 'they will fight' against the Lamb, but the Lamb νικήσει 'will overcome' them, because of who he is.

19:20a the false prophet In 13:11–18 the false prophet is called 'the second beast', but after 13:12 the first beast is simply called 'the beast', and 'the false prophet' is the term used for the second beast in 16:13.

by the rider on the horse The agent of the action is supplied to fill out the case frame. The most immediate potential agents in the context are those mentioned in 19b – the rider on the horse and his army. However, there is a potential inference from 17:14 and 19:21 that the Messiah himself is the only one who performs any action in the battle. This appears to be the reason why Bratcher and Hatton see the conquering Messiah as the agent of the seizing and of the throwing into the lake of fire. Certainly Christ is the agent in the final sense and it may be that more direct agents operating on the physical level are foreign to the mode of thought here. However, Düsterdieck, taking as an analogy 12:7 where the angelic army defeats Satan, thinks that the agents are the Messiah's army

19:20b The false prophet is the one who had performed miracles by the authority of the beast, by means of which he had deceived the people who had accepted the beast's mark and who worshiped its image This lengthy relative clause describing the false prophet serves the purpose of slowing down the narrative and focussing on the climax in 19:20c.

19:20c were thrown alive ... into the lake of fire 'Living', occurring first in the Greek clause, is emphatic. They contrast with kings and armies, whose human bodies were killed.

the lake of fire The term, which is used with the definite article, comes in 19:20, 20:10, 14, 21:8, and only occurs in Revelation. It is different from ἅδης 'Hades', the temporary place of the dead, which in 20:14 is itself cast into the lake of fire. The gospels refer to the fire of γέεννα 'Gehenna, hell' (Matt. 5:22), with Old Testament background, as in 2 Chron. 28:3. The lake of fire is to be identified with Gehenna. The fire is unquenchable (Mark 9:48). In 20:14 and 21:8 the lake of fire is also called the second death.

19:21a The rest were killed TEV translates οἱ λοιποί 'the rest' as "their armies". This is appropriate, especially if it includes the 'kings of the earth' (19:19), and if the officers and soldiers of those armies are at least potentially thought of as all of unregenerate humanity. Another option would be 'all the beast's followers'.

BOUNDARIES AND COHERENCE

For the initial boundary of paragraph 19:17–21 see the Boundaries and Coherence for 19:11–16. Paragraph 19:17–21 begins with the introduction of an angel announcing God's feast for the birds and it ends with the grim statement that the birds gorged themselves on dead bodies. This is an inclusio. The birds are not mentioned again after that. The marker of a new unit, καὶ εἶδον, occurs at the beginning of 20:1. It is true that there is also a καὶ εἶδον at the beginning of 19:19, introducing the beast and the kings of the earth with their armies, but the inclusio or chiastic structure (see above, Intent and Paragraph Pattern) shows that 19:17–21 forms a unit at some level.

Lexical items add to the coherence. The word "flesh" is used six times, five times in 19:18 and once in 19:21. Words that fit the idea of battle are: kings, captains, and horses (19:18), armies and fight (19:19), captured (19:20a), killed by the sword (19:21).

PROMINENCE AND THEME

In the narrative structure both the *problem* and the two parts of its RESOLUTION are naturally prominent. Here the *problem* (19:19) is given added prominence by the lengthy *setting* (19:17–18) and the RESOLUTION is given prominence by 19:20b (see the note). The *setting* indicates that God is behind all the action. Each of these elements is therefore represented in the theme statement.

SCENE CONSTITUENT 20:1–3 (Episode: Step₂ of 19:11—20:15)

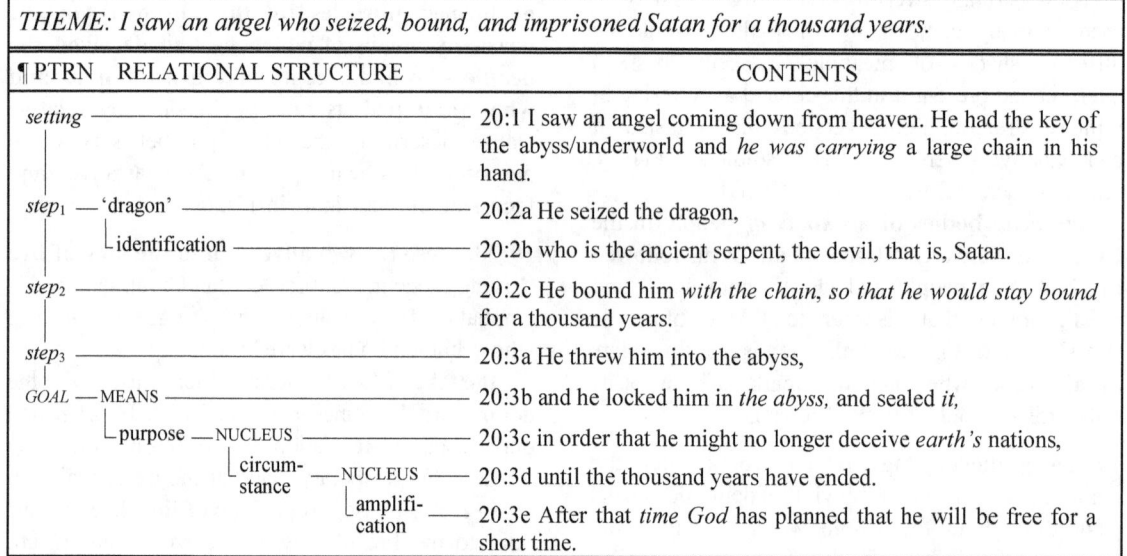

INTENT AND PARAGRAPH PATTERN

The intent of unit 20:1–3 is to show the intermediate fate of Satan, his being imprisoned by God for a thousand years. The intended effect is to encourage the believers. It is presented in a *step-GOAL* narrative paragraph pattern.

NOTES

20:1 the key of the abyss/underworld It is of great importance to realize that the abyss is fully under God's control. In 9:1 ἐδόθη 'given' is used in connection with the key to the abyss, referring to what God permits.

20:2a–b the dragon, who is the ancient serpent, the devil, that is, Satan He is identified here in the same terms as in 12:9.

20:2c He bound him *with the chain, so that he would stay bound* for a thousand years Although δέω can simply mean 'imprison' the mention of the chain in 20:1 implies that here Satan is being 'tied up' with the chain before being thrown into the abyss.

The Greek is literally 'bound him for a thousand years, but since 'bind' signifies an event, it is not the binding itself that lasts a thousand years here, but the duration of the period Satan is in the state of being bound.

20:3b and he *locked him in the abyss* The verb κλείω means 'to shut and lock' a door. 'Over him' in the Greek text signifies that Satan is down below, closed, locked and sealed in. It is similar to the English expression 'locked him in'.

sealed *it* The sealing refers to a mark or a sign being put on something that has been closed, to indicate it must not be opened without the consent of the person authorized to break or remove the seal.

20:3c deceive *earth's* nations It is difficult to know in what way the nations mentioned here are not included in those destroyed in 19:21, though there are many suggestions by the commentators. However, it is notable that in 20:8 Satan gathers the nations to make war on God's people, just as he did in 19:19. It may be that 'deceiving the nations' (i.e. all those who reject God) is to be regarded as the essence of all that Satan does, so the fact that he can no longer deceive anyone shows that he has become totally powerless.

20:3d After that *time God* has planned that he will be free for a short time That Satan is released is another of the necessities of God's purpose. The word δεῖ 'must' indicates something that will certainly happen in order that everything should follow the plan which God has predetermined.

The lack of a conjunction in the Greek, and the use of the present tense, show that this is a comment, not a further action on the narrative timeline.

BOUNDARIES AND COHERENCE

The use of καὶ εἶδον 'and I saw' and the introduction of another angel mark the beginning of a new paragraph. There is another καὶ εἶδον at the beginning of 20:4 which introduces thrones and those sitting upon them. The coherence of the unit is established by its *step-GOAL* progression of clauses with aorist verbs all having the same subject.

PROMINENCE AND THEME

In a *step-GOAL* paragraph pattern the *steps* and GOAL are thematic.

SCENE CONSTITUENT 20:4–6 (Paragraph: Step₃ of 19:11–20:15)

THEME: I saw that those who had been faithful to God received authority and reigned as kings with Christ for a thousand years. God will bless those who are in this first group that he has caused to live again.

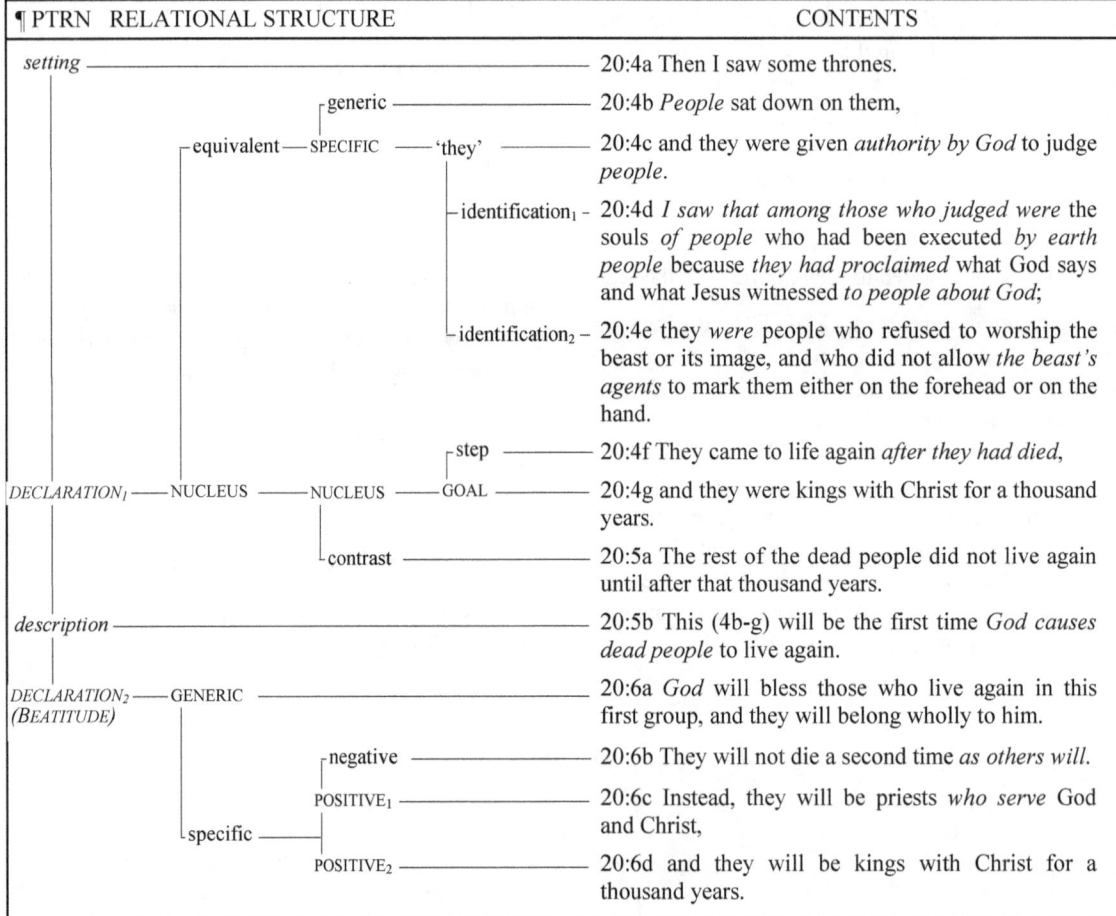

INTENT AND PARAGRAPH PATTERN

We might expect this paragraph about the thousand-year reign of the saints with Christ to have as its main intent the affecting of ideas, communicating what will happen during the millennium. However, the beatitude in 20:6 suggests that it has the main purpose of affecting the emotions, encouraging the saints regarding their glorious future.

In contrast to the aorist verbs in 20:1–3 indicating the *step-GOAL* narrative progression on the timeline, in 20:4–6 there is really only one possible event, the reigning of the saints with Christ. In addition to the verb ἐβασίλευσαν 'they reigned' (20:4g) this concept is also expressed as sitting on thrones (20:4b) and having authority to judge (20:4c). Moreover, the verb ἔζησαν 'they lived/came to life' indicates time prior to 'they sat upon thrones and judgment was given to them', so it seems that there is no a distinct timeline in this paragraph. Rather it appears to be descriptive of the state of the saints exalted to kingship with Christ.

There are thus two *DECLARATIONS* in the paragraph. The first, 20:4b–5a, focuses on the kingship of the saints who participate in the first resurrection. The second *DECLARATION* is the beatitude 20:6a.

NOTES

20:4a-b I saw some thrones. People sat down on them Literally the text is 'And I saw thrones, and they sat upon them'. None of those sitting upon the thrones are identified until 4d-e. This would suggest that the focus here is on the thrones as the *setting* of the unit. It is the opinion of Bratcher and Hatton, Caird, and Morris that the martyrs (20:4d) are the agents of the events of ruling (taking their places on the thrones, 20:4b), judging (20:4c) and reigning (20:4g). Some commentators think the twenty-four elders are intended as sitting on the thrones (Düsterdieck, Walvoord), but there is no reference whatever to them in this context. Others think that 20:4b refers to the saints in general and that the martyrs introduced in 20:4d are only one group within the saints (Ladd).

20:4c they were given *authority by God* to judge people The Greek text is literally 'and judgment was given to them'. No mention is made of who was to be judged by the resurrected saints, or of their actually passing any judgments. Also κρίμα 'judgment' in 4c is forefronted and serves as grammatical subject of the clause, showing that the event of judging is being focused on. It should be remembered that in the ancient world all rulers were judges. Therefore this proposition can be seen as in a *generic–specific* relationship with 20:4b and in an equivalence relationship with 20:4g.

20:4d *I saw that among those who judged were* The Greek starts with καί 'and', which shows that this does not refer to exactly the same group of people as 20:4b–c. However, the subject of 4b–c is not specified, and no different action is predicated of this second group, so it is most probable that John is here mentioning a particular subgroup of the general company of God's people who he saw taking up their kingship (Beale p. 999, Ladd).

the souls of *people* who had been executed This is not a reference to disembodied souls. John simply means that the people he saw had been dead but were now alive again.

The Greek verb πελεκίζω means 'to behead (with an axe)'. Most commentators take it here with a more generic meaning, 'execute', and TEV and JBP translate it that way.

because *they had proclaimed* what God says and what Jesus witnessed *to people about God* See the same or similar wording in 1:2, 9, 6:9, and 12:17.

20:4e they *were people* who refused to worship the beast or its image See 13:12–15. A question here is whether 20:4e is a further description of the martyrs or is a description of the faithful saints who were not martyred, as Swete and others maintain. However, there is nothing mutually exclusive between this identification and that in 20:4d, so it is more probable that they refer to the same group.

and who did not allow *the beast's agents* to mark them either on the forehead or on the hand See 13:16. The phrase 'the beast's agents' is supplied to fill out the agent of the action in the case frame.

20:4f They came to life again *after they had died* BDAG lists ζάω 'to live' in this verse under "of dead persons who return to life, *become alive again*". This is generally accepted by expositors to mean a literal living after having died.

20:4g and they were kings with Christ The verb is ἐβασίλευσαν 'they ruled/reigned', but it is interpreted in an intransitive sense here since there is no reference in this passage to any other inhabitants of the kingdom who could be ruled. The implication is that just as Christ is king, so the saints will also be kings together with him.

for a thousand years Although the proximity of this unit to 20:1–3 might imply the same thousand years during which Satan is imprisoned, the Greek here is χίλια ἔτη without any definite article or demonstrative, so the author is certainly not focusing on this connection. It should therefore be translated as indefinite—'a thousand years'.

20:5b This (4b–g) will be the first time *God causes dead people* to live again The term ἀνάστασις 'resurrection' is the term used for the Christian life after death. Those who, like Lazarus, were raised to continue their earthly life, all died again. It is said in this passage of those who live again that they will never die a second time and that they reign with Christ a thousand years. This is understood as identifying the first resurrection.

20:6a *God* will bless those who live again in this first group, and they will belong wholly to him 'Blessed and holy' are descriptions of the ones who will experience the first resurrection. These descriptions might be translated as actions or states: '*God will* bless *them* and *consider them* holy' or 'They are/will be happy and holy'. The states are the results of the actions. The context suggests that 'holy' here means belonging wholly to God, as in 14:10 where it is applied to angels. The descriptions which follow (20:6b–d) are the specific characteristics of their blessedness.

20:6b They will not die a second time This is literally 'over these the second death does not have authority', which is personification of an event. The second death is identified in 20:14 as the lake of fire. In 21:8 it is also described as the destiny of those who choose not to follow the Lamb.

as others will The Greek definite article in 'the second death' shows that John's readers knew there was such a thing as 'second death.' The message of 20:6b is that it only affects those who have rejected Christ, since the saints with Jesus are alive forever.

BOUNDARIES AND COHERENCE

The initial boundary has been discussed under the Boundaries and Coherence for 20:1–3. As for the final boundary, there is a new temporal point of departure at the beginning of 20:7, 'and when the thousand years were finished'. The coherence of the unit is shown by the topic of ruling/judging in 20:4a–c, 4g and 6d.

PROMINENCE AND THEME

The two *DECLARATIONS*, in 20:4g about the kingship of the faithful saints, and in 20:6a about God's blessing on them (the fifth beatitude of the book), are the most naturally prominent parts of the unit. They therefore comprise the theme.

SCENE CONSTITUENT 20:7–10 (Episode: Step₄ of 19:11–20:15)

THEME: When Satan was released, he deceived the nations into fighting against God's people. But God sent fire that destroyed them and Satan was thrown into the lake of fire.

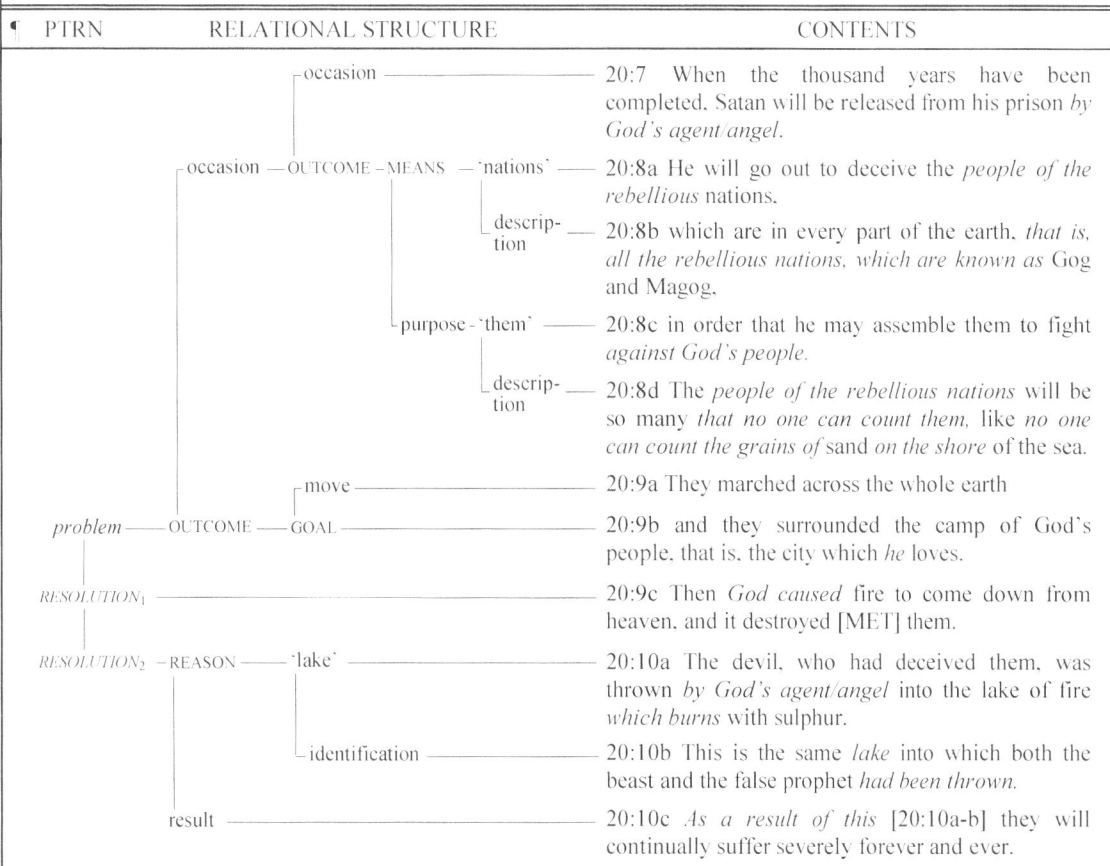

INTENT AND PARAGRAPH PATTERN

This unit has a narrative solutionality structure. The *problem* of Satan driving the nations into war against God's people is resolved by God destroying the nations and having Satan thrown into the lake of fire. In keeping with narrative structure the verbs on the main event line in 20:9a–10a are aorist, whereas the more backgrounded events of 20:7–8 and 20:10c are in the future tense.

NOTES

20:7 When the thousand years In 20:3e δεῖ 'must' signals God's purpose to which ὅταν 'when' in 20:7a points, showing God controls the time of Satan's imprisonment.

Satan will be released from his prison φυλακή 'prison' simply means the place where someone has been kept locked up – in this case, the abyss.

by God's agent/angel The agent of the releasing is not in focus and so does not occur in the Greek. The options are God's agent, or an angel (cf. 20:1–3), or possibly God himself.

20:8a will go out to deceive The word 'go out' in Greek, ἐξέρχομαι, does not necessarily focus attention on coming out of a place. Here it is used with reference to the extent of Satan's activity. He went throughout the world deceiving the nations.

the *people of the rebellious* nations The context shows that these are rebellious nations, willingly deceived into waging war against God and his people.

20:8b which are in every part of the earth As in 7:1 the Greek text has 'the four corners of the earth', meaning 'the whole world' (Beasley-Murray, Lenski, Mounce, Swete), though some feel it refers only to the distant pagan nations (Düsterdieck).

that is, all the rebellious nations, which are known as **Gog and Magog** 'Gog and Magog' are in apposition to 'the nations' as shown by the fact that there is no conjunction before 'Gog and Magog'.

In Ezekiel 38–39 Gog is a leader and Magog is the name of his people. But here the two names have taken on a more universal significance, referring to all of the enemies of God.

20:8c in order that he may assemble them to fight *against God's people* A second infinitive of purpose follows with no connecting καί 'and', which shows that his deceiving the nations had the purpose of mustering of forces for battle against God's people (9b).

20:8d The *people of the rebellious nations* **will be so many** *that no one can count them*, **like** *no one can count the grains of* **sand** *on the shore* **of the sea** In the display the simile is rendered in a non-hyperbolic fashion on the basis that an exact comparison is not intended.

20:9a They marched The verb here is ἀνέβησαν 'went up,' which was often used of journeys to Jerusalem (see 20:9b) because that city was higher than anywhere else of significance to the Jews. However, this is not an appropriate translation here, since this army is marching from both high and low places over all the earth.

across the whole earth Since 'the four corners of the earth' indicates an all-inclusive reference to the whole earth, it is not necessarily hyperbolic to see 'over the breadth of the earth' as a reference to armies moving over the whole earth to attack the camp of the saints.

20:9b the camp of God's people, that is, the city which *he* **loves** The word translated 'camp' can refer to a military camp or the type of encampment that the Israelites had in the wilderness. The picture has been understood by some to be that of an encampment of God's faithful defenders surrounding the city, but the more common view is that the encampment is the people of God as a whole.

Although the primary reference of 'the city that he loves' is to Jerusalem, as in Psalm 78:68 and Jer. 12:7, it also refers to God's people as a whole, so that there are two references to the same group, with καί 'and' having an epexegetical function: 'that is'.

20:9c Then *God caused* **fire to come down from heaven** Some manuscripts have not only ἐκ τοῦ οὐρανοῦ 'out of heaven' but also ἀπὸ τοῦ θεοῦ 'from God'. The UBSGNT text does not include ἀπὸ τοῦ θεοῦ 'from God'. However, there is no question but that God is acting, although throughout this unit God is never referred to explicitly. The focus is on what happened to Satan rather than on what God did.

and it destroyed them The Greek is κατέφαγεν 'swallowed, consumed', a common metaphor for complete destruction.

20:10a The devil, who had deceived them This phrase refers back to 20:8a, but it also refers to the whole history of Satan's deception of mankind. This statement of his actions coming right before his final punishment may function to highlight the main reason why God had to destroy him.

by God's agent/angel See the note under 20:7 for this same implied expression of agency.

20:10b This is the same *lake* **into which both the beast and the false prophet** *had been thrown* An alternative for this identification would be 'where the beast and the false prophet *already were*'. Many English translations use a similar clause.

20:10c they will continually suffer severely The future tense in the Greek shows that this is not on the main timeline of the narrative, but is a comment on 20:10a-b.

BOUNDARIES AND COHERENCE

In 20:7 the reference to the thousand years, as described in 20:1–6, is a tail-head connection and marks the beginning of this unit. The end of the unit is marked by the backgrounded reference to the punishment of Satan. 20:11 begins the next unit with a new setting and the characteristic new-setting marker καὶ εἶδον 'and I saw'.

The coherence of the unit is provided by the focus throughout on Satan and the rebellious nations. It is noticeable that although they are defeated and destroyed by God, he is backgrounded in the text and not once mentioned overtly in the Greek.

PROMINENCE AND THEME

The greatest prominence falls on the two resolving factors of the threat against God's people, that is, the fiery destruction of the hordes of rebellious nations and Satan's being thrown into the lake of fire. The theme thus includes the two *RESOLUTIONS* and the prominent parts of the *problem*, since a resolution cannot be stated without reference to its problem.

SCENE CONSTITUENT 20:11–15 (Episode: Goal of 19:11–20:15)

THEME: I saw God's throne with the people who had died standing in front of it. Record books and the book of life were opened. God judged each person by his deeds. Death itself and all whose names were not in the book of life were thrown into the lake of fire.

¶ PTRN	RELATIONAL STRUCTURE			CONTENTS
setting	NUCLEUS₁			20:11a I saw a huge white throne.
	nucleus₂			20:11b *I saw* the One who sits on the throne, and in his presence the earth and the sky/heaven disappeared [PRS]. They did not exist any more.
	NUCLEUS₃			20:12a I saw that the people who had died *were now living again and* were standing before the throne, both those of great social importance and those of little social importance.
step₁	NUCLEUS₁			20:12b The books *in which God had recorded what people did* were opened *by God* (*or, by God's agent/angel*).
	NUCLEUS₂			20:12c Another book was opened *by God* (*or, by* God's *agent/angel*), which *contains the names of those who live spiritually/eternally*.
step₂	NUCLEUS			20:12d The people who had died *and now lived again* were judged *by God* according to what they had done, just as *he* had recorded it in the books.
		occasion₁		20:13a The people who had died at sea *lived again in order to be judged*. [PRS]
		occasion₂		20:13b Every person who was in the place where people go when they die lived again *in order to be judged*. [PRS]
	EQUIVALENT	OUTCOME		20:13c Each one was judged *by God* according to what each one had done.
GOAL	NUCLEUS₁	'lake'		20:14a Everything that causes people to die, together with the place where the dead people had been, was thrown *by God* into the lake of fire.
		identification		20:14b This lake of fire is *the place where people* die the second time.
		condition		20:15a If any person's *name* was not found written in the book which *contains the names of those who* live *spiritually/eternally*,
	NUCLEUS₂	CONSEQUENCE		20:15b *that person* was thrown *by God* into the burning lake.

INTENT AND PARAGRAPH PATTERN

In the 20:11–15 unit the record books are inspected, the dead are judged, and those whose names are not found written in the Book of Life are thrown into the lake of fire. There is thus chronological progression and the paragraph is analysed as a narrative episode of the *step-GOAL* type.

In the *setting* (20:11–12a) it seems that the focus is on the throne and those who stand before it to be judged. In fact, it is noticeable that throughout the unit God is only referred to obliquely (e.g. 20:11b). Thus the focus here is clearly on those who are judged rather than on God who is doing the judging.

NOTES

20:11a a huge white throne Emphasis on size gives an aspect of dominion and majesty. The word translated 'white' may also be translated 'brilliant, shining'.

20:11b the One who sits on the throne From previous mentions of the throne (4:2–11, 5:1, 7, 13; 6:16; 7:10, 15) and especially from 19:4 it is clear that the One who sits on the throne is God the Father. However, some commentators understand Christ to be the Judge (Barnes, Lenski, Walvoord), based on other passages of scripture such as Matt. 25:31 and John 5:22, 27.

in his presence the earth and the sky/heaven disappeared BDAG lists this occurrence of φεύγω as 'vanish, disappear'. The figure of speech is personification, a figure used freely in this unit. The exegetical problem is whether John is speaking symbolically in order to convey the awesomeness of God which terrifies the universe or whether he is speaking about its actual destruction. In favour of the latter view is 21:1, 'And I saw a new heaven and a new earth for the first heaven and first earth had passed away'. John uses the vividness of personification to communicate the reality of the physical destruction of the universe.

A second question is whether ὁ οὐρανός should be translated as 'heaven' or 'sky'. Certainly we are not to understand the heaven which is the abode of God as disappearing, but there is also a possibility that 'heaven' here refers to the sky and everything which is physically above the earth. At the same time 'the earth and the heaven' may simply be a designation for the entire physical universe created by God.

They did not exist any more The expression in the Greek is 'no place was found for them'. Completeness and finality are what is expressed in this clause.

20:12a the people who had died The Greek says, 'And I saw the dead'. Many commentators (e.g., Alford, Bratcher and Hatton, Charles, Ladd, Mounce) say that this refers to 'the rest of the dead' as mentioned in 20:5 and defined by 20:4. However, identification of who 'the dead' are in the current verse depends on one's interpretation of 20:4.

1. Some interpret the dead here to mean all people except the martyrs (Bratcher and Hatton, Charles). If 20:4 refers only to the martyrs then the statement in 20:5 that 'The rest of the dead did not come to life until the thousand years were finished' suggests this.
2. Others interpret the dead here to refer only to the ungodly (Walvoord) on the understanding that 20:4 includes all believers.
3. Still others interpret the dead here to mean all human beings who have lived and died (Beasley-Murray, Lenski).

were now living again The people standing before the throne are certainly conscious, and John's calling the resurrection mentioned in 20:5 'the first resurrection' could well imply that there is a second bodily resurrection. The implied information '*were now living again*' appears in the display to indicate that the ones called dead are not still dead when they appear before the throne.

both those of great social importance and those of little social importance The expression is used to emphasize that all are included.

20:12b The books *in which God had recorded what people did* were opened This echoes Dan.7:10, where the books opened clearly contained the evidence that was to be put before the court. Mounce notes references in intertestamental literature to books in which the deeds of people are recorded for judgment. Here this is confirmed by 12d.

by God (or, by God's agent/angel) The agent is expressed here in order to fill out the case role for the benefit of languages that require the agent of an action to be explicit. Since God is the ultimate agent of all the activity which he controls, it is not easy to decide to whom events such as this should be attributed.

20:12c which contains *the names of those who live spiritually/eternally* See the note on 3:5.

20:12d The people who had died *and now lived again* were judged *by God* according to what they had done, just as *he* had recorded it in the books Some commentators complain about this statement not being in chronological order because it is followed by the remark that the sea and the grave released the dead people in them. However, the purpose of the flashback in 20:13a–b is to make the individual judgment clear and emphasize that it was universal.

according to what they had done, just as *he* had recorded it in the books One purpose of the resurrection of those who died without accepting the pardon provided in the redemption of Christ is that they may have opportunity to stand trial and God's justice may be vindicated before all the universe.

20:13a The people who had died at sea *lived again in order to be judged* Personification of the sea, death, and Hades giving up the dead is the figure used by John to express the emotional impact of what he was seeing. The use of ἔδωκεν 'gave up' implies a recipient or specific purpose, rather than a general and eternal return to life. Since the focus of this paragraph is on the judgment rather than on the Judge this is translated here as '*to be judged.*'

The sea is mentioned because of the belief that only those whose bodies are buried in the earth go to the underground world of Hades. It was thought that the souls of those drowned at sea stayed in the sea.

20:14a Everything that causes people to die, together with the place where the dead people had been, was thrown *by God* into the lake of fire The Greek text is καὶ ὁ θάνατος καὶ ὁ ᾅδης ἐβλήθησαν εἰς τὴν λίμνην τοῦ πυρός 'and death and Hades were thrown into the lake of fire'. There is a question as to whether death and Hades here refer to something abstract such as the principle of death (Alford, Beasley-Murray, Caird, Ladd, Lenski, Morris, Mounce, Swete) or refer to all unredeemed dead people (Walvoord). Since the ungodly are released by death and Hades in 20:13b and are resurrected for judgment and since their fate of being thrown into the lake of fire is described in 20:15, it seems best to understand death and Hades to be a personification of death itself.

20:14b This lake of fire is *the place where people die the second time* This refers back to 20:6b where the second death was mentioned but not identified.

20:15a If any person's *name* was not found written in the book which contains *the names of those who* live *spiritually/eternally* Though the first meaning of the Greek verb εὑρίσκω is 'to find after search', it is often used simply to express a state of being. But since the absence of the name in the registry is evidence for condemning the person, it is possible that there is stress here on the fact that an adequate search for it is made in order to validate the evidence.

BOUNDARIES AND COHERENCE

The 20:11–15 unit opens at 20:11 with the new setting marker καὶ εἶδον 'and I saw' as John sees the setting for the final judgment of mankind. Its closure, which coincides with that of the third act, comes at 20:15, at which point all rebellious earth people have been thrown into the lake of fire along with Death and Hades. There is another definitive 'and I saw' at the beginning of 21:1 as John sees a completely different setting: the new heaven and earth. The 'and I saw' at the beginning of 20:12 does not introduce a new setting but new participants: the dead, whose judgment, being in focus throughout the unit, gives it coherence

PROMINENCE AND THEME

The theme gives the prominent parts of the *setting* of the court scene, the *steps* of the judgment and the GOAL of the execution of the judged.

PART CONSTITUENT 21:1–22:5 (Act: Goal of Body)

THEME: I saw the Bride of the Lamb, the new city of Jerusalem, perfect in every way, where God will dwell permanently with his people. God declared that he had made everything new and everything was now accomplished. In the city God's servants have the abundant sources of eternal life, and they live forever as kings worshipping God in the light of his glory.

MACROSTRUCTURE	CONTENTS
NUCLEUS₁ (contraction)	21:1–8 I saw the new city of Jerusalem, where God will dwell permanently with his people and they will no longer experience suffering. Then God declared that he had made everything new and everything was now accomplished and he will provide abundant eternal life to all who trust him and punishment in the lake of fire for the wicked.
NUCLEUS₂ (amplification)	21:9–22:5 When I was told to come and see the Bride of the Lamb I saw the holy city, the new Jerusalem, perfect in every way. In the city God's servants have the abundant sources of eternal life, and they live forever as kings worshipping God in the light of his glory.

INTENT AND MACROSTRUCTURE

It is notable that once this unit has been reached, the Goal of the Body of Revelation, the action within John's vision ceases. The culmination of the vision is not an event but a state, a new creation replacing the first created universe – the new Jerusalem which John here describes in detail. The description focuses on the beauty of the new Jerusalem, the blessed state of God's people who live there and the fact that God dwells there permanently with them. The intent is clearly to encourage John's audience as they see the ultimate reward God has for them.

This new Jerusalem is introduced twice, in 21:2 and 10, so it is clear that the two parts of the unit are parallel. Each part covers the same topics, the beauty of the city, the presence of God and his people and the absence of all evil, but 21:1–8 is more like a summary of these topics, so it appears to stand in a *contraction–amplification* relationship with 21:9–22:5.

BOUNDARIES AND COHERENCE

The beginning boundary of this Act is discussed under the Boundaries and Coherence for Part Constituent 17:1–20:15. The Act consists of a description of God's new world, the new Jerusalem, but at 22:6 the topic changes to the imminence of Jesus' return to earth and the fulfilment of the prophecies of the book. For this reason 20:5 is seen as the close of the current unit.

The coherence of the unit is demonstrated by the several topics that occur in both parts of it: the new Jerusalem coming down from heaven (21:2, 10), the beauty of the city (21:2, 18–21), the presence there of God (21:3, 22, 22:3–4), the blessed state of God's people there (21:3–4, 6–7, 24–26, 22:2–5).

PROMINENCE AND THEME

Since the two parts of this unit stand in parallel with each other, the theme is a conflation of the two parts.

ACT CONSTITUENT 21:1–8 (Scene: Nucleus₁ of 21:1–22:5)

THEME: I saw the new city of Jerusalem, where God will dwell permanently with his people and they will no longer experience suffering. Then God declared that he had made everything new and everything was now accomplished and he will provide abundant eternal life to all who trust him and punishment in the lake of fire for the wicked.

MACROSTRUCTURE	CONTENTS
description	21:1–4 I saw the new city of Jerusalem, where God will dwell permanently with his people and they will no longer experience suffering.
DECLARATION	21:5–8 After declaring that he had made everything new, God declared that everything had been accomplished and that he will provide abundant eternal life to all who trust him and punishment in the lake of fire for the wicked.

INTENT AND MACROSTRUCTURE

The 21:1–8 scene is clearly descriptive, comprising a general *description* of the new Jerusalem (21:1–4) and a DECLARATION based on that *description* (21:5–8). In the DECLARATION God himself declares final fulfilment of all his purposes and the eternal blessedness of his victorious people in the holy city, which replaces the old creation and from which all evil is absent. The unit thus forms part of the climax towards which the discourse of Revelation has been building up. It has the intent of affecting the emotions of the readers with confidence in the goodness of the final reward that God has in store for them.

BOUNDARIES AND COHERENCE

For the final boundary of the 21:1–8 unit, there is a distinctive break at the beginning of 21:9 with the reintroduction of one of the angels of the seven bowls. This also initiates a much more specific description of various aspects of the New Jerusalem. The coherence of 2:1–8 can be found in the references to making things new 21:1, 2, 5, the passing away of the old 21:1, 4, 6 (γέγοναν 'it is done'), 8, and the relationship between God and his people 21:3, 7.

PROMINENCE AND THEME

In a *descriptive-DECLARATION* paragraph both constituents are thematic.

SCENE CONSTITUENT 21:1-4 (Paragraph: Description of 21:1-8)

THEME: I saw the new city of Jerusalem, where God will dwell permanently with his people and they will no longer experience suffering.

¶ PTRN RELATIONAL STRUCTURE	CONTENTS
setting — RESULT	21:1a Then I saw a new heaven and a new earth
└ reason — NUCLEUS₁	21:1b because the first heaven and the first earth had ceased to exist [MET]
NUCLEUS₂	21:1c and the sea no longer existed.
description — 'city'	21:2a I saw the holy city, which is the new *city of* Jerusalem. It was coming down out of heaven from God.
└ description	21:2b The city had been prepared *by God,* so that it was as beautiful as a bride *ready to marry* her husband.
┌ orienter	21:3a And I heard a loud voice *which spoke* from the throne *of God* and said,
NUCLEUS₁ REASON	21:3b "Take note! God now dwells [MET] with humankind, and he will *continue to* dwell with them.
NUCLEUS₂	21:3c They will be his people. God himself will be with them, *and he will be* their God.
DECLARATION	
┌ comparison	21:4a And it will be *as if he was* wiping every tear from their eyes.
RESULT — RESULT	21:4b They will no longer die or mourn or cry or suffer pain,
└ reason	21:4c because everything that existed before has ceased to exist [MET]."

INTENT AND PARAGRAPH PATTERN

This descriptive paragraph itself consists of a *description* and a DECLARATION. After a *setting* in which John sees the new heaven and new earth he describes the new Jerusalem that comes from heaven to earth. The heavenly voice declares that this is where God will now dwell for evermore with his people, who will never again experience any sort of suffering. To John's audience this would be the epitome of the consolation which his vision brought them in their time of troubles.

NOTES

21:1a Then As in many other places in the discourse structure of this book, καί 'and' has its temporal sequential sense here.

a new heaven and a new earth Commentators argue about whether the former heaven and earth are transformed and renewed or whether they are simply replaced by the new creation. However, it should be noted that the term καινός 'new' used here tends to refer to things that were not previously in existence (BDAG), and full weight must be given to the statement in 21:1b that 'the former heaven and the former earth had disappeared'.

21:1b because the first heaven and the first earth had ceased to exist For a discussion of the meaning of 'heaven' when it refers to something that will pass away see the note on 20:11b.

The Greek ἀπῆλθαν 'passed away' is a metaphor for ceasing to exist, as in 21:4c.

The reason proposition explains why the heaven and earth were 'new.' Note that there is no focus here on the destruction of the first creation, since attention is immediately switched to the new.

21:1c and the sea no longer existed Mention of 'the sea' separately from the earth fits with other references in Revelation where they are treated as different elements of creation (5:13, 7:2, 12:12 etc.). In 10:6, as here, heaven, earth and sea together indicate the totality of the inhabited creation.

There is no mention of a new sea in the new creation. This may be due to the negative view of the sea in the O.T., where it was a symbol of chaos and was sometimes thought of as 'the abyss' in which Satan and his angels were imprisoned.

21:2a the holy city, which is the new *city of* Jerusalem This is the focal constituent of the Greek sentence and is preposed to indicate that the writer's attention has now switched from the new heaven and new earth to the new Jerusalem. This is the topic of all the remaining descriptions in 21:1–22:5.

The new Jerusalem is also referred to in 3:12, "I will write on him the name of my God, and the name of the city of my God, the New Jerusalem which comes down from my God out of heaven (RSV)". Since 'holy' may be defined as that which belongs to God, 'holy city' and 'city of God' are very similar in meaning. Other NT writers also mention the heavenly Jerusalem in Gal. 4:26 and Heb. 12:22, and it is referred to obliquely in Phil. 3:20 and Heb. 11:10, 13:14.

It was coming down out of heaven from God The phrase 'from God' could be seen as representing a proposition, in which case the second part of 21:2a could be rendered as, 'It was coming down out of heaven, because God *had caused it to come down to earth*'.

21:2b had been prepared *by God* so that it was as beautiful as a bride The Greek text is ἡτοιμασμένην ὡς νύμφην 'prepared as a bride'. The identity of the agent doing the preparing is not explicit in the Greek text, but the city is coming from God and he is the only one who could prepare her worthy for her husband.

The reference to the new Jerusalem by the angel (21:9–10) as 'the bride, the wife of the Lamb', together with the mention of the bride and wedding of the Lamb in 19:7–9, show that there is a complex figure of speech here. There seem to be two images, that of a city and that of a bride, for the one topic of God's people. Or it may be that the bride is used as an image for two separate topics, that of the people of God and that of the holy city where they live.

***ready to marry* her husband** The statements that the new Jerusalem had been prepared and was dressed beautifully for her husband show that the underlying thought is that God has made his people worthy of living with himself and his Son.

21:3a I heard a loud voice *which spoke* from the throne Since the speaker refers to God in the third person, while the one sitting on the throne in 21:5 (obviously God) refers to himself in the first person, it is possible that God is not the speaker here in 21:3–4. The important thought is the authority of the voice, because it announces the fulfilment of a basic theme of the Old Testament (Lev. 26:11–12; Ezek. 37:26–27) which is repeated in Matt. 1:23: 'God with us'.

of God The nominal phrase τοῦ θρόνου 'the throne' is recognizable in Greek as referring to the throne of God, because of the use of the article and the central place of the throne of God in the heavenly scenario of Revelation.

21:3b-c Take note! 'Take note' is an attempt to render ἰδού, a word that is difficult to translate in many contexts but serves to signal attention and emphasis on the statement or event under consideration. Here it gives the reason proposition equal prominence with its result 21:4.

now dwells with humankind σκηνή 'tent' is here used in the sense 'dwelling place.' Beasley-Murray points out that for Greek-speaking Jews the word would have a special resonance since it has the same consonants as the Hebrew term 'shekinah' that was used of the glorious presence of God. This is probably reflected in the use of the noun (and its cognate verb) here and in John 1:14.

humankind 'Humankind' is a more precise rendering for τῶν ἀνθρώπων here than the more ambiguous 'people', since the idea is that the mighty God deigns to live with mere humans.

21:3c his people The UBSGNT reads λαοί 'peoples', classifying it as a 'B' reading, though Metzger (p. 688) remarks that it is difficult to decide between this and the singular form λαός. If the plural form carries any different meaning from the singular, it is probably implying that God's people are no longer from just one people, as the Jews in the OT, but they are now from all the peoples of the world.

God himself will be with them The subject of the Greek clause is preposed, giving it marked prominence.

***he will be* their God** Metzger says the UBS editorial committee found great difficulty in determining the actual Greek text in this clause. Their decision here was to bracket the final phrase 'their God' and call it a 'C' reading.

If 'their God' is included, we need to determine its relationship with what comes before it. Since 'their God' is the reciprocal of 'his people', it would seem that the relationship between 'they will be his people' and '*he will be* their God' would be a conjoined one.

21:4a *as if he was* wiping every tear from their eyes Sin caused the sorrow that brought tears, and there is no more sin. Although 'he will wipe every tear from their eyes' is figurative, its nonfigurative meaning is actually given in the rest of the verse, so it is retained in a literal form.

BOUNDARIES AND COHERENCE

The unit begins at 21:1 by introducing a new situation which is in strong contrast to all that had been seen before. It is marked by a double inclusio, which indicates its ending at 21:4 – in 21:1b and 21:4c the first creation has ceased to exist, ἀπῆλθαν; in 21:1c the sea is no longer there, οὐκ ἔστιν ἔτι, and in 21:4b there will no longer be, οὐκ ἔσται ἔτι, any form of suffering.

PROMINENCE AND THEME

As already noted, the *description* has marked prominence because of its preposed subject, and in the DECLARATION 21:3b–c has equal prominence with 21:4. The theme therefore consists of the *description* and the DECLARATION.

SCENE CONSTITUENT 21:5–8 (Paragraph: Declaration of 21:1–8)

THEME: *After declaring that he had made everything new, God declared that everything had been accomplished and that he will provide abundant eternal life to all who trust him and punishment in the lake of fire for the wicked.*

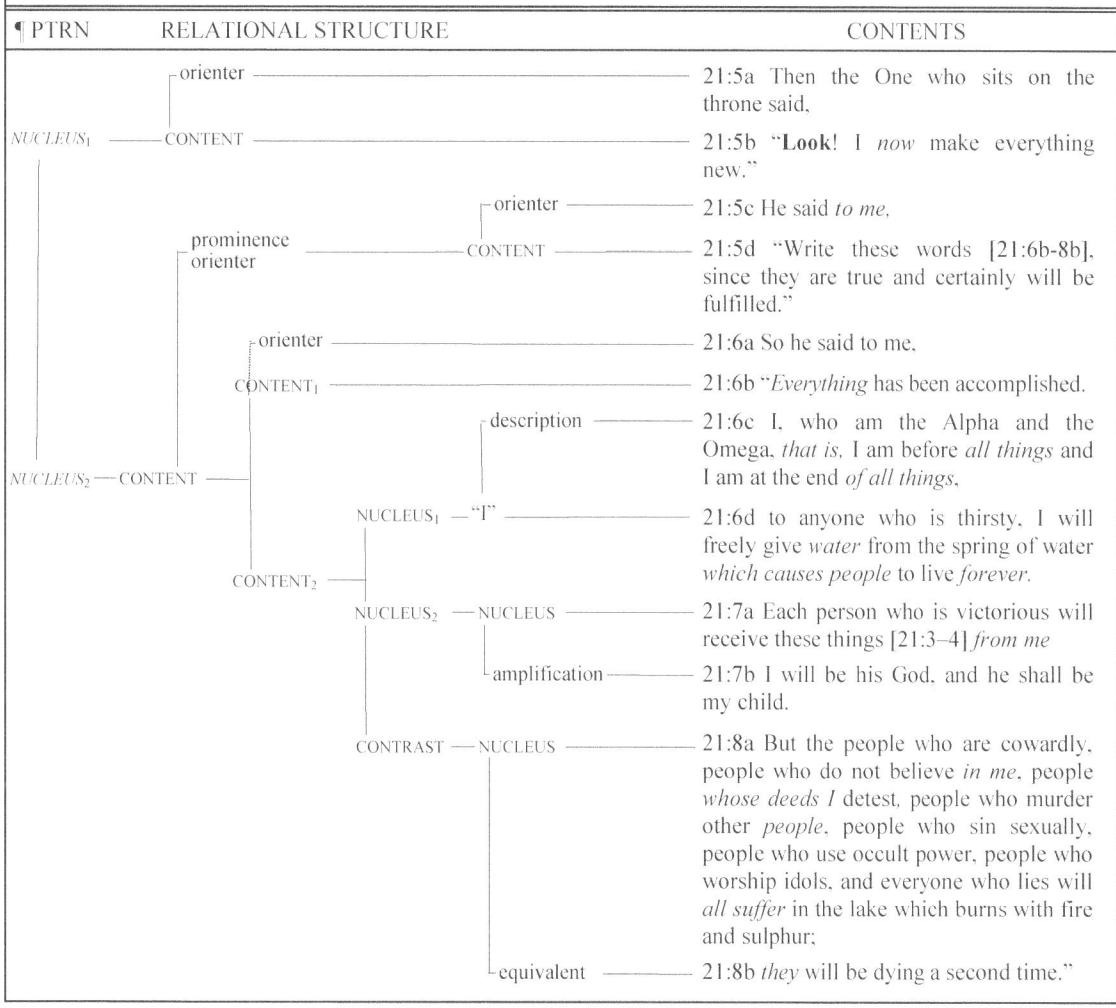

INTENT AND PARAGRAPH PATTERN

This declaration consists of two parts, both being the words of God (see the note on 21:5c). The second part, 21:5c–8, is introduced by a prominence orienter, which is appropriate since it constitutes the head of the first nucleus (21:1–8) of the Goal (21:1–22:5) of the Body of the Book.

NOTES

21:5b Look! The Greek word that focuses attention on what follows occurs here: ἰδού. In this context it seems that 'Look!' is more fitting than 'Take note!' since John was able to see the new heaven and earth.

I *now* make everything new The Greek has present tense, so '*now*' is added in the display to avoid the misconception that this is a statement of what God generally or habitually does. The emphasis of the sentence is on 'new', which is preposed in the Greek.

21:5c He said *to me* On the surface, the three quotes in 21:5–8 would all appear to be from God who sits on the throne, since no other subject is stated. The verbs of the orienters in 21:5a and 6a are aorists, but the verb in 21:5c is present tense. Because of this change and because other commands to write have been from a voice from heaven or an angel (14:13; 19:9), many commentators feel that the command to write must be from an angel or an impersonal voice from heaven. However, like most historic presents, λέγει 'he says' in 21:5c probably points forward, giving added prominence, in this case, to the next utterance. The function of the content in 21:5d is thus not to add new information but to mark the prominence and truth value of 21:6-8. As far as prominence and authority are concerned, it would be counterproductive to introduce an angel or impersonal subject as the speaker in 21:5c–d.

21:5d "Write these words [21:6b-8b], since they are true and certainly will be fulfilled." Most versions and commentators take ὅτι as signalling reason or grounds, although some consider it serves like quotation marks to introduce the following words. In addition it should be noted that statements such as 'these words are trustworthy and true' tend not only to stress the truth value of words referred to, but also to signal that they are highly significant. As in 19:9 the command 'Write,' refers forward to the next significant utterance (here 21:6b-8b), which is qualified by a statement about its truth value.

these words [21:6b-8b] There is debate about what this refers to. However, the fact that it refers to the following utterance is confirmed by the new speech orienter in 21:6. This fits with the Greek pattern whereby a speech orienter in the historic present (21:5c λέγει 'he says') that is pointing forward to another speech requires the following speech to have a new orienter.

certainly will be fulfilled When πιστός 'faithful' modifies statements, as here, it propositionalizes as 'these words ... certainly will be fulfilled'. So we find that both 'trustworthy' and 'true' are similar in meaning in this context and the repetition of the thought gives emphasis.

21:6b "Everything has been accomplished" The Greek text has here the one word γέγοναν (a plural form). It is a perfect active indicative form which is translated in most versions as "It is done" (KJV, RSV, NIV, TEV) or "They have come to pass" (ASV). The sense of the verbal form is actually adjectival, 'Everything is in a finished, accomplished state'.

Some commentators take the plural form to refer back to οὗτοι οἱ λόγοι 'these words' in 21:5. But others say that the pronominal suffix "probably refers to all the events that had to take place" (Morris), described more specifically as "the great work is accomplished; the arrangement of human affairs is complete. The redeemed are gathered in; the wicked are cut off; truth is triumphant, and all is now complete—prepared for the eternal state of things" (Barnes).

21:6c I, who am the Alpha and the Omega See the note at 1:8b. Here the meaning of the metaphor is made explicit in the following statement.

I am before *all things* and I am at the end *of all things*. There are various ways in which ἡ ἀρχὴ καὶ τὸ τέλος, literally, 'the beginning and the end', could be understood in this context:

1. They could be understood basically as a time orientation. As the Eternal One, God is both at the beginning and the end of all things. Thus ἡ ἀρχὴ καὶ τὸ τέλος, like 'the Alpha and the Omega', are to be taken and understood together as an idiom for 'the Eternal One'.

2. Rather than only being chronologically based, they have to do with actions that God takes as the Eternal One. The word ἀρχή can have the sense of 'origin' as in Psa. 110(111):10 in the Septuagint where we find that the fear of the Lord is the ἀρχή of wisdom. It was also a philosophical technical term meaning 'the first

cause' (BDAG). This is the sense of ἀρχή in Rev. 3:14 where Barclay translates ἡ ἀρχὴ τῆς κτίσεως as "the moving cause of God's creation". Thus it might be translated here in 21:6 as the 'originator *of all things*'. The word τέλος may have not only the meaning of 'end position', but also the meaning 'end result, goal, outcome'. Mounce says that God is the end of all things in the sense that he constitutes their goal or aim (as in 1 Tim. 1:5; Rom. 10:4).

3. With the context of the immediately preceding γέγοναν 'they are done/accomplished', and with the sense of ἀρχή as origin or originator of all things, τέλος may have the idea here of 'finisher/accomplisher/perfector (of all things)'. Compare the ideas in τὸν τῆς πίστεως ἀρχηγὸν καὶ τελειωτὴν Ἰησοῦν, 'Jesus the originator and perfector of the faith' Heb. 12:2.

The first option has been chosen for the display since it appears to be the more basic of the three options. The concepts in option (2) and (3) are latent in ἡ ἀρχὴ καὶ τὸ τέλος but not necessarily in focus here. Since 'I am the Alpha and the Omega' is a title, it is retained in the display text as such, i.e. in metaphorical form.

21:6d from the spring of water Rather than being strictly a metaphor, 'the spring of the water of life' has a visionary connection with 'the river of the water of life' which flows from the throne of God and the Lamb down the middle of the city (22:1–2).

which causes people to live forever As in 7:17 'water of life' is a genitive construction in which 'life' is an abstract noun and 'water' represents spiritual provision. This water causes or enables believers to live in some sense.

21:7a Each person who is victorious will receive these things [21:3–4] *from me* The verb κληρονομέω means 'to come into possession of something', as one does with an inheritance. But it contains no reference to the death of the donor, so 'inherit' is not a good translation here.

victorious The Greek has a participle form, ὁ νικῶν 'the one conquering'. See the note on 2:7b.

these things [21:3–4] Since ταῦτα 'these things' is plural while the most immediate antecedent, 'the water of life', is singular, 'these things' would appear to refer to those things promised in 21:3–4.

21:7b I will be his God, and he shall be my child While the Greek text says μοι υἱός 'a son to me', here and in certain other contexts this does not strictly refer to males only, and so 'child' is a better translation.

21:8a people who are cowardly This might also be rendered as 'people who are afraid to confess that they believe in Christ lest they suffer persecution'.

people who do not believe *in me* The meaning of ἄπιστοι is 'unbelieving' or 'faithless ones'. Mounce says, "The unbelieving are not the secular pagan world (as in 1 Cor. 6:6; 7:12ff; 10:27; 14:22ff) but believers who have denied their faith under pressure". There are at least two reasons why ἄπιστοι could be understood here as those who have renounced their faith, even though most references of ἄπιστος in the New Testament are to unbelievers in general. Firstly, the main hortatory theme of all of Revelation is to encourage believers to keep the faith no matter what the cost. Secondly the immediately preceding word in this list is 'cowards'. In the context of Revelation as a whole, 'cowards' also would most apparently indicate those who had renounced the faith because of their fear of persecution. On the other hand, the rest of the list appears to refer to the unbelieving world in general, so the best translation for ἄπιστοι would be one that is more general.

people *whose deeds I* detest BDAG shows that ἐβδελυγμένος means 'abominable, detestable', and that the related noun, βδέλυγμα, refers to anything that must not be brought before God because it arouses his wrath, everything connected with idolatry. As with the other items of the list in this verse, it is what people do that causes God to detest them, not who they are.

people who use occult power The word used here, φάρμακος, has the basic meaning of 'one who practices magic arts' (cf. NIV) and is associated with φάρμακον meaning 'a magic potion, charm' (BDAG). In a list like this where the context is not restrictive, everyone who practices magic arts and uses occult power in any way would be included.

and everyone who lies This eighth category is set off from the other seven by the use of πᾶσιν 'all'. Since in each category it is certainly implied that all people in that category are included in having their lot in the lake of fire, why is πᾶσιν added to the final category alone? The answer would appear to be either to stress this final category even more than the others or to stress the fact that all kinds of lies will come under God's judgment.

will *all* suffer The Greek τὸ μέρος αὐτῶν 'their part, share' refers to what they will experience, as in

20:6 'those who experience the first resurrection'. Here it stands in contrast to 21:7a κληρονομήσει ταῦτα 'will receive these things as their share'.

BOUNDARIES AND COHERENCE

The full introduction of the speaker, God, as 'the One who sits on the throne' in 21:5a marks the opening of this unit. It consists of three short speeches by God, which gives it coherence, and the end of the third speech marks the end of the unit. The following unit begins at 21:9 with the reintroduction of one of the seven angels who had the bowls of the seven last plagues and who then guides John in the detailed vision of the new Jerusalem.

PROMINENCE AND THEME

Both parts of the declaration are naturally prominent. However, 21:5c–d gives the second part marked prominence, so both its positive and its negative elements are included in the theme.

ACT CONSTITUENT 21:9–22:5 (Scene: Nucleus₂ of 21:1–22:5)

THEME: When I was told to come and see the Bride of the Lamb I saw the holy city, the new Jerusalem, perfect in every way. In the city God's servants have the abundant sources of eternal life, and they live forever as kings worshipping God in the light of his glory.

MACROSTRUCTURE	CONTENTS
setting	21:9 One of the seven angels of the seven bowls told me to come and see the Bride of the Lamb.
step	21:10–2 I was shown the holy city, the new Jerusalem, shining with God's glory, immense and perfect and constructed from amazing, beautiful and precious materials. The Lord God Almighty and the Lamb are physically present there and their glory provides the light by which the kings and peoples of the earth come to glorify them. The morally impure cannot enter the city but only those who are registered in the Lamb's book of life.
GOAL	22:1–5 In the city God's servants have the abundant sources of eternal life, and they live forever as kings worshipping God in the light of his glory.

INTENT AND MACROSTRUCTURE

In the scene 21:9–22:5 John is shown the new Jerusalem that has come down out of heaven from God, which is the bride, the wife of the Lamb. The two main parts of the unit are marked by ἔδειξέν μοι 'he showed me' in 21:10 and 22:1. These are in the aorist tense, as are the main verbs of 21:9. This shows that although much of the material in this unit is description it has an overall narrative framework of *setting*, *step* and GOAL. The progression from *step* to GOAL is marked by the switch from describing the physical appearance and polity of the city to its purpose and essence as the final, eternal state of fellowship and communion between God and his faithful people.

BOUNDARIES AND COHERENCE

The opening of the unit is marked by the reappearance of one of the seven angels of the bowls as an active participant who leads John to the next stage of his vision. The unit ends with the final description of the eternal state of the believers as reigning with God for ever and ever. See also Boundaries and Coherence for 21:1–22:5.

The coherence of the unit comes mainly from the fact that it consists almost entirely of descriptions of the city and what goes on in it. There are also constant references to glory, brilliance and light, as in 21:11, 18–21, 23–26, 22:1, 5.

PROMINENCE AND THEME

Since the unit has a *setting*, *step*, GOAL framework, the theme consists primarily of the GOAL. However, a summary of the *setting* and *step* are necessary to provide the narrative background.

SCENE CONSTITUENT 21:9 (Propositional Cluster: Setting of 21:9–22:5)

THEME: *One of the seven angels of the seven bowls told me to come and see the Bride of the Lamb.*	
RELATIONAL STRUCTURE	CONTENTS
─orienter	21:9a One of the seven angels who *previously* had the seven bowls which were filled with *the liquid/wine causing* the seven last terrible afflictions came and said to me.
CONTENT	21:9b "Come with me and I will show you the Bride *of the Lamb, that is,* the wife of the Lamb".

INTENT AND STRUCTURE

This short speech unit forms the *setting* of the scene and introduces its subject and main active participant.

NOTES

21:9a One of the seven angels who *previously* had the seven bowls which were filled with *the liquid causing* the seven last terrible afflictions came and said to me The wording of this verse is almost the same as that of 17:1, except that the identification of the angel is expanded with a reference to the seven last plagues, perhaps to increase the tension in this climax of the whole book.

***the liquid causing* the seven last terrible hardships** As in 15:7, an attempt has been made to handle the abstract idea of bowls filled with plagues.

BOUNDARIES AND COHERENCE

The propositional cluster 21:9 coheres as one sentence in the Greek, with an orienter-CONTENT relation. The most significant reason for seeing a boundary at the end of the verse is that 21:10 is clearly parallel to 22:1 (see above, 21:9–22:5 Intent and Macrostructure). Also in 21:10 the description switches from God's people as the bride to the new Jerusalem.

PROMINENCE AND THEME

The identity of the angel is significant and is included with the more prominent CONTENT.

SCENE CONSTITUENT 21:10–27 (Sub-scene: Step of 21:9–22:5)

> *THEME: I was shown the holy city, the new Jerusalem, shining with God's glory, immense and perfect and constructed from amazing, beautiful and precious materials. The Lord God Almighty and the Lamb are physically present there and their glory provides the light by which the kings and peoples of the earth come to glorify them. The morally impure cannot enter the city but only those who are registered in the Lamb's book of life.*

MACROSTRUCTURE	CONTENTS
description$_1$	21:10–14 I was shown the holy city, the new Jerusalem, shining with God's glory, having a great wall with twelve gates and twelve great foundations.
description$_2$	21:15–17 The angel measured the size of the city and its wall, showing their immensity and perfection.
description$_3$	21:18–21 The whole city and all its parts were constructed from amazing, beautiful and precious materials.
DECLARATION	21:22–27 The Lord God Almighty and the Lamb are physically present in the city and their glory provides the light by which the kings and peoples of the earth come to glorify them there. The morally impure cannot enter the city but only those who are registered in the Lamb's book of life.

INTENT AND MACROSTRUCTURE

This descriptive unit consists of three *descriptions* of the physical aspects of the new city of Jerusalem, leading up to a DECLARATION. This DECLARATION gives some salient details of life within the city. It shows that the ultimate destiny of God's people lies in a place where God and Christ are physically and eternally present, where all evil is excluded, and where everything is constantly focused on the glory of God. The intent of the unit is to influence the emotions of the readers, both by the wonderful *descriptions* of the city's beauty and magnificence and by the DECLARATION of the glorious setting of the destiny that awaits them.

BOUNDARIES AND COHERENCE

For the opening boundary of this unit see above, 22:9 Boundaries and Coherence. Its closing boundary is marked by the action of the angel in 22:1 ἔδειξέν μοι 'he showed me', parallel to 21:10, and the switch from a general description of the city to details of the relationship between God and his people there, echoing details of the Garden of Eden in Genesis 2 and 3. The constant focus on the magnificent, beautiful and glorious details of the city gives the unit coherence. It may also be significant that in each part of the unit there is mention of the city gates (21:13, 15, 21, 25), one of most notable features in any ancient city.

PROMINENCE AND THEME

The DECLARATION has several features of marked prominence (see 21:22–27 Prominence and Theme) as well as natural prominence. Since this is a descriptive unit the *descriptions* are also included in the theme.

SUB-SCENE CONSTITUENT 21:10–14 (Propositional Cluster: Description₁ of 21:10-27)

THEME: I was shown the holy city, the new Jerusalem, shining with God's glory, having a great wall with twelve gates and twelve great foundations.

RELATIONAL STRUCTURE	CONTENTS
┌ move	21:10a Then, while I was *specially controlled* by *the Holy* Spirit, *the angel* carried me to a large, high mountain.
GOAL ─── 'city'	21:10b and he showed me the holy city Jerusalem, *which was* coming down out of heaven from God.
├ description₁ ─── GENERIC	21:11a God's glory was present in it.
└ specific	21:11b It was shining like a very precious stone *shines*, that is, like a diamond that sparkles like crystal.
├ description₂	21:12a The city had a very high wall *around it*.
├ description₃ ─── 'gates'	21:12b The city had twelve gates *in its wall*,
├ description₁	21:12c at which were twelve angels.
├ description₂	21:12d Each gate had the name of one of the twelve tribes of the sons of Israel written over it.
├ description₃	21:13 Three gates were on the east *side*, three gates were on the north *side*, three gates were on the south *side*, and three gates were on the west *side*.
└ description₄ ─── 'foundation stones'	21:14a The wall of the city *was built* on twelve foundation stones.
└ description	21:14b Each foundation stone had the name of one of the twelve apostles of the Lamb *written* on it.

INTENT AND STRUCTURE

Within a simple narrative framework this unit is entirely descriptive. It gives the initial extended description of the city as seen from the outside. As John sees the city coming down from heaven he notes the details that would be obvious to anyone seeing an ancient city from a distance – its surrounding wall, its gateways, and the basis or foundation on which it was built.

NOTES

21:10a Then, while I was *specially controlled* by *the Holy* Spirit, *the angel* carried me See 1:10; 4:2; 17:3. John's experiences of heightened ecstasy seems to make a framework for telling his vision. (See Boundaries and Coherence for 1:9–22:11).

21:10b the holy city Jerusalem, *which was coming down out of heaven from God* The wording is almost identical to that in 21:2, indicating that the same event in John's vision is being referred to. Here it will be described in greater detail.

21:11a God's glory was present in it The phrase 'the glory of God' only occurs three times in Revelation. In 15:8 the reference is to "smoke from the glory of God," so it is clear that here and in 21:23 the glory is not equated with light (21:11b) but is the source of the light.

21:11b It was shining The asyndeton between 21:11a and 11b shows that this is not a separate description but a restatement, indicating how God's glory was seen.

like a diamond that sparkles like crystal The term ἴασπις, usually translated as 'jasper', is better translated as 'diamond.' See the note on 4:3a, which also refers to the presence of God.

21:12a a very high wall The Greek μέγα καὶ ὑψηλόν 'great and high' may mean 'thick and high' (Aune, and some versions) but the thickness of the wall might not be so obvious at first to an external observer. Bratcher and Hatton suggest it means 'very high'.

21:12b The city had twelve gates *in its wall* Mounce points out that πυλών properly denotes the gateway rather than the actual gate.

21:12c at which were twelve angels The angels' function is probably not to admit or exclude people from the city, since all God's people are in the city and all evil forces have been eliminated. Walvoord says that the angels serve as an honour guard.

21:14a The wall of the city *was built* on twelve foundation stones The Greek θεμελίους could refer to 'foundations' (as in Heb. 11:10), or 'foundation stones' (BDAG). The question here is whether there are (1) twelve foundation stones, each one being the foundation of the wall which goes from one gate to the next (Beasley-Murray, Swete), or (2) twelve layers of foundation, that is, built one upon the other, each one extending all the way around the city (Walvoord, p. 325). However, Aune points out that (2) gives an awkward picture and is not found in any other similar descriptions. So it may be better to think of one foundation consisting of twelve foundation stones.

BOUNDARIES AND COHERENCE

For the initial boundary of 21:10–14 see the Boundaries and Coherence for 21:9. In 21:15 the angel is reintroduced and the focus switches from a general description of the city to the measurements of it, which the angel takes. The unit 21:10–14 describes the radiance of the city, its wall, its gates, and its foundations. These would be expected in the first view of the city.

PROMINENCE AND THEME

Since this is a descriptive unit the naturally prominent constituent is the four main descriptions: of God's presence in the city, its wall, its gates and its foundations.

SUB-SCENE CONSTITUENT 21:15–17 (Paragraph: Description$_2$ of 21:10-27)

THEME: The angel measured the size of the city and its wall, showing their immensity and perfection.			
¶ PTRN	RELATIONAL STRUCTURE		CONTENTS
setting	MEANS		21:15a The *angel* who was speaking to me had a golden measuring rod,
	purpose		21:15b in order that he might measure the city, its gates, and its wall.
	contraction		21:16a The city was square *in shape*, that is, its length *was* as long as its width.
NUCLEUS$_1$	NUCLEUS		21:16b *The angel* measured the city with his rod and *reported that it was* 12,000 stadia in length and *that* its width and height were each equal *to its length*.
NUCLEUS$_2$	'measure'		21:17a He measured its wall according to the *cubit* measure that people *normally use and reported that it was* 144 cubits *thick*.
	identification		21:17b That was the measure which the angel used.

INTENT AND PARAGRAPH PATTERN

Like the previous unit, the 21:15–17 unit is essentially descriptive but with a narrative framework. It describes the size of the city with measurements that show not only its immensity but its perfection.

The narrative framework is provided by the two instances of the finite verb ἐμέτρησεν 'he measured', 21:16b, 17a. Since all the rest of the paragraph consists of non-events, it is clear that the description of the city is more focal than the events of measuring.

NOTES

21:15a a golden measuring rod This contrasts with the ordinary rod that was given to John in 11:1, with which he was told to measure the sanctuary, the altar, and the worshipers. Gold is appropriate for measuring the heavenly city.

21:15b in order that he might measure the city, its gates, and its wall The actual measuring of the gates is not mentioned in the text, but the gates are described in 21:21.

21:16a square *in shape* The balance and symmetry of the square here symbolize the perfection of the city. In the Greek τετράγωνος 'square' comes before the verb, to show that it is in focus.

21:16b *The angel* **measured the city with the rod** *and he reported that it was* **12,000 stadia** The Greek text is literally 'And he measured the city with the rod at twelve thousand stadia,' but this also implies an action of reporting the measurement so that John could record it.

12,000 stadia The στάδιον was a unit of length that varied in different parts of the Graeco-Roman world from 190 to 210 meters. This means that 12,000 stadia would equal about 2,400 kilometres or 1,500 miles. However, the symbolic function of the number 12,000 is undoubtedly of more significance than the exact length. It probably symbolizes the immensity and perfection of the city.

its width and height were each equal *to its length* This is generally taken to mean the city was cubical in shape, but it might also be interpreted as a pyramid. It may be significant that the holy of holies in the wilderness tabernacle and in Solomon's temple (1 Kings 6:20) were cube-shaped. The holy of holies was considered as the dwelling place of God, which is what the holy city is now shown to be, 21:3.

21:17a *and reported that it was* **144 cubits** A cubit is the measurement from the elbow to the tip of the middle finger or almost half a metre (about eighteen inches). This would give a measurement of about 65 meters or 210 feet. But again, the number 144, symbolizing perfection, as in the number of God's servants (7:4), is more significant than the actual measurement.

thick The Greek text only says 'he measured its wall a hundred and forty four cubits'. The question is whether this measurement refers to the thickness of the wall or its height. Many commentators take this measurement for the height of the wall and some consider that there is an inconsistency between the great height of the city (21:16) and the insignificant height of the wall (21:17). Moreover, it was stated in 21:12 that the wall is great and high.

However, it is known that the walls around ancient cities were very thick, and it might be expected that the thickness of the wall would be noted before its composition is described (21:18). In Ezekiel's vision (Ezek. 40:5) both the thickness and the height of the wall around the temple area were measured. For these reasons, many commentators understand the measurement given in 21:17 to be that of the thickness of the wall.

21:17b That was the measure which the angel used The measurement by the angel is said here not to be different from the standard human measurement, the cubit, which was based on the length of the human forearm, whatever we might think the size of an angel would be.

BOUNDARIES AND COHERENCE

This unit begins at 21:15 with the introduction of the angel and the measuring rod. It ends at 21:17b, where John explains that the angel used the standard of measure that people use. 21:18 begins the description of the composition of the city, the materials of which it is made. The measuring gives coherence to paragraph 21:15–17.

PROMINENCE AND THEME

The most prominent constituents are the two parallel NUCLEI relating to the measurements of the city and the wall. The theme gives the symbolic sense of the measurements rather than the actual figures.

SUB-SCENE CONSTITUENT 21:18–21 (Paragraph: Description₃ of 21:10-27)

THEME: The whole city and all its parts were constructed from amazing, beautiful and precious materials.

¶ PTRN	RELATIONAL STRUCT.			CONTENTS
DECLAR-ARATION	NUCLEUS₁			21:18a The city wall *was* made of diamond.
	NUCLEUS₂			21:18b The city *itself* was *made of* gold *which was* as pure as clear glass.
DESCR-IPTION	NUCLEUS₁	GENERIC		21:19a The foundations of the wall of the city were constructed from every kind of precious stone:
		specifics 1–12		21:19b–20 The first foundation *stone was a transparent stone,* diamond; the second *foundation stone was a blue stone,* sapphire; the third *foundation stone was a green stone,* chalcedony; the fourth *foundation stone was a green stone,* emerald; the fifth *foundation stone was a brown and white striped stone,* sardonyx; the sixth *foundation stone was a red stone,* sardius; the seventh *foundation stone was a yellow stone,* chrysolite; the eighth *foundation stone was a green stone,* beryl; the ninth *foundation stone was a yellow stone,* topaz; the tenth *foundation stone was a green stone,* chrysoprase; the eleventh *foundation stone was a blue stone,* hyacinth; the twelfth *foundation stone was a purple stone,* amethyst.
	NUCLEUS₂			21:21a The twelve gates *of the city* were twelve pearls. Each gate consisted of a single pearl.
	NUCLEUS₃			21:21b The open space in the city was *made of* gold *which was* as pure as clear glass.

INTENT AND PARAGRAPH PATTERN

The 21:18–21 paragraph is a detailed description of the material composition of the city, stressing its amazing and glorious beauty. All the propositions in the paragraph are stative, which is typical of descriptive genre.

The asyndeton between 21:18 and 19-21 marks the division of this unit into a general DECLARATION of the composition of the city and a more detailed DESCRIPTION of its foundations, gates and open space. Within the two parts of the unit the co-ordinate nuclei are marked by καί 'and'.

NOTES

21:18a The city wall *was* made of diamond 'Made of' is used in the display to express the verbal idea underlying ἐνδώμησις 'construction.'

See the note on 4:3a for the term translated as 'diamond'.

21:18b The city itself was *made of* gold, *which was* as pure as clear glass Ancient glass was generally quite impure, so it was often very clouded. Clear glass was unusual and very costly. Gold was also often impure, but unlike glass its purity was not necessarily obvious and usually had to be tested.

The repetition of καθαρός 'pure, clear' may imply "so pure that it looked like …".

21:19a The foundations of the wall of the city were constructed from every kind of precious stone The verb used is κοσμέω which may mean 'adorn, decorate.' Some have understood the precious stones mentioned to be adorning the foundation by being set into the foundation stones or covering them. However, the display follows those who interpret each foundation to be actually composed of one precious stone of enormous size. This accords with the basic sense of κοσμέω as 'arrange, set in order' as in Matt.12:44 and 25:7.

21:19b–20 Many, but not all, of the twelve precious stones mentioned here are the same as those in the high priest's breastplate in Ex.28:16–20 and 39:10–13.

However, there are several problems involved in translating the names of the different stones. One is that the English forms of some of the Greek names now refer to a different stone than the original Greek names did. Another problem is that in many languages, even English, most readers will not be familiar with many of the stones mentioned. Nevertheless, the overall theme of this part of the description seems to be that the foundations were composed of beautiful precious stones in a variety of colours. In the display the presumed colours of the stones are given along with the common English forms of the Greek names (except for the first).

For the first stone, ἴασπις, 'diamond' see the note on 4:3a.

For the second stone, the sapphire, both BDAG and *The New Bible Dictionary* say that the Greek name referred to what is now called 'lapis lazuli,' "a deep blue stone with golden flecks of iron pyrites". The modern sapphire is blue.

For the third stone, the chalcedony, *The New Bible Dictionary* says it is usually understood to refer to a green stone. BDAG says that it is uncertain what stone is referred to in Revelation.

The fifth stone σαρδόνυξ 'sardonyx' is a form of agate. The modern sardonyx has layers of brown and white. The ancient sardonyx was also layered, though the colours may have varied.

The sixth stone is σάρδιον 'sardius'. In the Septuagint, in such places as Ex. 28:17, σάρδιον translates a Hebrew term that is derived from the word meaning 'to be red'. There is little doubt that the stone intended in Rev.21:20 is red or reddish brown in colour.

The seventh stone is chrysolite. According to BDAG and *The New Bible Dictionary*, the ancient chrysolite is the modern topaz and the ancient topaz is the modern chrysolite. However, both are yellow stones.

The tenth stone is chrysoprase. BDAG describes it as "an apple-green, fine-grained hornstone (variety of quartz), coloured by nickel oxide and highly translucent".

The eleventh stone, the hyacinth, was undoubtedly blue in colour like the hyacinth flower.

The twelfth stone is the amethyst, "a purple variety of transparent, crystalline quartz" (*The New Bible Dictionary*). It was a well-known stone in antiquity.

21:21a The twelve gates *of the city* were twelve pearls. Each gate consisted of a single pearl In John's time the pearl was one of the most valuable gems. The description of the gates is given added prominence by the repetition of the numeral twelve and the fact that the second clause is almost a repetition of the first.

21:21b This description also is given added prominence by the use of redundant terms, 'of the city' and 'as pure glass.'

The open space in the city The πλατεῖα, literally 'the broad way, street', is the only internal feature of the city that John describes. Many commentators consider the singular to be used here collectively, meaning 'the streets' (Charles, Lenski, Walvoord). But in 22:2, the singular is again used, and there it is less likely to be a collective noun. Aune suggests that it means 'an open plaza or square.' This is more appropriate, since the concept of a 'street' is defined by buildings on either side of it, and there is no focus at all on buildings in the picture of the new Jerusalem. A large city square (as described in 22:1–2) might well have been just as obvious as the walls and gates to an external observer like John.

BOUNDARIES AND COHERENCE

The 21:18–21 paragraph is coherent in that it describes the materials with which the different parts of the city were built. In 21:18 and 21 the mention of 'gold as pure as clear glass' form an inclusio bracketing the unit. From 21:22 onwards there is no further reference to the composition materials of the parts of the city.

PROMINENCE AND THEME

The basic DECLARATION of the city's amazing construction has natural prominence. However, in this unit the DESCRIPTION is given marked prominence by the abundance of repetitive detail and redundant wordings, which emphasise the city's glorious beauty. In view of this use of repetition, the theme consists of a summary of the overall impact of the descriptive unit.

SUB-SCENE CONSTITUENT 21:22–27 (Paragraph: Declaration of 21:10-27)

THEME: The Lord God Almighty and the Lamb are physically present in the city and their glory provides the light by which the kings and peoples of the earth come to glorify them there. The morally impure cannot enter the city but only those who are registered in the Lamb's book of life.

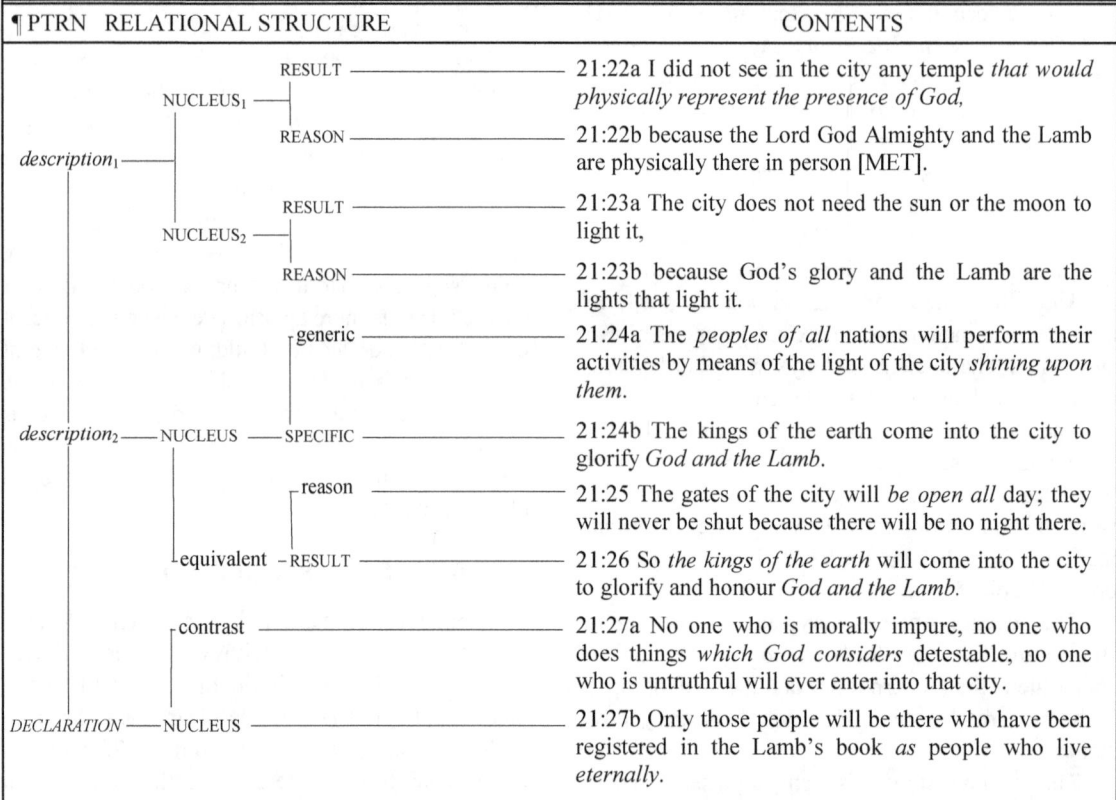

INTENT AND PARAGRAPH PATTERN

The description of the new Jerusalem culminates in this unit, which is concerned not with the physical appearance of the city but with its polity, who lives there. It consists of two *descriptions* leading to a DECLARATION. The *descriptions* cover the physical presence of God and the Lamb, who provide light, and thus life, to all in the city and who receive the glory and honour of all nations. The DECLARATION then provides the motivating force of the unit by showing that the only people who share the presence and glory of God and the Lamb in the city are the faithful believers.

NOTES

21:22a I did not see in the city any temple *that would physically represent the presence of God* The Greek is ναὸν οὐκ εἶδον ἐν αὐτῇ 'I did not see a temple in it'. What made the earthly Jerusalem both holy and precious in the eyes of the Jews was the fact that the Temple was there representing God's presence among his people. The absence of the Temple from the new Jerusalem is thus very startling and requires the explanation given in 21:22b. To make the logic of the connection clear the significance of the Temple is therefore spelled out in the display.

21:22b the Lord God Almighty In the Greek this comes before the verb, indicating its unexpectedness to anyone used to descriptions of the earthly Jerusalem. It also indicates the contrast between the actual physical presence of God in the new Jerusalem and the Temple in the earthly Jerusalem, which simply represented him. This gives marked prominence to the REASON, especially since the RESULT in 21:22a is a negative statement.

and the Lamb In 22:3 both God and the Lamb are specifically linked with the one throne.

physically there in person In line with the translation of 'temple' in 21:22a this represents ναὸς αὐτῆς 'its temple.' As Mounce says, "For John there is no temple because symbol has given way to reality".

21:23a The city does not need the sun or the moon In the Greek 'no need' comes before the verb, giving added prominence to this proposition.

21:23b God's glory and the Lamb are the lights that light it There is parallelism in saying that 'the glory of God illuminates the city and the Lamb is its light.' Since this is clearly not referring to two separate lights the translation here combines them. The parallelism gives the proposition marked prominence.

21:24a *peoples of all* nations As John turns to describe the activity that takes place in the heavenly city he uses terms 'nations' and 'kings' taken from O.T. prophecy about the restored Jerusalem (Isaiah 60:3). In Revelation these terms usually refer to the parties opposing God, but those parties have been destroyed in chapter 20. Here, therefore, the terms must refer to God's redeemed people who come from all the nations (7:9) and who rule the earth with Christ (20:6).

will perform their activities 'Walk' here is an idiom for behaviour or synecdoche for general activity. The light of the city will enable the nations to carry out their daily activities. Details of the nations' activities are given in the next proposition, so this is a generic–specific relationship. The verb is in the future tense, showing that it is less prominent than 21:24b.

shining upon them These implicit words are supplied in the display to make explicit the event of which 'the light of the city' is the agent.

21:24b And the kings of the earth come into the city to glorify *God and the Lamb* The Greek text φέρουσιν τὴν δόξαν αὐτῶν εἰς αὐτήν 'they bring their glory into it' could be understood to refer to their material glory and wealth, or to their non-material glory and power. It is a continuation of the allusion to Isaiah 60, where the kings of the nations show their submission to the restored Israel by bringing tribute to Jerusalem. In the present context 'bring glory' must be used in the non-material sense of 'glorify.'

The noun phrase 'God and the Lamb' as goal (object) of the event of glorifying is supplied to fill out the case frame.

21:25 The statement that 'the gates of the city will not be shut by day for there is no night there' seems to be just another description of the city. But it appears in the wrong place for an unconnected description, between 21:24b and its restatement in 21:26. One way to understand this is to take it as the reason for the possibility of the activity of 21:26. It is probably an echo of Isaiah 60:11, "Your gates will always stand open, they will never be shut day or night, so that men may bring you the wealth of the nations—their kings led in triumphal procession" (NIV).

the gates of the city will *be open all* day; they will never be shut The implied information is added to supply the ellipsed stage in the logic of the proposition.

21:26 So *the kings of the earth* The only agent reference in this verse is the third person suffix on the Greek verb. This probably refers to 'the kings of the earth' in 21:24b, which is the nearest antecedent reference to personal beings, though it may simply have indefinite reference 'they (people) will bring.'

will come into the city to glorify and honour *God and the Lamb* See the notes on 21:24b.

21:27a morally impure The Greek πᾶν κοινόν 'everything common' refers to the offense of sin in the Old Testament, which was represented by what was declared to be unclean and common, and therefore under a ban and forbidden in God's presence. It could be a thing or a person. Here people are in focus and the reference is not to ceremonial uncleanness but moral impurity.

no one who does things *which God considers* detestable See the notes for 21:8a. There is at least an allusion to idolatry in the use of βδέλυγμα 'abomination'.

BOUNDARIES AND COHERENCE

The opening boundary of the unit is marked by the switch of subject matter at 21:22 from the material construction of the city to the activity that takes place within it. The focus on who is in the city and what they do continues through the unit and gives it coherence. The beginning of the next unit in 22:1 is marked by a new action on the part of the angel, the main actor in this scene.

PROMINENCE AND THEME

There is a lot of marked prominence in this unit (see the notes on 21:22b, 23a, 23b, 24a, and the use of restatement in 21:24–26). In view of this the *descriptions* are included in the theme together with the DECLARATION.

SCENE CONSTITUENT 22:1–5 (Paragraph: Goal of 21:9-22:5)

THEME: In the city God's servants have the abundant sources of eternal life, and they live forever as kings worshipping God in the light of his glory.

¶ PTRN	RELATIONAL STRUCTURE		CONTENTS
description	NUCLEUS₁ — 'river'		22:1a *The angel* showed me the river of water *which causes people* to live *forever*.
	├ description₁		22:1b The water was as clear as crystal.
	└ description₂		22:1c–2a *The river was* flowing out from the throne of God and the Lamb, down through the middle of the open space in the city.
	NUCLEUS₂ — 'trees'		22:2b On each side of the river were trees *having fruit which causes people* to live *forever*.
	├ description₁		22:2c *The trees* bear twelve *crops* (*or, kinds*) *of* fruit; *they* produce a crop each month.
	└ description₂		22:2d The leaves of the trees are *a medicine* for strengthening/invigorating the *people of all* nations.
		┌ contrast	22:3a There will never be anyone or anything *there that God* has condemned.
	NUCLEUS₁	REASON	22:3b But the throne of God and of the Lamb will be in the city.
		RESULT	22:3c And *as a result* his servants will worship him,
		└ amplification	22:4 they will look *directly* on his face, and his name *is written* on their foreheads.
DECLARATION	NUCLEUS₂	RESULT	22:5a There will never again be night, and *God's servants* will not need the light of a lamp nor the light of the sun,
		REASON	22:5b because the Lord God will shine *his* light upon them.
	NUCLEUS₃		22:5c They will be kings forever and ever.

INTENT AND PARAGRAPH PATTERN

Unlike the descriptive paragraphs in 21:10-27, which focus on the city itself, this unit focuses on the relationship between God and his people in the city. It consists of a *description* of the river and the trees, the things which give God's people eternal life, and a DECLARATION of their eternal communion with God in worship, glory and majesty.

In this vision of the ultimate relationship of God and his people there appear to be echoes of the original relationship in the Garden of Eden: the river (22:1, Gen. 2:10), the tree of life (22:2, Gen. 2:9), mankind as rulers (22:5, Gen.1:26), the curse (22:3, Gen. 3:14, 17). However, some of the actual wording of the passage is drawn more directly from Zechariah 14:6-11, God's promise of a new Jerusalem: the flow of living water (22:1, Zech.14:8), no more curse of destruction (22:3, Zech.14:11), God as king (22:3, Zech.14:9), no night or need of lights (22:5, Zech.14:6-7).

NOTES

22:1a The angel showed me The subject of the Greek phrase ἔδειξέν μοι 'showed me' is not expressed, but the fact that the wording is identical to that in 21:10 shows that the angel of 21:9 is being referred to.

the river of water *which causes people* to live *forever* This is what is promised in 21:6d. See the note there regarding the display text.

22:1b clear The Greek word, λαμπρόν, has the primary lexical meaning of 'bright, shining', but where used to modify 'water', it has the meaning 'clear'.

22:1c–2a down through the middle of the open space in the city Some commentators (Beasley-Murray, Charles, Ladd) and many versions (JB, NEB, NIV, TEV, REB, NASB, NRSV, RSV) take ἐν μέσῳ τῆς πλατείας αὐτῆς 'in/through the middle of the open space of it', the first phrase of 22:2, as an extension of the sentence in 22:1c rather than as beginning a new sentence. This is followed in the display text. However, many Greek texts put a sentence break after 22:1, and some commentaries follow this (Alford, Lenski, Swete). (It should be remembered that the Greek was originally written without any punctuation at all.) But this sentence break is unlikely to represent the meaning of what John wrote, since elsewhere in Revelation he never begins sentences with prepositional place phrases like 'in the middle of' (Aune), and it yields a confused picture of what he is seeing in 22:2: "In the midst of the street of it [the city], and on either side of the river, *was there* the tree of life" (KJV). With the punctuation that the display text follows, the picture clearly reflects that of Ezekiel 47:1–12, where the river flows from the temple and the trees on either side of it produce both constant crops of fruit and leaves for healing.

22:2b On each side of the river were trees Although 'tree' in Greek here is in the singular, it is obvious that as far as the picture is concerned this is a collective use of the singular form. The use of singular may be influenced by the singular tree of life in the Garden of Eden.

having fruit which causes people **to live** *forever* See the notes for 21:6d.

22:2c *The trees* **bear twelve** *crops* (*or*, *kinds*) *of* **fruit** The Greek text is ποιοῦν καρποὺς δώδεκα 'producing fruits twelve', with no explicit word for 'kind' or 'crop', but either of these could be understood implicitly. Many commentators interpret the text to mean twelve kinds of fruit (Alford, Beasley-Murray, Ladd, Mounce). Others take it to mean twelve different crops of the same fruit (Bratcher and Hatton, Morris, Swete). The text of this verse is similar to that of Ezek. 47:12. In that reference there are many kinds of fruit trees, but both there and here in Rev. 22:2 the focus is on the constant plentiful supply of fruit. The second clause of 22:2c is thus simply repeating the meaning of the first part in different words.

they **produce a crop each month** In the Greek 'each month' is preposed for emphasis, since it is unexpected.

22:2d The leaves of the trees are a medicine for strengthening/invigorating The use of θεραπείαν, which means 'healing', comes as a surprise in a city where sin and its results have been abolished. It is a quote from Ezek. 47:12, but the meaning has to do with the context of the new Jerusalem. The interpretation taken here is similar to that of commentators such as Lenski, Morris, Mounce, Walvoord, who describe the leaves as 'health-giving' and associated with the complete absence of physical imperfection.

the *people of all* **nations** As in 21:24a, the reference here is to the redeemed people of all the nations.

22:3a There will never be anyone or anything *there that God* **has condemned** The question here is whether κατάθεμα refers to an action 'cursing, condemning to destruction' or to the thing which is cursed/condemned. The echoes of Genesis 2–3 in this unit may indicate that this sentence refers to the ultimate end of all that is sinful. There may also be an intended connection with οὐ μὴ εἰσέλθῃ εἰς αὐτὴν πᾶν κοινόν 'no impure thing will enter into it', 21:27, in which case 'accursed thing' would more likely be the intended meaning. However, Aune makes out a good case for the sentence to mean 'There will no longer be any threat that God's holy city will be condemned to destruction', since it is an almost direct quotation of Zechariah 14:11, where that is clearly the sense.

22:3c And *as a result* Though there is only a καί at the beginning of this clause, a reason–result relationship is at least inferred, but, following John's style, it is not explicitly marked. The use of καί may indicate that both the reason and the result are equally prominent.

his servants will worship him After the full noun phrase reference to God and the Lamb in 22:3b there is only third person singular pronominal reference to the Deity until 22:5c, where the nominal reference 'the Lord God' occurs. Beasley-Murray says, "God and the Lamb are viewed as a unity in so real a fashion that the singular pronoun alone is suitable to interpret them".

22:4 This verse echoes and amplifies 22:3b–c. God's people have intimate fellowship with him because he is intimately present in the city, and they worship him because they belong to him.

his name *is written* **on their foreheads** Throughout the book this has been recognized as symbolic of ownership. In 14:1, 4, ownership by God and Christ is attributed to Christ's redemption, which in this passage is pictured as completed.

22:5b the Lord God will shine *his* **light upon them** It is the glorious brilliance of the presence of the Lord that will shine upon them. See the notes for 21:23b. Although this is given as the reason for 22:5a, it has added prominence since it is a positive clause whereas 22:5a is negative.

BOUNDARIES AND COHERENCE

The unit begins with another reference to the angel, who shows John more about the city. The description ends at 22:5, and in the following verse the next move of the angel initiates an interaction with John relating to his visions as a whole.

The internal coherence of the unit is provided by its focus throughout on the life of God's redeemed people in the city, together with the sources of that life (22:1–2) and its attributes of worship, glory and majesty (22:3–5).

PROMINENCE AND THEME

The *DECLARATION* constitutes the main part of the theme, but it does not include the most significant component of the *description*, so this is also regarded as part of the theme.

PART CONSTITUENT 22:6–11 (Section: Denouement of Body)

THEME: God has verified this revelation and Jesus reminds his people that he is coming soon, so they must obey the message of this book in order to enjoy God's blessings. I, John, am the one who heard and saw these things, and the angel who showed them to me told me not to keep this revelation secret.

MACROSTRUCTURE	CONTENTS
NUCLEUS₁	22:6–7 God has verified this revelation and Jesus reminds his people that he is coming soon, so they must obey the message of this book in order to enjoy God's blessings.
NUCLEUS₂	22:8–11 I, John, am the one who heard and saw these things, and the angel who showed them to me told me not to keep this revelation secret.

INTENT AND MACROSTRUCTURE

This section functions as a denouement to the Body of the Book. That is to say, it is clearly part of the Body, but it does not extend the narrative of the Body. It consists of two verifications of the contents of the Body, a declaration by God and an attestation by John. These have the hortatory intent of persuading John's audience to accept his words and to act on them.

BOUNDARIES AND COHERENCE

Many commentators understand 22:6 to begin the epilogue of the book, but this is unlikely since 22:6 begins Καὶ εἶπέν μοι 'and he said to me' which is parallel to the beginning of 22:1 and has the same unexpressed subject in the verb. There is therefore no major break in the structure of the book at this point. The description of the heavenly city has ended at 22:5, and both parts of the current unit are concerned with the acceptance of John's account of his visions as a whole. They are joined by καί 'and' and both parts focus on the phrase τοὺς λόγους τῆς προφητείας τοῦ βιβλίου τούτου 'the words of the prophecy of this book' (22:7c, 22:10b). At 22:12 the discourse structure changes to a series of short units with asyndeton, in which the main speaker is Jesus himself.

PROMINENCE AND THEME

The theme statements of the conjoined equally prominent *NUCLEI* are both contained in the theme for the section.

SECTION CONSTITUENT 22:6–7 (Paragraph: Nucleus₁ of 22:6–11)

THEME: God has verified this revelation and Jesus reminds his people that he is coming soon, so they must obey the message of this book in order to enjoy God's blessings.

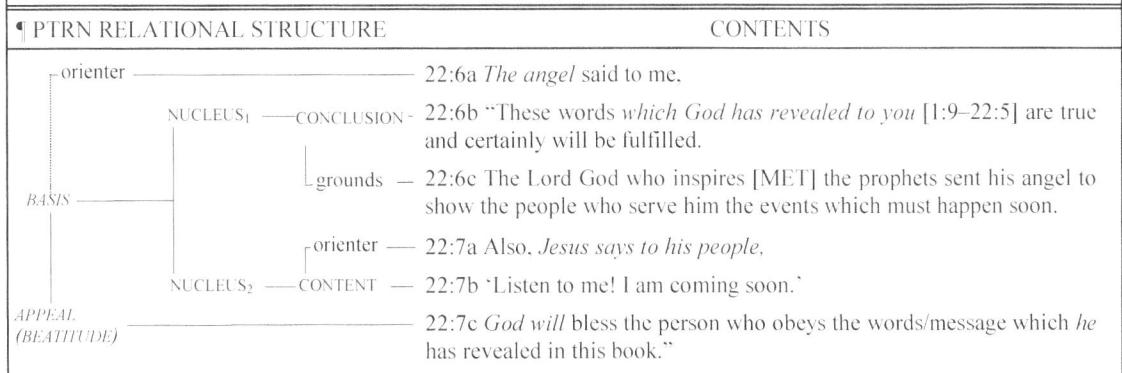

INTENT AND PARAGRAPH PATTERN

In the 22:6–7 paragraph, 22:6b-c functions as a validation or reaffirmation of the truth of the body of the Revelation discourse while 22:7c functions as a mitigated appeal in the form of a beatitude. In line with the hortatory intent of the whole book there can be seen to be a BASIS-APPEAL relationship between 22:6b-7b and 7c which would be expressed in unmitigated form as 'Since these things are true and Jesus will return soon, people should obey all the exhortations revealed in this book if they want to enjoy the glorious blessings also revealed in this book'.

The unit is thus very similar to 1:1–3 in intent as well as in paragraph pattern and content. Both units consist of a validation of the book (with the authority of both God and Jesus) forming the basis for a beatitude that functions as an appeal to heed the contents of the book.

Commentators and versions vary greatly in where they close the speech that starts with 22:6b, and in their attribution of the parts of 22:7. However, the BASIS–APPEAL structure of the unit (see notes on 22:7b and 7c) shows that it should be regarded as one speech unit. See the note on 22:7a for the attribution of that element to the angel, quoting Jesus.

NOTES

22:6a *The angel* said to me The text is Καὶ εἶπέν μοι 'And he said to me'. The third person singular reference may well be to the angel who has been showing John the holy city (21:9–10, 22:1) because no other speaker has been introduced and because 1:1 says that an angel was sent to show John 'the events that must happen soon' for the benefit of God's servants.

22:6b "These words *which God has revealed to you* [1:9–22:5] are true and certainly will be fulfilled These words are also found in 21:5. Here this strong affirmative is understood to apply to the main contents of the book (Alford, Düsterdieck, Lenski, Mounce, Swete) because of the echoes of 1:1c–e in 22:6c, and because of the reference to the whole book in 22:7c.

22:6c The Lord God who inspires the prophets The Greek is ὁ κύριος ὁ θεὸς τῶν πνευμάτων τῶν προφητῶν 'the Lord God of the spirits of the prophets'. Here 'spirits', being plural, is probably not a direct reference to the Holy Spirit but a metonymy for what enables the prophets to prophesy. Swete says, "the God from Whom prophetic inspiration proceeds".

The use of the term προφήτης 'prophet' in 11:10, referring to the two "witnesses", shows that in Revelation it means any Christian who becomes prominent in proclaiming God's word, either within the church or to the world outside.

22:7a Also, *Jesus says to all his people* The καί 'and' at the start of the verse shows that 22:7a-b are co-ordinate with 22:6b–c.

The words in 22:7b 'I am coming soon' are those of Jesus as the use of 'I' shows. They are the same as in 2:16 and 3:11, and they are repeated in 22:12 and 20. Here they form part of the basis for the appeal of 22:7c, so they are probably being quoted by the angel (Lenski). In order to clearly identify the speaker and addressees, the display makes these explicit here.

22:7b Listen to me! These words express the highlighting function of the Greek emphasis marker ἰδού in this context.

I am coming soon This is also highlighted by the use of the Greek present tense.

The repetition here of the term 'soon' from 22:6c shows that 22:7a–b stands in parallel to 22:6b–c as the basis for 22:7c.

22:7c *God will* bless the person who obeys the words/message which *he* has revealed in this book The fact that this APPEAL picks up the key terms 'words' from 22:6b and 'prophecy/prophets' from 22:6c shows that 22:6b–7b is the *basis* for it.

words/message which *he* has revealed in this book The Greek is τοὺς λόγους τῆς προφητείας τοῦ βιβλίου τούτου 'the words of the prophecy of this book'. Since 'obeying' presupposes commands, whereas 'prophecy' simply means 'foretelling', it is clear that the term here has its basic meaning of 'telling forth' or 'revealing' God's message. See the note above on 'prophet' 22:6b.

BOUNDARIES AND COHERENCE

The initial boundary for 22:6–7 has been discussed in the Boundaries and Coherence for 22:6–11. For the coherence of 22:6–7 see under Intent for this unit. As for the final boundary, 22:8 begins a unit where John is an active, rather than a passive, participant.

PROMINENCE AND THEME

In this hortatory passage, the *basis* of the APPEAL is given marked prominence by its references back to the superscription of the book, 1:1–3, and by the highlighting of 22:7b (see the note). Both parts are therefore included in the theme.

SECTION CONSTITUENT 22:8–11 (Paragraph: Nucleus₂ of 22:6-11)

THEME: I, John, am the one who heard and saw these things, and the angel who showed them to me told me not to keep this revelation secret.

¶ PTRN	RELATIONAL STRUCTURE	CONTENTS
OCCASION		22:8a I, John, *am* the one who heard and saw these things [1:9–22:5].
	circumstance	22:8b When I had heard and seen *these things*,
occasion — NUCLEUS		22:8c I prostrated myself at the feet of the angel who was showing me these things in order to worship him.
	orienter	22:9a But he said to me,
	negative — EXHORTATION	22:9b "Do not *worship me*,
	grounds	22:9c *since* I am your fellow servant and *the fellow servant* of your fellow believers *who are* prophets, and of *all the people* who obey the words/message in this book.
OUTCOME occasion — POSITIVE		22:9d *Instead* worship God!"
	orienter	22:10a He also said to me,
OUTCOME — OUTCOME — EXHORTATION		22:10b "Do not keep secret [MET] the words/message which *God* has revealed in this book,
	grounds	22:10c since, *because* the time *when this message will be fulfilled* is near.
	grounds	22:11a *there is now no time left for people to change their way of life,*
grounds — CONCLUSION — CONCLUSION		22:11b *so* those who are vile and act in an evil manner can continue like that [IRO]; *and* those who are holy and live righteously should continue like that."

INTENT AND PARAGRAPH PATTERN

As is appropriate for the last unit of the Body of the Book, 22:8–11 tells what happened after John received the visions. The use of the aorist tense in the Greek of 22:8b and the historic present in 22:9a, 10a confirms its status as narrative. It has an *occasion-OUTCOME* structure. However, the *OUTCOME* is delayed by an embedded *occasion-OUTCOME* unit 22:8b–9d in which John attempts to honour the angel and is rebuked. This interruption of the narrative serves to highlight the instruction, in 22:10b, that John should publish his visions.

The unit also serves as a validation of the Body of the Book. Not only does John attest that he was an eye-witness of the visions, 22:8a, but he is also given divine authority to publish them.

NOTES

22:8a I, John, *am* the one who heard and saw these things [1:9–22:5] The use of the first person pronoun with the name, Κἀγὼ Ἰωάννης 'And I, John,' identifies John as an eye-witness of what he has written. Mounce says, "John now attests that he has actually heard and seen all the things which are recorded in the book. His literary product is not the result of any flight of imagination". The addressees know John and trust him to speak the truth.

22:8b The tail-head linkage to 22:8a, 'heard and saw … heard and seen', marks the break between the *occasion* and the *OUTCOME* in structure of the unit.

22:8c I prostrated myself at the feet of the angel who was showing me these things in order to worship him 19:10 and 22:8c–9d are very similar. See the notes on 19:10 for a discussion of the details. In both instances John's reaction follows a statement verifying the authenticity of his vision.

22:9c your fellow servant and *the fellow servant* of your fellow-believers *who are* prophets, and of *all the people* who obey the words/message in this book Note that there is a καί 'and' before 'brothers' and before 'the people who obey,' but not before 'prophets.' This means that 'brothers' and 'prophets' are equated.

22:9d See the note on 19:10b. The Greek is identical here.

22:10b Do not keep secret the words/message which *God* has revealed in this book The Greek is literally 'Do not seal the words of the prophecy of this book'. This echoes Dan.12:4, 9, especially in the Greek Theodotion version. However, Daniel was told *not* to reveal his vision because of its reference to the end time. Here the command is *against* sealing up the book because the end time has now come. This is litotes, in which the negative command is used to strengthen the implied positive command that John must openly proclaim his visions.

22:10c the time *when this message will be fulfilled* is near The context shows that the time being referred to is that of the fulfilment of the message of the book.

22:11a Commentators (Alford, Beasley-Murray, Ladd, Mounce) agree that the statement of the nearness of time in 22:10c is the basis for 22:11. However, there is disagreement over the intent of 22:11:

1. Some commentators (Alford, Morris) say that the third person imperatives in 22:11b are ironic, with the sense that the speaker is ostensively telling the evil people to do the opposite of what he wants them to do. He means, 'Change while there is time.'
2. Others (Mounce, Bratcher and Hatton) still see irony as intended, but without the aim of affecting the behaviour of the evildoers. They can continue their evil ways because there is no time left for them to change.

This second interpretation fits better with the overall intent of Revelation, which is the reassurance of believers rather than the conversion of unbelievers. The implied information of 22:11a has therefore been added to the display to clarify the link between 22:10c and 11b.

The propositional cluster 22:10c–11b thus gives the grounds for the exhortation in 22:10b that John should publish his visions – since although publication will encourage God's people it cannot pre-empt the judgment and destruction of their enemies. This is confirmed by the fact that this verse echoes Dan.12:10, which also has this import.

22:11b This appears to address four groups of people. But there does not seem to be any distinction intended between ἀδικῶν 'unrighteous' and ῥυπαρός 'filthy,' or between δίκαιος 'righteous' and ἅγιος 'holy.' Rather the exhortations include everyone, both the unrighteous and filthy and the righteous and holy.

those who are vile Since spiritual impurity in the scriptures often refers to the contamination of worshiping idols or other gods, and in view of the contrast with ἅγιος 'holy, belonging to God,' it is possible that ῥυπαρός 'filthy' here refers to all those who have rejected the worship of God.

BOUNDARIES AND COHERENCE

From 22:8 the focus is on John and his role in relation to the visions. This ceases at 22:11. It may be questioned whether 22:10–11 forms a separate unit, but the focus is still on John and the visions and the phrase 'the words of this book' occurs in both 22:9 and 10.

PROMINENCE AND THEME

The use of the first person pronoun with the name in 22:8a gives it marked prominence, so it and the main OUTCOME in 22:10 form the theme of the unit.

BOOK CONSTITUENT 22:12–20 (Section: Epilogue of the Book)

THEME: Jesus warns that he is coming soon to recompense everyone according to their deeds. He proclaims that all who are free from sin will be blessed. He asserts that the message of this book has indeed come from him. The Holy Spirit and God's people respond by urging him to come. Whoever hears this is also urged to respond. Jesus then warns of the eternal consequences for anyone who tampers with the message of this book, and again declares that he is coming soon. I, John, respond by urging him to come.

MACROSTRUCTURE	CONTENTS
NUCLEUS$_1$	22:12–17 Jesus warns everyone that he is coming soon to recompense them according to their deeds. He proclaims that all who are pure and free from sin will be blessed by God. He asserts that the message of this book has indeed come from him, the Messiah. The Holy Spirit and God's people respond by urging him to come. Whoever hears this is also urged to respond and accept the gift of eternal life.
NUCLEUS$_2$	22:18–20 Jesus warns of the eternal consequences for anyone who tampers with the message of this book, and he declares that he is certainly coming soon. I, John, respond by urging him to come.

INTENT AND MACROSTRUCTURE

The final matter in many discourses is characterized by miscellaneous topics presented in brief statements. This is certainly true of the *Epilogue* of Revelation, and many commentators and versions simply divide it into short unrelated paragraphs, 22:12–13, 14–15, 16–17, 18–19, 20. But some structure can be seen in this unit if its nature as dialogue is taken into account. Several of its elements must be attributed to the words of Jesus because of the self-identification that they include (22:12–13, 16, 20a–b), and others are clearly responses by John, or by John on behalf of God's people (22:17, 20c–d). If the remaining parts (22:14–15, 18–19) are assigned to Jesus, as Mounce and others suggest, then the unit is seen to consist of two NUCLEI, each containing a speech by Jesus (22:12–16, 18–20b) and a short response by John or others (22:17, 20c–d).

Throughout the unit there is focus on the imminence of Jesus' coming and John's eager reaction to it which he expected his audience to share. The section is therefore expressive in intent.

BOUNDARIES AND COHERENCE

Whereas 22:11 marks the end of the Body of the Book, in which John reports the visions which he has "seen and heard", 22:12 is the beginning of the Epilogue, consisting entirely of short speeches, largely without speech orienters. At this point also Christ is reintroduced as a major participant interacting with John for the first time since 1:20. The unit ends at 22:20 with the termination of John's dialogue with Christ. The final unit of the book (20:21) is addressed by John to his audience.

Although this unit consists of a miscellany of topics, it does have coherence. This is partly provided by the parallel structure of the two NUCLEI with their speeches by Jesus and short responses by John. There is also reference in both NUCLEI to the same topics, Christ's authentication of the Book (22:16, 18) and the consequences of his return for all people (22:12) both for those who embrace the contents of the Book (22:14) and for those who reject or tamper with it (22:15, 18–19). The consequences for both groups are linked to the tree of life and entry into the holy city (22:14, 19).

PROMINENCE AND THEME

Both the conjoined NUCLEI are equally prominent. The theme therefore includes the prominent statements of each of them.

SECTION CONSTITUENT 22:12–17 (Paragraph Cluster: Nucleus₁ of Epilogue)

THEME: *Jesus warns everyone that he is coming soon to recompense them according to their deeds. He proclaims that all who are pure and free from sin will be blessed by God. He asserts that the message of this book has indeed come from him, the Messiah. The Holy Spirit and God's people respond by urging him to come. Whoever hears this is also urged to respond and accept the gift of eternal life.*

¶ PTRN	RELATIONAL STRUCTURE	CONTENTS
	orienter	22:12a *Jesus says to all people,*
	NUCLEUS₁ — COMMISSIVE — NUCLEUS₁	22:12b "Listen to me! I am coming soon.
	NUCLEUS₂ — CONGRUENCE	22:12c And I will recompense everyone
	standard	22:12d exactly according to what each one has done.
	basis	22:13 *I am* the Alpha and the Omega; *that is, I am* the first *one* and the last *one, I am* before *all things* and *I am* at the end *of all things*.
SITUATION	NUCLEUS₂ (BEATITUDE) — GENERIC	22:14a *God will* bless *those who have become pure and free from the guilt of sin, like* people who have washed their garments *clean;*
	specific₁	22:14b they will *be able to* eat *the fruit of* the tree *which enables people* to live *forever,*
	specific₂ — CONTRAST	22:14c and they will *be able to* enter through the gates into the *holy* city.
	contrast	22:15 But *people who are unholy like* dogs, people who use occult power, people who sin sexually, people who murder *other people*, people who worship idols, all people who enjoy lying and continually lie, they will never enter that city [MET].
	NUCLEUS₃ — DECLARATION — MEANS	22:16a I, Jesus, sent my angel
	purpose	22:16b in order that he might truthfully report *all* these things [1:9–22:11] to you(pl) *who are* in the churches.
	DESCRIPTION — NUCLEUS₁	22:16c I am *the one who is called* 'the shoot from the root of *King* David,' and *I am* the descendant of *King* David.
	NUCLEUS₂	22:16d I am *the one who is symbolized by* the bright morning star."
	APPEAL₁ — orienter	22:17a The *Holy* Spirit and God's people, the bride *of Christ,* say *to Christ,*
	CONTENT	22:17b "Come!"
	APPEAL₂ — orienter	22:17c Let whoever hears *this* [1:1-22:21] also say *to Christ,*
REACTION	CONTENT	22:17d "Come!"
	contraction	22:17e Also let the thirsty person *who hears this* come,
	APPEAL₃ — AMPLIFICATION	22:17f *that is,* whoever desires the water *which enables people* to live *forever*, let him take it as a free gift.

INTENT AND PARAGRAPH PATTERN

This unit consists of two speeches. The first is by Christ, focusing on his imminent coming and on his divine and human nature. The second speech is a response from the Holy Spirit (divine) and God's people (human). The response offers an emotional REACTION to the prospect of Christ's return and his promise of eternal life, so the unit can be seen to be expressive in intent.

Within the speech of Christ there is a loosely conjoined relationship between the parts, with no conjunctions linking the three NUCLEI, as is natural for this sort of final material in the book. The first NUCLEUS is a COMMISSIVE, the second a beatitude, and the third a DECLARATION authenticating the Book. Within the REACTION the three APPEALS are more closely linked by the conjunction καί 'and'.

NOTES

22:12a *Jesus says to all people* Almost all commentators understand the words of 12–13, to be those of Jesus. Whether Jesus is speaking only to believers or to people in general is difficult to know. While the addressees of the book as a whole are the believers in Jesus, its message has consequences for all people, as 22:12c shows.

22:12b See the notes on 22:7b, to which this is identical.

22:12c-d And I will recompense everyone exactly according to what each one has done The preposing of elements in the Greek sentence gives prominence to the recompense and its relationship to what each has done. Most commentators understand the recompense to be both to the good and the evil (Bratcher and Hatton, Ladd, Lenski, Morris, Mounce), according to their deeds, while others believe this refers only to believers (Walvoord). The use of ἑκάστῳ 'to each (one)' suggests both groups.

22:13 I *am* **the Alpha and the Omega,** *that is, I am* **the first** *one* **and the last** *one,* **I am before** *all things* **and** *I am* **at the end** *of all things* In Revelation the Alpha and Omega declaration is made in 1:8 and 21:6 as well as here. Here it is in its fullest form. (See note on 21:6c.)

The divinity implied in the use of these titles is the *basis* on which Christ can make the promise of universal judgment in 22:12.

22:14–15 Several commentators attribute these words to John, but Thomas and some English versions (NIV, NCV, GW, JBP) assign them to the voice of Jesus. They certainly continue Jesus' theme of the just reward for all people (22:12).

22:14a *God will* **bless** *those who have become pure and free from the guilt of sin, like* **people who have washed their garments clean** For the figure of speech used here see the note on 7:14e.

22:14b–c As in 14:13d (see the note there) the beatitude here is followed by ἵνα 'so that', indicating restatement. In this case two blessings are stated as *specifics*.

they will be able to *eat the fruit of* **the tree** *which enables people* **to live** *forever,* **and they will** *be able to* **enter through the gates into the** *holy* **city** The first blessing ('to *eat the fruit of* the tree of life') logically, or at least chronologically, would follow the second ('to enter through the *holy* city'). The order may have been reversed to highlight the contrast between the entry of the righteous (22:14) and the exclusion of the others (22:15).

For the 'tree of life', see 22:2a.

22:15 *people who are unholy like* **dogs** When 'dogs' is used in the New Testament as a derogatory term for people, its general sense is that they are spiritually impure and wicked. In Deut. 23:18 'dog' is used to refer to male prostitutes. Here it seems to be replacing ἐβδελυγμένοι 'detestable people' from the list in 21:8. (See the note on that verse.) However the use of the term 'dogs' in such references as Matt. 7:6 and Phil. 3:2, where sexual immorality is not in focus, shows that Rev. 22:15 need not be limited to the more specific sexual sense.

people who use occult power See the note on 21:8a.

they will never enter that city This is the non-metaphorical meaning of ἔξω 'outside'. However, it is not an indication that such people are living outside the city and are prevented from entering it. 20:15 and 21:8 show that all such people, unrepentant sinners, are consigned to destruction in the lake of fire. Moreover, the vision of 21:1–22:5 does not indicate that anything at all exists "outside" the new Jerusalem. The reference here must therefore be to the type of people who will never be found in the city.

22:16a I, Jesus The verse begins with the first person pronoun used to indicate the switch of focus to Jesus, with the name preposed in the Greek clause for emphasis.

sent my angel This refers back to 1:1–2, where it is stated that Jesus communicated the message to John by means of his angel.

22:16b in order that he might truthfully report The word μαρτυρῆσαι 'testify, bear witness' is significant here. It is used to indicate that the angel bore true testimony of what he had received from Jesus. See the note on 1:2.

to you(pl) *who are* **in the churches** The plural ὑμῖν 'you' is unexpected when John is the person receiving the message. But it is appropriate here in the Epilogue to the Book, since in the Superscription to the Book (1:1) it is made clear that the message is for God's people, and in the Opening (1:4) John addresses his book to the churches of Asia.

22:16c I am Along with the emphatic pronoun which begins this declaration, this use of ἐγώ εἰμι 'I am' gives prominence to the speaker's identification. It is the expression used by God in his revelation of himself to Moses and used frequently by Jesus in John's Gospel.

the one who is called **'the shoot from the root of** *King* **David** Here the Greek is ἡ ῥίζα καὶ τὸ γένος Δαυίδ 'the root and the descendant of David.' Some commentators maintain that Jesus is declaring that he is not only the offspring of David but also the root itself (Charles, Swete) of David's line. But see the note on 5:5c for the reasoning for taking 'root' to mean descendant. Here both ἡ ῥίζα and τὸ γένος refer to Christ being the Messianic 'descendant' of David. Most commentators take this view.

22:16d I am *the one who is symbolized by* **the bright morning star** A star was a symbol of the Messiah from the Pentateuch (Num. 24:17) onwards, occurring in extrabiblical writings to symbolize the coming Davidic king (*Testament of Levi* 18:3, *Testament of Judah* 24:1). The particular association with the morning star may be because the morning star, the planet Venus, is the brightest of the heavenly bodies after the sun and the moon.

22:17a *God's people,* **the bride** *of Christ* In 19:7-8 the church is called the wife of the Lamb.

say **to Christ** If, as has been assumed above (22:12–20 Intent and Macrostructure), the whole of 22:12–16 is the words of Christ, then "Come" in this verse is clearly a response to Christ's promise in 22:12, as several commentators state. Others, however, consider that this, like 22:17e–f, is an echo of Isa. 55:1 and therefore addressed to the world outside the church. But Revelation is not generally addressed to the world, and the uses of 'come' in this section (except 17e–f) refer to Christ's coming, not to people coming to him.

22:17c Let whoever hears *this* **[1:1–22:21]** Here and in the next verse, as in 1:3, those who hear the book read out are addressed.

22:17e Also let the thirsty person *who hears this* **come** It is unlikely that new participants would be brought into the discourse at this point, so this is probably a continued address to those who hear the book being read. They are being invited not to salvation but to take up their right of entrance into the holy city. Since the river of the water of life is featured in the description of the holy city, it is important that the figures of water and drinking are retained here.

22:17f *that is* **whoever desires the water** *which enables people to* **live** *forever* Since desiring water is the same as being thirsty, this is clearly a restatement of the preceding proposition in amplified form.

For 'the water of life', see 22:1a.

BOUNDARIES AND COHERENCE

The unit opens with the reintroduction of Jesus as a participant in dialogue with John and his audience. It ends with the response by that audience to Jesus' speech. The next unit begins in 22:18 with another speech by Jesus.

In both parts of the unit there is reference to the coming of Jesus (22:12, 17) and the subsequent reward of eternal life for God's people (22:14, 17).

PROMINENCE AND THEME

In this SITUATION–REACTION structure both constituents are thematic. Both parts contain parallel nuclei, which comprise the theme of the unit. In 22:16 both the declaration and the description are prominent (see note on 22:16c).

SECTION CONSTITUENT 22:18–20 (Paragraph Cluster: Nucleus₂ of Epilogue)

THEME: Jesus warns of the eternal consequences for anyone who tampers with the message of this book, and he declares that he is certainly coming soon. I, John, respond by urging him to come.

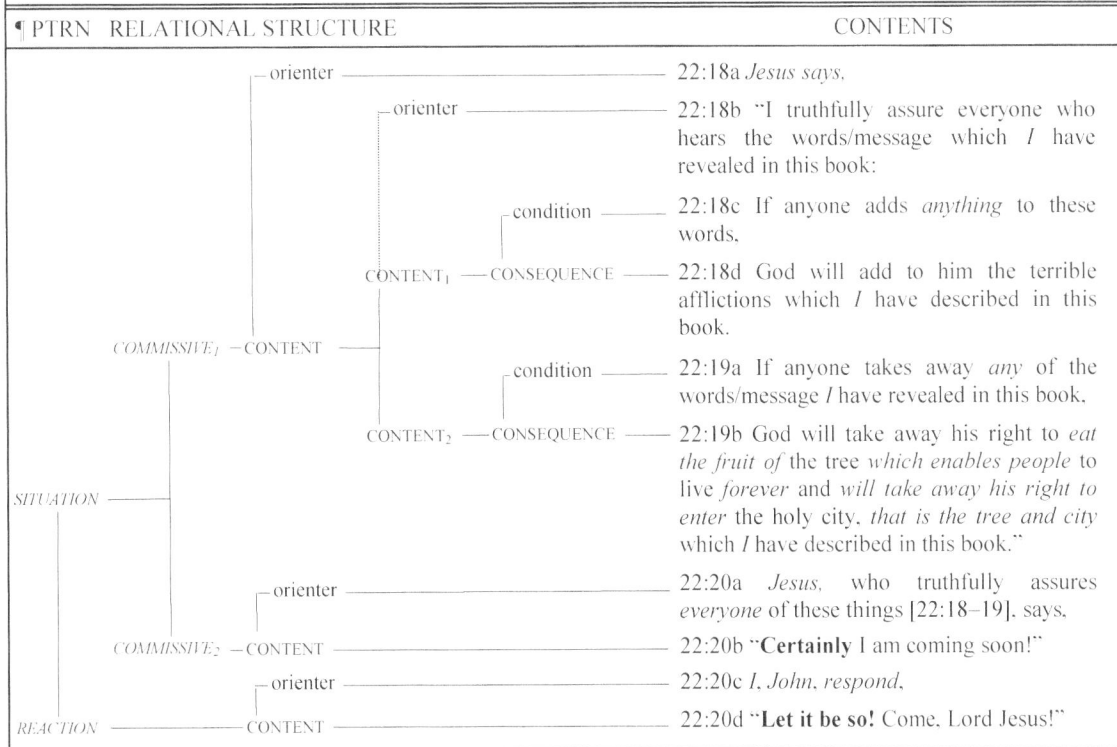

INTENT AND PARAGRAPH PATTERN

Like the previous unit, 22:18–20 consists of dialogue and has a *SITUATION–REACTION* structure. There are two speeches by Jesus, followed by John's response. At one level Jesus' first speech is a *COMMISSIVE* functioning as a mitigated exhortation, warning anyone against tampering with the revelation as contained in the book. However, it can also be seen as an expression of the authenticity and authority of all the warnings and promises in the book, since it comes in the context of repeated assertions of Christ's imminent return and the end of all things. To this John responds with an echo of the response in 22:17, showing that the overall intent of the unit is emotional expression.

NOTES

22:18a *Jesus says* The speaker is not explicitly identified in this paragraph. Several commentators (Beasley-Murray, Bratcher and Hatton, Caird, Ladd, Morris) understand that John is the speaker. But many others understand Jesus to be the speaker. Mounce says, 'The solemnity of the injunction suggests that the speaker is Christ himself.' Moreover, if 22:20 directly refers back to 22:18–19, then Jesus is necessarily the speaker here.

22:18b I truthfully assure Many versions (NIV, NRSV, REB, RSV) translate μαρτυρῶ here as 'I warn' or 'I solemnly warn' (TEV). For the basic meaning of the term see the notes on 1:2 and 22:16.

everyone who hears the words/message The hearing would probably be on the occasion of the book being read to a congregation as in 1:3.

22:18d God will add to him Here and in 22:19b, the verb of the condition is repeated in the consequence (ἐπιτίθημι 'add', ἀφαιρέω 'take away'). This gives marked emphasis to the warning.

the terrible afflictions For the meaning of the term πληγή 'blow, plague' here, see the note on 9:18.

22:19b to *eat the fruit of* the tree *which enables people* to live *forever* See the note on 21:6d.

22:20a Jesus who truthfully assures *everyone* of these things [22:18–19] Since the speaker of 22:20b must be Jesus the name is supplied here in the display. The Greek μαρτυρῶν 'witnessing' echoes the immediately preceding μαρτυρῶ 'I witness' in 22:18, and the demonstrative ταῦτα 'these things' will thus take its reference from the immediate context, namely the warnings in 22:18–19. However, some commentators (Beckwith, Thomas, Charles) think it refers to the whole of Revelation.

22:20b <u>Certainly</u> BDAG classifies this occurrence of ναί, as "in solemn assurance". Aune states that it confirms the truth of the statement that follows.

22:20c *I, John, respond* Though the orienter is implicit in the text, it is made explicit here. In view of the parallel with 22:17 it could be said that John is speaking on behalf of all God's people.

22:20d <u>Let it be so!</u> The affirming Hebrew 'Amen' is an emotional response to Christ's promise of his coming. See the notes on 1:6b and 7d.

Come, Lord Jesus The appeal ἔρχου κύριε Ἰησοῦ 'come, Lord Jesus' has its basis in the Aramaic *marana tha* 'our Lord, come', a liturgical expression used in the celebration of the Lord's Supper, attested by the Didache (10:6). Paul used it in 1 Cor. 16:22.

BOUNDARIES AND COHERENCE

The unit begins with the opening of Jesus' second speech, and ends with John's response to it. In 22:21 John is still speaking, but he is now addressing the audience of his book.

Although the subject matter appears to change between 22:19 and 20, the strong grammatical links between 22:20 and 18 have been noted (on 22:20a above). The coherence of the unit also lies in the fact that the speaker and addressees of 22:20b are the same as those of 22:18–19. Aune has adduced several examples (including 1 Cor. 16:22) where warnings or curses, as in 22:18–19, are immediately followed by the *marana tha* formula, indicating that this combination may be a stylistic feature.

PROMINENCE AND THEME

In this SITUATION–REACTION unit both parts are prominent. The marked prominence in 22:18c–d and 19 have been noted. The theme therefore comprises a summary of each element.

BOOK CONSTITUENT 22:21 (Paragraph: Closing of the Book)

THEME: *I pray that the Lord Jesus will bless you all.*	
RELATIONAL STRUCTURE	CONTENTS
┌─ orienter ───────	*22:21a I, John, pray*
└─ CONTENT ───────	*22:21b that* the Lord Jesus will act graciously to (*or,* bless) all *of you.*

INTENT AND PARAGRAPH PATTERN

Just as Revelation begins (1:4–8) with the typical features of a letter of its time, so it ends here, typically, with a benediction. As a benediction this brief unit is expressive in intent, conveying John's emotions to his audience.

NOTES

22:21a *I, John, pray* The benediction is verbless in the Greek, but semantically it constitutes John's prayer on behalf of his fellow servants of Christ.

22:21b the Lord Jesus It is noticeable that the title 'the Lord Jesus' is used only in the last two verses of the book, both of which are formulaic.

will act graciously to (*or,* bless) Again, the noun χάρις 'grace' occurs only here and in the formulaic blessing of 1:4b. See the note at that place.

all *of you* Since Revelation is a letter to the churches, it is natural that the full meaning of 'all' in a benediction to the addressees should be 'all of you'. Some manuscripts have the reading μετὰ πάντων τῶν ἁγίων '(be) with all the saints', which would have just the same reference to John's audience.

PROMINENCE AND THEME

The one statement is prominent and comprises the theme.

BIBLIOGRAPHY of works referenced

Abbott-Smith, G., *A Manual Greek Lexicon of the New Testament*; Edinburgh, T. & T. Clark; 1937
Alford, Henry, *Alford's Greek Testament, and Exegetical and Critical Commentary, Vol. 4*, (1875); Grand Rapids, Baker; 1980
Aune, David E., *Revelation* (Word Biblical Commentary, Vols. 52a,b,c); Nashville, Thomas Nelson; 1997 and 1998
BDAG, Arndt, W. F., and F. Gingrich; *A Greek-English Lexicon of the New Testament and Other Early Christian Literature*, trans. and adapted from Walter Bauer's *Griechisch-Deutsches Wörterbuch zu den Schriften des Neuen Testaments*; 2nd English edn., F. Wilbur Gingrich and Frederick W. Danker; Chicago, University of Chicago Press; 1979
Barclay, William, *Letters to the Seven Churches*; New York, Abingdon; 1957
Barnes, Albert, *"Revelation," Barnes' Notes on the New Testament*; Grand Rapids, Kregel; 1962 (reprint from 1861 ed.)
BDF, *see* Blass, F., A. Debrunner and R.W. Funk
Beale, G. K., *The Book of Revelation, A Commentary on the Greek Text* (The New International Greek Testament Commentary); Grand Rapids, Eerdmans; 1999
Beasley-Murray, George R., *The Book of Revelation* (New Century Bible Commentary); Grand Rapids, Eerdmans; 1978 (revised ed.)
Beckwith, I. T., *The Apocalypse of John*; New York, Macmillan; 1922
Beekman, John, John C. Callow and Michael F. Kopesec, *The Semantic Structure of Written Communication*, 5th rev.; Dallas, Summer Institute of Linguistics; 1981
Blass, F., A. Debrunner, and R.W. Funk, *A Greek grammar of the New Testament and other early Christian literature*; Chicago, Univ. of Chicago Press; 1961
Bratcher, Robert G., and Howard A. Hatton, *A Handbook on The Revelation to John*; New York, The United Bible Societies; 1993
Bruce, F. F., "The Revelation to John." in G. C. D. Howley, ed., *A New Testament Commentary*, pp. 629-666; London, Pickering & Inglis; 1969
Caird, G.B., *A Commentary on the Revelation of St. John the Divine* (Black's New Testament Commentaries); London, Adam & Charles Black; 1966
Callow, John, *A Semantic Structure Analysis of Colossians*; Dallas, Summer Institute of Linguistics; 1983 (2nd edition, 2002)
Callow, Kathleen, *Man and Message: A Guide to Meaning-Based Text Analysis*; Lanham, MD/Dallas, University Press of America and Summer Institute of Linguistics; 1998
Charles, R.H., *A Critical and Exegetical Commentary on The Revelation of St. John* (The International Critical Commentary); Edinburgh, T. & T. Clark; 1920
Chilton, David, *The Days of Vengeance : an Exposition of the Book of Revelation*; Fort Worth, Dominion; 1987
Dana, H.E., and J.R. Mantey, *A Manual Grammar of the Greek New Testament*; New York, Macmillan; 1957
Düsterdieck, Friedrich, *Critical and Exegetical Handbook to the Revelation of John* (Meyer's Commentary on the New Testament); New York, Funk and Wagnalls; 1884
Hodges, Z.C. and A.L. Farstad, *The Greek New Testament according to the Majority Text*; Nashville, T. Nelson; 1982
Hughes, Philip Edgcumbe, *The Book of Revelation (Pillar New Testament Commentary Series)*; Grand Rapids, Eerdmans; 1990
Kittel, G. and G. Friedrich eds. (TDNT), *Theological Dictionary of the New Testament* (10 vols.); trans. G.W. Bromley; Grand Rapids, Eerdmans; 1964
Ladd, George Eldon, *A Commentary of the Revelation of John*; Grand Rapids, Eerdmans; 1972
Lenski, R. C. H., *The Interpretation of St. John's Revelation*; Minneapolis, Augsburg; 1963
Levinsohn, Stephen H., *Discourse Features of New Testament Greek*; Dallas; Summer Institute of Linguistics;1992 (2nd edition, 2000)

Longacre, Robert E., "Exhortation and mitigation in First John"; in *Selected Technical Articles Related To Translation, Vol.9*, pp. 3-44; Dallas, Summer Institute of Linguistics; 1983

Louw, Johannes P. and Eugene A. Nida, *Greek-English Lexicon of the New Testament Based on Semantic Domains*; New York, United Bible Societies; 1988

Metzger, Bruce M., *A Textual Commentary on the Greek New Testament*; New York, United Bible Societies; 1971 (2nd edition, Stuttgart, U.B.S., 1994)

Moffatt, James, "The Revelation of St. John the Divine," in *The Expositor's Greek Testament, vol.5*, pp. 279-494; Grand Rapids, Eerdmans; 1951

Moore, T.W., *The book of Revelation; study and translation of the symbols*; Chicago, Fleming H. Revell; 1897

Morris, Leon, *The Book of Revelation: an Introduction and Commentary* (Tyndale New Testament Commentaries), Revised Edition; Grand Rapids, Eerdmans; 1988

Moule, C.F.D., *An Idiom Book of New Testament Greek*; Cambridge, University Press; 1953

Moulton, J. H., and G. Milligan, *The Vocabulary of the Greek Testament*; Grand Rapids, Eerdmans; 1974

Mounce, Robert H., *The Book of Revelation* (The New International Commentary on the New Testament) Revised ed.; Grand Rapids, Eerdmans; 1997

The New Bible Dictionary, Douglas, J. D. ed.; ; London, Inter-Varsity Fellowship; 1962

Pattemore, Stephen W., *Souls under the Altar: Relevance Theory and the Discourse Structure of Revelation*; New York, United Bible Societies; 2003

Robertson, A. T., *A Grammar of the Greek New Testament in the Light of Historical Research*; London, Hodder & Stoughton; 3rd edn. 1919

Schooling, Stephen J., *The Structure of the Book of Revelation: A Discourse Analysis Perspective*, PhD Thesis, Bristol University; PDF version 2005© Copyright Stephen Schooling

Sherman, Grace E. and John C. Tuggy, *A Semantic and Structural Analysis of the Johannine Epistles*; Dallas, Summer Institute of Linguistics; 1994

Swete, Henry Barclay, *Commentary on Revelation*; Grand Rapids, Kregel Publications; 1977

TDNT, *see* Kittel, G. and G. Friedrich

TH (Translator's Handbook), *see* Bratcher, Robert G. and Howard A. Hatton

Thomas, Robert L., *Revelation, An Exegetical Commentary*, 2 vols.; Chicago, Moody Press; 1992, 1995

Tuggy, John C, "Semantic paragraph patterns: a fundamental communication concept and interpretation tool"; in David A. Black (ed.), *Linguistics and New Testament interpretation*, pp. 45–67; Nashville, Broadman; 1992

UBSGNT, Aland, B., K. Aland, J. Karavidopoulos, C. Martini and B. Metzger eds.; *The Greek New Testament*, 4th edn.; London, New York, United Bible Societies; 1993

Van Otterloo, Roger, "Towards an Understanding of 'Lo' and 'Behold': Functions of ἰδού and ἴδε in the Greek New Testament"; in *OPTAT Vol. 2*, pp. 34-64; Dallas, Summer Institute of Linguistics; 1988

Walvoord, John F., *The Revelation of Jesus Christ*; Chicago, Moody; 1966

www.ingramcontent.com/pod-product-compliance
Lightning Source LLC
Chambersburg PA
CBHW080537300426
44111CB00017B/2761